The Button Box

University of Missouri Press
Columbia and London

The Button Box

A Daughter's
Loving Memoir of
Mrs. George S. Patton

Ruth Ellen Patton Totten

Edited by James Patton Totten
Foreword by Carlo W. D'Este

Cataloging-in-Publication data available from the Library of Congress
ISBN 0-8262-1576-9

∞ ™ This paper meets the requirements of the
American National Standard for Permanence of Paper
for Printed Library Materials, Z39.48, 1984.

Designer: Jennifer Cropp
Typesetter: Crane Composition, Inc.
Printer and binder: Thomson-Shore, Inc.
Typefaces: Minion and Snell Roundhand

Contents

Foreword

by Carlo W. D'Este

Ruth Ellen Patton Totten's *The Button Box* is an engaging memoir of the life of an extraordinary woman: her mother, Beatrice Banning Ayer, who was the daughter of Frederick Ayer, a self-made New England millionaire entrepreneur. Growing up in wealth and privilege, Beatrice Ayer was an accomplished equestrian, a skilled racing sailor, a talented musician and songwriter, and later in her life, a published author. By the age of eighteen, when she was first introduced into Boston society, Beatrice had matured into a confident, independent, strong-willed woman. Her father expected she would one day marry a man of proper social standing. Instead, Beatrice gave her heart to a young dyslexic Californian by the name of George S. Patton.

Her courtship by Georgie, as his family and close friends called him, began in 1902 and continued while he was a cadet at West Point. Frederick Ayer quite liked young Patton but deplored the prospect of his daughter marrying a lowly career Army officer with little money and few prospects in an era when Yankees like Ayer thought of soldiering as the last refuge of scoundrels, a profession of the "brutal and licentious mercenary."

Obsessed with a deeply held conviction that his destiny was to become a great battlefield commander, and that he would one day lead an army in a desperate battle, Patton steadfastly resisted Frederick Ayer's attempts to persuade him that he could have a successful civilian career of his own choosing. Failing that, Ayer turned his attention to dissuading Beatrice from marrying young Patton; and when that too failed, he vetoed the marriage. In response, his headstrong daughter locked herself in her bedroom and staged a hunger strike that soon led to her father's capitulation, and his blessing of the marriage. After a lavish wedding that was one of the noteworthy social events of 1910 on the fashionable North Shore of Massachusetts, Beatrice Ayer Patton entered into a new way of life for which nothing could have adequately prepared her. The young woman who had been the toast of Boston suddenly found herself an Army wife.

The life of a Cavalry officer's spouse in the "Old Army" of the early twentieth century was one of hardship and habitually Spartan living conditions. On the remote Cavalry posts of the American West where her husband was assigned the days were regulated primarily by the evocative sounds of the bugle and of horses. When the Pattons arrived at Fort Riley, Kansas, in 1913, traces of the old frontier army were still in evidence, including some grizzled veterans of the Indian wars of the nineteenth century. A sign on the parade ground read: "Officers will not shoot buffalo from the windows of their quarters. By order of the Commanding Officer."

For a time Beatrice questioned seriously if she was cut out for such an existence. Ruth Ellen writes that "She was beginning to feel she was a terrible failure as an Army wife . . . It all seemed very wild and crude and savage." The story of Beatrice Patton's epiphany in the wild, open spaces of Kansas and how it changed her life forever is one of the most heartwarming anecdotes in this memoir. Henceforth, Beatrice not only embraced her new way of life with the same passion she brought to every endeavor she ever undertook, but as Ruth Ellen writes, "Her inner eye had been opened . . . She had discovered the whole world."

Beatrice's role in Patton's life was indispensable, and throughout their turbulent thirty-five-year marriage her influence upon her flamboyant, mercurial husband was profound. She was also fiercely protective. Shortly after World War I Beatrice demonstrated the same warrior spirit as her husband at a white-tie dinner in Washington, D.C. As Beatrice waited in the foyer while Patton parked their car, a stout, unmistakably deskbound officer began making snide remarks about him. "Just look at the little boys they are promoting to colonel these days; look at that young chicken still wet behind the ears, wearing a colonel's eagle," he complained. The next thing Beatrice remembered was sitting astride the officer's shoulders, banging his head on the black-and-white marble floor tiles. It took Patton and another officer to pull her off the dazed officer.

Although he is not the principal character, the book also reveals a great deal about George S. Patton as a father and husband. As Ruth Ellen has noted, her father is "a twice-told tale, and Ma is a tale that has never been told."

Ruth Ellen Patton Totten was a singular, outspoken, and resolute woman with an irreverent sense of humor. I first met her in 1992 at the Patton family home in South Hamilton, Massachusetts, while researching my biography of her father. She not only told me about her parents and her late husband, an Army general, but also spoke thoughtfully about herself. I learned of her photographic memory, her belief in reincarnation, and her philosophy of life. Both George and Beatrice Patton believed passionately in reincarnation, and that conviction seemed to rule Ruth Ellen's life. Death to her was merely a passage to a new life in another time and place. My visit with her remains one of the most exceptional and unforgettable days of my own life.

The reader will find this book poignant, amusing, and enormously entertaining. For example, the anecdote the author relates of how her father taught her and her sister, Beatrice, to memorize and recite his ribald version of "Itsy Bitsy Spider" in front of a roomful of eclectic characters like Ellie, with her mass of tinkling bracelets, and the elderly lady with an ear trumpet, remains the most uproariously funny tale I have ever read.

Originally written for the edification and amusement of her family, is the insightful portrait of a remarkable American family. Its publication will serve as a lasting testament to a very unique woman, to a bygone era we will never again see, and as a portrait of some of the most interesting characters that one could hardly invent any better in an E. L. Doctorow novel.

The Button Box

Introduction

On a spring day in 1960, I was weeding the front lawn of our house in Washington, D.C., when the two little Nixon girls came maundering by. Richard Nixon was then the vice president of the United States, and he lived across the circle from us. This was a great convenience, as, when there was a snowstorm, Forest Lane always got swept clean first thing so that Mr. Nixon could get to his office.

The girls were on the teen-turn. They went to school with our younger son Jamie, who was thirteen, but they were a grade or two ahead of him. I knew them very slightly, asking them to our children's parties on Halloween and New Year's Eve along with the other kids on the street. They were well-mannered, beautifully dressed, and quiet. Jamie had not quite discovered girls, so they didn't run in and out of our house, but I often saw them around the circle. On this day, Tricia, the older one, stopped beside me and asked: "Mrs. Totten, wasn't your father a very famous man?"

"Yes, I guess he was pretty famous," I replied, and she went on: "Did it bother you much?"

"No, it didn't, because he wasn't famous until after I got married and left home."

Tricia shrugged and looked at Julie: "Well, our father's famous, and it bothers us a lot."

Recently, I was reminded of that long-ago conversation, and I realized that while my father's fame had not bothered me much outwardly, it affected me in many ways. Thinking about my life as a child of General George Smith Patton, Jr., and Beatrice Ayer Patton is like looking through my button box. I can pick up one button and remember that it came off a very pretty green and white suit I wore on my honeymoon. Another button, and I remember that it came

1

from a blue woolen reefer that belonged to one of the children; I tore the house apart looking for it, and when I couldn't find it, replaced all the buttons—a double row of them—with buttons that never looked as nice as the originals. Then another button, from our daughter's first-day-at-school dress, and another button, a pink quartz turtle, bought in a Japanese store in Honolulu during my green and salad days—all of my life brought back to me by buttons!

This reminiscence will be like looking through a button box. A proper biography has letters and dates and footnotes, but this is a loving memoir, not in perfect sequence, nor in perfect order, but offered with gratitude and affection. There will be too much "I" and many "me's," but, after all, these are *my* buttons.

Remembering further my little conversation with the Nixon girls, I realize that there was never a moment in our lives that we were not reminded that our father was the finest, bravest, most gallant, and best-looking man who ever lived and that he was destined for unimaginable glory. This we took for granted. Being our father's children was a special influence in all our lives, but the greatest, most pervasive, and most interesting influence in my life was Ma. She was not famous, but from the time I can remember, she made her Georgie famous to us. (There were three of us children—the "we" of whom I speak: my beautiful sister, Beatrice Ayer Patton, born in 1911; myself, Ruth Ellen Patton, born in 1915; and our longed-for and prayed-for brother, George S. Patton, IV, born in 1923—of all things, on Christmas Eve!)

Our father was Apollo at Delphi—the king of the castle—the perfect knight. When we read of Achilles, we knew that Georgie looked like him. Beowulf was in his image; Roland was Georgie; and Siegfried, with his sword and his blond curls, was his very picture. His is a twice-told tale, and Ma is a tale that has never been told. I wanted to write this as a memoir of our mother, but as it is quite impossible to separate her from her husband, it will have to be a joint affair.

—Ruth Ellen Patton Totten, 1981

Part I

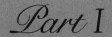

Tell me the tales I delighted to hear
Long long ago, long long ago
Sing me the songs that were dear to my ear
Long long ago, long long ago

Chapter 1
Granfer Ayer and Ellie

This book is mainly about my mother, Beatrice Banning Ayer—Ma—who was born in Lowell, Massachusetts, on January 12, 1886.[1] She was the eldest child of Frederick Ayer and his second wife, Ellen Barrows Banning.

"No man is himself who has a thousand ancestors," so I must, in all fairness, start "way back when" with the Ayers and the Bannings in order to tell about Ma, the flowering of many generations. Ma was very proud of her family: after listening to the interminable tales of the ancestor-worshipping Pattons, she would strike in with "but don't forget—every man in *my* family could write Esquire after his name."

Frederick Ayer (or Granfer Ayer, as we called him) was the son of Frederick Ayer and Persis Cook of Groton, Connecticut. His father died when Frederick was a boy, and he always recalled the sight of his father, stretched out on the bed, being bled by the doctor into a yellow bowl. The treatment probably shortened the poor man's life, and it certainly made a deathless impression on his three-year-old son.

After his father's death, Persis Ayer left Frederick and his older sister, Fanny, with the Ayer grandparents and took her other two children, James and Lovisa,

1. "Ma" is neither disrespectful nor a diminutive. It is one of the names of the Great Goddess, the Archetypical Mother. She had other names: Isis, Hathor, Cybele, Ops, Demeter, Kore. She exists in all phases of earliest human religion and mythology—as the Three In One, the One In Three, Virgin, Nymph, and Crone, equated with the phases of the moon. Her name is as eternal as her being. The first cry of an infant is "mm mm," "ma ma."

In Anatolia, Ma was the supreme Goddess, and today, after more than two thousand years, her huge bas relief still exists, sculptured into a cliff near Sardis by the Hittites. Her faceless head peers down into the valley below her, tear-streaked with the rains of the centuries. Her great knees can support a human body. Her handless arms are folded across a vast bosom.

to her family's home. Fanny stood the life at the senior Ayers' for a few months and then went home to mother and her Cook grandparents, leaving Granfer Ayer with the Ayers. Grandma Hope Ayer was loved by one and all—the Fannings were a much "softer" family—but even she couldn't do much with old Elisha. Granfer Ayer wrote:

My grandfather was a very industrious man and could never endure to see anyone about him idle. Though only four years old, with him I was never too young to work . . . There would be stones to pick up in the garden, sticks to pick up around the place, and when this was done to perfection, [he] would always find something else that a boy my size could do. I can't remember that I was ever too small to drive the cows to pasture and bring them home; to carry lunches and water to the men in the fields; to bring in wood; build fires, turn the spit and help at all sorts of work around the house and kitchen. I could always feed the cattle and it was early found that I could milk, which called for early rising and late work. My grandfather had large flocks of merino sheep from the ones my uncle had brought home from Spain. These sheep are very delicate and had to be housed during storms and in the winter. My evening's work during the winter was to help the men slice up several bushels of turnips and carrots for their feed. The Groton Indians used to pass thro' the place going to and from Preston City where they got their rum and tobacco, and they generally stopped on their way to quench their thirst with cider, which was always free and abundant and which it was my duty to draw for them. After school in the winter I had to go to a barn a mile-and-a-half from the house, through a lonely wood, to feed the band of sheep that were kept there. This barn was on the Indians' route to their reservation and I was always expecting to put a pitch fork into one of them who had gotten too tired to go further and taken lodgings for the night in the hay.

One of the squaws used to spin flax in our attic and had crazy spells, and would mutter to herself and was really quite wild, but not considered dangerous. Her peculiarities, however, made a deep impression on my young mind and did not add to my happiness. She spun a good deal of the thread used by the family, and all the linen. The tow she spun was made into shirts for me, and were never washed until I had given them a good airing. The memory of their scratching is very distinct.

My grandfather did not believe in fun. There was always so much to do that the time was filled up without it. . . . At one time there was a muster of the militia to take place five miles from us, and I was finishing up the binding and the shucking of a field of buckwheat. The day before I asked Grandmother Hope to intercede for me for a permit to go. She said she was afraid Grandfather would never consent unless I could get the buckwheat all up. That night, by moonlight I worked until one o'clock, which won me permission to walk five miles to the muster next day. I must have been about eleven years old.

Granfer Ayer had some fascinating uncles. One of them, his father's older brother, also named Elisha, was greatly admired by all his nephews and nieces.

When his fiancée broke the engagement, he "turned wild" and "went to sea." Elisha became a privateer, and some years later he came home with a load of merino sheep that he had smuggled out of Spain. The reason for this particular cargo, according to family legend, is because there was a death penalty for exporting merino sheep and Elisha wanted to show the world what a false woman could do to a good man. He was a gay blade, rich for the times, and on one unforgettable occasion, to show off, he threw his gold watch and chain into the open fire that heated the ballroom where he was attending a party.

Granfer Ayer used to say, "There was no bad blood in the Ayer family, but I won't say there hasn't been a wag or two."

Another favorite uncle was Elkanah Fanning, Grandma Hope's brother, who "occasionally indulged in the use of West India goods" (meaning rum and molasses), and he directed it in his will that he was to be buried in a chestnut coffin so that he "might go snapping and cracking through hell." He must have been one of the wags. Once, when he was hoeing his garden, a man rode up and said, "I would like to inquire the way to Mystic." Elkanah rested on the handle of his hoe and replied, "I have no objection."

Elkanah also wrote the classic poem, "The Spider":

> Venom in his snout,
> Poison in his pout
> The old grout.

Uncle Elkanah's brother, Charles Fanning, was "a most exemplary man." An original member of the Society of the Cincinnati, he enlisted in the Continental Army on May 8, 1775, and served seven years and eight months, rising in rank from sergeant to captain. He was a great friend of the Marquis de Lafayette. Granfer Ayer wrote of Captain Fanning: "I remember him as one of the few people I ever saw who habitually wore the old-fashioned buckled shoes, long stockings, buff waistcoat and blue coat with silver buttons and a white pigtailed wig."

Granfer Ayer's mother, Persis Cook Ayer, worried a lot about Granfer Ayer. She had left him with the Ayers because she didn't feel she could handle him, but Fanny's description of the little boy's life upset Persis so much that in 1834, when Granfer Ayer was twelve years old, she married again to give him and the other children a home. Her new husband was a tailor named Ripley Parke. Granfer Ayer said the marriage was a milestone in his life, as he wore his first suit of clothes—made by his new stepfather—to the wedding.

The Parke marriage, meant to bring the family together, slowly became a disaster. Mr. Parke was always on the move, looking for better places and better jobs. Persis and the children followed him however they could. After two little Parkes were born, Persis and William, Granfer Ayer's mother could not get enough money out of Mr. Parke to feed the family, so she sold their house and, taking the five hundred dollars they got for it, joined a "community" that contracted to care for the member families for life in return for services. However, the experiment failed—and they moved on.

Mr. Parke eventually had to be "put away" for a year or two. Granfer Ayer, though a young boy, was the man of the house and had to take his stepfather to the asylum. When they reached it, while Granfer Ayer was paying for the cab, Mr. Parke ran up the steps into the building and committed Granfer Ayer, who was taken away by attendants and kept confined until his mother came and straightened out the situation. When Mr. Parke got out of the asylum, he studied phrenology and supported himself for the rest of his life by lecturing on the subject. He never came home again.

Granfer Ayer took on the support of his mother and the two Parke children. After he married Cornelia Wheaton in 1858, he sent the little Parkes to good schools and took his mother home to live with him and his bride. According to Granfer Ayer, Persis was an exceptional mother and loads of fun. The only other thing that is written about her is that she refused to be buried in the same cemetery with her brother-in-law, George Ayer, because after she became a widow and was living alone in the house with her four young children she heard noises in the night and "knew" he was trying to scare her.

Granfer Ayer's life was really a prototype of the Great American Dream. He started very small, sleeping under the counter of the store where he worked, and ended up owning the store before he was thirty-five years old, but he always insisted to his family that he never made a dollar in his life of which he was ashamed. In 1855 he went into partnership with his brother, James Cook Ayer, in the patent medicine business in Lowell, Massachusetts.

The Ayer brothers' medicines—Ayer's Sarsaparilla, Hair Vigor, Cathartic Pills, and Cherry Pectoral—were household names all over the country. Ayer's Cherry Pectoral had one-sixteenth of a grain of heroin in each bottle and was, indeed, a boon to harassed mothers as well as harassed coughers. Ma discovered that a teaspoonful to each child at the beginning of a long trip ensured peace and quiet. People now, myself included, collect the medicine bottles and the posters. One issue of Ayer's Hair Vigor came in a most beautiful sapphire blue bottle with a fancy top. One of the advertisements for Hair Vigor stays always in my mind. On the label is a picture of a gentleman with his suspenders hanging down and a horrified expression on his face. His lady wife, in bustle and pompadour, looks equally appalled, and the object of their concern is the marble wash basin, which is sprouting hair under a broken bottle of Hair Vigor.

Granfer Ayer's marriage did not interfere with his life pattern of hard work. On a visit to Washington, D.C., Granfer Ayer and his associates decided to drop in on President Lincoln at the White House. They found the president "hard at work in his office, tieless, vest unbuttoned, and in his shirt sleeves, wet with perspiration." Granfer Ayer recalled that "Mr. Lincoln received us standing, and looked terribly tired, bored and lifeless until, after introducing myself and our friends, I said, 'Mr. President, I have called to pay our respects to our President, but none of us has a favor to ask, not even a country post office.' At this, he woke up and rushed at me with both hands, took both of mine, and shaking them vigorously said, 'Gentlemen, I am glad to see you. You are the first men that I have seen since I have been here that didn't want something.'"

Granfer Ayer's life leapt from peak to peak, with the necessary valleys in between. He lost his beloved Cornelia when their fourth child, a daughter, Louise, was just a baby. He was involved in a family feud with his sister-in-law, the widow of J. C. Ayer, about money. Mrs. Ayer made much of this and went to every member of the family in turn, telling them that they would have to choose between her and the Frederick Ayer family. Granfer Ayer won that contest, so Mrs. Ayer took her family and her Lares and Penates and went to live in New York and, later, Paris.

There was a difference of thirty years in the ages of Ma's parents, but theirs was a true love story that lasted until the end of their lives, which came just a few weeks apart in 1918.

Granfer Ayer's account of his meeting with his second wife is very calm stuff compared with Ellie's version. Frederick wrote that he was visiting his sister-in-law in St. Paul, Minnesota, in 1883. She was anxious for him to marry again, and presented him with a list of young women whom she considered eligible. "One day I said to her, 'What is the matter with Miss Ellen Banning?' I found she considered her (Ellen Banning) more highly than any other girl of her acquaintance, though a little young for such responsibilities, and having previously made up my own mind, I was pleased to be agreed with in this fashion."

Ellie's account of their meeting was characteristic. She told Ma that she had been invited to a very special party to meet an older man, a widower who was very rich and was considered a "great catch." She accepted the invitation, and then found that Edwin Booth was playing *Hamlet* on the same evening. Ellie was an amateur actress and diseuse, much involved in the local theatre, so she wrote her hostess a note explaining her reasons for changing her mind, and went to see Booth. As she came out of the theatre, "the handsomest man . . . I had ever seen walked up to me and said, 'Are you Miss Ellen Banning?'"

As the young ladies of her day were never "picked up," she replied very stiffly that she was, and started to move off with dignity, although, as she told Ma, "Once I looked into those piercing blue eyes, if he had said 'Ellen Banning, will you follow me to the world's end?' I would have gone right with him just as I was."

He walked along beside her and said, "Miss Banning, when I understood that there was one young lady in the town of such good sense and judgment that she preferred going to see a performance by America's greatest living actor to going to an evening party, I decided that she should have both treats, and I have come for you in my carriage with a chaperone to take you to the party."

Ellie said he was "like a knight in armor" and her name for him was always "Sir Frederick." Comparing Ellie with the lovely and gentle Cornelia, I have always felt that Ellie was the dessert course of his life and that he lived as long as he did because she made him laugh so much.

My grandmother was very strictly raised. The Bannings were not wealthy, but she was the kind of person who treated rice pudding as if it were ambrosia, and her mind transformed the world into gorgeous scenery with a suitable backdrop in front of which she was usually the leading lady; not aggressively so, but with a certain flare. Ma once asked Granfer Ayer how he could have loved both of his wives as much as he said he did, and he replied, "Little daughter, they were both extraordinary women in their way, and I loved them both with all my heart, but perhaps the Frederick Ayer that fell in love with Cornelia Wheaton would never have looked at Ellen Banning. When Cornelia left us, I kept on living and developing and, when I met your mother, she was just right for this Frederick Ayer. Perhaps the Frederick Ayer that married Ellen Banning would never have looked at Cornelia Wheaton."

But how could he have resisted the authoress of the poem that Ellie had privately printed?

FREDERICK AYER
EBA
DECEMBER 8, 1912
Cambridge, Riverside Press, 1913
1.
Born to be loved and to command
Was ever such a soul?

He'll weep with one, he'll laugh with one
He'll help one to the goal

2.
I waited for you, Frederick Ayer
And in my home did stay
No man could share my heart with you
I saw you on the way

3.
And when I met your eyes sky blue
And heart as fresh as mountain dew
I followed you, I followed you
I followed Frederick Ayer

4.
You made a heaven for my heart
Earth's flowers tell your love
I would not leave your paradise
No, not for that above

5.
With power and mind that never sleep
You fly, my own, while others creep
Your dear ones on your wings you bear
My life, my love, my Frederick Ayer!

Ellie was as unforgettable as Granfer Ayer. She left a tremendous impression on all who met her, especially her daughters. She also left her mark on a great many of her descendants—drama all the way!

Ellie's father was William Lowber Banning, a Philadelphia lawyer, and her mother was Mary Alicia Sweeney. The Bannings moved to St. Paul in 1855. The Banning name is of Danish origin, applying in early times to a class called "hero worshippers." Reference to it is found in the earliest ballads on record, "Scot and Bard Sons," in which one song begins with "Becca ruled the Bannings." They were probably Vikings. Eventually, they moved from Denmark to Holland, and then to England. Rembrandt painted one of the Bannings in "The Night Watch." The gentleman in the foreground, in the yellow suit, is Captain Banning-Coq. His father-in-law, the apothecary Coq, was so horrified that his daughter was marrying one of the "wild Bannings" that he insisted on hyphenating the name.

The first American Banning came to America from England and settled in Dover, Delaware, where his son, John, was born in 1740. John Banning was a staunch patriot and cast Delaware's vote for George Washington as president. When the Continental Army was disbanded after the Revolution, and was paid in depreciated scrip, John Banning stood on the steps of Dover Academy and paid the Delaware men in hard money from his own fortune.

John Banning married Elizabeth Alford Cassons, a widow who was reputedly the most beautiful woman in America. There is a fascinating story about the Alfords, who were from the West Indies. Elizabeth's maternal grandmother died when Elizabeth was a small girl. As one of her older sisters lived on another island, they delayed the funeral until the sister could arrive. After her arrival, they were starting to nail down the coffin lid when the corpse began to move, and soon came back to life. In memory of this event, the reborn lady took her children to the cemetery each year, on the anniversary of her close call, and they had their tea on her tombstone.

Ellie's mother was the daughter of Frederick Morgan Sweeney and Rachel Ormsby Norris. Rachel was a widow, with two young Norris children, when Sweeney swept into Dover and swept her off her feet. I can't imagine that that was very hard to do, as Mr. Norris had been "very fine and very stern" and the only man in the Norris family to marry at all, which his family considered "very daring." On the other hand, there was Sweeney, gay and full of fun, with a clear Irish tenor voice; a great chestnut stallion, called "Red Fox"; and a bullet hole through the brim of his hat. He bragged, in his cups, about being descended from Brian Boru, who drove the Danes out of Ireland in 1014 AD at the battle of Clontarf. He was most probably from Northern Ireland, and a Protestant, as he had no saint's name. He gave her four children—Mary Alicia, Kathleen, Robert Ormsby, and Emmet—and then rode off to fight in the Mexican wars, where he died. Rachel soon died of a broken heart and the children were raised by her Quaker friends and family. Even though we know a lot of the ancestors from whom Ma sprang, we come to a dead stop at Frederick Morgan Sweeney. Maybe that is where we get the dramatic skills and the intense love of music and musicianship. Ellie had them all; she was a consummate actress all her life, and her children not only thrived on it, they inherited it.

Ellie's father died full of years, and Alicia Sweeney Banning lived out her time in Los Angeles with her daughter, Katharine, who had married her first cousin, also a Banning, and her unmarried daughter, May. Ma remembered Alicia well. She went one night to say good night to her grandmother. As she had just been given a knee-length strand of crystal beads, which I still have, she was proudly wearing it, and old Mrs. Banning looked her up and down and said, "Well, my dear little Beatrice, I suppose that every woman is a squaw at heart." That phrase has been passed down ever since from mother to daughter as a gentle signal that one is a bit overdressed.

In St. Paul, Ellie belonged to several drama societies and acted in scenes from Shakespeare, all of which were rewritten for her so that she was never alone on the stage with a man. This reflected the conventions of her day. During the love scene from *Romeo and Juliet,* the nurse sat and knitted away for the whole act.

Ellie earned money with her readings, as she "entertained" at teas and ladies' sodalities. I have the book from which some of her readings came—*My Recitations* by Cora Urquhart Potter, published by Lippincott in 1886. Ma gave marvelous imitations of Ellie, and would have us in tears with her rendition of Charles Kingsley's "Lorraine Lorraine Lorree," where the cruel husband makes Lorraine Lorraine Lorree ride the colt, Vindictive, although she has just had a baby. She says, quite understandably, that "I will not ride Vindictive with this baby on my knee! He has killed a man, he has killed a boy, and why must he kill me?" But she does, and he does, and "No one but the baby cried for poor Lorraine Lorree."

Then there was Hood's "Bridge of Sighs" and "The King in the Ulster Coat"— and one special one we loved that I cannot find anywhere, about two poor children who hear a piano for the first time and cry, "Open the box, please, lady, and let us see the bird." These poems and certain lines from them became part of the "family language," such as the striking line from "Berth Gelert"—"Hell hound, by thee my child devoured?" When there was a sudden flux of relatives, Ma would plaintively recite, "Pibroch of Dhonal Dhu, Pibroch of Dhonal! Wake thy wild cries anew, summon Clan Connell!"

The Pattons, who were very different from the Ayers, had several stories they told about Ellie—I don't think they ever knew quite what to make of her. The Pattons' most memorable account concerned a dinner she and Granfer Ayer attended at Lake Vineyard when they were visiting the Bannings. The family was so huge that in those days they thought nothing of sitting down to dinner with thirty places.

At this particular party, everyone was already seated at the dinner table waiting for Ellie. They were all talking politics—the Patton clan lived and breathed politics, as did so many of the families who had been uprooted by the Civil War. They, of course, were raving, tearing Democrats, and the Ayers were, of course, staunch Republicans, but this just made it more exciting.

Ellie was late, which was to be expected as she always "made an entrance." She appeared shortly after they were seated, gauzy with lace shawls and wearing the inevitable rose in her pretty curls. She stood in the dining room door long enough to command an attentive silence, and then seated herself at Mr. Patton's right. The conversation immediately turned on again, and back to politics, which did not quite leave Ellie in the center of attention. Our aunt, Nita Patton, then a young girl, had never seen anything quite like Ellie before and couldn't take her eyes from her. She said Ellie looked around the table in a rather calculating way, and when she had decided who was the furthest person seated from her, she rose gracefully and walked around the table to her intended victim, who happened to be Aunt Annie Banning. Ellie paused, and so did the conversation. She took Annie's chin in one be-ringed and dimpled hand, and turning up her face, said to her in tones of low and thrilling register: "Annie, dear, what do you think of life?" No one in the family ever got over this. All our lives, when things in the family come to an impasse, all anyone had to do is ask "What do you think of life?"—and we all returned to normal.

In February 1918, Granfer Ayer died of pneumonia caught while out riding his horse in the rain. He was ninety-five years old. Ellie died three weeks later. Ma was running the house in Thomasville for them and for a number of other relatives who joined them there. The double tragedy broke her up. She knew her father was living on borrowed time simply because of his age, and she knew her mother had a heart condition, but she had no idea that Ellie was in such very poor health. When she asked the doctor why her mother had died so suddenly, he said that he could only tell her that Ellie (like her grandmother, Rachel Ormsby Sweeney) had died "of a broken heart."

One consequence of her parents' death so far from home was that Ma developed a lifelong hatred of undertakers. She discovered, while making preparations for the shipment of their bodies back to Boston, that the largest undertaking parlor in Boston had sent down to the funeral home in Thomasville, on the same train on which the Ayers had traveled, the two most expensive bronze coffins in the Boston warehouse, with the notation that these were for Mr. and Mrs. Ayer.

I remember very well the day that Granfer Ayer died. Bee and I were taken to Ellie's room where she sat, as usual, on her huge puffy bed with loads of lacy pillows and scarves around her, her lovely white hair piled on top of her head and a rose tucked into her curls. She told Ma later that she wanted to look nice in order "not to upset the little girls." She gave us each a present—to soften the blow, I suppose. My sister got a Red Riding Hood doll, which I greatly coveted. I don't remember what I got. Ellie told us, with tears in her beautiful eyes, that "Granfer Ayer has slipped away to Heaven." As soon as I could get away, I ran down the hall to his room to see for myself, as it seemed a most unlikely tale. But sure enough, his bed was empty and there was no one in the room, so I weighed myself on his weighing machine (a totally forbidden act)—not that I could tell how much I weighed, but the little platform you stood on wiggled so deliciously.

I was only three years old when Ellie died, but I remember her in clear living color. She was very sentimental, and had the gardener make wreaths of fresh flowers every day for my sister Bee and me to wear on our heads. They were prickly and slippery. Ellie was "pink and plump and pretty" with lovely dimpled hands, covered with jewels, and a gold bangle for every year of her married life—thirty-three in all—on her left arm. These slipped up and down and tinkled. She smelled delicious, and was great on hugging and kissing. Once or twice, in Thomasville, we went out in the carriage with her and were taken to some place where she bought "real" ice cream. It was a long time that I realized that meant ice cream without any gelatin or filler in it. At the time I thought it was a put-on—that ice cream was ice cream—and Ellie was just showing off.

I remember her best in Thomasville, where she and Granfer Ayer died. We all lived in an enormous house—and it must have been as big as I remember it because the inhabitants were Ma; my sister and me; our nurse, Taty; Ellie and Granfer Ayer; Ellie's two nurses, one of them the inimitable Miss Crowley; the man who looked after Granfer Ayer; my aunt, Nita Patton; both Patton grandparents; and Annie Ruggles and her brother, Will, cousins of Granfer Ayer's.

Thomasville and the winter of 1918 made a great impression on me. Ellie gave Bee and me a little white kid, who developed quickly into a young goat who butted people from behind. We were afraid of him until one day he butted Bee's lady tutor and knocked her down. After that, we admired his gall, but we always kept our faces toward him.

One day Bee and I were playing in the grape arbor, and we found an old, old colored woman, with her head between her knees, rocking back and forth, howling and calling on "Sweet Jesus" with all her might. We thought for a moment that she might be "Howley Mary, Mither Uv God" to whom our nurse, Taty, made frequent reference, but Bee realized she was in trouble and ran to fetch a grown-up. She came back with Dr. Washburn, Ellie's physician, who quieted the old woman and led her away. We heard later from Ma that she told Dr. Washburn she remembered being a slave, and how the Yankee soldiers came, and how, as a little girl, she had been working in the cotton fields when "the stars fall out of heaven." Dr. Washburn said that there had been a well-known shower of meteors in Alabama at one time, and that if the old darky really did remember it, she was well over one hundred years old.

The death of her parents within three weeks of each other, while Georgie was away in the Great War, broke Ma up. It was as if someone pulled the arbor out from under the grapevine. She was thirty-two years old, but there had always been somebody there. Fortunately, she loved and was much loved by the Pattons. No one ever took the place of her "Ma" and "Pa," and she talked about them to us all of our lives as if they were still nearby. When we were old enough to understand, she bade us remember Granfer Ayer and Ellie every night in our prayers and told us that whenever we had a special treat or were able to buy something very nice, to "thank Granfer Ayer in our hearts" because he had worked all his life so that his children and his grandchildren could be comfortable. We always have. She explained to us that the possession of wealth was a responsibility, not a privilege.

Ma was extremely musical. In fact, her gifts in that direction were closer to genius than to just talent. She played the mandolin, the steel guitar (later in life), the piano, and even the musical saw. She also wrote music, and had a total understanding and command of harmony. In her middle years, she gathered the songs she had written into a little book, which she had published and gave to the family and close friends. One of these songs is dedicated to "E.B.A."—to Ellie. Whether Ma wrote the words herself or found them in some old sentimental book I don't know. I have never found the words anywhere but in her little songbook, so I assume she wrote them. They expressed her feelings about her mother.

> ABSENT
> I feel I am not all bereft of her so dear
> For when she went away she left her laughter here,
> A spirit in this room it dwells, and every night
> When I sit here alone, it tells of her delight.
> Her joy in life, it was so wild, that all her days
> She never ceased to be a child, with her wild ways,
> A child, and yet a woman too, could laugh, could weep—
> Her heart was pure, her friendship true, her passion deep.
> Her gentle laughter, soft and low, is in the air.
> None else can hear it, but I know that it is there.
> B.A.P.

Ellie was a great gift giver and she was absolutely mad about having everything engraved. There were initials and dates on all her little silver boxes. (I don't know what people kept in those little oval- and heart-shaped boxes, embossed with cupids and garlands of roses, but she had a plethora of them). I had an umbrella with a battered silver crane's head for the handle. I am sure it was once very handsome, but its glass eyes are long gone. It is engraved "Beatrice forever. EBA." I also have a silver-handled paper knife, now the property of my daughter Beatrice, engraved "BBA from EBA, á ma fleur qui pense"—for my flower who thinks. Ellie had chosen the name "Beatrice," meaning "one who blesses": that was one of Ellie's pet names for Ma, and the one that suited her best.

For all Ellie's drama, she had a genuinely loving heart, and it showed up at all times—sometimes to the intense embarrassment of the object. Ma and Georgie, after their beautiful wedding, had to spend the night in a hotel in Boston before making connections for their honeymoon in Europe. Ma was a lot like Ellie in many ways, but Georgie was shy. The morning after the wedding, they rang for breakfast, and when the knock came at the room door, who should precede the trays but Ellie, carrying a single perfect white rose in a crystal vase, followed by several brothers and sisters, all of whom had risen early for their long train ride to Boston to be there when "the children" awoke. Ma thought it was terribly thoughtful, but it almost killed Georgie.

With this constant change of scenes to "standing-room-only performances," no wonder Granfer Ayer lived to be ninety-five! How could he have borne to leave the audience any sooner? I have often thought it was the only real fun he ever had in all his good, useful, and unselfish life.

Chapter 2
"Like Birds on a Telephone Wire"

Ma was quite a big girl before she realized that her four much older, much loved brothers and sisters were "halves," the children of Granfer Ayer and his first wife, Cornelia Wheaton. Cornelia died of cancer in 1878, and her loss was deeply felt. Her four children were Ellen (born in 1859); James, or Jamie (born in 1862); Charles, or Chilly (born in 1865); and Louise, born in 1876. Florence Wheaton came to Lowell to take care of her dying sister, and stayed on and kept house for the family until Granfer Ayer married Ellie in 1884. Thereby hangs a tale.

Before Cornelia died, Frederick built their dream house in Lowell. It was to last forever as a home, a landmark, and a memorial. There were vast rooms filled with vast furniture, lots of stained glass and inlaid parquet floors, and a cellar under the cellar (for root vegetables). If I had been taken there as a new bride, as Ellie was, I would have sat down upon the vast front steps and gone into what Georgian ladies called "a fit of the whoops." But Ellie was made of stronger stuff. She had visited Frederick there with her sister, May Banning, before her marriage. When she came home from her honeymoon, she was met on the steps by Florence Wheaton and little Louise Ayer, both dressed in full mourning and wearing gloomy and deprived expressions. Perhaps Miss Wheaton expected to marry Granfer Ayer; in any case, she succeeded in turning little Louise against Ellie completely and it took some time for that breach to heal. Miss Florence had been very explicit about Cinderella and the wicked stepmother, and Louise was scared to death.

One day, sometime after Ellie and Granfer Ayer were married, she went to her sitting room and found an old rag, covered with uneven stitches, a few odd beads sewn at random across it, and a small prim person standing admiring her handiwork pinned to the back of Ellie's velvet-covered arm chair, saying: "I have made an antimacassar for you, Mama."

Ellie left the object pinned to her chair for years, and she became Louise's "rose friend."

Ellen Ayer Wood was Granfer Ayer's oldest child. She helped to nurse her beloved mother through the last stages of cancer, and was traumatized by the experience. Ellen was a beautiful, high-strung little woman with the heart of a lion and the constitution of an eggshell. She was for a long time engaged to a Dr. Greenleaf, who was apparently a very understanding man and did not want to rush her into marriage until she had recovered from the loss of her mother. This was his undoing.

Granfer Ayer had, as a manager of the Washington Mills in Lawrence, a highly intelligent and capable man, the son of a Portuguese seaman from New Bedford. William Madison Wood entered the business world much as the Assyrian came down like a wolf on the fold. He was a dashing man, swarthy, mustachioed, emotional, generous, shrewd, passionately devoted to his family and, of course, very much on the make. He was a self-made gentleman, and had had to learn how to do everything correctly: how to dress, how to order wine, how to help a lady from her carriage—and all with great vitality, the kind that generates sex appeal. He saw a good deal of Ellen Ayer in his dealings with her father and, finally, after a whirlwind courtship, he came one night into the room where she was sitting, and took out his watch, announcing: "Miss Ellen, I shall give you exactly five minutes in which to accept my heart and hand in marriage." And she did. Whatever became of Dr. Greenleaf is unrecorded, but there is a backstairs story that one night a loud voice proclaimed from behind the closed doors of the master bedroom: "Ellen Wood, there are three people in this bed—you and me and Greenleaf—and one of them has got to go."

Ellen and William had four children: Rosalind, William, Jr., Cornelius, and Irene. Rosalind, who was called Diddah, lived all of her life on an emotional tightrope of wild enthusiasms, eccentric beaux, passionate opinions, and violent tantrums. In her thirties she married a perfectly delightful Italian named Mario Guardabassi, from Perugia. They were well matched in temperament, and had histrionic battles that ended in blissful reunions, which managed to include all the family whether or not they wished. Diddah produced two sons, and Mussolini made Mario a count, which pleased everyone enormously.

William Wood, Jr., beautiful, fast, and spoiled rotten, married a belle from Louisville. He gave her a son and a daughter, and got himself killed in a car accident. Ellen never got over that sorrow. On top of that, her look-alike gentle and lovely daughter, Irene, died in 1918 during the flu epidemic. Ellen stood this hatchment of ravens as long as she could—they were all dark and intense like William—and, finally, after the death of her two darlings, took to her bed and became an invalid. During these years—and there was, undoubtedly, some reason for her ill health besides her children and William—she had a severe stroke, from which she totally recovered while in her eighties.

Her description to Ma of how she felt while supposedly unconscious is thought-provoking. She said she could see and understand everything, but she could not communicate in any way. She heard everything people said about her and her condition, and they said a lot of things they would not have said if they had realized she was mentally alert. She told Ma she felt as if she were trapped in a ruined building, unable to tell her would-be-rescuers where she was so that they could come to her aid. After she got well enough to function again, several people who had considered themselves faithful servants, to be rewarded at her death, were surprised to find themselves fired.

Ellen's long unhappiness led her to try to communicate with her two dead children. She was fleeced for thousands of dollars by mediums and fortune-tellers. Finally, her Ayer common sense surfaced and she got wise to what was going on and did an about-face. She gave great assistance to Joseph Dunninger, whose investigations exposed many fake spiritualists. She told Ma that *she* could afford to be robbed, but at the séances she had attended she saw so many poor people being gypped that it made her furious. It was during this period that Ellen Wood met Maude Piper, the only medium of the time who could never be faulted. Like Cassandra, Priam's accursed daughter, Mrs. Piper was not believed in as she did not put on a great act with trumpets and ectoplasm. She and Ellen became great friends, and Ellen helped her financially when she was old and blind and fell on hard times.

Poor William Wood. He had everything he had dreamed of—money, power, a family, a place in society—but he was at the end a desperately unhappy man. He had done everything in the world for his own family. He had set up his brother, Otis, who was a dear, his carbon copy without the spark, in a printing business; one sister was a schoolteacher, and the other was in the best mental institution money could buy. He sent his mother money every week of her life (his father being long dead). Old Mrs. Wood was a classic Latin beauty. From the stiff photographs of her day, she fairly blazes out at you. She would never move from the little house in New Bedford where she had been wife, mother, and widow; until she became bedridden, she would never allow her sons to hire any help for her.

When she was dying, they sent for William. By the time he arrived, she was beyond speech, but she kept pulling at the neck of her nightgown until he lifted her hand and found she was groping for a key that hung around her neck on a chain. She gestured toward the old-fashioned trunk that stood in the window niche, and when he opened it, he found thousands and thousands of dollars in coins and bills, some very old. It was every penny that he had ever sent her. She had never trusted banks, and had kept the money in case someday he might need it.

William Wood was the soul of generosity, and he loved to give stunning gifts. When Ma became engaged to Georgie, he took her to the best jeweler in Boston and told her to pick out anything she liked as a wedding present. When she hesitated between a small diamond crescent brooch and a pearl and diamond bracelet, fashioned like a slender vine, he bought them both for her.

William Wood was disappointed in Ma's engagement to Georgie, as he had wanted her to marry his son's tutor, Bennie Smith. William adored Bennie in an emotional way, and treated him like another son. There was to be a fancy dress ball for some great occasion and William persuaded Ma to go as Columbine. He had bought for Bennie a fabulous Pierrot costume of satin. Poor Bennie died just before the ball. William was overcome with grief and had Bennie buried in the Wood family vault in his Pierrot costume. Bennie's death added to his measure of unfulfillment. His Ellen had taken the light of her presence from him and had become an invalid; his elder son, his heir, his pride and joy, was dead; his gentle Irene, so like her mother, had died—at any rate, he was out driving with his chauffeur one day at his winter place in Florida, and had the car stopped so he could walk in the woods. There, alone with his thoughts, he shot and killed himself.

After his death, and a decent interval, Ellen Wood arose from her invalid's couch and had a quiet but happy life with her remaining children and grandchildren. She entertained the clan at Sunday luncheons that were remarkable for their length and their calorie content in her remarkable house on the North Shore. Outside, it was straight New England; inside, it was a Portuguese peasant's dream. The walls of the living room and billiard room were upholstered in red brocade. There were three sets of curtains on every window—glass curtains, lace curtains, and red velvet drapes with tassels. There were vast oils of peasants driving oxen down vaguely European village streets with laughing maidens bouncing their skirts provocatively, or fishermen barely escaping storms of enormous proportions. The highlight of the decor were three life-size, white marble busts of William, Billy, and Irene, whose sightless eyes followed every move of the living from their pedestals.

James Cook Ayer was Granfer Ayer's second child and eldest son. He was one of the most charming men who ever lived. He looked just right; talked just right; and smelled of British tweed, Havana cigars, Yardley's after-shave lotion, and the very best brandy—a fragrance that no parfumerie could ever duplicate; he smelled like a GENTLEMAN.

A graduate of Harvard, and a doctor, he wrote the textbook on erysipelas that was a classic for years. But he was really a playboy. He wanted to be an artist, and had some talent, but that was too un-Ayer-like for Granfer Ayer, whose elder sons called him "the Governor." Jamie was given a few years' leeway for his painting (to his father a boyish foible—a "wild oat") and then told to settle down to his profession. So, Dr. James C. Ayer did just that, although he didn't really practice. He fell in love with a divorcée—unheard of. Jamie broke off their relationship and she killed herself. Years later, he married the widow of his doctor.

Jamie adopted his wife's son, Dick, and they had a son of their own, Frederick II. Jamie's wife, May, was very attractive and very social. When Ma and Ellie first met her, they were both astounded to see that she was the living image of the dead divorcée.

Jamie and May Ayer lived in New York and Nassau, and were the "beautiful people" of their time. May was my godmother. (Ma asked her, as she thought it would please her adored brother.) When I was in boarding school, at Dobbs Ferry, in New York, they invited me for Thanksgiving dinner. I was terribly impressed. Their apartment was on Park Avenue, and was a decorator's delight. But to me it had no warmth—or heart—or soul—frigidity in impeccable taste. One wondered where they spent their private time.

The Thanksgiving dinner that I attended was served in their beautiful little dining room, catered by the restaurant downstairs. It made an unforgettable impression on a greedy schoolgirl, all primed for the turkey and fixings. There was Consommé Florentine, squab, braised endive, and a sherbet served from a swan sculptured in ice that had an electric light in its gizzard. After lunch, they didn't know quite what to do with me, so Dick Ayer, who was a darling, took me to see Charles Laughton in *The Wives of Henry VIII,* and put me on the train back to school. I could never describe that Thanksgiving dinner to Ma, as she worshipped her brother, and it would have broken her heart to think of him living in such an atmosphere.

My wedding present from Aunt May was a gold and platinum powder compact, set with square sapphires—just the ticket for a first lieutenant's bride on her way to her first station. On our way to our Bermuda honeymoon, we took it back to Tiffany's and exchanged it for a number of useful and exciting things; one of them being a sterling silver police whistle which my husband, Jim, used with his troops for years. No one but us knew it was silver (it was a private joke).

When Jamie Ayer finally decided to die, he went to the best hospital. I don't know what killed him off, high living or boredom. Ma got him a huge aquarium full of exotic fish, because he had gotten quite senile and couldn't read or do anything much, and she thought it would be nice if he had something pretty to look at.

Ma was distraught when he finally died and said, weeping, to Georgie: "You know, Jamie would be alive today if it hadn't been for his liking for 'West India goods.' To think of my darling Jamie, dying so young!" Georgie asked her how old he was, and she thought for a moment, then sobbed: "He was only seventy-seven."

Uncle Jamie, as a young man, had his own little rendezvous with the unknown. I include it in Ma's story because it was so contrary to the common-sense Ayers and their ways—and yet such strange things happened to nearly all of them. Uncle Jamie had a sporting friend named Willie Mackay, an uncle of Mrs. Irving Berlin, the wife of the composer. Willie was killed under rather unusual circumstances. One day a lady, who said she was a medium, came to Uncle Jamie's office in New York and asked to see him personally. She said that she wanted no money, but that a spirit who called himself Willie kept interrupting her séances, saying that he had died before making up a quarrel he had had with his mother, and asking her to get in touch with "Jim Ayer" and give him the following message: "My mother has wept pitchers of tears; tell her that her tears are keeping me back." The medium had gone to every "J. Ayer" in the telephone book, looking for one who had recently lost a friend named Willy. Uncle Jamie undertook to deliver the message to Mrs. Mackay, and he said, "It brought great comfort."

Granfer Ayer's third child, Chilly, was the most upright and unbending of all the Ayers. Diogenes would have loved him: he was a totally honest man. For some years he was in charge of the family's western holdings and forest properties. Then "the Governor" decided that he too had sown his "wild oats" and summoned him back to Boston and the family office. Chilly said that he never really liked it, but he was an excellent businessman. On holidays he went rattlesnake hunting in Maine. At one point he became engaged to a handsome Boston beauty of the first water. The engagement was about to be announced, and in an excess of feeling, he bought her a grand corsage of orchids and daringly approached her to pin it on her magnificent bust. She backed away from him with little maidenlike screams, and thinking she was just being coy, he advanced on her and pinned the orchid firmly to her shoulder, whereupon he was startled by a long hissing sound as one side of her lovely bosom slowly deflated. She was wearing water wings under her corset cover! Chilly broke the engagement, or rather, let the young lady break it. He said he couldn't marry a woman who was living a lie.

It took Chilly Ayer some time to find another bride after that shock, and he was quite the man about Boston and much in demand at all parties. Finally, he met, courted, and married the beautiful Theodora Ilsley from New York. Her family were old New York—Beekmans and the like. They were poor, but very proud of their inheritance and their significance. Theodora was beautiful, very social, and very condescending. She tried for awhile to be patronizing to Ellie, her stepmother-in-law, who was, after all, a nobody from St. Paul (of all outlandish places), but that did not work. Ellie could out-queen them all, and she also had the biggest aquamarines in Boston.

Chilly and Theodora built a beautiful house in horse country called Juniper Ridge. It was a triumph—hothouse flowers always perfectly arranged, priceless family portraits (Theodora's family), and superb food and drink. In time they had two extraordinarily beautiful daughters, Theodora and Anne Beekman.

Chilly hunted, rode, rode in steeplechases, drove a snappy rig, and went to Boston to the office five days a week. Theodora also rode—sidesaddle, of course—in English tailored riding dress of darkest blue, with an adorable veil fastening down her lady's style top hat. She entertained lavishly in the country, and in her Dartmouth Street mansion in Boston, and raised her daughters to be belles. She was an adoring mother. One enchanting thing she did for the girls when they were small was to organize the "Patchwork Hunt." All of Theo and Anne's little friends met at Juniper Ridge, with their ponies and their pet dogs. There would be a short drag-line laid, over small fences, with some sort of smell in the drag bag that appealed to poodles and pekinese alike, and the little dogs would go screaming off, followed by the little girls on their little ponies, a groom at every fence to rescue any casualties among dogs or girls.

The housekeeping at Juniper Ridge was perfection itself, and was presided over by a lordly Irish butler named Herne. This many-faceted man could make the best martinis this side of Fiddler's Green; could make a centerpiece of water lilies stay open all night (by dropping warm candle wax into the center of each flower so that it could not close); and could do anything any butler out of the best English novel could do—but there was another Herne deep down, and two glimpses of that Herne proved that "one touch of nature makes the whole world kin."

Anne Ayer was to be a bridesmaid for an older friend—some maiden lady of about twenty-five. On the day of the wedding Anne came down to breakfast and said to Herne, "What a lovely day for Miss Florence's wedding." To which Herne replied, "Indeed it is, Miss Anne, and now she will never die wondering."

Herne really made his mark on Boston society at Anne's formal debut. Theodora insisted on only the best for her two beauties, and when the time came for this momentous happening, the Ayers hired the ballroom of the Copley Plaza Hotel (known locally as the "Costly Pleasure"). The dinner before the ball was to be held at the Somerset Club, which is the Inner Sanctum in Boston. It is on Beacon Street, halfway up the sacred hill, and is gradually falling down in a classical and considerate way. The club has always served the best food and drink in the city. But Theodora would always out-Herod Herod, and so she insisted that the wines, liquors, and liqueurs to be served were to come from Chilly's own cellars. Herne brought the wine to the Somerset Club some weeks before the party to be sure that it was settled and fit to drink. He was also put in charge of the whole affair, even to bossing the club's superior staff. Everything went swimmingly.

After dinner the ladies retired to the ladies' retiring room, and the gentlemen forgathered in the gentlemen's likewise, to fortify themselves with cigars and strong waters for the ordeal of the ball. Herne took the last order for the last drink, lit the last cigar, then came up to Chilly with the most benign expression, and, taking a highball from a passing tray said, "Well, Chil, old boy, what a bloody good party that was!"

Chilly told the story all over Boston, and Theodora never recovered from the shame of it. Herne recovered, although as the years went by the chink in his armor of starch widened and his nose grew redder and redder.

With two such devastating daughters to show for it, many of the friends and family wondered why Chilly and Theodora had stopped at two children. Ma told me the reason that she had been given, although she never said who told it to her. When Anne was born, Theodora expressed some surprise that she had not gotten any messages or flowers, except from the senior Ayers and the brothers and sisters, and Chilly said, "Oh, it may be because I never said anything about it. It was only another girl."

Chilly was a marvelous storyteller, and the annual Hunt Breakfast at the Baldpate Inn was never really launched until he told his story of the Blue-Eyed Boy, which is not very funny written down but is hilarious when told, as if by a man with a cleft palate. He told Ma and her younger brother and sister wonderful stories—ones that continued all the time they were growing up—about when he was a "little girl" and lived in Mexico on the side of the volcano, Popacatepetl, and cooked his lamb chops by lowering them into the volcano on a string. He loved the music halls, and would teach the younger ones all the latest popular songs, such as "The Bird in the Gilded Cage" and "She Is More to Be Pitied than Censured" and "You Wouldn't Dare Insult Me, Sir, If Brother Jack Were Here." Ma said he was the most truthful man she ever knew. She quoted him with awe as once answering Ellie's question, "Is it still raining, Charles?" with "It was when I came in, Mamma."

Chilly was too old to fight in World War I, although he did his bit and Theodora did hers, in a madly becoming Red Cross uniform, tailor-made. Life went on as usual. Both daughters went to the Foxcroft School in Middleburg, Virginia, which was the most stylish school of the time, concentrating on fox hunting and fascinating. Theodora entertained and had the expected flirtations, copied from English society. One of her beaux was the rich Bradley Palmer, owner of United Fruit, and a near neighbor in the country. Her other beau was a fellow exile from the faster New York society in which she had been born and had blossomed. He was the editor of the most important newspaper in Boston, and a very clever and sophisticated man, but, unfortunately, he was married to one of the chips off of the Plymouth Rock, whose Pilgrim inheritance did not take kindly to even a coy glance. She was not only old family, but old money, and had four children. A further complication was that the two families were connected by marriage as well as by membership in the same sacred clubs. This particular flirtation (no one ever knew just how far it went) caused a lot of heartbreak and bad feeling, and gave Theodora a black mark in the county society, which she probably considered dull—but even if it was dull, it was all there was.

The two girls married within six months, both to the obvious men—prime Pilgrim beef on one hand, and the worn and trodden grapes of a once good New York vintage on the other. But both bridegrooms were gentlemen with outside incomes and impeccable lineage. *Happy* marriages were not the first priority on Theodora's requirement for her beautiful girls.

After Theodora died, Chilly married again—at a suitable interval—the agreeable and lovely secretary of a school that some of his grandsons had attended. His two sons-in-law were his groomsmen. Chilly's last years were not lonely. He went to the office every day, and as he got older and slightly forgetful, he sometimes went on Sunday. He constantly compared his new wife's excellent housekeeping with Theodora's—which he had never seemed to notice when Theodora was alive. This kept the new wife on the verge of hysterics, which kept the remaining brothers and sisters hovering helpfully in the wings. Herne trickled from the scene, and things ended gently for Chilly with Death's dark nurse.

> Wisdom is folly,
> The elder man's dolly,
> They dandle and play
> With dolly all day
> Till Death's dark nurse takes their dolly away.

Granfer Ayer's fourth child and second daughter was Louise. She was about ten years older than Ma, and as well as being half-sisters, they were devoted lifelong friends. Louise was beautiful in a fragile, distinguished way, and had a "very good mind." Ellie's first meeting with her stepdaughter Louise on the steps of the Lowell mansion was the one stage-managed by Louise's Aunt Florence. It was unfortunate for them both. But there is a poem often quoted by Ma that must have been one of Ellie's life maxims—and it goes:

> He drew a circle and shut me out; heretic, rebel, a thing to flout,
> But love and I had the wit to win—we drew a circle and took him in!

Louise was very shy and would never let the family have parties for her, nor would she drive in the open carriage, because she thought it was showing off. She had one or two intimate girlfriends, and Ellie encouraged them to visit Louise and made things delightful for the little girls. She really "drew the circle and took her in."

For all Louise's shyness, she had a great many young men who were seriously in love with her. She chose her half-brother Fred's tutor, young Donald Gordon, and they had a short but happy marriage. Donald had to put himself through Harvard as his father—a medical missionary in Japan—was not affluent. The Gordons were grand people, amusing, cultivated, and very spiritual.

Donald and Louise had two children: Jean, who was just three weeks older than I and who was my best friend; and Crawford, who was younger, but only in years. They lived at Drumlin Farm in Lincoln, Massachusetts, where Donald ran a model farm and Louise raised Welsh terriers. Donald died of leukemia when Jean was about ten years old. He was deeply mourned by the whole family, especially Louise. "The Lord loveth a shining mark."

After Donald's death, Louise's health broke down and she became somewhat of a recluse. Jean Gordon spent a great deal of time with us—almost as a sister. In due time, Louise remarried to Donald's best friend, Conrad Hatheway. He was a widower with one daughter, darling Mabel. She was a real daughter to Louise and it was a happy family, its greatest tragedy being that Louise lived just a few years too long.

Ma's younger brother, Frederick Ayer (Fred), was her joy and her delight. He was a couple of years younger than she was, but that made less and less difference as the years passed. They were as close as a brother and sister could be—and another blessing was that he and Georgie were devoted lifelong friends. Fred went to the Hill School and then, of course, to Harvard. He took the considered-a-must world tour after college and shot a rhinoceros and a lot of lovely harmless horned creatures in Africa, whose innocent heads hung all over his house in Wenham for years. He married the beautiful, spirited Hilda

Proctor Rice from Ipswich, and they had five children. Hilda was really "cold roast Boston." Proctors and Rices are buried in every old meetinghouse cemetery in the best small towns in the New England area.

The baby of the Ayer family was Mary Katharine, four and a half years younger than Ma. She had dark hair, sparkling blue eyes, and was always most exquisitely groomed and dressed—her taste was incredibly good in everything she ever wore or said or did, and she had a marvelous sense of fun. In due time, after an exciting courtship that had the audience on tenterhooks, she married dark, dashing, debonair Keith Merrill, a Yale man. He was in the foreign service, and Kay had a fascinating life abroad—and made the most of it. They had three of the best-looking children in the whole connection, bringing Granfer Ayer's descendants to seven children and twenty grandchildren.

The Ayer family was quite famous in Boston for their devotion. Someone said that at a party the Ayers all got together "like birds on a telephone wire" and they kept in close touch all of their lives. Ma's brothers and sisters were truly her best friends, not just relatives. I know that to Ma they were always, next to Georgie, "the closest kin there is."

Chapter 3

Growing Up

In 1896, Granfer Ayer's doctors recommended that he retire from active business. He protested vigorously, saying that, after all, he was only seventy-three years old and in his working prime. Ellie, with loving tact, suggested that all they needed was a change of scene and a good long holiday—she, from the responsibilities of running a huge establishment, and Sir Frederick, from his business interests. She also felt it would be a good opportunity for the four children (she counted her stepdaughter, Louise, as one of them) to learn to speak perfect French. So, complete with outriders in the form of two governesses (Boombi, the German governess, and Gogo, the French governess) and a tutor for Freddie, Ellie and Sir Frederick and the children went "abroad" for two wonderful years.

One of the gifts this sojourn gave Ma was a complete familiarity with classical and conversational French. Years later, when they were stationed in Hawaii, Ma published a book of Hawaiian legends translated into French. She spoke to Georgie and to us in French, particularly at meals, so we all grew up bilingual, but none of us could compare to her. Another long-lasting gift, which now belongs to her great-granddaughter, Beatrice Waters, was The Doll—Marguerite. Ma earned this doll by not speaking a word of English for three months. Marguerite is not the most beautiful doll in the world, but she is surely one of the most beloved and most traveled. She is about ten inches high, with very shiny blue-glass eyes, real auburn hair, and a slight flaw in her porcelain nose. Ma picked her because of this flaw—she said that other little girls might be put off by it and not see the real doll underneath. She was Ma's totem, and went everywhere with her—frequently in a matching costume. Marguerite had real kid gloves with tiny buttons, real tortoise shell hairpins and a comb, and underwear embroidered with the letter "M"—as well as an ermine toque and muff for opera wear. She is definitely a doll's doll.

Another unforgettable memory of the year in Paris was the sub rosa visits to the Bois de Boulogne to see their Aunt Josephine (their uncle J. C. Ayer's widow) drive by in her stylish landau. The lady had long been estranged from the Frederick Ayers, by her own wish, and was cutting quite a figure in Paris at that time. Scarlet fever, or some other childhood disease, had left her completely bald, but she rose above that and had a wig to match every costume. She also had her poodles rinsed to match her color-of-the-day. Aunt Josephine was the first lady Ma ever saw who wore false eyelashes and eyebrows, although these were ordinary in color. The French governess, Gogo, took them on these walks, but it was clearly understood that it was not to be talked about at home. Gogo had a sense of the dramatic that fitted in well with the family.

During the years abroad, the whole family spent one winter on a houseboat on the Nile in Egypt. It was a big, comfortable, clumsy boat with a square sail. Going up the Nile it was pulled by mules and horses on a towpath beside the canal. The older half-brothers and sisters came for part of the time, and one of Ma's most vivid memories was of her half-brother, Jamie, taking a palm thorn from the foot of an Egyptian laborer. Word spread up the river that there was a doctor on the boat, and whenever they went up to tie to the shore at night, the banks would be crowded with the lame, the halt, and the blind, wailing and praying for aid, and holding their sick babies up in the air for the doctor to see. Jamie did not have any of the equipment he needed (he could have used a trained staff and an operating room), but he did the best he could. However, some of the cases were beyond the scope of any doctor—there were lepers, horribly deformed children, cases of gangrene, and nameless disfiguring diseases. Finally, the Ayer children were taken below decks at landing time, but there they would fight for the best places to see through the curtained windows what was going on. This only ended when Jamie's vacation was over and he went back to the United States.

The archaeological discoveries in Egypt were just beginning to be of worldwide interest at this time, and there was a climate of discovery and excitement. The children were allowed to go ashore with their governesses, and the boatman's son went along with them as an interpreter. He was a boy of about thirteen, and a great favorite with Ma and Freddie. One day he showed them a newly opened tomb. Ma rushed up and was about to jump down into it, "in case she might find something" (a quality of curiosity that lasted all her life), and only the Egyptian boy's strong arms kept her from leaping into a recess filled with cobras. She said when the snakes heard the commotion they came out from the recesses of the tomb, hissing and spreading their hoods and staring up at the children with soulless eyes.

But they did get into another tomb, where the mummy was lying outside of its case, partially unwrapped from its four-thousand-year-old grave clothes. Ma stole his big toe, which we still have. It doesn't look like much of anything, as the ancient linen is more or less embedded in the aromatic gums they used in the process of mummification. It is kept in a jelly jar with a tight lid, and when you first open the jar, you can smell, wafted as a memory down the ages, the faintest fragrance of something like tar, and something sweeter and more lonely. Ma used to tell us it was "the odor of eternity."

Ma had another near-adventure as the result of a birthday gift of ten dollars from her other half-brother, Chilly. She had long admired the tattoo on the back of the boatman—the father of her friend—who steered the barge. With the guidance of her young friend, she took off with her ten dollars for the tattoo parlor where the boatman had been decorated, planning to have a full-rigged ship tattooed across her chest. Her guide quite agreed with her that it would enhance her beauty no end. The governess discovered she was missing just in time.

After their return from Europe, the family removed from Lowell to Boston. Ellie thought the long commuting from Lowell to Boston to the office was too much for Sir Frederick in the winter. They lived in a rented house until Granfer Ayer built a house at 395 Commonwealth Avenue that was the wonder and envy of all. It had every modern convenience—bathrooms, an elevator, a dumb-waiter, electric light, a telephone—everything. It was otherwise a typical Boston town house of the time—miles high with rooms front and back, and stairs and hall up the center; full of Tiffany glass, marble inlay, parquet flooring, and velvet draw-curtains over lace curtains, over translucent window curtains.[1] It was very handsome, though considered brash and nouveau by the "old money" families with their jade collections and their Georgian antiques, brought back in the clipper ships from faraway places.

Ma and Kay continued with the governesses for some time, although Ma did spend a term or two at the super-fashionable Miss Carroll's School, but it didn't make enough impression on her for her to ever talk about it.

---

1. In 2005 it was a woman's residence for Boston-area colleges and universities, and a fund-raising campaign is under way to restore many of the Louis Comfort Tiffany features of the house.

There was, of course, a dancing school that everyone who was anyone attended. Ma had outgrown it by the time Freddie and Kay went there, but she used to tell us about their meeting with a starchy little boy named Ernest Simpson. None of the girls liked to dance with him because his poor little hands always sweated right through his kid gloves. He grew up to be the second husband of a Baltimore belle named Wallis Warfield.

And then there was the great sport of Pearson-baiting. J. C. Ayer's daughter had married a fine man named Pearson, but as far as Mrs. Pearson was concerned, the feud with the Frederick Ayers was still on, and her son, Freddy, was told that he must never speak to any one of the Frederick Ayer children: if they spoke to him, he was to come straight home. Kay and Freddie Ayer used to draw lots to see which one would go up to poor Freddy Pearson. As soon as one of them did, Freddy had to leave the party.

The winter in Egypt had been a tremendous influence in the lives of Ma and Kay, and they loved all things Egyptian. Granfer Ayer's great friend was Theodore M. Davis, the famous American Egyptologist, who lived in Newport, and they wanted very much to accept his frequent invitations to spend a week at his house there. There was the call of Egypt, but there was also the call of Newport with its fabulous "cottages," its high-flying society, and, although neither of them was "out," they longed to see the "beautiful people." They were a little in awe of Mr. Davis, who was the only person they knew to call their father "Ayer," but he had always been very kind to them, and he had given Ma, as a christening present, a silver porringer with amoretti and roses on it in bas relief from which she had eaten her porridge every day of her life. After a good deal of talking it over, the Ayers decided that the girls could spend a week with Mr. and Mrs. Davis, as they had been invited so often. On the day they were to leave, while they were eating breakfast, Granfer Ayer put down his newspaper and said, "Your mother and I think you should be told that Mr. and Mrs. Davis have not spoken directly to one another for thirty years."

It was a week Ma never forgot. A distant cousin named Mrs. Andrews lived with the Davises, and when Mrs. Davis said something to the effect of "Theodore, I would like to take the Ayer girls for a drive this afternoon, may I have the carriage?" Mrs. Andrews would answer, "Mr. Davis, Mrs. Davis would like to have the use of the carriage this afternoon to take the young ladies for a drive." Mr. Davis would reply, without looking up from what he was reading, "Mrs. Andrews, please tell Mrs. Davis she is most welcome to use the carriage for the pleasure of our young guests." And so it went.

The highlight of the visit was when Mr. Davis took the girls into his study to show them his private collection, and gave them a taste of honey from the tomb of an Egyptian queen who had been dead for four thousand years.

Toward the end of the week, Ma and Kay would go down to the rocky boulders on the beach and scream at the top of their lungs to get it out of their systems. Glorious Newport! The hub of society! Ma never forgot it.

Ma was a real "Pocket Venus." She had very beautiful blue eyes and exquisitely marked brows, a softly rounded chin and long, rich, dark auburn hair. All this was in addition to being talented, witty, and, of course, a considerable heiress. She started having serious beaux some time before she made her debut. Two that we particularly liked her to tell us about were the musician and the Russian count. The musician,[2] who remained a lifelong friend, wrote lovely songs, many of them based on American Indian music. Our favorite was "From the Land of the Sky Blue Water." Whenever I felt sad, I would sing it, which would make me feel even worse, and to this day I wonder, was the Indian girl a real mute, or just mute from homesickness?

The count had stunning mustaches and wore seed pearl tassels on his boots. One day Ma remarked, playfully, that she had heard that if you scratched a Russian, you found a Tartar. Immediately, the count rolled up his sleeve and ran his long shiny fingernails down his arm until blood flowed from the welts and cried, "Scratch me, Meees Ayer, scratch me!"

Ma had met her real beau, almost, when she was a very little girl. On the Ayers' first visit to California in 1892, they stayed with the Bannings in Wilmington, which was by the ocean, and they decided to take a day and drive to Los Angeles to see Ellie's sister, "Kash" Banning, who lived in the Banning mansion there—the one called "The Barn."

This fantastic house was actually built on top of a stable. The horses lived on the ground floor, which surrounded a court, and all the horses' doors looked out onto this grassy space. There was a huge carriage house on one corner, where they had retired Ellie's uncle Phineas's great transcontinental coaches. These were kept in mint condition and had a most wonderful smell. We used to be allowed to play in them when we were little—there were even bullet holes in some of them, where outlaws had tried to hold up the mail in the old days. Above the stable were the living quarters—beautiful big rooms with intricately hand-carved fireplaces, cornices, and ceilings—all done by a retired ship's carpenter—for the Bannings had gotten in on the ground floor of the California shipping business.

2. Charles Wakefield Cadman (1881–1946).

Ma refused to go on the excursion to Los Angeles. She always got slightly carriage sick, and, anyhow, she had a new book she wanted to read, so they left without her. When they got back to Wilmington that night, they all talked about their wonderful visit with all the Banning cousins, including young Hancock Banning's new wife, who had been a Miss Smith. Her father, Colonel Smith, had been in the party, and with him were his stepchildren, the Pattons, and, among them, the dearest little boy, whose name was "Georgie" and who was just a few months older than Ma. He had big blue eyes, and beautiful golden curls, and was such a *good* little boy that he would have never let his father and mother and brother go off alone just so he could read a book—he would have come with them. Ma decided that right there Georgie Patton must be a little prig: she told her parents she hoped she would never meet him and if she did, she would certainly not play with him.

Chapter 4
The Pattons

When the various interrelated families started west, headed by Georgie's maternal grandfather, Benjamin Davis Wilson (called "Don Benito"), and Ellie's uncle, Phineas Banning, they found very few people of "their sort." There were many fine Spanish families and Mexican families, and a great many Indians of high and low degrees—all Catholics. There were not many Americans from the East. So the pioneer families stuck together, married each other, and were a separate society for many years. After the Civil War, many of the southern relatives went west. There was nothing left for them in the ruins of their politics and their plantations—and their way of life.

Andrew Glassell, a well-known lawyer, left Virginia before the Civil War, as Eliza Patton had refused his hand in marriage twelve times; when she did it the thirteenth time, he took her refusal to heart and left home forever. After the war, his widowed sister, Susan Glassell Patton (Eliza's sister-in-law), was left with four small children; her old father, who was blind; and her gallant brother, Commander William Glassell, commander of the submarine *Little David* in the battle of Charleston Harbor, who had been captured and imprisoned by the Yankees at Fort Warren, and was dying of tuberculosis. Brother Andrew was not rich, but he sent them all he could to help pay for their journey west, and Susan sold everything she owned except her husband's sword, saddle, gold watch, and Bible. Willie sold what he had, and old Mr. Glassell had already given his worldly goods to the Confederate cause. The family made their way west by ship and crossed the Isthmus of Panama (what a story that is!) and joined Andrew in Los Angeles. Andrew by this time was married, with a large family, and things were very difficult for a few years.

Then, up from the south, from Mexico, came the "Knight In Shining Armor"—and that he was—to all who ever knew him. Colonel George Hugh Smith was the first cousin, beloved companion, and Virginia Military Institute classmate of Colonel George Smith Patton, Susan's husband, who had been killed in the battle of Cedar Creek in 1864. Colonel Smith had never married because he had always been in love with Susan. Andrew Glassell took Colonel Smith into his law firm with great enthusiasm—Colonel Smith was a very brilliant man—and in 1870 Colonel Smith married the Widow Patton, adopting her four children, who adored him. Colonel Smith and Susan had two children of their own—the redoubtable Annie Ophelia, who married Hancock Banning, and Eltinge, who died as a young boy "full of promise." Poor little Eltinge died of lock-jaw and, for this reason, none of us were ever allowed to go barefoot in California.

Susan died of cancer in 1883 and Colonel Smith brought up the five children as his own. He was a noble and generous man, and he raised them on stories of the heroism of George Patton, the real father and grandfather they never knew. His stepson, George William (later Smith) Patton, married Ruth Wilson, daughter of Don Benito, so that huge Spanish-American family was added to the clan as well. George and Ruth's son was that good little boy of Ma's first California visit, Georgie Patton.

Old Phineas Banning would meet all the boats that arrived at Wilmington, and when there were passengers of distinction, he would send a vaquero on a horse to notify Don Benito Wilson of their arrival. A coach would be standing at the door of the Banning house in Wilmington, with a vaquero hanging onto the bridle of each blindfolded bronco in harness. When the passengers were in the coach, the blindfolds would be whipped off by the vaqueros, who would leap aside, and the horses would be off at a run across the unbroken country to Lake Vineyard, often with Phineas Banning as whip.

The fence around "The Barn" was of cast iron, made like a row of cornstalks, the stalks painted green, and the finials, which were ears of corn, painted yellow. The Barn really belonged to Captain William Banning, Aunt "Kash" Banning's brother-in-law, an old bachelor who had never married because, according to the family story, he too was in love with Kash who married his brother Joe. However, all the Bannings lived in The Barn and Kash kept house for them. The one stipulation William Banning—"Uncle Captain"—made when Kash took over his house was that she would serve ice cream at every meal. He even had it for breakfast on his porridge. We thought this was really living!

Ruth Ellen Patton Totten (February 28, 1915, to November 24, 1993) with a friend.

Frederick Ayer and Ellen Banning Ayer on their wedding trip, Paris, 1884.

Beatrice Banning Ayer, 1908.

Cast of *Ondine,* Catalina Island, 1902. Left to right: Georgie—Kuhlborn, Katherine Ayer—Hulda, Anita Patton—Huldebrand, Bee—Ondine.

Ayers, Bannings, and all the connections at Catalina Island, 1902.

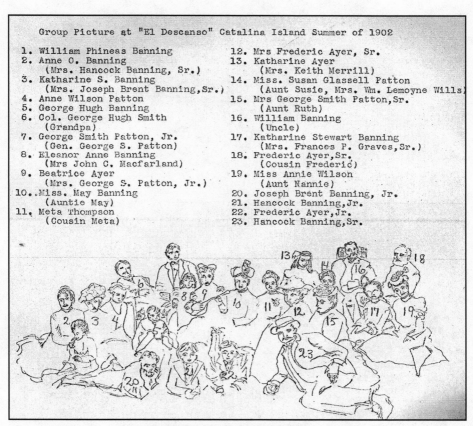

Group Picture at "El Descanso" Catalina Island Summer of 1902

1. William Phineas Banning
2. Anne O. Banning
   (Mrs. Hancock Banning, Sr.)
3. Katharine S. Banning
   (Mrs. Joseph Brent Banning,Sr.)
4. Anne Wilson Patton
5. George Hugh Banning
6. Col. George Hugh Smith
   (Grandpa)
7. George Smith Patton, Jr.
   (Gen. George S. Patton)
8. Eleanor Anne Banning
   (Mrs John C. Macfarland)
9. Beatrice Ayer
   (Mrs. George S. Patton, Jr.)
10. Miss. May Banning
    (Auntie May)
11. Meta Thompson
    (Cousin Meta)
12. Mrs Frederic Ayer, Sr.
13. Katharine Ayer
    (Mrs. Keith Merrill)
14. Miss. Susan Glassell Patton
    (Aunt Susie, Mrs. Wm. Lemoyne Wills)
15. Mrs George Smith Patton,Sr.
    (Aunt Ruth)
16. William Banning
    (Uncle)
17. Katharine Stewart Banning
    (Mrs. Frances P. Graves,Sr.)
18. Frederic Ayer,Sr.
    (Cousin Frederic)
19. Miss Annie Wilson
    (Aunt Nannie)
20. Joseph Brent Banning, Jr.
21. Hancock Banning,Jr.
22. Frederic Ayer,Jr.
23. Hancock Banning,Sr.

Who's who in photo, opposite page.

Old Lake Vineyard.

Bee's debut, 1908. Left to right: Elizabeth Dunn (Buford), Beatrice Banning Ayer (Patton), Katherine Ayer (Merrill), Frederick Ayer (Granfer), James Cook Ayer (Jamie).

Ellen Banning Ayer, Beatrice Banning Ayer, wedding day, May 1910.

Beatrice Ayer, 1910.

Lieutenant and Mrs. George Smith Patton, May 26, 1910.

Mr. and Mrs. Frederick Ayer

request the honour of your presence

at the marriage of their daughter

Beatrice Banning

to

Mr. George Smith Patton, Junior

Lieutenant 15th United States Cavalry

on Thursday afternoon, May the twenty-sixth

at half after three o'clock

Saint John's Church

Beverly Farms,   Massachusetts

Wedding invitation.

Mr. and Mrs. Frederick Ayer

request the pleasure of your company

immediately after the ceremony

at Avalon, Prides Crossing

Please reply

Train leaves North Station, Boston

for Beverly Farms at 2.15 P. M.

Returning leaves Prides Crossing at 6.53 P. M.

This card admits to Special Car

Reception and travel instructions.

Left to right: Katherine Ayer, Frederick Ayer, Jr., Beatrice Ayer, 1908.

Left to right: Katherine Ayer, Ellen Banning
Ayer, Beatrice Ayer Patton, 1911.

Anne Wilson Patton, Tinta, 1920.

Little Bea's christening, 1912.

The Pattons, 1918. Bee, Ruth Ellen, age three, Georgie, and Little Bea, age seven.

Little Bea and Ruth Ellen, Avalon, 1918.

The photo Bee gave Georgie to take with him to France in 1918.

Charles Fanning Ayer, Chilly, 1918.

Tank—the deaf bull terrier.

Ruth Wilson Patton, Bama, 1884

Nannie Wilson, Aunt Nannie, 1885.

George S. Patton, Bamps, 1890.

Little Bea with the infamous goat who butted her tutor, Thomasville, Georgia, 1918.

Georgie dressed for parade, VMI, 1903.

Georgie and Fred Ayer, Jr. (Bee's brother) at the Farm, 1908;
they were best friends throughout their lives.

James C. Ayer and May Ayer with their son, Frederick.

Avalon.

395 Commonwealth Avenue, Boston.

Chapter 5
Georgie

When the Ayers returned to California in 1902 "in the [train] cars," there was quite a crowd to meet them at the station. Young Georgie Patton was included in the reception committee because he was just Ma's age, and everyone thought it would be nice for her to have a young man to introduce her to his friends. Georgie's younger sister, Anita, was included in everything, and was my greatest source of information (after Ma) of the California good times.

Ma, who was sixteen years old at this time, had already had three proposals of marriage; she got off the train to be smothered with Banning kisses and admiration. She wore her long auburn hair in a braid that reached the hem of her skirt, and under her arm she carried her constant companion, Marguerite. The girl and the doll were dressed alike in smart suit dresses of crash linen, suitable to the California climate. But Georgie took one look at the much-touted "Belle of Boston" and backed away in disgust. In California "young ladies" of sixteen had their hair up and most certainly did *not* play with dolls. If anyone thought he was going to escort this little kid around, they were making a big mistake. His friends would laugh him off the face of the earth!

It was a wonderful summer, anyhow. Georgie was soon to go off to Lexington, Virginia, to be a gentleman cadet at the Virginia Military Institute, and all his doting aunts and cousins and his father, who idolized him, were going to give him a summer to remember—and so they did. That was the summer when Uncle Captain Banning, on July 4, filled one of the old Catalina Island ferries with fireworks, and at dusk set fire to it so that for hours the sky was filled with rainbows and stars and fiery Catherine wheels, and great explosions that seemed to mark the end of an era and the beginning of a new one. The family watched and picnicked from the new ferry.

Then the clans went off to their cottages on Catalina, which, at that time, belonged to the Banning family. There was sailing and swimming and fishing, picnics, tennis, and sing-songs; all the young men went camping and goat hunting.

The highlight of the summer was a play put on by the young people. They chose "Ondine," a fantasy by De La Motte Fouqué. It is a romantic and touching story about a water sprite named Ondine who was adopted by an old fisherman and his wife. Ondine won a human soul when she was beloved and married by the knight Huldebrand. But when Huldebrand was lured away from her by the wicked Bertalda, Ondine turned back into a water sprite.

The programs were printed (I have one here before me now).

PREFACE
This is the story of the Knight Huldebrand of Ringstetten and of Ondine, telling how the knight wedded with a water sprite, and what chanced therefrom; and how the knight died and was buried; and how Ondine returned to her element beneath the Mediterranean Sea.

CAST

Ondine, a water sprite	Miss Beatrice Ayer
Bertalda, a lady of rank	Miss Katharine Banning
Hulda, wife of a fisherman	Miss Katharine Ayer
Huldebrand, knight of Ringstetten	Miss Anita Patton
Rudlier, a fisherman	Mr. Joseph Banning, Jr.
Father Heilman, a priest	Mr. Frederick Ayer, Jr.
Kuhlborn, a water spirit	Mr. George Patton, Jr.
Rolf, a page	Miss Katharine Ayer

Act I	Interior of a Fisherman's Cottage
Act II	The same, a month later
Act III	Three months later; Castle Ringstetten
Act IV	A Boat on the Danube River; Moonlight
Act V	A year later, Castle Ringstetten

Miss Banning—Stage Manager

New Scenery   Grand Orchestra   New Costumes

Opening Night, Friday, September 5, 1902

AVALON

Santa Catalina Island

By the end of the rehearsals, the play, and the summer, Ma and Georgie were in love—as they would be for the rest of their lives.

There is a letter from Ma to Mrs. Patton, mailed on November 14, 1902, that shows she was most definitely leaving all her doors open.

395 Commonwealth Ave.
Boston, Mass.

Dear Aunt Ruth:

Thank you very much for your letter—it gave me a great deal of pleasure.

I am sorry to have to write you with this ink [it is bright purple, even now] but someone has put water in my black ink. . . .

I am pretty busy now but have not much studying to do, out of lessons, as I have it all to do in the afternoon. I am not allowed to work by lamplight, although that is what I am using now.

I went to see [Eleonora] Duse three times while she was here and think she is a wonderful actress. You have seen her, I suppose.

I have been to two football games this fall—one, a Harvard-Pennsylvania game which Harvard lost 11 to 0, and one game at Fred's school.

Frederick has been having extra lessons too, so I think he could sympathize with Georgie—I hope Georgie's are all over by this time.

We had a Hallowe'en party the other night, and had a fine time playing all the ghostly games which belong to that particular night. I am sorry Ormsby Phillips broke his arm and hope it will soon be well.

I know that Georgie's birthday comes sometime this month, but not the exact date. When it comes, please, spank him seventeen times for me and give him my very best birthday compliments.

I am sorry that this letter is so blotted and badly written, my writing is famous for its untidiness. Please give my love to your dear family.

Yours lovingly,

Beatrice

P.S. You asked me about coming back this winter. I don't really expect we shall, but shall do my best to have the family go to California in the early spring or summer. I don't know anything about it though.

BBA

P.S. Katharine sends Georgie her wishes too.

The summer over, the Ayers went back to Boston. Granfer Ayer had taken up four-in-hand driving, in addition to his other hobbies of swimming, rowing, and horseback riding. Granfer Ayer loved horses and had had a way with them since his childhood on his grandfather's farm. He rode with Ma and Kay, on the bridle-path in the center strip of Commonwealth Avenue in Boston, after they built the house at 395. He was insistent that his girls ride in divided skirts— very daring, indeed—as he felt that side-saddle riding was bad for their backs.

The stable for 395 was in the mews in back of the house, and Ma always had a soft spot for their coachman, Henry. When he was hired by the Ayers, he told Granfer Ayer that he would never want a regular day off, just permission to attend all public hangings.

Of course, the horses went wherever the family went, which was 395 in the winter and "The Farm" in Newton, Massachusetts, in the summer. Ellie once told Granfer Ayer that the only gifts she would ever really want were roses. So when "The Farm" was remodeled, extensive gardens and greenhouses were added to it. When Louise Ayer first became fond of her stepmother, Ellie, she would not call her "mama"—she called her "my rose friend."

However, "The Farm" was near water and Ma caught malaria while they were there so Granfer Ayer put it on the market.[1] That malaria was a cause of great chagrin to Ma later in life, as she was never allowed to give blood to the blood bank.

If "The Farm" was out of favor, Ellie decided that Sir Frederick still needed a summer retreat, and so she took the train from Boston to all the points within an easy commute of Boston. She finally chose the small seaside village of Prides Crossing, near Beverly, Massachusetts, and there they built her their last house, "Avalon-By-The-Sea," in 1905.

Prides Crossing was a very clannish place, inhabited by "cold roast Boston's best"—the old whaling and sailing families, the descendants of the shipmasters. When the Ayers bought the old Robbins place and tore it down to build "Avalon," the neighbors were appalled at the vulgar "new money" coming into their sanctum. "Avalon" was a ducal mansion in the Italianate style, with stucco walls and bas reliefs of cherubs over the French windows. The circular staircase rose up from and around a marble paved hall, lit by a giant skylight. The enormous living room ran the length of the back of the house, with tall windows framed in wisteria, and there was a musician's balcony over the grand piano, which stood at the end of the room opposite the fireplace—large enough to "roast an ox." Under the musicians' gallery was a room strictly for flower arranging, with a chute to the basement for dead flowers and trash. It was a most improbable house, but one of the loveliest in America.[2] The whole downstairs always smelled of lilies and roses, and ghosts of happy summers.

The next-door neighbors, the Misses Kay and Louisa Loring, decided that while they could not stop the Ayers from coming, they could certainly stop them from spreading and mingling, so they asked their brother, Judge Loring,

---

1. It was still owned by Frederick Ayer at his death in 1918.
2. Following Katharine Ayer Merrill's death in 1981, the house passed out of family hands. It was recently taken down and moved in train cars to Ohio, where it is scheduled to be rebuilt.

to have a fence put up on the rocks that stretched out into the sea between the two beaches. This was done forthwith. One day Judge Loring, who was a giant of a man, went out onto the rocks and tore the fence up with his own hands. He told his sisters that he had met Frederick Ayer on the train to Boston several times and that he was a "capital fellow." So that was that. However, no one in the Ayer family ever went onto the Lorings' beach without a direct invitation from one of the numerous Lorings. This was not a great privation as there were as many Lorings as there were Ayers. The generations grew up together and mingled. Eventually, Miss Kay and Miss Louisa came to Avalon for musical afternoons and tea. In 1943 Aunt Kay Merrill's daughter, Rosemary, married Caleb Loring, Jr. The holes where the fence was fastened are still there, bored deeply into the rock and full of barnacles now.

Ma made her debut in Boston when she was the right age—approximately eighteen—and was taken into the correct "sewing circle." She had a marvelous time. It made her feel very grown up to have her name on Ellie's calling cards:

> Mrs. Frederick Ayer
> Miss Ayer
> Thursdays

It also meant that she had to be at home on Ellie's "at home" days, when the other ladies and their daughters came to call and drink tea. Kay was away at boarding school, Miss Masters', in Dobbs Ferry, New York, and Freddy went from the Hill School to Harvard.

A very close friendship had formed between the Ayers and the Pattons; and Georgie, who was at VMI for a year, and then for five years at West Point (and, later, Nita Patton and young Kash Banning, who were at Miss Spence's School in New York), spent short vacations at the Ayers'.

Georgie went to VMI in 1903. He was right in Patton country: his grandfather and his six great-uncles had all been educated there, and his father had been the "Number One Graduate" in the Class of 1877. One of Georgie's cousins was a professor at the Institute. The Lexington cemetery was full of dead Pattons, Slaughters, Strothers, and Williamses, and Georgie wrote to his father, "I have so many kinfolk here that when I am not walking on them, I am kissing them."

The Virginia Military Institute was still suffering from the aftereffects of the Civil War, so when Georgie was offered an appointment to West Point (thanks to his father's unceasing efforts) he transferred to the Military Academy, as he and his family felt it would give him a better start in the military career on which he had set his heart. For his entire college career, which lasted for six years, either his mother or his doting Aunt Nannie lived in nearby lodgings. They wanted to be near "the boy" in case he needed anything.

There are some pathetic letters between Georgie's parents, written during that time, telling each other how they miss each other, and how someday, when the children are grown, they will be together, never to part. There are many references to "walking hand-in-hand into the sunset." In the meantime, they encouraged each other to stay near "the boy," and then near "little Nita," and bear their mutual loneliness as best they could. Aunt Nannie, of course, loved "the boy" above all things. He was the be-all and the end-all of her life, the child she never had.

Aunt Nannie's story is a sad one. Back in the 1870s both the Wilson girls, Nannie and Ruth, fell in love with the dashing young George Patton—even before he attended VMI and then afterwards, when he went into his uncle's and stepfather's law firm. Young George chose Ruth Wilson. To make it sadder, they all lived together in old Lake Vineyard. When the Pattons finally built their own home, Aunt Nannie, as a matter of course, moved right in with them. So all her life she lived in the house with the only man she had ever loved, and she lived vicariously through his son Georgie. When George Patton died in 1926, she moved out and built her own house. I have often wondered how Georgie Patton grew up to be the man he was with two strong-minded women (his mother and his aunt) baby-sitting him until he married Ma. Fortunately, Ma, a member of a large family, loved them all and took their constant presence for granted.

As a cadet at West Point, Georgie wrote to his mother, "The Ayers are so awfully nice that it is positively oppressive. We ride, swim, sail, motor and see *Bee.* Be sure though, I have not told her that she is the only girl I have ever loved, but she is—though it would be fatal for me to mention that fact now or perhaps ever. She is very nice to me and I think likes me for she has been wearing my favorite color dresses ever since I said I liked them. Gosh, those skirted bipeds at Catalina, who pawn themselves off as girls, aren't in it with her shadow. But, O Lord, what an ass I am!"

Georgie's college career and the courtship were long. As a West Point freshman, or "plebe" (cadet slang for freshman), he failed math and had to repeat the truly grim "plebe" year. He always stood among the top ten men in the class for discipline and military aptitude, but he had a real handicap. Because of this and because Aunt Nannie had decided that he was "delicate," he did not learn to read or write until he was twelve years old. We now know he was dyslexic. Aunt Nannie liked to read aloud to him. It must be admitted that her choice of reading material was admirable: *Pilgrim's Progress,* Plutarch's *Lives, Pausanias,* the *Iliad* and the *Odyssey, The March of Xenophon, The Ten Thousand, Alexander the Great*—anything and everything about Napoleon. He had Siegfried and Beowulf for his heroes, along with Robert E. Lee and Stonewall Jackson. The stories of the Civil War he heard right from the men who had fought in it: his stepgrandfather, Colonel Smith, and the Confederate guerilla, J. S. Mosby, who had migrated to California and was partially supported, in his old age, by the Pattons. Georgie lived and played in the company of heroes, dead and alive.

This, however, did not help his spelling or his math. When he was twelve years old, his father finally rebelled against the "hands that rock the cradle" ruling "the boy," and sent him to the local grammar school, run by Mr. Clark, a famous Latin scholar and historian. But Georgie never really caught up, and got through his six painful college years by memorizing the textbooks. When he found out that Napoleon couldn't spell, he quit trying himself.

His failure to pass his sophomore, or "yearling," year was extremely traumatic to everyone. He was terribly afraid that Ma wouldn't wait for him. His father wrote him a wonderful letter, in it referring to Ma as a "fine little woman," and assuring him that if she was worth having, she would wait. It never occurred to Georgie that Ma was in love with him—he was too humble at that point in his life—and his failure to pass had humbled him even more deeply, but I am sure his parents knew she loved him, as did hers.

But aside from the difficulties of getting an education, Georgie's college years afforded him great good times. He "dragged" Ma to many football weekends, with dances (or hops) on Saturday night, and picnics where she was the undoubted belle. Georgie was on the varsity football team, but he never made the Navy Game—the great moment of the year at West Point—because by the time *the* game came along (near Thanksgiving weekend) he had tried so hard that he always had a broken bone. He spent most of his short leaves with the Ayers, and Ma visited the Pattons and the Bannings in California during several of the summers, and, as in all things, the happy times were remembered, and the long cold days of study and drill faded into the background. Georgie and Ma wrote to each other constantly. He worried also about how he looked, and was always wishing that she could have seen him on such-and-such-a-day. His beautiful golden curls were disappearing and he worried a lot about losing his hair—which, of course, he eventually did, although he loyally used Ayer's Hair Vigor for years and years.

Ma's letters are very cozy and girlish, and full of little anecdotes about how she mounted a ladder to dust the top of the highboy, and how well her strawberry jam turned out—a sort of subconscious advertisement of her wifely traits. In addition to visiting Georgie at West Point, she was having a wonderful time in Boston. There were balls, parties, beaux, concerts, art exhibits, theatres—all the things young ladies did—and, of course, Freddie was at Harvard, so the house was full of his friends and classmates, and Ma was included in all the college fun.

Ma played the piano in many better-than-amateur concerts, and the family went in for theatricals in a big way. She also did volunteer work in a "settlement house" with the children of the immigrants. This was thought very daring by other Boston mothers, and Ellie was considered very "avant garde" to let her daughters work there where they might "catch a disease."

In the summers Ma crewed for her nephew, Cornelius Ayer Wood, who was a first-class racing skipper, and had two racing yawls called the *Silver Nutmeg* and the *Golden Pear.* Ma was a great racing sailor herself, and had a fine understanding of the tides, winds, and local conditions and their effects. The family belonged to the two fanciest yacht clubs in Marblehead—the "Eastern" and the "Corinthian"—and there were a lot of social occasions there.

In the autumn there was hunting with beagles at the Myopia Hunt Club, a few miles inland, as well as fox hunting for the fearless and marvelous "hunt breakfasts." There were amateur race meets there, and an entirely different crowd from the "shore crowd"—people who played polo and had horse shows and model farms. There was wonderful bird hunting and skeet shooting and tennis; and in the winter, skating and tobogganning and skiing, and fabulous house parties over the long winter weekends. Those were, indeed, salad years after the Civil War, with World War I only a bugaboo in the minds of a very few long-sighted statesmen and businessmen who had too much sense to talk about it.

During Georgie's first class year, when he was a senior at West Point, Ma wrote Georgie's parents that "Our visit to West Point . . . was a surprise party to him. We went up to the Yale game there but did not let him know our presence until the game was over. He bore up well under the shock, however, and it was great fun watching him prance up and down the field at inspection, chest bulging and chevrons shining, serenely unconscious of the two pairs of cousinly eyes anxiously fixed upon him. He seemed by far the most military person on the post that day; our only anxiety was that he might break in two at the waistline."

During the time that Georgie was at West Point, Ma had an emergency appendectomy that was high drama indeed. With Ellie in charge, no illness in the Ayer family was a minor illness, so of course no surgery was minor surgery. But Freddie and Kay got the most out of it, not excluding baskets of grapes and the latest books. They wrote a song that they used to hum, when Ma was acting up, until the end of her life. The tune is something like "Reuben, Reuben"—and the words were:

> Georgie Porgie, so they say
> goes a-courting every day
> Sword and pistol by his side
> Beatrice Ayer for his bride
> Doctor, Doctor, can you tell
> What will make poor Beatrice well?
> She is sick and she might die
> That would make poor Georgie cry.
> Down in the valley where the green grass grows
> There sits Beatrice, sweet as a rose
> And she sings and she sings, and she sings all day
> And she sings for Georgie to pass that way.

And pass that way he did. He was spending his senior year Christmas furlough at 395 Commonwealth Avenue, with the Ayers, and, finally, after six years of longing and loving, he brought himself to propose to Ma. He was so afraid that she would refuse his suit that he had a telegram in his pocket ordering himself back to West Point immediately in case this terrible catastrophe took place.

He had written to his parents that he was about to take the fatal step, but I have never seen that letter. I quote from the letter to his mother, written January 4, 1909—the punctuation is his.

Dear Mama:
   As I am somewhat calmer than when I last wrote and have been thinking along two lines, both of which tend to the same result. First, no one on earth has a better right to know truths from me than you and Papa, and second that if I don't tell somebody I will bust. I had a peach of a time in Boston except for the fact that every time I saw B I wanted to kiss her and had a hell of a time not to every time I went driving or walking but as when so occupied I was sort of on honor I could do nothing besides I thought she would refuse and that my position but particularly hers would be very awkward so I postponed it until Wednesday and as God or brains of the family ordained we were left in the library all afternoon. I am not a coward but this business of pointing a gun at yourself and pulling the trigger in order to prove it is not loaded is not particularly enjoyable especially when you really think it is loaded, and had she refused it would have been for me. Well, I did it and it was a very empty gun. Thank God! Oh she was dear, still is and ever will be never have I spent such an afternoon it

went like a flash but were I never to smile again I still had not lived for nothing. The strange part is I think she has known it a long long time six years. She said I should have known it too what an ass I have been, but we are not engaged. I would not let her say a promise for I am going to the Islands first and she might want to forget and be held by foolish notions of honor so it is better that I alone (as I ever have been) be bound. For no matter should she never love me or marry me I am decided how I shall always act. I guess though that she will not forget me as she has told her parents and they said they knew it before she told them and didn't mind. I would rather that you say nothing to Mrs. or Mr. Ayer, or to Beatrice as the less said about it until I come back the better besides I would rather talk to you about it. Of course if they say anything why fire otherwise pretend you know nothing trust to me for I am on the spot and should know.

your devoted son George Patton

Please do what I ask

If there is any point on which I can enlighten you let me know

your devoted son

How much more fun a courtship was in those days when "a glance, a bird-like turn of the head, the pressure of a hand" was as much thrill to the suffering lover as getting right into bed is nowadays. They could savor every moment, and forever!

Georgie's remark about going to "the Islands" refers to service in the Philippines, which was practically automatic for the graduating officer of his period at West Point.

His next letter was written on Tuesday, January 9, 1909.

Dear Mama:

I just got the enclosed from Bee and she asks you to excuse it as she wrote it on the way to the train. Of course don't tell other people but I know you won't. She got up at seven o'clock to see me off and I never saw the hotel so full of people it was jammed. She was pretty nice to get up though as she had no watch and had to stay awake from two o'clock to do it. It is rather hard to express in writing how much she loves me really it scares me to death. I guess I love her as much only I am not part Banning so don't show it so much. I suppose you may as well write to Mrs. Ayer if you think it is proper of course I don't know who should write first.

Your devoted son George S. Patton, Jr.

Ma's note, to which he refers, reads:

Darling Aunt Ruth:

Georgie will not be telling you and Uncle George anything that will be a great surprise to you—but we love each other very much indeed and since we have

found our tongues to tell one another, you are next in our hearts. Papa and Mama and Aunt Nannie are the only others. Please give my dear love to Uncle George.
Always your loving Bee

Georgie also wrote Granfer Ayer, asking for permission to "speak." The answer to that letter, which has disappeared, is as follows:

My dear George
Your letter of the 18th is very clear and comprehensive. Your ambition I admire. Your "plan of life" is alright if you can have a command for a year in God's country and not in the Philippines.

Fighting malaria is not war. After all, as the civil life is what you finally fall back upon for an indefinite period, the question may occur to you whether this first year will not be worth more to you in that than in any command you can get. That is a question no one can decide for you. You too can best judge how much opportunity a year's command will give you to investigate and decide upon another occupation. Always keeping in mind that the younger a man starts in business the easier it is for him and the better his chance for success.

In regard to speaking to Beatrice, there are times in one's life when one feels impelled to speak and to follow that impulse, which comes after long thought, is natural and generally wise.

Hoping you will pardon the above suggestions, I am
sincerely yours
F. Ayer

The next letter from Granfer Ayer must have been in answer to Georgie's second letter.

The Farm, Jan. 10, 1909
Mr. George Patton
West Point, N.Y.

My dear George
Your frank letter of the 3rd inst. deserved an earlier reply but absence in New York and the pressure of important matters, since my return, have prevented.

It is no wonder to me that you, and I may say, Beatrice, have felt a growing admiration for each other, and I admire the delicate way in which you have treated the matter.

Beatrice has a pretty well developed mature mind of her own and can speak for herself.

Referring to your profession, I believe that it is narrowing in its tendency. A man in the army must develop mainly in one direction, always feel unsettled, and that his location and homelife are, in a measure, subject to the dictation and possible freak of another who he may despise or even hate.

This is no reflection on your educational institution which I suppose to be one of the best.

It appears to me that a man like you should be independent of such control. His own man, free to act and develop in the open world.

I would compare the military man to a tree grown in the forest as against one in the field with plenty of room to spread. Should you, at any time, adopt civil life, I have no doubt that your skill and patriotism will be in requisition with equal chance of preferment, as if you had remained in the service.

You will pardon me for this commenting on an occupation known to be most respectable, earnestly sought, and won with great labor; and this without suggesting a better one; but I do it from the point of a free man—always at liberty to go and come—governed only by surrounding conditions, consideration for others, and my own judgement.

The above views I give from my experience and observation. Every independent man should choose his own course in life but must think carefully as to the road, and where it may lead him. The searchlights of reason and experience may well be applied to the unknown and uncertain future.

I believe that the qualities of a good soldier—and let me add—the training will help a man to win in whatever calling he may choose.

> with affectionate regards I am
> yours very sincerely
> F. Ayer

P.S. My letters are all dictated, can't use the pen and ask you to excuse the pencil. FA

His next letter to Georgie, in reply to another letter no longer extant, was written on February 9, 1909.

My dear George:

On returning from New York I find your favor of the 3rd. inst. My absence will account for delay in acknowledging same.

You state very fully and clearly your position and decisions, upon which I have very little comment to make. Your high position in your profession (as it comes to me) shows that you have a taste for it and that you have devoted yourself to the business which makes it natural that you should want to continue and reap the benefits, or at least, continue along a little further into the future to enable you to guess at the possibilities.

> very sincerely yours
> F. Ayer

Granfer Ayer, as had been his custom, was slowly drawing in the net that he had used on his own three sons, to put Georgie in the niche that he was fashioning for him. In addition to the desire to have all his connections under his sway, he had the typical New England view of the "brutal and licentious mercenary."

Of course, one went to war when the long roll sounded on the drum of the local militia, but in New England the military was not a way of life as it was in the South. In his heart of hearts, the Yankee always thought of the Army as the refuge for thieves and murderers. The Navy! Ah, now that was another chapter in the maritime states.

However, from the unrecorded letters it can be seen that Georgie was ruffling his feathers, with the help of Ma, who was the most strong-minded of the Ayer children; she always got her way in the end.

After graduation, Georgie was ordered to Fort Sheridan, Illinois. He arranged for Ma to come there for a visit, and she stayed with his commanding officer and his wife, Captain and Mrs. Frank Marshall. Fort Sheridan was a very civilized "outpost," being on the outskirts of Chicago. When he was ordered there, Aunt Nannie took an apartment in Chicago to be near "the boy."

Captain and Mrs. Marshall had no children of their own, and they really loved Georgie, and their love was returned. Frank Marshall, one of the earliest victims of a military plane accident, was one of Georgie's heroes, and Mrs. Marshall was one of the greatest ladies of the "Old Army." They invited Ma to visit so that she could get a firsthand view of Army life. It was certainly different from Boston! In fact, at some point during her visit, Ma offered to break their engagement as she didn't think she could ever make a good Army wife. Georgie kissed her out of that fancy. But the following letter to his mother, apparently enclosing a letter to him from Ma, makes plain his state of mind:

Fort Sheridan, Illinois
Feb. 20, 1910

Dear Mama [the punctuation is Georgie's]:
From the enclosed letter which you should read before going further you see things are happening. As to her plan I am in doubt but not in very great doubt. First I think that the only way a second Lieut. can ever get a house is to get married and arrive then have to do something if he waits until something happens he is apt to wait until it is cold in Hell and as O'Brien said no second lt. has ever been forced to camp in the fields for want of a house.

Again even if she did have to live in the club it would not kill her at all it would not be easy but it could be stood and it might do her good to have to stand something. If we get married say the last part of June I would not get back here until the latter part of July and we would be here not a month before the maneuvers which she could go to and stay at a hotel. And see something of the army not the soft side of it either. Then in September we should certainly get a house or something. At least we would be no worse off then than were we to wait until then to get married.

Of course it is asking a lot of a girl raised as B has been to do these things but there is no help for it she is not made to go and if she does she will have to take it as it is sent and not as I should like it to be.

I suppose her family will be morally sure she is a martyr and I am a monster but let them be.

Gosh I do hate to get the poor kid into a life so different from that to which she is accustomed but what can I do and as Mary says she is getting thinner every day and something must be done and I guess it will be too. As I have said I feel a reluctance to take the plunge but it is the natural moment of [panic] that one always feels before changing conditions.

As the declaration of independence says "All history hath shown mankind is more prone to bear evils which evils are sufferable than to correct them by altering fixed and established facts."

Hence I have historical sanction for my hesitation and indeed it is not for myself but for her that I hesitate—

> Much love your devoted son
> George S. Patton

In the Army of those days—and even much later—there was a horrid custom that an officer coming to a post could "rank out" another officer from his quarters, even by such a small thing as a date of rank, or a few files. A lot of lifetime feuds were started by this custom, and Georgie decided that he would not put himself in the embarrassing position of being "ranked out" of anything, so he applied for the smallest and the worst set of quarters at Fort Sheridan, which were assigned to him.

Ma never ceased talking about those quarters, especially when many years later her own two daughters had any complaints. The first thing she would mention was that the closet shelf in their bedroom was so narrow that Georgie had to stand his straw boater on edge so that they could shut the closet door. The dining room could only hold four chairs. There was no room in the bathroom for the clothes hamper. The final touch was that while Georgie and Ma were on their honeymoon, the quarters were supposed to be painted, which they were. When they returned from the three blissful months in Europe, and Georgie carried Ma over the doorstep into their first home, the whole downstairs was painted peacock blue. The paint had been left over after painting the railway station, and the quartermaster wanted to use it up.

On March 7, 1910, Granfer Ayer wrote the following:

Lt. G.S. Patton, Jr.
15th U.S. Cavalry
Fort Sheridan, Ill.

My dear George:

I thank you for your letter and statement, the latter of which I return herewith.

Am sorry that you have hesitated to write me or that you should have any misgivings about doing so. Also sorry that Beatrice should have had any hesitancy about speaking to me freely on any subject pertaining to herself or her interests. I have always endeavored to cultivate the most confidential relations with my children and to make them feel free to confide in me and consult me in all matters. I invite you to the same confidential relations and freedom of intercourse.

You know how Beatrice lights our lives and how dearly we all love her. Our beloved younger children, so full of promise, will always remember Beatrice, who brought happiness as a shining example, who strained every nerve to do her best to be the light of our house, to be the moving spirit for the good of all, to improve every gift, and never to withhold from father, mother, sister or brother the constant expression of her love and devotion.

She has no discounts, no minus traits—all is to the good. She has made us all happy always, and we hope she will always be a joy to you, as she has always been to us. Of course we feel that half the house will be gone when our Beatrice goes, and we confide her to you with our love and fullest confidence. Her frequent return to us we shall look for with longing.

Will you keep this ever in mind?

I know that your accommodations are not what you would have them in private life but think Beatrice enjoys roughing it to some extent, as all good soldiers and sailors must, and you know she is a pretty good sailor.

I did not know you had such a fine nest egg in your property. I would not sell the land.

It has been my custom when my children have married and left our home to give them a monthly income, and shall do the same to Beatrice and the younger ones. This is without regard to their circumstances and for reasons which I will explain later.

I am hoping to take Beatrice to Chicago, and if so, will, of course, see you but it is not certain. I admire your firmness of purpose in sticking to the army until more strongly tempted by another occupation, and with every good wish for your early and steady advancement, I am

> sincerely your friend
>
> F. Ayer

Between this letter and Ma's visit to Fort Sheridan—as I assume this letter was written before she went—there was a short interlude of the kind of drama that the Bannings thrived on. I think of the above letter, in fact, as a "calculated withdrawing action to reassemble forces."

Granfer Ayer was not going to allow his darling to be taken off to a godfor-saken Army post in the middle of nowhere (who do you know who lives in Chicago, of all places?). If Georgie really cared for precious Beatrice, he would do the decent thing, resign his commission and take a job (one which was waiting for him) in or near Boston. This became more and more evident. Granfer Ayer had not had his own way for nearly ninety years without getting accustomed to the feeling.

Georgie retaliated with heated despair (if there is such a thing). He said that if he could not marry Ma he would never marry anyone, but that the Army was his chosen career and his profession and he was going to stick to it, and serve his country in the way he knew best.

Ma took a more direct course. She went on a hunger strike. She locked herself in her bedroom on the third floor and refused all suggestions to change her mind. As was to be expected, every night on the stroke of midnight, there would be a basket dangling down the stairwell on a string to be filled by Kay with the choicest pickings from the larder, and which basket, when full, would be drawn up to the third floor in thrilling silence.

Beatrice was her mother's daughter. She seemed to grow paler and more fragile each day; she could be seen leaning sadly on her windowsill. After about a week of this, Granfer Ayer capitulated to his concerted womenfolk, and gave permission for the wedding to proceed.

But Granfer Ayer had the last word, of a sort. I have never seen the letter he wrote to Georgie, but it was quoted to me by Ma and by Nita Patton, who said that it literally changed Georgie's life. Granfer Ayer said that he was persuaded that Georgie's vocation lay in the military, and so they would henceforth each do the thing they did best: he would earn the money, and Georgie would earn the glory.

The favorite gift in the Ayer family was, next to flowers, jewels. But Ma's engagement ring was her symbolic reneging of the diamond halter. Her engagement ring, which she wore to the grave, was a gold miniature of Georgie's 1909 West Point class ring, set with a topaz, which was Georgie's birthstone.

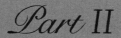 *Part* II

When all the world is young lads
And all the trees are green
And every goose's a swan, lads
And every lass a queen

Chapter 6

Orange Blossoms

Ma's and Georgie's wedding, on May 26, 1910, was the wedding of the year. It was also the first military wedding on the North Shore since the Civil War. Ma wore the wedding dress that had been made for Ellie in 1884. It was trimmed with real orange blossoms from Lake Vineyard, brought on the train by the Pattons in a box of wet cotton. Georgie and the ushers, except for Fred Ayer, wore their full dress blue uniforms, and all the bridesmaids but one were family.

The only shadow on the festivity was that the day before the wedding Georgie's mother came down with severe influenza, and had to stay in her hotel room in Boston, which must have been a cruel blow to her. It was Aunt Nannie's shining hour. She lived her dream as she stood in the receiving line, next to the only man she had ever loved, with her adored Georgie marrying a girl that she herself truly loved.

The newspaper description of Ma's wedding is well worth repeating.

MISS AYER FIRST BRIDE OF NORTH SHORE SUMMER SEASON
Miss Beatrice Ayer made, as everyone knew she would, a rarely lovely bride, when, in the warm sunlight of Thursday, she was married in the St. John's Church of Beverly Farms to Lt. George Smith Patton, Jr., 15th United States Cavalry. The decorations in the chancel were entirely confined to spring blooms, the coloring white and green. No more effective background could have been devised to set off the bridesmaids' gowns of cream lingerie and lace and their wonderfully novel and becoming hats and the full dress uniforms of the Army and Navy Officers who made up the majority of ushers. An added touch of color was the scarlet hood on the Oxford gown worn by The Reverend Doctor Gordon who shared the services with the rector, The Reverend Eugene Huiguin. Further

picturesqueness and impressiveness was given by the arch made with the crossing of the ushers' swords, beneath which the bride and bridegroom passed from
the chancel after the service. The bride's gown was her mother's wedding dress—
the same in every particular except clusters of fresh orange blossoms. The bridesmaids wore cream lingerie and lace over satin. The hats were of cream Neapolitan
tied with blue ribbons and trimmed with tiny wreaths of pink roses and forget-
menots—very smart and Parisian in effect. The maid of honor, the schoolgirl
sister, Miss Katharine Ayer, was in cream lace over blue satin with dainty hat to
correspond. All the group carried 1830 bouquets.

The only shadow upon the occasion was the inability of the bridegroom's
mother, Mrs. Patton, to be there. She came on from California with her husband,
and was taken quite ill at the Touraine shortly after arriving. Mrs. Ayer wore a
gown, the perfect taste of which was as conspicuous as was its beauty. It was of
palest blue satin, so pale as to have the effect of gray and veiled with chiffon in
the same tone. The hat was of white crin with clusters of white feathers. No jewels were worn beyond a single string of pearls and a pendant.

Mr. and Mrs. Ayer received at the entrance of the spacious living room, which
with the library on one side, and the dining room on the other, covers the entire
floor of the beautiful country seat, Avalon. Mr. Patton and his sister-in-law, Miss
Wilson, stood with them. Farther on in the room the bride and bridegroom surrounded the bridesmaids, received their congratulations.

A full orchestra was on the broad terrace which overlooks the water and where
seats were scattered about for the guests. Later, there was dancing in the library,
and just before the majority of the guests left, was the pretty ceremony of the
bride cutting the wedding cake with her husband's sword, followed by the army
cheers given by the classmate ushers and the band's playing the "Star Spangled
Banner." A special train brought the guests from town. Carriages were in readi-
ness to take them back to the church and house and back to the train.

Lt. and Mrs. Patton left for New York later in the afternoon. They are to have a
month's honeymoon in Europe before they return to Lt. Patton's post of duty at
Fort Sheridan, Illinois.

Ma and Georgie had a wonderful wedding trip in Europe. On the boat going
over they met an Englishman who made a remark that Ma never forgot. He
said, "Come to Europe for the history, my dear, not the scenery. You, North
Americans, have the finest scenery, and more of it, in the whole world."

When the young couple returned in late June, they went to Fort Sheridan via
Prides Crossing and Avalon, which was quite a contrast to Quarters 92A. Kay
went along with Ma to keep her company; when Georgie went off on maneuvers in July, both young ladies hastened back to Avalon.

When Ma rejoined Georgie at Fort Sheridan in the middle of September, she
joyfully announced that she was pregnant. To Ma, this was the ultimate goal of
woman's life: to find love, to have it returned, and to be able to bear a child to

sanctify that love. She had been raised in a close-knit, loving family, and she always felt "the more, the merrier." Georgie, on the other hand, felt a shadow creeping between himself and his golden girl. He wanted her to himself, and he was slightly resentful that they were to be joined so soon by another.

Ma sensed this, of course. Both families were thrilled with the news. The Ayers obviously belonged to "the more, the merrier" faction, and the Pattons were always obsessed with the thought that "the Name" must be preserved. They had never recovered from the physical and spiritual losses of the Civil War, when so many Pattons and their kin had died on the bloody fields of Gettysburg and Winchester, and in nameless battles at leaf-choked creeks and stubbled fields, and in the stinking hospital tents that were actually more deadly than the battles.

With all of this in mind, Ma asked Georgie, "Will you mind terribly if this one is a girl?" He gave her the perfect answer—because he loved Ma with all his heart: "What do *you* think, Beaty? I married one, didn't I?"

Ma had been given a great deal of advice when she persisted in marrying this wild westerner and going off to the desperate frontier. Of course, everyone knew there was a city called Chicago—this was where you changed trains to go to California. There was just time, between trains, to go to the Blackstone Hotel and have a hot bath and a meal and then go to the Field Museum. But aside from Chicago, what was there in Illinois (or was it Iowa? sometimes pronounced Ohio)? Indians? Saloons? Card sharps? Corn?

Of course, the senior Ayers knew the Middle West well. Ellie was from Minnesota, and Granfer Ayer had, as a young man, taken Ayer's patent medicines all over that part of the world, driving horse and buggy and selling them to the general stores.

But Ma's contemporaries and Ellie's friends were filled with alarm at Ma's western trek-to-be. She was given some very cogent advice. One lady told her never to leave her house without a hat on, as the sight of her long auburn hair might rouse some Indian local to go on a scalping spree. She was warned against the drinking water, and told to be sure to ask the butcher if the meat was fresh (which, of course, would have made it too tough to eat). Ellie gave her some sound advice that is as good today as it was then: never get intimate with your next-door neighbors; never borrow anything; never confide in anyone but your husband, your doctor, your pastor, and of course, your mother.

When Ma got back to Fort Sheridan, happily pregnant, she was very reluctant to go to the post doctor. He was there mainly to treat the soldiers, and if she went to the infirmary she would have to sit in the waiting room among complete strangers, and then be questioned, poked, and prodded by a complete stranger; also, the post doctor had a beard. Why she should have let the beard worry her, she never knew. Her adored father had a beard, and her doctor brother, Jamie, had an enormous mustache—but there was something about the post doctor's beard that she couldn't stand—maybe it was because he chewed tobacco.

Ma wrote to her family doctor in Boston for the name of a doctor in Chicago, which was, after all, just a short ride on the streetcar from the post.

Ma was preoccupied with keeping house and running her servant and trying to make Quarters 92A into something like she thought a home should be. She had absolutely no experience in this field. Ellie had always had a housekeeper, a tremendous character named Mamie Ryan, who had a set time to see Ellie every day to discuss menus and what flowers were available from the gardens and greenhouse—in fact, all the trivia of housekeeping boiled down into a situation report for which Ellie only had to make the final decisions.

Ma didn't know the Army ladies very well. She almost always had either her sister, Kay, or Georgie's sister, Nita Patton, staying with her for company; and they had a terribly gay time with Ma chaperoning them. Her only "Old Army" friends, Captain and Mrs. Marshall, had left shortly after Georgie and Ma came back from their honeymoon.

One day in February of 1911, she saw, to her infinite horror, the colonel's wife, Mrs. Gerard, flanked by the two lieutenant colonels' wives, who were in turn flanked by four majors' wives, coming up the walk to her front door—the seven senior ladies of the regiment! There was no one room in the house that would hold eight people, and she was not sure she had enough chairs, but she pulled herself together and met them at the door and invited them to come in. They appeared to be almost as ill at ease as she felt. Mrs. Gerard, who later became a great friend and ally, started the ball rolling conversationally by mentioning the weather, then worked around to the fact that they did not see Ma at many of the regimental functions, then inquired how she was feeling, how she was getting along in the Army, did she like it, and, finally, how was she getting along with Mr. Patton. (All lieutenants were addressed as "Mister.") Ma got stiffer and stiffer, and more and more New-England-rock-bound-coast, and finally Mrs. Gerard shrugged her shoulders and burst out laughing: "My dear little Mrs. Patton, you must think we are a bunch of old busybodies, sticking our noses into other people's affairs, but we have all been thinking about you, and, since you have confided in no one, not even the post doctor, we got up our courage to come and tell you that we think you should know that you are going to be a mother in a very short time."

And—so it was. Beatrice Ayer Patton came into the world on March 19,

1911, just at sunset. The flag had just been lowered in the Retreat Ceremony, and the band was playing the last bars of the "Star Spangled Banner."

Ma, who had wanted this baby above all things, also wanted to share her joy and their triumph with her Georgie, so she insisted that he be there for what turned out to be a difficult birth. The little bedroom was crowded with mother, doctor, the nurse the Ayers had brought from Boston, and Georgie. The Ayers, themselves, stayed outside on the landing. To everyone it was an occasion of supreme joy, except to Georgie. He had to stand there and see the beautiful girl he had been married to less than a year being torn to pieces (in his eyes) by a monstrous stranger who was not pretty or appealing or very much wanted, by him. He had seen plenty of kittens and puppies and calves and colts born on the ranch, but he had never seen anything as awful and revolting to all his sensibilities as the birth of his first child, and he never got over it. When they tried to put the baby in his arms, he rushed out of the room and ran downstairs, and was sick in the kitchen sink. The family, all crowding in the cheer, felt that he was showing very suitable and sensitive emotions. No one knew how he really felt.

The Ayers stayed in Chicago and the nurse invaded the house until all was well. Georgie felt that he would never be alone with his Beaty again. Then, all the Pattons and Aunt Nannie arrived on April 11 and slept in Chicago, but took over the house, and he was definitely the outside man. Bee was the first Patton grandchild and the Pattons were firmly resigned to her being a girl, as they felt that Ma was such a wonderful little mother that there would be plenty of time for others, mostly boys, of course. They even called the baby "Smith."

The post ladies were all very helpful and the colonel's wife, Mrs. Gerard, especially so, except for one incident. It occurred one day about noon. Ma was not expecting Georgie home for lunch, as he was out on the rifle range teaching the new recruits to shoot. She was not surprised when she saw Mrs. Gerard had some sort of a message to impart. She asked politely after both families, and after Bee, and, then, with a little awkwardness, she began to ask Ma if the baby had made any difference in her marital happiness. Were she and Mr. Patton getting along happily? Was all well "in the bedroom"? Ma was very embarrassed and beginning to be slightly offended, when Mrs. Gerard broke down and said, "I know you must think me an interfering old woman, Mrs. Patton, but when Colonel Gerard came home at noon for his lunch, he mentioned the fact that Mr. Patton had been standing on the rifle butts all morning, between the targets, and he wondered if some circumstance had occurred of such a nature that Mr. Patton was trying to take his own life without causing any comment, perhaps because of some misunderstanding at home. As you know, the recruits were firing this morning and they are very green."

Ma was able to set Mrs. Gerard's mind at rest about any marital problems, but when "Mr. Patton" got home from rifle practice that evening, he found an infuriated Mrs. Patton all packed up, baby, maid, and all, ready to take a taxi to Chicago to get on the east-bound train. It took him quite a while to persuade her that he was only trying to find out what George Washington had meant when he wrote to his "dearest Patsy" that he had heard the bullets whistling past his ears and that "indeed, there was something very merry in the sound." He also wanted to see if he would be scared while being shot at. Ma was persuaded to unpack, but she was not amused.

Ma had very few friends at that time among the other wives and she thought it was probably her fault. She noticed that the other ladies dropped in on each other without notice—not done in Boston—and she decided she had better try to be more outgoing. So one morning she got Bee into her carriage by the back door, and pulled herself together preparatory to "dropping in" on her neighbor in the other half of the house. Just as she was about to knock on the door, Lieutenant X appeared, half of his face still covered with shaving lather, his suspenders hanging about his knees, his razor gripped firmly in his right hand, and running as fast as he could around the corner of the building; after him came his wife, in her dressing gown, with her nightcap still on and her rolling pin clutched firmly in her right hand. They were so intent on this silent pursuit that neither of them saw Ma. She stood fastened to the ground—wondering whether to disappear, or call the military police, or the hospital; while she stood there uncertain as to what to do, the back door opened again and the officer in question appeared, shaven and neatly buttoned into his blouse. When he saw Ma standing there he touched his cap to her, and strode off toward the stables. This put the quietus on Ma's idea of dropping in on people. Shortly after this incident, the warm weather began and Ma was shipped home to her parents. Ma spent June with "Smith" at Avalon, because Illinois was considered unhealthily warm, but she missed Georgie terribly and she wanted to share Smith's every drip and coo with him, so she hurried back to Sheridan at the end of July and stayed there until he had orders for a change of station, at which time they all went to California.

While the Ayers were building Avalon at Prides Crossing, Massachusetts, the Pattons were also building their dream house in San Gabriel, California—the new Lake Vineyard. The old house, built for Georgie's grandmother, was sadly out of date, shabby, and hard to run. The walls were made of the local adobe brick, and they did not stand up very well during the earthquake season. Georgie's mother, "Bamma" to us children, remembered one night in her childhood when an earthquake woke her up and she saw the wall of her bedroom falling away and found herself gazing at the stars.

The new Lake Vineyard was built with all the conveniences that "Bamma" had always longed for and it was, to me, the perfect house. The whole downstairs, except for the kitchen wing, was surrounded by a deep veranda. The rooms were spacious with high ceilings. Every room had a fireplace, and the mantels had been hand-carved by the same ship's carpenter that had carved the panels and mantels in the Bannings' "Barn." The huge living room was paneled almost to the ceiling in walnut that had been cut and cured on the estate. The front door was made of cleverly joined planks of olive wood, surrounded with a carved wreath of leaves, and the door frame was a wreath of olives and their leaves.

Upstairs were five huge bedrooms, each with a bath, and two sleeping porches. The rooms, both upstairs and downstairs, were built around a great hall which made the air circulation so successful that there was never any need for air-conditioning. The third floor consisted of a large bright room for the weekly seamstress who came and did the mending, made the clothes, and altered anything that needed to be done. There were also two great attics that were the grandchildren's secret dens and rainy-day playrooms.

The cellars were also thrilling. Georgie's father, "Bamps" to us children, had his office in the cellar, with large area windows out onto the lawn, and a door with an iron grille through which he would enter the house when he had walked up the brick path across terraces that led right down to the entrance of the place, on Huntington Avenue, where the streetcars ran. The rest of the front part of the cellar was filled with trophies from his and Georgie's lives: the saddle on which Colonel George S. Patton, C.S.A., was riding when he received his mortal wound at the battle of Cedar Creek in 1864; the saddle and bridle of the Mexican bandit, General Cardenas, whom Georgie had killed;[1] the suit of armor that Aunt Nannie had given Georgie when he was a little boy; a huge turtle shell with the harpoon hole in it; innumerable stuffed fish, photographs, guns, helmets, Indian baskets—a living museum. Of course, when the new Lake Vineyard was built these things were not in the cellar, but they were there during my earliest memories. The stuffed fish were a novelty in the early 1900s. Game fishing had just come into style about the time Georgie was ready to go to VMI. Before Zane Grey found out that it was fun to catch billfish, they were called "boo-hoos" because they made you weep "boo hoo" when they stole your bait. Zane Grey had fishing headquarters on Catalina Island and he taught Georgie the joys of game fishing.

Upstairs Bamma and Bamps had the largest bedroom, with two dressing

---

1. Both saddles currently located at the U.S. Army's George S. Patton Museum of Cavalry and Armor at Fort Knox, Kentucky.

rooms, and a private sleeping porch on one corner of the second floor. Nita had a lovely room facing the mountains, which you could see in those days. Ma and Georgie had the room opposite the top of the stairs; Aunt Nannie had the huge bedroom right next to Georgie's with the door from her bathroom opening into Georgie's room. Someone, probably Bamma, had tactfully put a large immovable armchair against it—on Georgie's side of the door. My sister and her nurse had the fifth bedroom with a door that also opened into Aunt Nannie's room.

There they had a wonderful visit, Georgie visiting with his own enormous clan. They went out to family parties every night, drove with Uncle Captain Banning in the six-horse stage coaches, and took the ferry to Catalina.

The Patton-Banning bunch were all deeply serious about, and involved in, politics. One occasion at Lake Vineyard made a deathless impression on Ma. The talk at the dinner table turned inevitably to politics (in Boston, they left that to the men along with the port and cigars). However, the Pattons and Bannings couldn't wait till the ladies had left the table; and the ladies usually had something to say, too. On this occasion, the gentlemen had taken frequent glasses of the very fine wine raised at Lake Vineyard, as well as some of the excellent port laid down by Don Benito Wilson in the fifties, and the language got very high falutin' and tempers flared. Several Browns went and got their wraps, vowing never to return if certain other guests were present; several Bannings suggested getting the situation cleared up at dawn, with bare fists, and seconds, under the live oak trees. Everyone started talked at once, and there was a good deal of shouting and "By God, sir," and the like. Ma noticed that neither her mother-in-law nor the other older ladies were even noticing, but were sitting quietly at the far end of the room talking about their own concerns.

All at once, the Dick Whittington clock over the fireplace chimed nine o'clock, and there was a general scramble to get coats, hats, and sticks. Raised fists were lowered to arms that clasped shoulders; voices were suddenly calm; and arrangements were made for the same party, with a few additions, to meet at one of the other family houses the following Tuesday, where they would, as Bamps said, "continue the damned argument to its natural conclusion, as gentlemen." Agreed.

Ma never got used to the amount of wine that flowed at Lake Vineyard. The ladies rarely indulged, except at dinner, perhaps one glass, but there were always decanters on the huge mahogany sideboard, and Bamma told Ma that when she was a little girl there had always been a silver-bound bucket of wine in the front hall, with a silver-handled gourd dipper, and that when the gentlemen came in from their estate management, or their hunting or riding, they quenched their thirst at the bucket, which was kept filled by one of the Mexican helpers. Of course, the wine was all made on the place, and, although it was all gone by the time I grew up (a vine disease had killed the vineyards and Bamps had replaced the dead grapevines with orange trees) I was always told that there was nothing like Lake Vineyard wine—nothing this side of Paradise.

The Pattons and the Bannings were all very staunch churchmen. They went to church every Sunday, paid their tithe, and either built the first Protestant churches in that part of California—as Don Benito did—or were on the building committees. The fine men of the church were in and out of their houses along with the Confederate veterans and the retired Mexican bandits. One of their dearest friends was darling Bishop Johnson, who was, at the time of this story, the Bishop of California. He and Mrs. Johnson had been to dinner at Lake Vineyard, and after dinner Ma saw Bishop Johnson and Georgie walking up and down the lawn in deep conversation. Bishop Johnson, who was five feet tall, had his arm around Georgie's waist, and Georgie had his arm draped across the Bishop's shoulders. They were so rapt in conversation that Ma sneaked up to listen, and she heard Bishop Johnson say, "Yes, indeed, Georgie, I quite agree with you. You would have made a wonderful Bishop if you had had the call."

One of Georgie's childhood dreads was that he would get "the call," like his father's first cousin, Robert Patton. Robbie Patton was reputed to be "the worst boy who ever graduated from the University" (of Virginia, of course). "Worst" must have been a purely comparative adjective, as Robbie once told my sister Bee and me that he had never known that girls had legs until he went to the University. His sister, Sadie, had told him that they just had springs under their dresses, and that was why they moved so gracefully. When he got "the call," he was kneeling by his bed and saying his prayers. He told us all about it, with a genuine enthusiasm that never left him. He said that he was saying his prayers, when he felt Jesus touch him on the shoulder. My sister asked, wide-eyed, "But Cousin Robbie, how did you know it was Jesus?" Cousin Robbie smiled: "Honey, when Jesus touches you on the shoulder, you just know who it is!" Then Jesus said to him, "Robbie Patton, I want you to come and work for Me." "How did you know it was Jesus?" Bee asked. And Cousin Robbie answered, "Darling, when Jesus speaks to you, you just know who it is."

So Cousin Robbie, who had planned to go to law school, switched over to the seminary and became a minister of the Gospel and lived a long, happy, impoverished life, marrying his dear Janie Stringfellow and raising two beautiful daughters. He started the Episcopal School for Negroes as he felt that, as the son of a slave owner, Jesus particularly wanted him to work for the Negroes and be their friend.

Georgie had been brought up on this story, and every night when he was a little boy, saying his prayers on his knees, he would pray that Jesus would not call him, because he wanted to be a soldier.

Georgie was the fair-haired boy at Lake Vineyard. Nothing was too good for him or, later, for Ma. He was adored by all his cousins. He was the great adventurer who had cut loose and gone off into the wilds of the unknown East, where fame and glory awaited him—they all hoped and felt sure.

From Fort Sheridan, via Lake Vineyard, Georgie and Ma went to Fort Myer, Virginia. Fort Myer was once one of the prettiest and most interesting posts in the U.S. Army. It was part of General Lee's estate, "Arlington"—now the National Cemetery—and it was so close to the capital that the social life was varied and quite glamorous. Ma and Georgie met a lot of interesting and important people. There was polo, fox-hunting in nearby Virginia and Maryland, and race meets in the spring. Ma, a city girl, fit right into the Fort Myer–Washington life, and Georgie was beginning to grow greater in his own esteem. With Ma at his side, who knew all the mores of the so-called Sophisticated East, he became more self-confident. Ma was able to entertain and do the things she had been brought up to do with style and verve.

Finally, Fort Myer was a prestigious post and only the most promising young officers were sent there. Georgie realized this and it did him good. He was beginning to be chosen from the herd.

The first really all-world Olympic Games were scheduled to be held in Sweden in 1912, and Georgie was picked to represent the United States in the pentathlon. This is the most truly Olympic of all of the competitions, calling for the man who excels in fencing, swimming, shooting, riding, and running. Georgie was a superb horseman; he was a well-trained and dedicated swordsman; a swimmer all his life, he was always in top physical condition, so foot racing was along the lines of his training. He started his serious training in May of 1912, and it was terribly hard on everyone. He went on a diet of raw steak and salad: according to Ma, he was simply unfit for human companionship. But he had to push himself, as he had such a short time in which to get into shape. Ma and Georgie, and his parents and Nita, took off for Sweden on June 14 on the ship *Finland.* Smith, now called "Little Bee," was left with the Ayers.

Georgie felt he should go on with his training on the ship, so a canvas tank 20' x 8' x 4' was rigged up on deck and he swam in it for twenty minutes a day with ropes tied around his waist against which he swam. This really ruined swimming for him as a sport and he never enjoyed it again.

The whole family fell in love with Sweden. Georgie and Nita, big and blonde from their Hereford inheritance, were frequently taken for Swedes, and the people were courteous and hospitable. There were marvelous parties, attended by the king and queen. The king's aide, Colonel Bjorling, became a great personal friend. The last photograph ever taken of Georgie was taken in Sweden in 1945 with this same fine officer.

The Olympic Games were marvelous. The great American Indian athlete, Jim Thorpe, was on the U.S. team. Georgie did well, finishing in fifth place in the pentathlon, being beaten by four Swedes. His score was brought down by the pistol shooting. The day before the competition he made a perfect score. The day of the competition, one of his bullet holes could not be found on the target. The Swedes, great sportsmen, insisted that the missing bullet had gone through a hole made by a previous bullet—and they never could find any bullet that had gone wide of the target—but rules are rules, and Georgie did not win the pistol shooting because he was one bullet hole short.

Ma took the entire blame for his not winning the pistol shooting. Her Georgie could not have failed on his own. She always said that she must have stayed too late at the party the night before the competition, or perhaps that she danced too much—or had too good a time. She firmly maintained that if she had taken him back to the hotel earlier in the evening, he would have won the prize.

The foot race was another chapter. Georgie tried so hard that he actually passed out as he crossed (in third place) over the finish line. He came to hearing his father asking the trainer if he thought "the boy" would live. The trainer replied that he thought he might as he was a very strong young man and in good condition. The trainer had given him what Georgie called "hop" before the race, to help him. That may have been the reason why he passed out—or, for that matter, why he lived. In those days, it was not against the law.

Georgie was an expert fencer. During the Games he became more and more interested in all the facets of sword exercise. There are many kinds of fencing, from the more or less game with the light epee, to the really serious fencing with the saber, another category altogether. A saber is a heavy sword with a sharp edge, not just a pointed stick with a button on the end. It takes a strong arm and a fine sense of timing to maneuver with the saber—it is a deadly weapon. The Swedes and the Germans were expert swordsmen with that terrible swift sword, and Georgie became interested in it as a thrusting weapon, as well as a cutting one as used in a Cavalry charge.

All the expert fencers told him that there was just one great teacher, the "beau sabreur" of the French Army, Adjutant Clery, who taught fencing at the Ecole Militaire in Saumur, France. He was the professional champion of Europe in the use of the foil, dueling sword, and saber. So, Georgie decided to get himself detailed to the school at Saumur.

That tour of duty at Saumur was one of the greatest times of Ma's and Georgie's young lives. They were alone at last, with no family whatsoever. Ma spoke perfect French—at times she even thought and dreamed in French. She loved the French people and understood them, and her love was returned a thousand fold. Georgie was associating with some of the greatest warriors of the nineteenth and twentieth centuries—the heroes of his youth in the flesh, the "beaux gallants," the "beaux sabreurs," the flower of the French Army, so soon to be mowed down by the trampling Bosch hordes. These were men of legend. There will never be their like again. They reminded Georgie of the descriptions of the Southern cavaliers who had fought in the Civil War, and had been immortalized for him by his stepgrandfather, Colonel Smith.

In addition to studying the art of fencing with the saber under the Adjutant Clery, Georgie came to know other soon-to-be heroes. One who was to feature later in his life in both world wars was Lieutenant Houdemon, a descendant of one of Napoleon's marshals.

The terrain around Saumur has been fought over for a thousand years. Caesar and his legions marched through it in 40 BC, Attila the Hun ravaged the land, and many other lesser men followed their bloody trails. Georgie and Ma followed their routes by foot, by horseback, and by car. Georgie was convinced that he had fought over this terrain before, and would fight there again. His intention was to study it "for the next time around." He said that wars had been lost and won in these fields and hills through knowledge of the country; that history had already picked the battlefields, that it was the greatest teacher. One of his mottoes was "There are no practice games in life."

Ma was entranced with the history of Saumur, which had been ruled since time immemorial by the notorious Fulke family. The first Fulke noted in the histories was Fauke Novra, Count of Anjou. The Fulkes were not nice people to begin with and had many eccentricities—all of a rather horrid nature.

Ma dug all this fascinating history out of the records in Saumur, and later Georgie used them to write the most horrible novel for us children. With his tremendous knowledge of history and life in the Middle Ages, he put in plenty of detail. We learned history the interesting way—because he "told it like it was."

In addition to following the campaign routes of the conquerors, Ma and Georgie visited museums and out-of-the-way towns, and did some very interesting collecting. One of the treasures they brought home was a Gothic high seat, or wooden throne. On its back is an obscure coat of arms with the bar sinister across it. The seat opens up very handily and it can be used for a wood box, but there are very few rooms that can take the height of the chair. They also bought a horsehide trunk of the time of Henri IV, decorated with brass studs, making a two-headed eagle. Ma always kept the sheet music in it.

They had to return in the first part of September. Packing their acquisitions was quite a job, and it was left to Ma, as Georgie had to attend the fencing academy. She wore herself out with the unaccustomed task and the attendant red tape. The day before they left, when she thought she had everything packed, sealed, and ready to deliver, Georgie strolled in and said, "I hope you remembered to pack all those swords under the bed." She looked under the bed and saw about thirty-odd swords and scabbards, which he had been collecting, and she said that something inside of her snapped. The next thing she remembered was chasing Georgie through the rooms with a sword uplifted in her two hands, and Georgie running madly ahead of her, jumping over chairs and tables, and his hands clasped over his head to guard off her stroke, yelling, "Don't! Don't! Please don't!"

She almost caught him, bringing the sword down so hard that it stuck into the edge of a table. Georgie helped her to pack his collection.

From Saumur, they went to Fort Riley, Kansas, where Georgie was Master of the Sword in addition to other duties. He served under Captain Guy V. Henry, later chief of Cavalry, and one of the Army "greats." There were a lot of real characters at Riley, such as Jupe Lindsay, who fell in love with the photograph of a young lady that he saw on the mantelpiece of a friend, sought her out, and married her; and Tommy Tompkins, who could lengthen one swear word into four or five syllables. Many of the officers at Riley had been children when their fathers went off with Custer to Little Big Horn.

Ma and Georgie and Little Bee went to California for Christmas of 1913, and then back to Fort Riley. Ma and Little Bee spent a part of the following summer at Avalon, and Georgie was there with her when they heard of the assassination in Sarajevo. This was to change their lives, and the lives of unborn generations. Back to Fort Riley. At that time Ma's constant prayers were answered, and she was able to tell both families that another little Patton was on the way. After the birth of Little Bee, Georgie was not at all anxious to have to go through such misery again, but Ma, who had always had her heart set on a big family, kept after him. Whenever he asked her what she wanted for Christmas, or her birthday, or their anniversary, she would always say, "I want a baby." She finally wore him down.

Ma's years at Riley were a turning point in her life. It was the place where she said she "finally woke up." Fort Riley is a post that is a long way from anyplace except Junction City, Kansas, which is rightly named—a train junction. Ma's years at Fort Sheridan had been packed with newly wedded bliss—learning to keep house, her first baby, her first taste of independence. Fort Myer had been glamorous, Saumur even more so, and Fort Riley seemed pretty dead in comparison.

Ma didn't speak the same language that was spoken by the other Army wives. Her interests had always been music, the theatre, racing boats, her family, the life of a cultivated Eastern heiress. She had never had to worry about money or "making do," and she didn't understand the gossip or wistful references to "olden" days. In those days the "Old Army" was a club, with an inner circle of people who were the sons and grandsons and daughters and granddaughters of Army officers; its members knew each other from the cradle to the grave. Having a great deal of her mother Ellie's acting ability, she could put on a good show, but her heart wasn't really in it, and she was lonely—and even a bit bored.

Ma went home to the Ayers quite often for visits. Her father was very old and her mother, still a notable actress, was always working that fact into letters, which made Ma feel guilty about neglecting her parents. She reasoned that, after all, Georgie was in the field a good deal of the time, and would not miss her too much. (In this she was quite wrong.) Her days at Fort Riley were stratified in many ways. She would push "Little Bee" down to the flag stand in time for the Retreat Ceremony, to hear the bugle call and watch the flag come down (surely one of the most touching of all the military customs), and there she would wait for Georgie to walk up from the stables.

The flag stand was near the Officer's Club, and there the old soldiers who were "fading away" would be waiting for their wives, or their orderlies, to come and get them. One old lady and her maiden daughter always came pushing a wheelbarrow, in case the captain was unable to walk home to his quarters. There was still a sign on the parade ground that read "Officers will not shoot buffalo on the parade ground from the windows of their quarters. By Order of the Commanding Officer."

It was, after all, only thirty-seven years since the disaster at Little Big Horn.

One of Georgie's idols was a Captain Brown, who was missing all the fingers from his left hand and the first joint of his right thumb. He had been captured by Indians during a sortie, at which time the chief's son was also captured. The Indians bargained for the return of the young chief, using Captain Brown as the prize. When the Army showed reluctance to make the exchange, they sent one of Captain Brown's finger joints to the commanding officer every day, as a means of persuading him to make up his mind. When that worthy finally realized that the next finger to come would be Brown's trigger finger, he made the exchange. During his captivity, the young Brown made such an impression on his Indian captors that they unofficially adopted him and he became an interpreter, working as such for the government for the rest of his life.

It all seemed very wild and crude and savage to Ma, and she began to wonder if she had been intended for Army life. There didn't seem to be anything to stimulate her imagination, or give her anything about which to talk to Georgie when he came back from the stables. The other ladies on the post made her feel shy because she didn't know what they were talking about; many of them had strong Southern accents, which she associated with the servant class, and she didn't live the way that most of them did. She had a couple, Hannah and Kane, whom she had brought with her from home and who did all the work, so she didn't know how to cook or to talk a good recipe game, and she was beginning to feel she was a terrible failure as an Army wife and mother. In fact, she was getting desperate. One experience she never forgot (although in the end she thought it was funny) was part of her "waking up."

She had been east with her parents for a month, and came back to Fort Riley unbeknownst to the neighbors, as Georgie had motored in to Kansas City to meet her train. It was so hot at Fort Riley in the summer and fall that everyone lived on the front porch. Ma and Georgie were sitting on their front porch, holding hands, when a voice coming from a house down the street and belonging to the deaf mother-in-law of one of Georgie's classmates broke the comparative stillness by a shrill "What say?" Another speaker, probably the long-suffering daughter-in-law, repeated something inaudible, and again came: "What say?" Whereupon the daughter-in-law shouted: "I said that with that pretty little Mrs. Patton gone so much to see her folks, Mrs. Merchant seems to be getting her hooks into young Mr. Patton."

One same-ish sort of day, the day she said changed her life, Ma was walking the carriage with "Little Bee" along a path up above the quarters where she could look out over the prairie, with its grass blowing like waves in the wind that never stops blowing in Kansas. The endless blue sky stretched over the endless green-gray-gold-prairie. She looked down at a ridge of chalky white rock that cropped up across the path. She knew it was called "rimrock," that it rimmed the gullies all across the prairie, and was just one more thing that was alien and far from the New England granite. She looked at it, and suddenly she saw that it was not a rock, it was thousands and thousands of tiny shells, melded together with sand, and she was not standing on a prairie in the Middle West, she was standing on the shores of a dead sea, millions of years gone dry. She ran as fast as she could push the carriage, handed the baby to Hannah, and sat right down and wrote to Lauriat's, a bookstore in Boston, to send her immediately all the books they had on American marine fossils. She found out, after reading several volumes, that Kansas had once been the bottom of the Permian Sea during the sixth period of the Paleozoic Era, a period that had lasted for three hundred and fifty million years. No longer were the plains of Kansas bleak to her. They were a treasure house to be explained, explored, and exploited. That one minute, she told us, changed her whole life. Her inner eye had been opened. She never again in her life had a dull moment, or a single regret for the fun and games of her girlhood. She had discovered the whole world.

As soon as she thus found herself, things began to sort themselves out for Ma. Not every lady at Fort Riley was on a different wave length. It was not long after that when one of the most delightful ladies she was ever to know came by the quarters with a cage full of five finches. It was Mrs. Hoyle, wife of one of the senior captains. The Hoyles had had orders and were transferring, and Mrs. Hoyle had dropped by to invite Ma and Georgie to a dance they were having the following evening, and to leave the little birds as a present for baby Bee. She told Ma that they always had a dance when they left a post, after the furniture had been packed and moved out of the quarters because there was plenty of room.

Mrs. Hoyle was a legend in her own time, and a great influence on Ma's life. She was as wide as she was high; she played the piano like an angel; she had a marvelous contralto voice, both for speaking and singing; and she was one of the real inner circle of the "Old Army." Mrs. Hoyle was descended from René de Russy, who had come to the United States during the Revolution, and had taken a commission in the American Army after the war. He married several times, and marked most of his descendants with the most beautiful eyes— heavy-lidded, slanted down at the outer corners with thick dark lashes all the way around—as the Irish say, "eyes put in with a dirty thumb."

The Hoyles come again and again into Ma's story, but the invitation to the dance was their first meeting. Of course, Ma and Georgie went to the party and Ma saw her first real "Old Army" gathering, where everyone knew everyone else, or was married to their cousin, and it was almost like the family at home in Boston. One of the greatest joys of Ma's life, the year before she died, was to see her only son married to the beautiful great-granddaughter of "her" Mrs. Hoyle. She lived long enough to see, also, their first child, lovely Margaret de Russy Patton with her enchanting de Russy eyes.

Mrs. Hoyle was famous for her charm and her hospitality. She was too large to sleep in a Pullman berth on the train, so had to spend nights in hotels along the way to join Captain Hoyle in his various stations, but she was the apple of his eye, and adored by her son and her four daughters.

One of the first stories Ma heard about her was of the young lieutenant, attending his first Saturday night hop at a new post, who saw Mrs. Hoyle, besieged, as always, with partners, tripping lightly from waltz to polka to mazurka like a soap bubble. He gasped out, "Good Lord, who is that enormous woman?" A very handsome, well set-up, richly mustachioed man standing next to him turned and said severely, "That is my wife, sir, and I love every ounce of her."

In order to clothe the four Hoyle daughters, material was bought by the bolt, and one day Helen, the eldest, who was trying to make bloomer skirts for herself and her sisters, brought the pattern to her mother to ask for some help. Mrs. Hoyle picked up the silver bell that always stood on the table beside her couch and rang it violently, calling out, "Mr. Hoyle, Mr. Hoyle! Come and hear what your daughter Helen has to say!" Captain Hoyle appeared, and Helen was asked to explain what she had been demanding of her mother. Then the bell was rung again, until all the family was assembled, and their father said, "Helen, Margaret, Fanny, Imogene and de Russy, I want you to know that this lady," bowing toward Mrs. Hoyle who reclined in queenly silence on the couch, "has done me the honor to be my wife, lady of my house, and the mother of my children, and that nothing more is to be demanded of her."

The Hoyle girls all grew up to be belles, almost as charming as their mother, and equally efficient at getting things done. Their charm is imperishable and, fortunately, inheritable.

Chapter 7
The Great War

Ma, Georgie, and "Little Bee" spent the Christmas of 1914 in California, and Ma promised to return in February, when the new baby was due (for this time it would surely be "the boy") to be sure that it was born in the same bed in which Ruth Wilson and Georgie Patton had both been born. This was an extraordinarily ugly bed, bought in 1856 for the second Mrs. Wilson, when Don Benito was furnishing the new ranch house he had built for her. The new baby was to be born in the new Lake Vineyard, but the old bed was still there, relegated to the attic but quite usable.

The Pattons went into a fever of activity, preparing for the great event. They planted the gardens so that they could be seen from the bedroom, with pink and white flowers—pink for a boy. The exquisite hand-woven, hand-embroidered baby clothes made for Georgie and Nita by the nuns at the San Gabriel Mission were all washed and sunned. Aunt Nannie, who had the best bedroom, was sent somewhere to visit and her bedroom was turned into a production room for the first grandson, to be the proud bearer of the name of George Smith Patton, IV.

While Ma was still able to travel, they took her to Lake Vineyard, along with "Little Bee," and she sat and rested on the veranda, contemplated the pink and white flowers, sniffed the intoxicating odor of the orange blossoms, drank milk from the Lake Vineyard Jersey herd, and awaited the birth of royalty.

Georgie, back at Fort Riley, was not so happy. He wrote to his father, "Tell the doctor if there is any question between her life and the life of the child, the child must go." He also said that if the doctor would not agree to that, they must get another doctor.

The great moment came on February 28, 1915. After a long and exhausting labor, the longed-for baby turned out to be just another girl. There was not even a name ready for her except, of course, in the back of Ma's loving heart. Ma loved her mother and her mother-in-law, so the baby was named Ruth Ellen. Georgie's suggestion that they name the baby Beatrice II, like a racehorse, was ignored.

That evening, when the inevitable mess attending a home birth had been cleaned up and Ma was set up on pillows with a room full of flowers and telegrams, her mother-in-law, our Bamma, came in to offer good comfort and good cheer. Ma, fully aware that she had failed the Pattons again, said, "Well, Aunt Ruth, better luck next time!" Bamma turned to her with a horrified expression and said, "Beatrice dear, please don't mention 'next time' to your Uncle George. He has had a very hard day!"

The Pattons had employed the very best doctor in the area, but apparently he was a butcher, as Ma had a hard time getting over her second child. In addition to her discomfort, this doctor said that it was not right for a baby to nurse as long as it wanted to, that it should only have ten minutes at each breast. This was patently not enough for Ruth Ellen, as I cried incessantly, got thinner and thinner, and was probably the ugliest baby—there are photographs which do not lie—that had ever come into the family. (Ma always insisted I was cute, though.)

Back at Fort Riley, I was not a bundle of joy. I had everyone mad at everyone else because I never stopped my crying. Finally, in desperation, Ma took me to the local civilian doctor in Junction City, a great-hearted man of genius, Dr. Fred O'Donnell. He took a look at me and said, cheerfully, "Well, Mrs. Georgie, I think we can save this little lady if we start right now. She's starving to death."

Doctor Fred put me onto a formula of cream laced with a little brandy, and in a week's time I was the best baby at Fort Riley and did everything I was supposed to do, including keeping quiet and sleeping a lot.

Eventually, and as inevitably as death and taxes, orders came for Georgie to report to the 8th Cavalry at Fort Bliss, Texas, under John J. Pershing. Ma took her two small daughters back to Avalon to her parents and joined Georgie at Fort Bliss.

With all the Mexican excitement and the shadows of impending war, somehow Ma and Georgie ended up in a little town called Mineral Wells, in the only house in the town that was for rent. Ma was fascinated by life in Mineral Wells. There were seven Love brothers, who owned ranches all around and also ran the town. One of the Love brothers was the sheriff for the simple reason that he was the best shot in that part of Texas. Years before his wife had run off with a traveling man and he had vowed he would never cut his hair until she came back. As she never came back, he had waist-long hair, which he wore in a bun, tied up in a bandanna. He had had to become a pistolier so that no one could laugh at him.

There was also a sweet-faced, white-haired old man named Dave Allison, who was town marshal because he had killed the Mexican bandit Orasco and four of his men. Then there were Mr. and Mrs. Van Buren Hogan. Mr. Hogan ran the saloon and Mrs. Hogan was the only "lady" in town—by her own reckoning. She was very gracious to Ma, and suggested that she come and sleep in the saloon on Saturday nights when the cowhands came into town, as the saloon had brick walls and the merry makers shooting off their guns at imaginary, unfriendly forms could not shoot through the walls. There was also Van Buren Hogan, Jr., a great strapping boy of ten months, who had his whiskey toddy every morning with his grandpa, as they sat on the stoop outside the saloon, watching the traffic go by.

Dick Love, the sheriff with the long hair, was very taken with Ma and Georgie. He wanted Georgie to retire from the Army and go into the health resort business with him in Mineral Wells, a town that was aptly named.

One night Dick Love invited them to dinner at the only hotel in town with some local businessmen to discuss the project. Suddenly, during after-dinner coffee, a gun went off. Instantly, the lights went out, Ma was grabbed by a strong hand and dragged under the table, and there she found the rest of the party. After a decent interval, and no more shots, the party disentangled and surfaced. They decided the wisest move was to disperse and meet again some other day.

Ma was so stunned by the speed of it all that she had little to say, and got into the car with Georgie to drive home. It was a bright moonlit night, and the desert shone like day—and, to her great surprise, Georgie drove slam-bang into a cattle gate across the road in plain sight. She looked at him: there were tears rolling down his cheeks; he was actually sobbing: "God dammit, you don't give a damn about me! That was my pistol that went off; I might have been killed, and you didn't even say anything or ask me if I was all right!"

When he calmed down enough to explain, it appeared that he had tried wearing his pistol in his trouser-fly—the way all the local gunmen did when dressed up for an occasion—and that in sitting down or moving around he had somehow triggered it off and it had shot a hole right through his trouser leg and into the floor.

Ma was not at Mineral Wells when the crime of that year took place, but she heard about it on her return from Mrs. Van Buren Hogan. One of the ranch owners sent his cattle to the cattle pen beside the railroad track to wait for the train on which they were to be loaded. The cowhand who worked for the owner of the pen told the hand in charge of the other cattle to get them the hell out. When the hand demurred, saying he would as soon as the train came, the pen owner's hand shot him dead. When Ma got back, the family of the dead man was chasing the killer and his family across the plains of Texas with retaliation in mind. Ma was horrified, and said there must have been another reason for such a dramatic crime. Mrs. Van Buren Hogan, with a conspiratorial smile, replied, "Oh no, Mrs. Patton. You know how the gentlemen are!"

When Ma and Georgie finally left Mineral Wells, the town gave them an unforgettable party. It took place in a private home. At the door stood Dick Love, behind a large table. As each gentleman entered the scene, he removed his gun and put down his flask of liquor on the table before going into the house. The coats, and the babies, were all stored in the bedroom on the double brass bed. The babies had been swaddled carefully in blankets so they couldn't move, and were stacked like cordwood among the coats. There was barbecue, music supplied by the local fiddler and the blacksmith, who played the accordion, and there was square dancing (round dances like waltzes being a bit on the racy side for respectable couples). Ma and Georgie danced with everyone in town. There was a genuine regret on all sides that they were leaving and going back to Fort Bliss.

Being back on an Army post again seemed the height of civilization. Hannah and Kane had left the team somewhere along the line, so Julia Gould was sent from Avalon to take care of the kitchen, and there was a Chinese houseboy who nonplussed Ma one evening by telling her that he had done everything on the list except to "feed the bugs." It took her awhile to figure out that he had meant he had not spread around the roach poison. And finally, Katherine Breen, our "Taty," was sent along from Avalon as nurse for the children, and was a fixture in our lives for some happy years.

I don't remember Julia Gould, but I do remember her impact. Ma decided one day that the quarters were in need of a good straightening out, and she pulled herself together to "speak to" Julia Gould. Ma was a bit in awe of Julia, who had "known her when" and had been Mamie Ryan's right hand at Avalon. She said, as firmly as she could, "Julia Gould, this house is a mess!" "Indade it is, Miss Beetruss," said Julia stoutly. "Tis high time we were having a visit from Miss Kath-run!"

Julia's manifesto has been used in the family ever since to indicate a state of chaos. Kay Ayer was an exquisite and meticulous housekeeper, and it was a matter of pride in Ma's case to have everything just so when she arrived.

Ma always remembered Fort Bliss with affection, and as a place where she learned a lot. At some point, she decided to keep a cow in order to have fresh milk. The lady in the adjoining set of quarters was agreeable to the idea as long as Ma would share the milk with her—as there seemed to be ample, the cow co-existed between the quarters for some months. They were supposed to share the cost of the cow's food, but Ma said she ended up thinking she owned the front end of the cow, where the food went in, and her neighbor had claim to the back end, but only to the part where the milk came out.

Ma had a green thumb, and loved to garden. Georgie's orderly helped her with the heavy work, especially in distributing the cow manure, but Ma was a black dirt gardener and went down on her knees with the rest of the dedicated weeders of the world. One day the lady next door came over to observe Ma "toiling in the vineyard" and remarked, somewhat scornfully, that she didn't see how Ma could bring herself so low, that *her* folks had always kept a hired man. Ma said that the velvety green acres of Avalon—the rose garden, the winter garden—had never seemed farther away from her than at that moment, but she thought of her "Pa," at four years old, picking up all those sticks and stones for his grandfather, and she said, "Well, you see, my grandfather was a farmer." The lady snorted and moved away. Apparently, that explained everything.

It was also at Bliss that Ma met a dear friend, the fabulous Carol Vidmer. She was Ma's first experience of the really truly Southern belle. The first time that they met, Mrs. Vidmer was sitting on a loveseat with a lieutenant, smoking a cigarette, drinking a cocktail, and knitting a pair of booties for her first grandchild. The lieutenant was smitten, the cigarette and cocktail were definitely "fast," but the booties were exquisite and Colonel George Vidmer, Carol's husband, was obviously proud, devoted, and pretty damn fascinated himself. He was the best left-handed fencer in the Army, and almost impossible to beat. He said he had had to be, to protect his wife's honor. Their daughter, Eleanor Vidmer, was married to Joe Aleshire, one of Georgie's dearest friends, and the families have always been close.

It was during one of Nita's frequent visits that General Pershing began to pay her marked attentions. He was a widower, having lost his wife and daughters in a disastrous fire in their quarters some years before. His only son, Warren, had survived, and when they were at Fort Bliss his sister, Miss Pershing, kept house for him and Warren.

Nita Patton was a tall blonde Amazon with an enormous capacity for love and loyalty and great good sense. In fact, she could have been Georgie's twin. Pershing was a handsome man, very dashing, and capable of great charm. He, too, was larger than life. The general and Nita were drawn together inevitably. Georgie was one of Pershing's young officers, and they saw a lot of Pershing, officially and socially.

Mexican troubles were on the increase at this time, and Georgie requested a job as Pershing's aide, if the troops were to go into Mexico. He had been aide to General Leonard Wood at Fort Myer, and had the experience.

The troops marched off to Mexico on March 16, 1916. Ma stayed at Fort Bliss with us children, and her world was full of rumors, alarms, and excursions. During this campaign, Georgie, on May 17, killed the Mexican officers Cardenas, Lopez, and Garcia, who were aides to the insurrecto, Pancho Villa. He pursued them to their ranch and killed them fair and square. Georgie was lionized in all the papers and made a hero. That was all very well, but the point was missed by the press—that Georgie's attack and victory at the rancho in Rubio was the first motorized warfare on record. They drove up to the rancho in cars, and came back with the bodies of the dead Mexicans tied over the hoods of the automobiles—like slaughtered stags.

Georgie always maintained that the very first armored action was when John the Blind of Bohemia fastened the shields of his knights onto the outside of his battle wagons and ran the wagons downhill into the enemy mass, while bowmen shot out from between the shields—but in truth Georgie was the first officer to use motor-powered vehicles in an attack. Great oaks from little acorns grow.

Forty-eight years later, when my husband was stationed at Fort Sill, Oklahoma, the Mexican General Staff came for their biannual visit to see our missiles and check the latest weaponry. They came in all ranks, ages, and sizes, with their wives, and it was great fun. They spoke their imperfect English, and I spoke my bad border Spanish, but we got along beautifully. The last night we were there, we had a large formal dinner. I was seated next to the dearest little old Mexican general—quite pear-shaped—with lots of curly white hair and twinkling eyes like little hot coals. There was a lot of whispering and chuckling among the members of his staff and, finally, the chairman for the Mexican delegation said that one of the other members wished to propose a toast to my husband and myself, as their hosts, and to my family. My little old general got up, and in very practiced English said, "I weesh to toast not only thees lady and her fine hoosband, but to her fader also, I knowed him well!" I said, in surprise: "You knew my father?"

The rest of the Mexicans began to laugh, and then roared with delight, as he continued, "Oh yess, I knowed your fader well. I shoot at him many times— from behind walls, from behind haystacks, from behind houses—I was weeth Pancho Villa!"

But to get back to Ma and 1916. The American troops returned to the U.S.A. in August, and Ma and Nita Patton met them in Columbus, New Mexico, for a great reunion and rejoicing. The troops went back into Mexico, and Ma and

Nita and the girls—us—went to California to wait for the next development, which was not long in coming. Georgie, out in the field, pumped up his gasoline lantern to the point where it exploded, burning him severely on the head, face, and neck. He was driven to Columbus, where Ma met him and escorted him back to California. The dressing on his wounds had not been changed during the trip to Columbus, and she had to change and redress his burns. This made her very sick to her stomach, which embarrassed her terribly. She felt it was wrong to have such a reaction—not a bit like Florence Nightingale. She felt helpless and inadequate because she had never done anything like that before, and poor Georgie had to tell her what to do while she seemed to be "pulling yards of skin off his face."

Georgie had a month's sick leave in California and his uncle by marriage, Dr. Billy Wills, took over the care of his burns. Extraordinarily enough, with all this changing, Georgie was left unscarred, except that he always felt the cold on his ears after that.

They had a wonderful family time in California, even though his whole head was bandaged like a mummy's. Bamps took Georgie to all his clubs and favorite haunts to show off his "hero son," the bandit killer. Georgie and his father were as close as any father and son could be. They adored each other.

Georgie had sent Ma a poem he had written while he was in Mexico, before he blew himself up. It was as bad as the rest of his poetry, but Ma treasured it always.

TO BEATRICE
O! Loveliest of women
Whate'er I gain or do
Is naught if in achieving
I bring not joy to you

I know I often grieve you
All earthly folk are frail!
But if this grief I knowing wrought
My life's desire would fail!

The mandates of stern duty
Oft take us far apart
But space is impotent to check
The heart which calls to heart

Perhaps by future hidden
Some greatness waits in store

If so, the hopes you praise to gain
Shall make my efforts more.

For victory, apart from you,
Would be an empty gain
A laurel crown you could not share
Would be reward in vain

You are my inspiration
Light of my brain and soul
Your guiding love by night and day
Will keep my valor whole.

It was while Georgie was in the field at this time that he met the Mormons. The Mexicans were harassing the Mormons who had built farms across the border, and the American troops were escorting out those who wanted to leave. Georgie, with his usual curiosity, got one of them to lend him the *Book of Mormon,* which he read with great interest. He always felt that it was intelligent to hear both sides of any story, particularly when a religious cause was involved. One of the families he moved was that of the Mormon Bishop Crow. He said that "that old procreator" had four wives at least because every time he went to escort a Mrs. Crow across the border, it was a different lady.

In January of 1917, Georgie wrote Ma, "I hate to get old and also for you to get old. It is true you look just as young as you did when I went to West Point, but I hate to have us out of the twenties [he had turned thirty-one on November 11 and she would be thirty-one on January 12]. Since we have lost a year of each other, it almost seems we should not age."

Getting older was always a worry to Georgie. He worried about losing his hair. He worried about losing his figure, and used to try on his cadet uniform to see if he could still get into it. On his fiftieth birthday, he refused to get out of bed, as he said his chances of being a hero were over; Caesar had conquered Gaul when he was in his thirties and forties; Alexander had conquered the known world in his thirties; Napoleon was finished at fifty. Ma finally got him out of bed by persuading him that he had been fifty for a whole year without knowing it.

Ma never worried much about getting old—she was too busy. I only remember once, when she was in her late forties, I found her weeping bitterly in front of her dressing table mirror. When I asked her what was wrong, she wailed, "Oh, no one that ever sees me now would ever know what a pretty girl I was!" Ma had aged naturally. She didn't wear makeup, and she refused to tint her hair because she had a great, if concealed, contempt for women whom she referred to as "mutton dressed as lamb." But to know her was to love her, and she was certainly of "infinite variety."

The Mexican expedition finished itself off, more or less, in January of 1917, and Ma and Nita met their dear ones again at Columbus at the end of the month. General Pershing had especially requested that Nita come to the reunion. Georgie loved his sister dearly, and General Pershing was his idol, but the way things were building up between them disturbed him very much. He had visions of what would be said about himself, if the romance blossomed—that Georgie Patton had climbed to rank and influence on the coattails of his commanding officer. He wanted Nita to be happy, but, oh, he did want to be his own man!

In February, Georgie and Ma went with the 7th Cavalry for station at Fort Bliss. The 7th Cavalry is a terrific regiment—just as full of esprit de corps as an egg is of meat; those not so fortunate as to be members of that august crew say that it is very interesting that the 7th Cavalry's main claim to fame is that it got chewed to pieces at Little Big Horn by Sitting Bull's painted savages. The 7th Cavalry pays no attention to such petty jealousy.

El Paso is one of my first memories, and I can carry on from there by memory and not just "tales my mother taught me." One of my two most vivid memories of the time must have taken place when I was about three years old. It still unfolds across my inner eye like a color movie. I was playing on the porch at Fort Bliss under the eye of my sister Bee. She was with her doll family, behind the red garbage cans, and I was watching traffic go by, such as it was. Three cows, attended by a sort of collie dog, came across the yard, and I knew immediately that if I could just put my hand on them, I could bring them to Ma. I waited until Bee was down behind the garbage cans, and then I sneaked off the porch, across the road, following them. I must have known I was being bad, because I glanced up at the windows of the quarters opposite, and saw what looked like two little lights twinkling through the lace curtains on the stair window. It was lucky for me that those little lights happened to be the reflections of Colonel Rhodes's spectacles as he came down the stairs; because when the hew and cry began for a lost child some time later, he remembered that he had seen a very small person in a brown suit heading that-a-way. They found me quite a long way off on the prairie. The cattle were still in sight, and I was still intent on bringing them home to Ma.

The other incident is still a green spot in my life. Ellie, as aforementioned, was always the drama artiste and was always writing to Ma reminding her that Granfer Ayer missed his "thinking flower." She constantly played on Ma's feelings about coming home for a visit. I don't think she did it to devil Georgie: I think she really felt what she wrote. Ma was always torn between her conception of her duty to Georgie and her duty to her parents.

So Ma decided to take another trip home, taking Taty and her girls with her. Life was much as usual at Avalon, except that Granfer Ayer now breakfasted in his room. We were all immediately absorbed into the familiar routine.

A few days before we left Texas, Georgie took Bee and me aside and asked Bee if Ellie still asked us if we had a new "piece" to recite. The Ayers were great on recitation. Bee said that Ellie did, so Georgie said he was going to teach us a piece that was a big secret, and we were to tell it to nobody until Ellie asked us to recite.

Shortly after we got to Avalon, this came to pass. Ellie was serving tea in the great long living room that faced the sea—as she did every afternoon. She sat in the tall green velvet armchair with its back to the fire, and the tea service was on a low table in front of her. One of the things we liked best about Ellie was the way her many bracelets tinkled when she moved. Quite a few people were there for tea: Cousin Annie Ruggles; Uncle Otis Wood, William Wood's ever-obliging and hanging-on brother; and, best of all, Ellie's old friend, Mrs. Obrig, who used a real ear trumpet. It was shaped like a trumpet with a slight curve in it, and when anyone spoke to Mrs. Obrig, she put the small end into her ear.

We had been brought down to be admired. We were dressed alike in our handmade dresses with real lace insets, each of us with a huge hairbow. For Bee, this was fine, as she had natural ringlets that looked like bouncy sausages which were curled every morning around Taty's finger. For me, it was a wasted effort, as I had dandelion-blow fluff, perfectly straight and not much of it. But Bee and I knew we were beautiful, and we had perfect self-assurance in those years.

Ellie saw our entrance and said, "Beatrice dear, do the girls have a nice piece that they could recite for our friends?" Ma said she was sure we did, so there was a hush while we said our new piece that Georgie had taught us:

> There was a goddam spider
> Lived up a goddam spout
> There came a helluva thunderstorm
> And washed the bastard out
> And when the sun came out again
> And dried up all the rain
> Damn, if the old son-of-a-bitch
> Didn't climb up that spout again!

I was looking right at Ellie, and saw the bangle-covered arm holding the teapot suspend itself in midair. There was a great silence. Bee thought an encore was indicated, and we started the piece again, but were gently removed.

The next morning Ma was called in to have coffee with Granfer Ayer. He was trying not to smile as he said, "Little daughter, I feel that I have had some sort of communication with George that he wants his little family around him, and that is quite understandable. You must remember that I have passed my three-score-years-and-ten, and that every day thereafter has been an added blessing with the love of your mother and our wonderful children. I cannot expect them to be all about me forever. Georgie needs you and his little daughters, and I have taken the liberty of purchasing these tickets for your return to Texas on the first of the week."

There are not many details I remember after that, except that General Pershing went to California to ask for Nita's hand in marriage, which made lots of talk and excitement. Georgie was still not very sure how he felt about having his commanding officer as a brother-in-law, but Ma was all for love. Bamps also had grave doubts, but Nita was of age and very set on it. I have General Pershing's letters to Bamps and Bamma, and to Aunt Nannie Wilson. The relationship at that time seemed very easy and comfortable.

War was declared by the United States on Germany on April 6, 1917. Family fermentation began, all over America. On April 11, Ma and Georgie, who took emergency leave, and we girls took off for Massachusetts. Granfer Ayer had pneumonia. On May 18 Georgie was told to report to Washington, D.C., as General Pershing's aide. Ten days later, Ma, the Pattons, and Aunt Nannie saw Georgie off to France. There were millions of men involved in that war "to end wars," but to every family there was only one real live participant. For us, it was Georgie.

I don't remember any of that scene. I just remember being told about it. But I do remember we had our pictures taken for a newsreel as "Women Working for the War." We were all knitting in the movie, and my sister and I wore little overseas caps. I didn't know how to knit, but I certainly knew how to mug the camera.

After Granfer Ayer and Ellie died, Ma was distraught for a long time. She went through the whole program of grief, from blaming herself to wishing she had been a better daughter, and that she had expressed her love more often and more deeply. From my point of view, I don't see how she could have done more or better than she did as their daughter, but she finally sank to the point of visiting a well-known medium in Washington to see if she could get in touch with her parents and tell them she had loved them.

She almost never spoke of her experience, as to her it was a mind-shattering one: she could not truly believe in ESP. She said the medium was an ordinary sort of man who took her into an ordinary sort of room and sat and talked to her for awhile, and then began to hum, and then to sing a song. It was an old ballad that begins, "Come rest in my bosom, my own stricken dear." Ma had never heard it sung by anyone except by Ellie, who sang it very occasionally. It was certainly not a well-known song. While Ma was still in shock from this, the medium took a pencil and wrote the name "Fredk Ayer" in very shaking writing. Granfer Ayer had suffered from palsy for years and the writing was, as far as Ma could tell, his writing. She said she was so horrified at what might happen next that she jumped up and ran out of the room and later sent the medium a large check for his services.

She told me that she had thought about it for years, and her only explanation was that a medium had a mind like a bucket which he would lower into the mind of his subject and draw up, not knowing what the bucket would contain. The whole idea appalled her that another person could delve into her mind, careless of what might come to the surface.

Georgie had a good time the first months of the war. He was stationed in the Tower of London, which thrilled his history-loving soul. The Seneschal of the Tower allowed him to try on some of the ancient armor there. He was very interested to find that the only armor that fit him was that of the so-called "giant," a freak from the court of one of the Henrys. The armor of the heroes of his youth was too small, although Georgie was not overly big for his own times; he was 6'1" tall, and his fighting weight was about 160 pounds.

I won't go into Georgie's first war. There have been a great many books written about that, and most of his correspondence with Ma and others has been sifted and catalogued. But I will tell some of the stories he brought home with him, and with which we grew up.

In December of 1917, Georgie was finally made part of the tank corps that he had so passionately advocated. He and his friend and fellow tanker, Colonel Elgin Brain, had to find a place to live near the tank center, which was at Bourg. They finally rented the ground floor of the hôtel of the Comtesse d'Aulan, in nearby Langres. The hôtel had been built in the early 1300s, and, according to Georgie, had not been modernized in the intervening years. Langres is a jewel of a town, unadvertised and untourist ridden. I have not been there since 1938, when my brother George and I went there with Ma while we were touring the battlefields of France. In 1938 the town was much the same as when Georgie had been billeted there. It is a walled town, with gates that are shut at sundown. One of the gates—still in use—had been built by the Romans. Georgie's hôtel was a small-town chateau, and there was no one there to let us in, but it looked suitably ancient and blended in with the other old houses and cobbled streets. Georgie had described it as having a banqueting hall, with the remains of tattered standards hanging from staffs. There was a well in the kitchen. An old woman and her two daughters cooked and cleaned for Georgie and Colonel Brain. When Georgie went to rent the ground floor, he asked the agent about the owner and was told that he had been killed in the war. When Georgie asked the name of the fatal battle, it appeared that the owner had been killed in the eleventh crusade. The family preferred living in Paris, or some of their other estates, and the hotel had been empty for some time—say, about three hundred years.

Georgie and Brain slept on camp beds in one downstairs room with a large fireplace, which they needed. One night, during a heavy storm, the ceiling began to leak into their quarters. Georgie had never had time to examine the upstairs, but he took a bucket and flashlight and located the leak in the empty room above, put a bucket under it, and went back to bed. Several days later the agent dropped in to collect the rent and to say that the old housekeeper was missing her bucket, and asked the colonel if he knew where it was. Georgie remembered the storm and said he would go and get the bucket. As he and the agent went up the wide stone staircase, Georgie told the agent that he thought he should be aware that some of the young people in the town were using the hotel as a trysting place. When he had gone up with the bucket on the night of the storm, he had heard two voices—that of a woman crying and of a man apparently trying to comfort her. The agent stopped dead on the stairs, and said "Mais, mon Colonel, that is impossible! There is no one in the city of Langres who would come upstairs in this hôtel!" Georgie insisted that he had certainly heard the voices, and the agent asked him to show him where they had come from. They went into the chamber where the bucket stood still, and Georgie indicated that it was in there. The room contained a huge mouldering bed on a dais, and some other cobweb-covered pieces, and was a part of the main tower, the curved front of the room made up of long narrow windows alternating with deep alcoves. The agent looked at Georgie with horror, and said, "Then, mon Colonel does not know the story?"

Georgie said no, he didn't know any stories, and the agent pointed dramatically to the alcove on the far left of the windows. It was bricked up nearly to the ceiling and the material was not the same as that of which the original walls had been constructed. The agent said that the story was, as everyone in Langres could testify, that when the owner of the hôtel, a Comte d'Aulan, came back from some crusade, he had found the Comtesse in that very bed with a page, and he had bricked them both up in the alcove on the left, and had gone back to the wars from which he never returned. This might explain why the family didn't want to live in the hôtel. Georgie said that he had never heard the story— all that he had heard was a woman crying and a man trying to comfort her.

Ma never really got over the fact that he hadn't explored the hôtel.

The officer in command of the American tank force was General Rockenback. He was famous for his razor-edged tongue and his martinet-ship. His wife, Emma, was a breezy aristocrat, and a notable horsewoman. When she was asked why on earth she had married "Rocky," she replied, "I married him for his conformation, of course. Did you ever see a finer piece of man-flesh?"

I remember them both, as a small child at Fort Meade, Maryland, where the tanks rolled to their long rest between the two world wars.

The Tank Corps, such as it was, proceeded toward the real war, and Georgie's letters were full of it. He wrote one to Ma in February of 1918 in which he said, "I am getting to talk to you about my battalion as much as you used to talk to me about the children. I objected to that. I will stop this."

It was about this time that he acquired one of his great treasures. He had always been fascinated by the sword, not only as a weapon but also as an object of veneration. He was at a tailor shop in France and saw on top of a pile of clothes a sword, the type of which he had never seen before. He inquired about it and the tailor told him that it had been brought in with the clothes by the valet of a gentleman who had recently died, in payment of his debts. Georgie bought the sword for a small sum. It was, and is, a slender damascened blade with some small gold inlays. He found out when he tried to identify it that it was the sword of a regiment of the Swiss Guard which had defended Marie Antoinette against the mob in the Tuileries, and that aside from a single blade in the museum, all the other swords had passed down to the families of the Swiss Guard.

The war was all around him when he wrote Ma a letter, which shows a side of him that she always saw, but that few others, outside his immediate family, ever knew existed.

He wrote to her that he had been inspecting a battlefield at night, and that the dead soldiers, as yet unclaimed by the burial teams, were lying there in the moonlight. He said it was hard to tell the Americans and British from the Germans, as they all looked alike—very young and very dead—and he began to think how often their mothers had changed their diapers and wiped their noses, and suddenly the whole concept seemed unbearable, and he decided that the only way to survive under such a stress was to try to think of soldiers as numbers, not as individuals, and that the sooner the allies won, the sooner the slaughter of innocents would cease. However, no matter what he said, he could never quite do that. To him his men were individuals, people and responsibilities always. At the time he wrote that letter, he also wrote a poem which he later sent to Ma.

THE MOON AND THE DEAD

The roar of the battle languished
The hate from the guns grew still,
While the moon rose up from a smoke cloud
And looked at the dead on the hill.

Pale was her face with anguish
Wet were her eyes with tears,
As she gazed at the twisted corpses
Cut off in their earliest years.
Some were bit by the bullet,
Some were kissed by the steel,
Some were crushed by the cannon
But all were still, how still.

The gas wreaths hung in the hollows
The blood stink rose in the air
And the moon looked down in pity
On the poor dead lying there.

Light of their childhood's wonder,
Moon of their puppy love,
Goal of their first ambition
She watched them from above.

Yet not with regret she mourned them
Fair slain on the field of strife
Fools only lament the hero
Who gives for faith his life.

She sighed for the lives extinguished
She wept for the loves that grieve
But she glowed with pride at seeing
That manhood still doth live.

For though the moon is winsome
In wisdom she is old
Nor grieves she for the fallen
Nor grudges she the bold.

Her years are for the hero
Her hate is for the cur
Her utter loathing for the hound
That shrinks from righteous war

The moon sailed on contented
Above the heaps of slain
For she saw that honor liveth
And manhood breathes again.

A lot of the poetry Georgie wrote, as he frankly told Ma, he wrote to cheer and inspire himself. He was always worried—as he had been that long-ago day at Fort Sheridan when he had stood on the target butts—that he would not be able to face the song of the bullet that had his name on it. He told us, while he was teaching us to shoot, that you never heard the bullet that killed you as the missile travels faster than sound. I suppose he had heard that hard soldier's comfort and fastened to it.

But the tests came. He knew firsthand that "there are no practice games in life."

There was the bridge at Essey over the Rupt de Mad. This bridge was rumored to have been mined by the Germans, but the engineers on the Americans' side could not spot the wires or connections. Georgie volunteered to walk across it, taking a chance at tripping any wires, before he would allow his precious tanks to be threatened. He wrote Ma that he knew instinctively that it was mined, and that every step he took might be his last. As he put his foot on the bridge, he was suddenly separated from the little uniformed figure he could see walking stiffly and carefully across the bridge, lifting his feet and putting them down with exquisite precision. After a moment, he knew he was watching himself. He saw the figure step off the bridge at the far side, duck down under it, and then come up with something in its hands; and then he was standing there with the broken connections, ordering his troops to cross. The bridge had been mined at the far side, and the trip wires were not visible from the approach.

His date with his destiny, so long anticipated and dreaded, came on September 26, 1918. It has all been written up with details and orders and comments, but this is how he told Ma about it. He was to lead a tank charge. He was crouching at the foot of a low hill, sending hand signals to his tanks. The Germans were getting the range from the far side, and the grass was flying up under their fire—just as if it were being cut by a lawnmower. He said that all he could think of was Jesus Callahan mowing the lawn at Lake Vineyard. He knew the Germans were expecting the tanks and had the range. He was afraid. His hands were sweating and his mouth was dry. There was a low bank of clouds behind the rising ground, and he looked up and saw, among the clouds, his ancestors. The ones he had seen pictures of looked like the daguerreotypes and the paintings; there was General Hugh Mercer, mortally wounded at the Battle of Princeton; there was his grandfather, Colonel George Patton, mortally wounded at the Battle of Cedar Creek; there was his great-uncle, Colonel Waller Tazewell Patton, mortally wounded at the Battle of Gettysburg; there were other faces, different uniforms, dimmer in the distance, but all with a family look. They were all looking at him, impersonally, but as if they were waiting for him. He knew what he had to do, and continued to take action.

Georgie was wounded at 11:15 a.m. Five of the six men with him, not in the tanks, were killed. He was shot in the groin, the shot emerging through his buttock, leaving a hole about the size of a teacup. One of his runners, Joe Angelo, stayed with him and dressed his leg with his own first-aid kid and one off a nearby corpse. Later, his sergeant missed him and came looking for him. Georgie told the sergeant to tell Colonel Brett to take command of the outfit and not to come after him as this would attract enemy fire.

Georgie was finally picked up about 3:30 p.m. He said his wound did not pain him—he was numb from the shock. He felt great calmness of mind and spirit, and he kept thinking that he was nearly thirty-three years old, and that his grandfather Patton had been thirty-three years old when he had taken the shell fragment in his belly at Cedar Creek, and how young he had been, and what a waste it all was. Georgie said that he knew he was alive, but that part of him had died; he was a little bit in both worlds. In his own words, "I was overwhelmed by a deep feeling of warmth and peace and comfort, and of love. I knew how profoundly death was related to life; how unimportant the changeover was; how everlasting the soul—and the love was all around me, like a subdued light." And, he knew then, that when St. Paul said "and the last enemy that shall be destroyed is death" (Corinthians 15:26), the saint really meant "the fear of death" because when you are so close to Thanatos, you cannot fear him; you know you have known him before.

Georgie's wound took some time to heal. It became septic and had to be drained and he was in the hospital much too long to suit him. Ma wrote to him every day, and he wrote her almost as often. She had obviously not given up hope of a larger family and must have mentioned in her letters about what a good mother she was, and how she loved her role as such, because he wrote to her, "Your childish proclivities, of which you boast, do not interest me at all. I love you too much and am jealous, or something, of the children. Your only chance to have another child is accident or Immaculate Conception. You ought to be complimented. But being pig-headed, I suppose you are not. I love you too much." She was pigheaded.

In the meantime, Nita's romance with General Pershing was going on the rocks. He had written to her that "the feeling" was gone and suggested that they do nothing about announcing their engagement or getting married until "the feeling" came back. On top of that, she was not sent a ticket to the Victory Ball.

Nita was staying with Kay and Keith Merrill in London at that time, and Keith called General Pershing's headquarters to see if there had been an oversight, and was told by a flustered aide, after a long wait, that the Merrills had been expected to bring Nita to the ball. Nita's letters to her parents at this time were staunch, but full of underlying despair. She broke her engagement to Pershing, returning his diamond ring before he could further humiliate her. She was a lady of high degree.

There are two sides to every story, even to the prejudiced. General Pershing had been under a terrible strain for the war years and had done a fantastic job. As the war drew to its successful close he was wined and dined and flattered and praised by the great and the near great; some of the most beautiful women in Europe were not above falling at his feet to gain something for their hearts' interests. He had a Caesar's triumph. Nita with her blonde Viking looks and carriage and her predominantly good sense, was just there and could be more or less propped in a corner until he had time to regroup and reconsider. Only Nita removed herself with all flags flying.

There is a letter on the sorry subject from Georgie to his mother, written from Camp Meade, Maryland, on September 6, 1919. The family used the code name, "Henry" (spelled in this case by Georgie, "henrie") for General Pershing.

I am going to command the tanks in the Pershing "Triumph" in Washington September 16. I seriously doubt if any of the tanks finish the parade as we are using American tanks and the engine usually jumps out after about five miles. Nita sent Bee a copy of henrie's letter to her and her reply. I think her letter was fine and I will bet that H got the surprise of his life when he received it. My own opinion is that he is being purely selfish wanting to let the affair rest for awhile to see if his feeling revived. It is perfectly possible that his mind, driven as it has been for nearly three years, is incapable of emotion. Or it may be that the war has aged his mind so that like a very old man he can only live in the past. I would not be at all surprised to see him renew his suit, especially if he is not successful here. I am not in a position to judge what Nita's action should be in that eventuality. She has acted so well thus far that I feel sure she will always do right.

Years later, when Georgie was stationed at Fort Myer and General Pershing was living in the suite a grateful government had built for him at Walter Reed Army Hospital, he used to dine fairly often with us. He was still arrestingly handsome, but there was something vital missing. We had, of course, heard about our beloved Tinta's broken romance, and were a little bit mad at General Pershing for having "broken her heart," although Nita herself never referred to it: she had gone on and made a full life for herself. Bee once asked Ma how Tinta could ever have been in love with "that silly old man." Ma got a very sad look on her face and said, "The John J. Pershing you children know is not the Black Jack Pershing that Tinta fell in love with. Lots of men die in wars, but some of them who have very strong bodies go on living long after the person inside of them, the real them, is dead. They are dead because they used themselves all up in the war. That's one of the most terrible things about war."

When General Pershing came to dinner he was always darling with us children, and he and Georgie talked about the old days in Fort Bliss and in Mexico. Best of all, he told us stories of when he was a brand new young lieutenant and fought in the last of the Indian skirmishes. He could be perfectly charming. One night I well remember, General Pershing and Georgie had washed down their reminiscences with many a fine libation, and the general began to weep, "Georgie, Georgie, if I hadn't been such a damned egotistic fool, my children would have been just a little younger than your children with the same beautiful blonde hair, and the same true blue eyes."

Before Georgie came back from France he wrote to Nita several times, urging her to come to Europe and have a "dignified reunion" with General Pershing, but for Nita it was over. Bamps was the only person really pleased by the break-up. He did not consider General Pershing good enough for Nita. Among other reasons, he said that Pershing's father had been a brakeman on the railroad. Georgie was relieved too, at having the taint of favoritism or nepotism removed from whatever his future might hold.

The war to me is only a few flashbacks, but I do remember the false armistice. We were all at Avalon where Ma was sorting and packing up the house, very subdued by memories of her parents, which, she felt, she was folding and putting away. All at once the church bells everywhere began to ring, and Ma burst into tears and cried, "The war is over! The war is over! Your father will be coming home!"

Chapter 8
Camp Meade and Fort Myer

Georgie came back to the United States in the middle of March in 1919. I have been told that he was walking with a cane because of his wounded leg, but that when he saw Ma standing on the dock, he laid down his cane and walked down the gangplank unaided.

I am sure there were lots of visits and reunions at that time, but I don't remember anything except Camp Meade, Maryland, where the tanks were sent to their eternal camping ground. The "war to end wars" had been fought; the swords had been beaten into plowshares; the military appropriations had been cut—all was to be well.

Camp Meade had been a wartime post so there were no officers' quarters, but Ma had had enough of separation. Somehow or other, a barracks was requisitioned, which Ma turned into an unforgettable home. The only paint available at the quartermaster stores were the Cavalry colors, blue and yellow. So, the whole part of the barracks we lived in was painted blue, yellow, blue and yellow, yellow and blue. This barracks was in the middle of a sandlot, so Ma planted oats to keep the dust down. The latrine presented a problem in decor, but she solved this by planting wandering Jew and trailing ivy in the urinals, and just using the two sit-down toilets with doors.

There was a post ordinance that no cooking could be done in the quarters because of the fire hazard (the barracks were made of boards covered with tarpaper). After a week or so of eating in the mess (canned corn, canned corned beef, canned tomatoes, canned butter, commissary ham, lethal apple pies) Ma put her foot down and said she *would* live at Camp Meade and she *would* have a kitchen.

A day or so after her "pronunciamento," a much harassed Georgie appeared in a tank, hauling a timber sled on which was a small signal house he had found abandoned on the range. We had prisoner labor in those days. Any soldier-prisoner not sinful enough to send to Fort Leavenworth worked off his AWOL and drunk charges by making roads, cleaning latrines, digging garbage pits, or doing what came next. These prisoners, always accompanied by a soldier carrying a rifle, were mostly young and cheerful types who welcomed a break in the Army routine. Bee and I knew all the prisoners; they were great friends of ours.

With prisoner labor, Georgie put a foundation under the little house and built a covered boardwalk between it and the room we used as a dining room, and we cooked and ate at home. Ma was very happy about it. She insisted the arrangement reminded her of Mount Vernon where the food was always carried into the house from the detached kitchens. Bee and I missed the mess hall. None of the food there had been "good for you," and we both had developed a lifetime passion for canned corn.

We all loved Camp Meade, aside from the fact that "Daddy was home." (This, of course, did not apply to Ma.) Bee and I had been led to expect so much—a knight in shining armor, a playmate, a fearless killer of the dreaded Hun, a teller of tales. What we got was far below our expectations. In remembering Georgie, I realize now that he was in considerable pain at the time, worried about his future in the tank corps of his creation, and having a hangover from the war, which is a very real thing. A man goes from the command of thousands of men where his judgment means victory or defeat, life or death, and where the very air, corpse-tainted though it may be, holds eternal excitement and danger, to the shrinking command of a handful of men, and the narrowing horizons of peacetime duty with not enough money and not enough troops, and the tender trap of home and family—and it is a letdown. I guess things didn't come up to Georgie's expectations either.

My sister remembered him from before the war, but I did not. I thought he was an ogre. Everything I did was wrong. I will never forget the first time he ever spoke directly to me. I had rushed into the house not knowing he was there, and he was sitting on the living-room floor among a lot of dismembered guns that he was cleaning and reassembling. He looked up at me as I hovered in the doorway, and with his really charming smile said, "Hello, little girl." I was so overwhelmed with the attention that I burst into tears and howls, and he began to yell at Ma to "come and take the baby away," that she was "making a goddam awful noise," and that he hadn't touched her. It was shortly after that incident, probably at Ma's insistence that he develop some rapport with his children, that he got us our first dog—something we had prayed for steadily. He was a white bull terrier puppy, named, of course, "Tank." We didn't find out until Tank was firmly established in our lives that he was stone deaf. This did not disturb Tank in the least, and we took it for granted that we communicated with him by banging on the floor. He was always able to distinguish the vibrations of our car, and was always at the door to meet us. Being deaf, more or less, cut him off from other dogs and he was totally devoted to us for all of his eleven years. As he was deaf, he didn't hear the challenges of other dogs upon whose territory he trespassed, and this led to some notable dog fights, which Tank nearly always won. The dogs would attack him, and with true bull terrier technique he would dispatch them and come to us, bleeding and wagging his tail to be mended and sewed back together again.

Our playhouse at Meade was a real tank, standing in front of headquarters. It had been brought back from the war because it had a record number of bullet holes in it. It never occurred to Bee and me that men had died in it. We played soldier there and kept the other kids out.

In back of our quarters was a disused trunk line leading to empty warehouses. Every evening an old gentleman, father of one of the warrant officers on the post, would take his evening constitutional up and down the line. Bee and I would follow him at a respectful distance, admiring the round bald patch on the back of his head as the result of his scalp having been taken by Indians years before when he was a recruit.

The Dwight Eisenhowers lived down the line from us. Bee and I found Mrs. Eisenhower the most glamorous creature that had ever appeared in our lives. She insisted, very daringly we thought, that we call her Mamie and not Mrs. Eisenhower, as she said she wasn't that old yet. Ma didn't approve of our first-naming grown-ups, but there wasn't anything she could really say. Also, Mamie wore filmy negligees most of the day, and drank a lot of iced tea, which she stirred by swirling it around in her glass. We thought this was the ultimate in sophistication, and tried to do the same with our milk, with bad results. Their little boy, Icky, was just my age, and he spent a lot of time at our house. He got up and wandered at night, so when he went to bed his shoes were tied on so he couldn't take them off. All of the post children fished like mad in a ditch near the quarters, with bent-pin hooks and grasshoppers for bait. One day Icky caught a fish. He carried it around all day in his hand to show people and, finally, that evening, he brought it to our house and asked Ma to cook it for him, as Mamie didn't know how to cook. By that time the fish was pretty run down. Me told us to go and play. Pretty soon she came out with Icky's fish on a piece of buttered toast, garnished with a sprig of parsley and a lemon wedge. Icky ate it in ecstasy. Ma told us later that she had opened a can of sardines and dressed one of them up for the occasion.

Our big dissipation was the movies on Friday nights. Our nursemaid, Taty, was with us, and if there was a William S. Hart movie, we could go with her to see it. William S. Hart, with his long horse face and his Army look, was our hero. We didn't want to grow up and marry him. William S. Hart never married anyone; he never even kissed the curly-haired girls he rescued from bears and Indians and villains; he just rode off into the sunset. Sometimes he kissed his horse—that seemed the thing to do.

Ma and Georgie came home from a party one night and woke us up and Ma, very dramatically, told us that she now *really* believed in fairies because that very night someone had put earphones on her ears and she had listened and heard voices coming out of the air. It was her first experience with a radio.

Prohibition was at its zenith, and the "dries" were going to save the world in spite of itself; so, of course, every red-blooded American was making beer in the woodshed. Georgie made up a batch and put the bottles in the covered walkway to the kitchen shack. One night there was a regular rattle of machine-gun fire, and great soft BOOMS. Georgie fell on the floor so fast and so flat that we all just stood there and stared while the cook screamed in the kitchen that all the beer was exploding and getting all over everything. Georgie got up, rather shamefacedly, and explained that it had sounded so much like hostile fire that he instinctively had taken cover. Ma laughed and laughed and called him "my hero," and he got very red.

Bee and I were devoted but totally different, and our eating habits were opposite. Ma pinned on the curtains across from my seat in the dining room a large sign that said "CHEW," and opposite Bee there was a large sign on the wall that said "SWALLOW." The night she had General and Mrs. Rockenback to dinner she was so flustered that she forgot to remove the signs and didn't notice them until the guests were being seated. Mrs. "Rocky" took it all in, and said, "We have the same trouble at our house too, Mrs. Patton. The general never stops chewing, and I never stop talking. So you see, we can still learn from the young."

We were not very long at Camp Meade—not long enough. The tank corps had folded its tents like the Arabs and silently stolen away, leaving its iron horses to cosmoline baths and dusty shrouds. The "war to end wars" had been fought and won and, while they were not quite sure of what to do with the Army, they knew they would never need tanks again in this best-of-all-possible worlds.

Georgie went back to the Cavalry, and we rented a house in Washington at 1920 23rd Street. (We had to memorize the address.) Our faithful Taty was with us and we got so fired up at her terrible tales of the cruelty of the landlords in Ireland to the simple peasants—of which Taty was one—that we were totally confused when Ma talked about our landlord, and we decided to ruin his house for him. ("Sure, this is the way we treat the Kings, and spoil their pleasures, the dirty things!") We didn't get much further than tearing strips of wallpaper off our bedroom walls and crayoning the stairwell. In an excess of zeal, I cut off the entire ball fringe on Ma's antique bedspread, thinking that that too was the property of the landlord, and at this point Ma stepped in and persuaded us that there was a difference.

At about that time, the Irish hero Terence McSweeney went on a hunger strike in the Washington area to call world attention to the sorry plight of the Irish, and the loyal sons of Erin picketed the White House, singing, "And shall McSweeney die? And shall McSweeney die? Then fifty thousand Irishmen will know the reason why!"

Georgie, on this great day, was with a troop of mounted Cavalry, keeping peace among picketers, when he saw his two daughters "with shining morning face," dressed alike, and with matching hair ribbons, marching along with the crowd. Taty was with us in her white starched nurse's uniform, beaming. There was nothing he could do where he was, but he finally located a policeman and told him, for God's sake, to contact Mrs. Patton at such-and-such-a-number, and tell her to come and get her daughters out of the picket line. Bee and I could not understand the subsequent fuss. We had been having a ball and, anyhow, Ma had told us often enough that her grandmother's name had been Mary Alicia Sweeney, and it was Sweeney for whom we were picketing.

This was just one of the many problems that Taty inaugurated, and the last straw came soon after the White House ploy. Ma found out that Taty had given the Catholic chaplain ten dollars for the poor so that he would tell us that dogs went to heaven, as we were very firm about not going to heaven unless Tank, the bull terrier, could go with us. Taty wanted to convert us to Catholicism in order to save our souls as a true act of faith. I don't think Ma was as angry with Taty as she was with the priest because when she closely questioned him as to whether he believed that dogs went to heaven, he had to admit that he did not, and she told him that he should know better than to lie to little children. But Taty, having been involved in this lie, had to go, and it broke our hearts.

Ma had a very definite and modern sense of religion. Her own mother had been raised very strictly in one of the less imaginative sects, and she had wanted her children to choose their own church, so Ma and her brother and sister had attended all the different churches in Boston, and Ma had decided on the Congregational faith. She also had a true feeling for prayer and depended on it all her life. In her religion she was not a mystic, as was Georgie, but it was certainly a foundation in her life. And truth was one of its cornerstones.

After Taty left, we embarked on a series of French governesses that both Bee and I hated. We got rid of several of them by acting like fiends—something that Georgie had taught us when he wanted to get rid of Bee's piano teacher, Miss Polkenhorn. But Ma got onto our scheme and the last one she employed, Mlle. Henri, was even more of a fiend than we were. I think Ma had warned her about us because she was adamant and unsurprisable. She was also a spiritualist. Her bedroom was between our bedroom and bathroom, and we thought we could hear her talking to her dead parents at night, so we got afraid to go to the bathroom, and even more afraid to tell anyone why, which led to a disastrous situation. We were driven to use chamber pots and when they were full we dumped the contents out the bedroom window. Ma, who had a sense of smell like a beagle, caught onto this and took steps. She moved Mlle. Henri into our bedroom and put us in the room next to the bathroom.

Our religious experiments in those days were rich and full. Georgie was a devout, tithing, church-going Episcopalian but Ma, remembering her own upbringing, said that we could try all the Sunday Schools at Fort Myer. Bee and I finally settled on the Baptist Sunday School: firstly, because it served cocoa and cookies, and secondly, because the Baptist hymns were so great. We would come home singing them and Ma, who had never heard them before, was crazy about them and, in fact, took the "Old Rugged Cross" as one of her lifelong favorites. Baptist hymns are grand for harmony, so we sang a lot of hymns on Sunday evenings. I sang soprano; Bee had a thrilling alto; and Ma filled in with snatches of all the other voices, including a bit of bass. Ma was full of music. She could pick up a tune and transpose it into any key and play it on the piano with the correct chords. The Pattons were all monotones, which was a shame. When Georgie was a cadet he had to learn the beat of the various bugle calls that ran the service life in the days before loudspeakers, so that he could tap them out with his fingers. It filled us with awe to learn that when he was a plebe at West Point he had stood up when the band played the "Dashing White Sergeant," and had sat down when it started the "Star Spangled Banner." We were as full of music as Ma was, although not so gifted, and Georgie's lack was incredible to us.

The post chaplain put out a plea in the daily bulletin for Sunday School teachers and Ma, in an excess of zeal, volunteered. She even volunteered to take the "big boys," who were the chaplain's despair. When Ma's class got the banner for attendance and recitation week after week, the chaplain finally couldn't stand it any more and came right out and asked her the secret of her success with the terrible "big boys." Ma was terribly embarrassed but finally admitted that when she saw how unruly they were, she told them that any boy who learned his collect for the day, and was present for four consecutive Sundays, could come home and put his finger in the notches in the butt of the pistol with which Major Patton had shot the Mexican bandits. I don't know what the chaplain said or thought, but Ma continued to have the largest and quietest Sunday School in the post chapel.

About the time we parted with Taty, Georgie got quarters at Fort Myer, Virginia. This was wonderful for all of us. The quarters were large and built of brick. There was plenty of polo and other horse activities. There were loads of children of all ages. There was also Arlington Cemetery. Lee's beautiful house is there on the hill overlooking the city. It is one of the loveliest of the antebellum houses in the South and, in those days, it was a quiet and wonderful place to walk and to play. Ma took us there one very nice day; it was there that she taught me to read by tracing out the letters on the gravestones—both capital letters and small ones, Roman numerals included. It never seemed a sad place to us as Ma said that a cloud of glory hung over it. We had our special walk and our favorite places.

There was a nice little tomb on the Washington side that had a roof and two little benches of marble under it with a dry fountain in the center. This was our house. There was a tombstone near the Fort Myer gate that was simply a huge boulder of rose quartz with a bronze nameplate on it. There were angels of all shapes and sizes; broken swords; torches plunged upside down; the topmast of the battleship *Maine;* the Confederate memorial with all the bronze people around it, marching off to war. There were the actual earthworks of the real Fort Myer built to protect Washington from the Confederates. It was lots of fun to slide down their grassy slopes into the ditch. There were statues of mounted soldiers on horses. My sister chose as her special hero the one-armed General Pat Kearney on his prancing horse near the old bandstand by Arlington House. I remained faithful always to a beautiful recumbent bronze officer, one of the Benet family—John Rogers Meigs, age twenty-two, chief engineer of the Army of the Potomac. He lies as if asleep; his useless Colt pistol by his outstretched hand, a horse's hoofprint in the bronze near his head.

In addition to its beauty and park-like charm, Fort Myer was noted for being the production center for the big (and small) funerals of political and military servicemen. The whole post was geared for these events: from the Artillery horses that drew the caisson for the coffin to the charger who went behind an officer's funeral to the band and the bugler and the firing squad. We were all used to the sound of the Dead March from Saul booming out three or four times a day—and oftener during a flu season. And we were used to the band marching back from the burial to the brisk quickstep march "The Girl I Left Behind Me." Bee and I attended all the funerals possible. Our quarters at that time were next to the hospital, which was conveniently next to the cemetery, and across the street from the chapel. We would follow discreetly behind the cars and were once, according to Ma, found dancing solemnly behind the tombstones to the hymn "Abide With Me," as played by the Army band.

There was something basic and terrible and splendid about the flag-draped coffin on the caisson and, in the case of an officer's funeral, the curveting charger with the rider's empty boots turned backwards in the stirrups (to confuse the ghost, Georgie told us) led by a soldier who, in the olden times, would have been the dead warrior's squire, leading the favorite horse to be sacrificed on the tomb so that he could join his dead master. The terrible throb of the music reached us as nothing else ever had—I know now that it was the sound of inconsolable grief.

Ma was passionately fond of flowers, having grown up among greenhouses and gardens. Georgie always gave her flowers on every occasion, and it gradually occurred to Bee and me that there were an awful lot of flowers going to waste in the cemetery. So—after the funerals were over and the band had marched away, and the mourners were gone, we would go to the graves and very choosily pick the best blossoms to take home to Ma. She was charmed. It never occurred to Ma that she had produced two ghouls.

Every big post in those days had a post greenhouse, and if the colonel's wife was not having a party, or there was no official reception in the offing, the post gardener would gladly give the flowers to anyone who asked for them. In those days nobody in the Army had any spending money, but they had everything that money could buy: polo, hunting on the border posts, racing, horse shows, skeet shooting, tennis, a hop at least once a month, prize fights for the enlisted men, football and baseball, even enlisted servants, called "orderlies" or "strikers," usually picked because they were too stupid to do anything else, and, of course, the post greenhouse. The poor old American taxpayer footed the bill for these goodies, but he certainly got an efficient Army out of it! One that won him at least two wars.

Of course, Ma thought the flowers we brought her were from the post greenhouse, and she told us we were dear thoughtful little girls. But the day finally came when we overreached ourselves.

Bee, who was nearly four years older than I was, thought it a poor idea from the start, but I would not be denied, so we took our red coaster wagon and hauled it for what seemed like miles and miles to the site of a funeral which we had attended that morning. It was the funeral of some Civil War hero with a big name, and he had been loaded with flowers and palms and laurel wreaths. Among these floral tributes was a wreath made of red, blue, and white flowers (he must have been a Yankee) with a gold ribbon wound around in it, and a swatch of red, white, and blue bunting with gold letters and numbers on it. I thought it was stunningly beautiful and could just picture it over the mantel-piece in the living room in our quarters. We took it off its easel and hauled it, tired and footsore, back home where we proudly presented it to Ma. The effect was not what we had expected. (Bee said, "I told you so.") Ma turned quite pale, gasped at the weight of it, and rushed it around the back to the rack of trash cans in the alley. (That rack was another happy memory of our youth because among the cans marked "ashes," "bones," "cans," etc., was one marked "edible garbage." We always wondered who ate it.)

Ma couldn't get the wreath in the can, so she wrapped it in newspapers and dragged it down to the cellar where the fire always flickered in the coal furnace that heated the hot water, as well as the house in winter. Ma jammed and hacked the wreath into the coals with the long "devil stick" used for breaking up clink-ers. We were white to the gills by this time—and so was she.

When Georgie got home that evening, he had to be told. The shock was so great to him—it appeared to us—that he had to leave the room for awhile. When he returned, he was wiping his eyes and his face was very red, so we thought he must have been crying. Georgie got down on his knees and put his arms around us (by this time we were bawling like stuck pigs) and explained that flowers from funerals were "government property," a phrase we perfectly understood to mean "no-no"; and that while he, too, thought we had made a truly lovely gesture toward Ma, he didn't think "they" would like it. We under-stood about "they" too: "they" said "Keep Off The Grass" and "No Parking" and "Keep Out," and no one in their right minds would cross "they."

The Commanding Officer of the 3rd Cavalry at Fort Myer at that time was definitely one of "they." He was a Colonel W. C. Rivers. (Bee and I thought that his name was a joke of outstanding scatology as a toilet to us was a "W.C.," and having the added attraction of that last name was just too much.) Mrs. Rivers was known throughout the Army as a holy terror, and Colonel Rivers was re-putedly under her formidable thumb, but she and Ma were quite compatible because of an incident that had taken place some years before when both fam-ilies were stationed at Fort Riley, Kansas.

Ma looked out of the window one morning and saw Bee picking up all the heads of Mrs. Rivers' tulips in her yard. Ma went all to pieces and called Bee in, gave her a hearty scolding, and sat down to write a note of apology to her neighbor with the terrible reputation. She went to the front door to take the note over in person and saw Bee, tears streaming down her face, trying to stick the blossoms back on the stems. Mrs. Rivers was standing on her front porch, laughing. When she saw Ma, she said, "Don't worry about me, Mrs. Patton. We don't have any children of our own, and I dislike children very much, but I know your little girl didn't ruin my tulips to be mean. I am perfectly easy to get along with, no matter what they say. If I think I am going to have any trouble with anyone, I just stop speaking to them."

There must have been a soft side to the terrible Colonel Rivers because one day in the daily bulletin, a mimeographed paper that was delivered with the mail each day, the last item of the day read, "Every dog on duty at Fort Myer will be given an extra ration today because it was observed that no dogs attended the funeral of Major General Smith by order of the Commanding Officer, W. C. Rivers, Colonel, USA."

There were other incidents during that tour at Fort Myer that made a deathless impression on us. Some we were aware of at the time, and some we only heard about later. Bee and I were both at the dinner table the night Georgie's dear friend, Colonel Emile Cutrea, and his wife and mother-in-law came to dinner. Colonel Cutrea was a Cajun from Louisiana. I can still remember his long eyelashes and his dark, almost Indian good looks. Mrs. Cutrea was a shy little woman, but her mother was a real tiger. The mother-in-law—I don't remember her name—was very much impressed with our family. (I suppose that everyone knew we were rich.) Both Ma and Georgie "smelt good and spoke good English," so this awful woman was playing the "me against them" game, telling Ma how much her poor dear little daughter had to put up with by associating with the barbarians that made up the officer corps of the U.S. Army— this included her son-in-law, whom she obviously disliked. She bridled and said archly to Ma, "And do you know, Mrs. Patton—of course, you and I know the better things of life but my poor little girl here—when she and the Colonel moved to Camp Meade they had to move into a set of quarters that was all painted blue and yellow inside!!! Can you imagine what kind of people would do a thing like that!"

Ma changed the subject with her imaginative tact and Georgie started talking very fast to Colonel Cutrea, who had turned the darkest red I have ever seen. How well all remembered those quarters! What fun we had there!

During that winter, an especially heavy snowstorm caved in the roof of the Knickerbocker Theatre in Washington and a lot of people were killed. The troops from Fort Myer were sent to help out in the dire emergency—among them Georgie. He came home late that night, dirty and sick and very pale, and told us all about it—in fact, his stories nearly turned us against the movies forever. He told us that he and a soldier were trying to free a lady from a collapsed wall and, as they pulled her body out by the legs, her head came off. Ma protested that we were too young to be subjected to such things, but Georgie said, "Bee, goddammit, they've got to know things like that do happen. They can't go through life with blinders on."

One of our near neighbors was Captain Summerall, later chief of staff of the

Army, and a very great soldier. His wife was the daughter of an "Old Army" family. Her maiden name had been Mordecai and the Mordecais were great munitions people—experts on heavy gunnery and mortars. Her father and mother were very old and living with the Summeralls, and Mrs. Summerall very seldom got out. Ma went over to see her one day to tell her that there was a sale at Woodward and Lothrop, Washington's fanciest department store, and that if she wanted to go, she, Ma, would sit with the Mordecais. Mrs. Summerall was pleased in her solemn way, and said that she would like that very much. The next day Ma went over at the proper time. As Mrs. Summerall got into the taxi, she said, "I forgot to tell you, Mrs. Patton, that my parents are quite senile, and they love to set little fires. You have to be careful." Ma went into the Summeralls' quarters and saw General and Mrs. Mordecai sitting in two rocking chairs on each side of the fireplace, looking very tiny and old. She said that they looked like a couple of "dried up crickets." Ma introduced herself to them, and they began to perk up and look around, and then Mrs. Mordecai said in a whisper to her husband, "Is SHE gone?" When he indicated that SHE was, they both turned to Ma with winning smiles: "Dear Mrs. Patton, do you have any matches with you, by chance?"

One of Georgie's warrant officers was a tall thin man whose name was Officer Hellencroiz. Georgie thought the world of him and told Ma more than once that he suspected that Mr. Hellencroiz was more than he seemed to be, that he was sure that he had served in some other Army at some time because he was so correct and had such military bearing. He was a handsome man, nearly bald, with a guard's mustache, and when he had occasion to speak to Ma, he always leaned over. (She said that she always thought he was going to kiss her hand.) One day, shortly before we left Fort Myer for our next station, Mr. Hellencroiz came to the front door and asked if he could speak to Ma. He was carrying a long package. When Ma came to the front room, she was very flustered. She said later that she thought he was going to ask to borrow some money and she didn't know what to say. She did say, however, that maybe he would like to speak to the captain, who was not in at the moment, but she would be pleased if he would wait. Mr. Hellencroiz said, "No, Madame, I intentionally waited until the captain was on duty as I wished to ask you to ask him to do a favor for me." At this point, Ma shut the door and I went on doing whatever I was doing when I had answered the door. A little while later Mr. Hellencroiz came out and marched away—very stiffly—and Ma came out and looked after him. She had been crying and she was wiping her eyes.

Ma told Georgie that night that Mr. Hellencroiz had unwrapped his package and removed from it a curved scimitar in a red glove leather sheath, ornamented with gold. He had unsheathed the scimitar and showed it to Ma, the damascened blue near the hilt gleaming, and said, "This sword is of Damascus steel, Madame. It was presented to my grandfather by King Charles XII of Sweden on the field of Poltava. I wish to ask you to ask the captain to accept it. It is right that he should have it as he will know how it should be treated."

Ma, who knew a good deal about swords from her association with Georgie, was deeply moved: "Mr. Hellencroiz, the captain will be much moved when I tell him, but this is a family heirloom; it is a priceless relic. Shouldn't you give it to your sons?" Mr. Hellencroiz drew himself up to his full height: "Madame, I am a soldier in the United States Army, and my sons are sergeant's sons. This will mean nothing to them, and when I am gone, they will pawn it for a pint of beer. It will mean something to the captain. I want him to have it." Then he gave her the saddest smile, saying, "I was not always as you see me now," and put the sword into her hand. Georgie was speechless with emotion when she told him the story that night. He said that he had always suspected that Hellencroiz was an assumed name and that the man had been an officer and a gentleman in times past, but he had too much respect for him to either refuse to take the sword or to investigate his past. So, the sword, which is still in the family, is a mystery that will never be solved.[1]

A story that Ma told us later always stuck in my mind as an example of what lay behind her small stature and elegant looks. She and Georgie were attending a dinner party at a marvelous Washington town house—now the Sulgrave Club just off Dupont Circle. It was a very stylish white-tie, long-gloves dinner, and Georgie took Ma to the door and went off to park the car. Ma was standing in the foyer waiting for him, and there was an older desk-type officer standing beside her waiting for his wife to leave her coat. At this time, Georgie was still wearing his wartime brevet insignia of colonel. (It is quite correct to wear a full dress uniform to a white-tie party, and most Washington hostesses encouraged it, as a uniform makes a party more colorful.) Ma was thinking how splendid Georgie was looking when the officer beside her said disparagingly, "Just look at the little boys they are promoting to colonel these days; look at the young chicken still wet behind the ears, wearing a colonel's eagle." The next thing Ma remembered was that she was sitting astride the gentleman's shoulders and had his head on the floor, banging it against the black and white marble tiles while Georgie and several others were trying to pull her off.

Some years later at another dinner party, she noticed the man on her left looked vaguely familiar, but she didn't place him until he said in a desperate

---

1. The sword is currently on display at the U.S. Army's George S. Patton Museum of Cavalry and Armor at Fort Knox, Kentucky.

whisper, "I am awfully sorry, Mrs. Patton, that you had to sit next to me. If I had realized it was going to be that way I would have sneaked in and changed the placecards. I don't suppose you will speak to me." Then, Ma recognized him as the gentleman she had "decked" at the other party and, although she said she really held no grudge, she entered into the thing and said, "No, I won't speak to you, but we can't embarrass our hostess, so when the table turns, we will recite the multiplication table to each other, antiphonally." And they did.

That tour at Fort Myer brought two never-to-be-forgotten imaginary characters into our lives, Chinquapin and Cigarette McCarthy.

Chinquapin was a fairy who lived in a mouse's nest that we once found out walking in the cemetery. It was woven of grass, with a lovely soft lining of milk-weed fluff, and Ma made us put it back where we found it because she said it belonged to a fairy. We begged her for a story, so she invented Chinquapin, and for years her adventures would crop up in the conversation: she often had the same experiences that we did. One of us had to have an enema at one point, and the whole trauma was eased by the story of when Chinquapin had to have an enema which was administered by a careful white-footed mouse, who used an empty acorn for the enema bag. Chinquapin learned to swim when we did, but her waterwings were made by a friendly spider. She also had to eat prunes for breakfast, but her prunes were dried elderberries.

Cigarette McCarthy was more in evidence—a very dashing member of the group. He was made of a twig and his head was an acorn, and he lived in a dish garden that we made with moss and partridge berries and tiny winter plants. You could always make a new Cigarette McCarthy if the old one got thrown out or eaten by the dog. Ma said it didn't matter which twig or which acorn, that Cigarette McCarthy was just *there* when you wanted him to be. We still have him around, especially when there are children in the house.

Another great event of those years was the inauguration of what was called "The Society Circus." The horses and troops at Fort Myer were highly trained and nearly all regulars—horses included—as they were the "household troops," and used for funerals, parades, inaugurations, visiting heads of states, and the rest. The soldiers had thought up lots of fancy trick rides and Georgie, who was always trying to do something about the enlisted men (as a young lieutenant at Sheridan, he started the first soldier football and baseball teams), thought that if the troops put on an exhibition ride at the riding hall at Fort Myer, and charged for tickets, they could make some money for the soldiers' rest and recreation fund.

The idea took hold with a vengeance, and, eventually, was one of the seasonal events of the Capitol, with the debutantes of the year riding in some of the easier rides, and all of their parents, and other worthies, buying boxes and having parties, which ended with their daughters marrying the handpicked young officers. But it began in a smaller way—back in the early 1920s—and Georgie was the moving spirit. Ma had luncheons and there was a tea after the event at the Officer's Club, and all the congressmen and senators would bring their constituents and families and have a great afternoon. Bee and I nearly wore ourselves out attending every practice, every rehearsal, and every performance. It was terribly exciting, and we liked to watch Georgie "doing his stuff." We could always tell whom he liked, and whom he was trying to impress whether he liked them or not—usually not—because he would smile what we privately called his "sissy-baby smile" (sissy-baby was the worst word in our sisterly language). It was a dead giveaway all his life. His smile would go so far around the corners of his face that his ears would lie flat, and he would crinkle his eyes and show his teeth, but his eyes inside were not smiling. It always amazed us that strangers did not recognize it, because even the dogs did.

In the spring of 1922 Ma's beloved baby sister, Kay Merrill, who was living in Madrid, almost died of child-bed fever. She was so very ill that the Spanish doctors gave her up for lost, so Uncle Keith took her to London on a stretcher to a famous doctor. All of the brothers and sisters, without consulting each other, found some reason to go to Europe to be near baby sister. Ma took off first. (Georgie could not go as he was on the U.S. Army polo team.) The senior Pattons in California, knowing the close tie between the sisters, turned up in Washington after Ma had left, and Bamps announced he had always wanted to take his family to England for the summer.

Ma had moved right into the Merrills' apartment in London, and was keeping house for Keith, and keeping an eye on the two older children, Keith and Rosemary, with their redoubtable Nanny Dalby, and the new baby, Eugenia.

Bamps rented the most wonderful house: an Elizabethan manor, Turville Park, near Henley-on-Thames. It came complete with servants, gardeners, a dairy farm, greenhouses—all the storybook attachments. It was meant to be a place where Ma could come and rest, but I know our grandfather really rented it to fulfill a dream of his: to be, for a time, a real country gentleman. The neighbors were very kind, and Nita Patton met a very serious beau named Mr. Brain, who used to take her punting on the Thames, serenading her with his guitar and singing "Juanita." As the Pattons were totally tone deaf, this made little impression on Nita, but it made a tremendous hit with Bee and me. On looking back, it probably hurt Nita deeply to hear that old song as, at the height of their courtship, General Pershing had always requested that the band play the tune when he was dancing with Miss Patton.

I came across a letter not long ago, written to Aunt Nannie Wilson from Turville on June 25, 1922. Nita writes:

> I am fated to be free, for this day I have definitely told Harry Brain that never can I be his wife. He is such a dear, so good, true and tender, that I d— near said "yes" but my guardian angel came to me and showed me in a vision of the night; that unless I could mate with a master, I'd better stay clear of the shoals. So, you'll have me back on your hands for keeps. And the worst of it is I'm glad. Love is not for such as I. But life is so full of a number of things that I'm like the jolly miller on the river Dee. It is very late but as my other well loved parent I had to send you the dope.

Dear Nita—she was not like the miller on the river Dee, who "care for nobody, no, not I, and nobody cares for me." She spent the rest of her life taking care of everyone.

Bee and I did not like the English custom of having high tea instead of dinner, but Bamps loved the formality of it, so we spent the summer like little English girls. However, we were allowed the come to the grown-up dinner table after the "sweet" and have nuts and raisins.

We were forbidden the greenhouses, but were terribly impressed when the first ripe peach of the season was brought to Bamma in a little silver basket on a bed of cotton wool.

Nita, our Tinta, soon got onto the fact that Mille. Henri was really a beast. So, poor Ma, with everything else she had on her mind, had to find us an English governess. The first one she interviewed and liked was a Miss Horsefall, but she said simply she could not hire her to live on a Cavalry post with a name like that. She finally found our beloved Miss Marguerite Dennett, who suited everyone, even Bamps. She had a brilliant mind, and the same fine sense of history that he did. With the assistance of Kipling's "Puck of Pook's Hill" and "Rewards and Fairies," she made the countryside come alive for us.

Kay Merrill took a long time getting well, so we saw very little of Ma that summer, but we didn't miss her. It was a never-to-be-forgotten time. Bamps read us Kenneth Grahame's *The Wind in the Willows* and then took us punting on the Thames. He read us *Ivanhoe* and *Treasure Island* and *Kidnapped,* and took us to visit the places in the books—or places very like them. When we finally had to leave Turville, the servants, including the butler, were nearly in tears. I don't know whether it was because of the American-sized tips Bamps left, or if they really liked us. We were the first Americans they had ever met. I taught Holland, the butler, to sing "Someday I'm Going to Murder the Bugler," and he said he would never forget me.

Back to Fort Myer we went; then to Fort Riley for a little while; then to Avalon to visit the Merrills who had come back from Europe. This was because Ma's "pig headedness" had triumphed, and she was pregnant. ("This really IS the last time!") She stayed with the Merrills to be near good medical facilities while Georgie reported to the Command and Staff College at Fort Leavenworth, Kansas.

There is a letter from Ma to Aunt Nannie, written from Avalon in June of 1923 that is an insight. We were all at Avalon—Georgie was there on leave.

Georgie and I leave for Leavenworth Sept. 1st but the house and kids will run till Oct. 1st anyhow as its easier to settle without 'em.[2] What with swimming, fishing and spending all available time in the sweet little 17-footer we've just rented, I am pretty busy. Yes, indeed, you can bring something for George and Martha [that was how she referred to the expected baby, who turned out to be just "George"].

He [Georgie] is having a grand time here and is busy every minute. He seems like his old self again—he has been so changed since the war I feared it was permanent! But this summer he is just like a kid—every stern line has gone out of his face and he fished on the pier with the kids till 7 last evening. They are having a grand time with him. He and B. are out riding now and I must take R.E. out. She is the funniest thing! She apparently cannot sunburn but is turning the color of weak cafe au lait which makes her hair look funnier than ever. She sticks it full of roses and dances solemnly before the mirror! William [the house man] and B. have built a play house where we have our 11 o'clock lunch etc. called the Do Drop Inn. R.E. painted the sign.

Miss Dennett and Bee and I lived on the third floor at Avalon, so we did not hear the excitement on the night of December 23, 1923, and didn't know until that next morning that Keith Merrill had driven Ma to Boston in the middle of the night, and that our longed-for and prayed-for baby brother, George Smith Patton, IV had been born the day before Christmas.

As soon as Ma could do it, she went to Fort Leavenworth to be with Georgie with their baby son, and we were left with the long-suffering Merrills for the rest of the winter. We were rather horrid little girls, and we also felt abandoned to the English discipline and lifestyle of the Merrills, of which, incidentally, Miss Dennett thoroughly approved. The great front hallway of Avalon was of black and white marble squares, highly polished, and we would lean over the railing of the circular stairs, from our third-floor eyrie, and try to spit on one

2. When they got to Leavenworth they found the quarters so small that it was arranged for Bee and Miss Dennett and I to stay on with the Merrills, as there would not have been room for all of us plus the coming baby.

of the squares. We didn't get caught until one day the Merrills' Italian butler, Umberto, was coming from the pantry with a laden tea try, and he hit the wet square and went down with all hands. The sights and sounds were worth the punishment that followed.

Ma and George and Georgie survived life at Leavenworth. It is the hardest station in the Army, as the men are studying for their very lives—their military future depends a good deal on their standing at graduation from the slaughter mill. More homes are broken up, there are more suicides and more cases of battered children from the tour at Leavenworth than anyone will ever officially know. Ma had one experience that she never forgot. Georgie was called before the board and told that he had been accused by a fellow student of using auxiliary aids in his studies that the other officers did not have. Georgie was amazed. He was working very hard, and standing very high in the course, and he was an honorable man. Even if there had been some way of improving his standing, he would not have used it. He asked what evidence had been presented and the board members muttered in a rather embarrassed way about a mysterious light. Georgie said he would find out about it, as he was not aware of anything out of line in his manner of conduct. To make a long story short, and to explain a mystery that was a nine-day wonder, Ma suddenly bethought herself of a purple light that Georgie had bought—in a slightly shamefaced way—because he had read that it would stimulate the growth of hair, and he was getting quite bald. He had been studying at night with the light shining on his head—"hope springs eternal"—and some classmate, walking his dog, or herding his child back from a Scout meeting, had noted same. It was very embarrassing to explain to the board. He stopped using the light—he went on getting bald.

In the spring Georgie graduated from the school at Leavenworth leading his class. To everyone's delight, he was ordered to the Army base in Boston. Georgie and Ma rented a house near the Beverly beach called "Sunset Hill," near Avalon, and Ma settled in for a blissful long family time.

Sunset Hill was quite an establishment. It had its own stables and paddocks, and there were many good riding trails along the shore and across the road. We also had a full complement of English servants who had come back from abroad with the Merrills, but preferred our less formal way of life. In fact, for years, all of our servants were ex-Merrill employees. (The Merrills insisted on the men servants wearing livery.) We had Ernie Booker, who had been gassed at Ypres during the war. Before that he had been a poacher, and during his convalescence he had learned to cane chairs. He was all cockney and our hero. His wife, May Lucette, was Alice Holmes (little George's Nanny)'s best friend. She not only was a perfect maid but also taught us cockney music-hall songs. There was also a cook named, of course, Fry. Ma was in her element. She had her family and old friends nearby—and Boston with the theatre and symphony—all the little refinements she had missed. And she had, at last, her little son. She realized that she could never talk Georgie into any more children, so she spread herself on us.

Little George, who was everything my sister and I had hoped a baby brother would be, had his Alice; and Bee and I had Miss Dennett. We had school at home, and Miss Dennett—we called her "Denty"—was great on taking us to Boston to the theatre and the ballet. We saw Anna Pavlova do the "Death of the Swan," and both of us died all over the living room for months and months, with much encouragement from Ma. We sang a lot, and Miss Dennett, who played the piano, gave us both piano lessons. Bee was very good, but I never amounted to much, except four-note accompaniments, as I loved to hear myself sing. Ma had several acts that she perfected with us. Our best one was an old English song to which we danced and sang in harmony.

> Begone, dull care, I prithee begone from me—
> Begone dull care, thou and I shalt never agree
> Long time has thou been tarrying here, and faith thou wouldst me kill
> But in faith, dull care, thou never shalt have thy will
> For too much care will make a young man gray
> And too much care will turn an old man to clay
> My wife shall dance and I shall sing, and merrily pass the day
> For I do think it the wisest thing to drive dull care away!

She also had two songs she encouraged us to sing in harmony at cocktail parties. (She had a wicked wit.) These were two songs her brother Chilly taught her, from the pre-Prohibition music halls. We sang them with lusty gestures at cocktail parties.

> We are the Temperance Advocates, we STAND for the right!
> Our subject we will agitate and stir up a fight!
> If you, and you, and you, and you
> With us will take a stand
> AGAINST the Demon Alcohol, we'll drive him from the land!
> Who'll join our band? Will you? Will you?
> Who'll join our band? Will you? Will you?
> If you, and you, and you, and you with us will take a stand
> Against the DEMON ALCOHOL, we'll drive him from the land!
> On every hand we see the work of rum, gin and wine

It spareth neither rich, nor poor, your dear friend or mine
So put your shoulder to the wheel and with us take a stand
And soon our flag triumphantly will wave o'er all the land!

We had another favorite, which we used as an encore—the end words were spelled out.

Oh, some people hop up and down all night at a D A N C E
And then they go to church next day to show their H A T
They cover their face with a coat or two of P A I N T
And then they laugh at folks like us who are S A V E D.
Oh, it's G L O R Y
To be S A V E D
And I'm H A P P Y
That I'm F R E E D
I used to be B O U N D
In the toils of S I N
But it's V I C T O R Y
To know this peace within!

On top of the theatre, ballet, a baby brother, and a lovely house, we had innumerable Ayer cousins to play with, and for once we were not "different," because we had all been brought up alike and wore the same sort of clothes and had the same kind of table manners and read the same books and had graduated from nannies to governesses to tutors.

That was the year of my mouse period. Miss Dennett was really used to older children, and she and my sister were very close. In Miss Dennett's eyes, I was still "in the nursery." Alice Holmes was "the nursery" but she had little George, and I refused to submit to her ministrations as I was not a baby, so I was a mess. The Ayers had "Nursie" who took care of the little ones, and a sort of tweeny before the children were old enough for the governess, but Ma couldn't face a tweeny just for me, so I was slightly unkempt, a little bit dirty where it did not show, and I raised mice. My idea was to have thoroughbred mice with a stud and a bunch of female mice, and to keep a studbook on them, as they did in the Cavalry with the horses. Somehow my mice strayed from their appointed stalls and paddocks, and there were mice everywhere. Ma had a hard time adjusting but she was game. I think she felt I might be jealous of George and feeling left out because he had usurped my place. All this went on until the morning when Georgie went to put on his boots (Cavalry officers wore boots even when they had office jobs) and one of my mice bit him on the toe. Poor

thing, it was scared of his great woolen sock! That crisis over, he had his breakfast and put on his overcoat and officer's cap to leave the house when he let out
a terrible howl. Throwing his cap violently to the floor revealed another mouse
running around and around on his bald head. After that, my mice lived in the
stable.

The great event of that winter happened on Ma's birthday. We were told by
Georgie that there was a very special surprise, and we were to stay upstairs and
keep Ma with us until he rang the bell. When the bell rang, we raced down, and
there standing on a sheet by the dining room table was a big black mare! Ma
had been learning to jump a horse over hunting jumps, and Georgie had located this splendid creature—whose name was Dinah—and saw that she was
just right for Ma. He had brought her in through the French windows from the
terrace. Many things happened in life that get forgotten, but a horse in the dining room is unforgettable!

We had a wonderful time at Sunset Hill, but it ended sooner than anticipated. Georgie got orders to go to Hawaii. These orders, though something of
a disappointment to Ma, as she had anticipated a longer stay on her native heath,
solved one difficulty that was growing daily: Miss Dennett had fallen madly in
love with Georgie.

Ma didn't like to fire Denty, as she really was a wonderful teacher, but Georgie was getting sticky about it. We were a family of readers and Georgie, especially, was always doing research for the articles he wrote for military journals,
and he liked to have us all together after dinner. He didn't mind when Ma read
aloud to us; in fact, he loved it. He would pretend to be reading his own books,
but he would be listening to her a good deal of the time.

Ma picked fascinating books for us: *Uarda,* the story of a slave girl in the
Egypt of the Pharaohs; *Unknown to History,* about Catherine the Great's illegitimate daughter; *The Dove in the Eagle's Nest,* about robber barons in Germany;
Michel Strogoff or the Courier of the Tsar, a real bell-ringer! The most incredible
things happened to Michel. At one point his enemies set fire to the Volga River
to keep him from getting "the message" through to the tsar, but Michel took a
deep breath and swam across under the flaming oil.

Of course, we had *A Little Princess* and *The Secret Garden* and *Nobody's Boy*
and *Little Lord Fauntleroy,* and lots of Louisa May Alcott. Ma's ability to read
aloud was one of her many gifts.

If we were not reading, we went into the room with the piano and sang. We
all three had perfect pitch and were a very merry trio. As Georgie was tone deaf,
he did not join us in the music room; he would stay in the living room and
read, and Miss Dennett would stay and try to entertain him. Ma first noticed

the rumbling of the volcano when Georgie would come into the music room and try to read there. Miss Dennett would follow him and be amusing. Georgie finally gave out an ultimatum: either Miss Dennett went or he did. All of this was solved by the orders to Hawaii. We were sent a plan of the quarters and there would not be a room for a governess. Ma felt very brave, like a pioneer. Her girls would have to go to school. But as Georgie said, other girls had gone to school, and it hadn't done them any permanent injury; anyhow, it was time we grew up.

Georgie decided to go ahead of the family with the horses and the furniture. Ma had had a hard time having George, and her doctor wanted to give her some minor repairs before she took off for foreign parts.

The transport bearing Georgie and our worldly goods had a fire in one of the holds that was put out by turning in the sea. It happened to be the hold where all our furniture was stowed, and when Georgie jumped down to see if he could estimate the damage, he landed on a huge box marked "Major George S. Patton, Jr. Piano." The piano had been one of Ma's wedding presents from her family. The piano, a Chickering, could have been a total loss, but one of those delightful coincidences occurred that make life worth living. The only piano tuner in Honolulu had been trained at the Chickering factory as a boy, and he put it all back together again in two years' time.

When Ma finally took off with Bee, me, little George, and Alice Holmes, we left on a Dollar Line steamer called the *President Adams*. It was a cruise ship and went through the Panama Canal. Ma was dying to see the canal as she had been there as a girl before they "turned the water on." We all shared a cabin, which was great fun. Ma really came to life once aboard the steamer—she loved the sea. She immediately made friends with the other passengers and started working on a ship's concert. Al Jolson, the famous black-face singer, was one of the passengers. He was along for a rest, but he and Ma hit it off at once, as they were equally bubbling over with music—each in their own way. It was all very exciting. I immediately fell madly in love with the Chinese cabin boy, whose name was Sing Ling and who was about my age.

When we finally arrived at the Panama Canal, it was thrilling. The sister of Mrs. Marshall, Georgie's first commanding officer's wife, was married to the commanding officer of the Canal Zone, General George Simonds. Mrs. Marshall had written the Simondses that we would be passing through, so they came down to the banks of the canal to greet us. We couldn't get off the steamer until we got to Colon, but this did not deter Mrs. Simonds, who trotted along the cement embankment as the locks were filling up and gave Ma all the local and personal news in a piercing south Texas voice—one which would have gone far in the cattle-calling trade. Her main interest was in her daughter Marjorie's bladder, and other equipment not usually discussed at far range. Pretty soon the *President Adams* had such a pronounced list to port that the purser had to come and urge some of the passengers to go over to the starboard side and see the view.

General Simonds walked alongside his family, looking "silent upon a peak in Darien"—a look he often had.

When we got to Colon, Mr. Tracey Page, Mrs. Marshall, and Mrs. Simonds' brother met us and took us all over town in a horse-drawn caretta, treating us to ice cream at the hotel. We ate seven different kinds of ice cream made from exotic tropical fruits, and Bee and I were sick all night.

The final highlight of the trip was pulling into Honolulu Harbor, hearing the beautiful Hawaiian voices singing. Georgie arrived on board with armloads of flower leis, and little George kicked off his shoe into the water. I was ten years old.

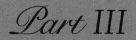

Part III

We are strong and are better
Under manhood's sterner reign
Still we feel that something sweet followed youth with flying
And will never come again.

Chapter 9

Schofield Barracks

Georgie had drawn a really nice set of quarters at Schofield Barracks, an inland post about a two-hour drive from Honolulu. The house on 27 Funston Road was U-shaped with a court in the middle. The front door opened into a large room, screened and open, called a "lanai." On the left was a living room with a fireplace, a dining room, pantry, kitchen, maid's room and bath, and trunk room. On the right were four bedrooms and two bathrooms. At the end of the road on which we lived was a gate that led off the post and at the other end a giant barracks complex. We could tell the time by the bugle calls, and it was very romantic. Each regiment—there were three in a row—had a "signature tune," of which one or two bars would be played after each bugle call. Our barracks belonged to the 27th Infantry, and their tune was "Oh, We Won't Go Back to Cuba Anymore."

Ma had done a lot of reading about the Islands while she was waiting to join Georgie. She took a special interest because a lot of the missionaries who had gone out to Hawaii had come from around Boston. In fact, they had gathered for their partings at the Park Street Church. The Hawaiian man who had started the missionary fervor in Massachusetts had been found weeping on the steps of Harvard College, saying that his people had no gods, and his pleas had started the whole movement. So, Ma felt very close to the brave and ignorant missionaries, and could hardly wait to see the fruits of their labors in the vineyards of their Lord. But none of her reading had prepared her for what she found! With Ma it was a case of love at first sight. It was as if she had been waiting for Hawaii all her life.

Georgie was enchanted by the Islands, too, but in a different way. He found there every sport he had enjoyed as a boy in California, plus a climate similar to the one he had been raised to love. The Army society was splendid, but the Honolulu society was made to order for all his tastes and his upbringing and his pleasure. Kay Merrill had been to school with Louise Gaylord, who was married to one of the most important and influential men in the Islands, Walter F. Dillingham. He was also one of the most handsome, attractive, and enchanting human beings who ever lived. Everyone loved Walter—his nickname, translated from Hawaiian, was "The Man of Oahu," and that he was. "Uncle Walter" was the grandson of missionaries and seamen, but he was completely an islander and the Hawaiians loved him as one of their own. He could entertain European royalty with distinction and dance a rousing hula, on separate occasions or in one evening. Louise Dillingham, his wife, was a queenly woman—a little bit frightening at first, but with a great and understanding heart under her aristocratic looks and bearing.

The Dillinghams took the Pattons to their collective bosom immediately and a lifelong friendship grew.

"Aunt Louise" was extraordinary in her manipulating of life and lifestyle. Walter was just as irresistible to the Queen of the Belgians as he was to the gardener's wife. His flirtations, and rumors thereof, were legion. That was one of the reasons the Hawaiians felt so close to him, as, in spite of the missionaries, they are a completely amoral people in the delights of love. There was one song they used to play at parties he attended that made for lots of good-natured laughter:

> I love a pretty Maui girl, she lives at Waikapu
> With rosy lips and pearly teeth and lovely nut brown hair
> Her waist is so slender, her opu [stomach] so much nui nui
> [very very]
> Of all the wahines [girls] I ever did aloha [love] Sweet Maria
> beats them all.

The Hawaiian love of double entendre comes in there as Waikapu means "forbidden waters." The song never bothered Louise, although everyone in Honolulu pretended to know who the pretty Maui girl was.

I think one of the reasons that Walter Dillingham was so fond of Ma was that she never found anyone but her Georgie irresistible, and so he had no trouble with her.

Looking back on the nearly six years we spent, altogether, in Hawaii, I realize that the social set there was probably one of the fastest groups that ever gathered in one spot, but neither then nor from '35 to '37, when we were there on our second tour, did I ever hear one word about Ma and Georgie being involved in what Ma's Hawaiian friend, Emma Taylor, called "naughty Polynesian fun."

Aside from the Dillinghams and their innumerable kin, the other person who loomed large in getting Ma started on her "Hawaiian act" was a great big handsome "cracker," Captain Douglas Crane. He had played his way through college on football teams, and was a sportsman to the bone. He knew all the Hawaiian fishermen and hunters and foresters, and took Ma around to meet them in their native haunts. It was through him that Ma met Haumanu Kalili, a magnificent example of the pure Hawaiian. A man in his sixties, with white hair and a deeply carven face, he had the body and reactions of a teenager. He lived and fished on the windward side of the island. Douglas took Ma and Georgie to meet him and to pick up some live lobsters he had ordered for a party he was having. Kalili was able to dive off the cruel lava rocks—there are two kinds of lava: the aa, which is like broken glass, and the pahoehoe, which looks like melted chocolate—and bring up the big Hawaiian lobsters in his bare hands. He would stand on the rocks in his bare feet and time the waves, finally slicing through one to get his prey and surface as it receded, as otherwise he would have been sliced to mincemeat on the rocks.

Kalili was a prominent member of the Mormon church. The Mormons had come to Hawaii after the original missionaries had done the legwork in converting the Hawaiians to Christianity, and they persuaded the Hawaiians that they were members of the two lost tribes of Israel. Many of the Hawaiians became staunch Mormons, partly because they could continue having lots of wives, as they had before Jesus came.

Ma struck up a friendship with Kalili, and he took her to meet his old aunties and other ladies of his family. These fascinating and shapeless women with their beautiful voices and their telling, liquid eyes, sat around making quilts and pounding poi, and, when encouraged—as Ma encouraged them—telling endless stories about the old days. The Hawaiians had had no real music until the missionaries came with their hymns. Music was in them, though, and overflowed when the outlet was offered. When Kalili's old ladies found out that Ma was musical, they sang her little songs and chants, which she wrote down, greatly to their pleasure. Ma could have gotten true confessions from a lizard, if left alone with one, because she was truly interested and extremely curious. These ancient people of a dying race recognized this quality in Ma, and they told her things they did not tell most strangers. The fact that she was being told things other travelers didn't know inflamed her imagination and got her going. Ma had the greatest of all gifts—she was a concerned listener.

We went to several luaus—Hawaiian barbecues—with Doug Crane and his wife, Emily, and some of them were unforgettable. These were the real thing, not tourist attractions, and Ma was fascinated because they went on the same theory as a New England clam bake. The food was put in the ground, on red hot rocks, in the morning and, after a day of games, swimming, and drinking, eaten around dark. The food was served on a "tablecloth" of ti leaves, spread on the ground, and the poi was served in coconut shells. One night, never to be forgotten, we had just started to eat when Ma, after peering into her coconut shell, said: "I do believe there's a hairpin in my poi." One of the hostesses, a tall and lovely woman in a red and white holoku, stooped over and looked: "Mine, I believe." She removed it from the poi and put it back into her coil of shining black hair.

Ma was greatly infatuated with poi because she thought it was what gave the Hawaiians such beautiful teeth. It is the fermented paste of the boiled taro root (taro is an edible elephant-ear plant), and as soon as Ma discovered a supply she started serving it every day for breakfast. It is definitely an acquired taste, and Georgie never acquired it, but Ma insisted that she loved it, and Bee and I ate it so that we could tell the other post kids, who thought we were queer anyhow, that we had poi for breakfast.

I thought the whole island life was wonderful and exciting, but my sister was not as enthusiastic. She missed Miss Dennett and her music lessons. She had never liked change very much, and Ma embarrassed her because she was so enthusiastic. Ma did dig up a ballet teacher, and Bee loved that. She had toe dancing shoes, and a pink tutu, and she was very graceful, and got to dance in the front line at the recitals. But it was pure torture for me, and I was much happier when Ma had me take lessons in dancing and hula and playing the guitar. She, herself, took up the steel guitar and became quite accomplished.

In addition to discovering the island and going to school, we had another mission. We had never been allowed to have ponies, as Georgie said they spoiled one for a real horse: in fact, we had never really been taught to ride. When we got to Hawaii, he was immediately drawn deep into the excellent polo. As he had to have his ponies exercised, Bee and I were taught to ride exactly the way he wanted them ridden. He had brought some of them with him—Barbara Breeze, Javelin, Starshell, and Bull Run—and he bought some more. Georgie was most particular about keeping his horses' mouths "soft," so we learned to ride seriously with a stirrup strap around the horse's neck for us to grab in case we lost our balance and were tempted to haul in the reins. We were shown how to keep light contact with the horse's mouth so that our hands moved with every movement of the horse's head, but never to take a firm hold or to jerk the reins. We were taught by Georgie and by the groom, an ex-soldier named Riley, a bowlegged little man with a squashed face who almost never spoke. The rumor among the troops was that Riley was a famous baseball player who had been struck in the head with a baseball and had lost his wits. He was a man of infinite patience, and all animals and children loved him. Georgie brought Riley with him from the States, and he also picked up two more grooms—soldiers from out west who had a modicum of riding experience. Their names were Button and Kent. Kent stayed with us for more than twenty years, but after we got back from Hawaii, Button got the local police chief's daughter in trouble and had to leave town.

Kent was one of the best friends I ever had. I don't think he was much more than ten or twelve years older than I was. He was very American-cowboy-looking with a lantern jaw and slicked-down black hair. He came from Oklahoma and said he was part Indian. His stories of his youth were very vivid. I remember his telling Ma that when he was growing up, a cowboy never rode into his hometown on a Saturday night without a bottle of Peruna in his hip pocket. Ma said that Peruna must have had as much alcohol in it as Lydia Pinkham's Pink Tonic for Pale People, and Kent allowed that it about did. Kent introduced Bee and me to contemporary music. I realize now that he could not carry a tune, as I have run into some of his songs and the tunes to which I lustily chanted them in my youth are not the tunes they came with, but his songs were certainly different from "To a Wild Rose" and "Beautiful Dreamer."

He had one ditty that was to me the utmost in sophistication:

> When your husband tells you what his first wife used to do
> Don't break up all the dishes in the flat
> Just take him by the hair, throw him down the stair, and say
> Did your first wife ever do that?

He also introduced us to Sophie Tucker and Ruth Etting, and Ma, who had never heard this facet of American music, thought they were great. Kent's favorites were "Some of These Days" and "Out in the Cold Again." Bee thought they were common. In fact, the whole boy-girl bit confused her.

Kent usually rode with us, and we really covered the cane and pineapple fields around Schofield. We had to come back to the stables past the barracks and, one day, when we were riding by the 27th Infantry barracks, we saw a naked soldier on the upstairs porch displaying himself. I called Kent's attention to him, and asked why the soldier acted like that; Kent, who had turned bright red, said very casually: "Aw, he just wants you to look at him, Miss Ruthie. He's just lonely and looking for attention."

When we got home, Bee told Ma all about it. Ma liked Kent's attitude. She explained to us a little bit about why people did things like that, adding, "Kent was right, just pay no attention."

Kent always called us "Miss Ruth" and "Miss Bee" unless the crunch was on. One day, when we were riding around the edge of Wheeler Field at the Air Base, the pony I was on decided to run away with me, and I can remember Kent screaming, "For God's sake, Ruthie, hold on and keep her going around the outside of the field; there's a plane fixing to land and he don't see you!"

I went to Kent for comfort and advice for years. I was terribly worried that I wouldn't be beautiful and charming like Bee, and that I would be an old maid. Kent perpetually reassured me, and finally made a bet with me that he would keep track of all my dates, and we would wager a silver cigarette case that I would end up just as attractive and popular as Bee—the debt to be paid when I was twenty-one years old.

We were on our second tour in Hawaii when I was twenty-one, and Kent was still with us. I told Ma about our long-ago bet. I had not checked it out with Kent to see if I had made the grade, and Ma said I would be putting Kent on the spot if I didn't pay up, as he couldn't possibly afford to buy me a silver cigarette case; anyhow, I didn't smoke. So I went to the best jeweler in Honolulu and bought one and had it engraved the way Ma told me to—with his name, the date, and the word "Craps." When I gave it to Kent on my birthday, he smiled: "I told you so."

When I got engaged, I told Kent before I told the family. His verdict was, "It's OK, Miss Ruth, I've checked him out with the troops. He's a real man. But your Daddy isn't going to like it." I asked Jim about the check-out and he replied, "Well, I did wonder. He certainly asked me a lot of searching questions. He might as well have been your father for all he wanted to know."

The last time I saw Kent, I was a widow and a grandmother. He had come east for what he said was his last visit with his friends. It was wonderful to see him after at least thirty years. The only thing that disturbed me was that he was not much bigger than I am. When I was a little girl I thought he was as tall as the church steeple.

We rode every day after school until it was time to come in and do home-work. On weekends Ma insisted that we got to the beach and that we learned to swim. Beautiful Haleiwa Beach was about twenty miles from the post, and we all loved it. My sister was a good swimmer, but I had gotten off to a bad start. When I was about four years old we were at Avalon for a visit, and Georgie announced to Ma that all little animals swam naturally. To prove his point, he threw me off the float into Salem Harbor. When I went down for the third time, Ma pointed out to him that there was one little animal who did not swim naturally. He had to dive in to get me, and ruined a new pair of white flannel trousers—a loss he brooded over for years.

But in the warm, champagne bubbling water at Haleiwa Beach, I learned to swim at last. Nearby were tethered three enormous sea turtles, who rested under the palms until we climbed on their backs, and then they would go for the water and swim out as long as they could—until they reached the end of their ropes. At this point, they would dive and we would have to swim back to the shore.

Bee was going on fifteen years old and a very pretty girl. Many of the recruits, who also swam at Haleiwa, were not too much older than she was, and we had two friends who used to help us hunt for cowrie shells on the rocks. We had a huge collection of cowrie shells at home, very smelly, that we planned to make into shell leis.

One day, at lunch, Georgie told us that a soldier swimming at Haleiwa the day before had apparently been swallowed by a shark. The boy had been standing on the reef, the water only up to his knees, when suddenly he threw his arms above his head, screamed, and vanished. Georgie's classmate, Major "Red" Miner, who was on duty with the swimming party, had swum up and down on both sides of the reef for an hour, looking for the body, with no luck.

About four days later Captain Doug Crane came by to tell us that our friend Kalili had caught a giant shark on his ulua lines that he had set out the night before. The ulua was a large and tasty local fish, worth good money at the market. Most Hawaiians were very superstitious about sharks, as their mythology told them that there were many of them mystically related to the shark and under its protection, but Kalili was mad at this one, which had swallowed all his ulua. He killed and gutted the shark, and in his belly found the large arm and leg bones of a human, a partial human skull, and some bathing trunks with the laundry mark still legible. These trunks were identified as those of our soldier friend. Bee and I were terribly shocked, but Ma, who was curious about everything, decided to drive to Kalili's and see this giant shark that had swallowed a man. Her curiosity wasn't morbid—she just didn't believe it was possible. By the time we got there, the shark had been butchered and carried away (the Chinese were very partial to shark meat), and Kalili had the jaws hanging in a tree, propped open with a stick. They were at least three feet in diameter. Kalili was unmoved by it all, but several old ladies in the village were having a little ceremony of propitiation, as they were sure a shark of that size was some relative and that his sons might take revenge on their sons out fishing.

At Kalili's request, Ma was allowed to attend the ceremony: the Hawaiians were a little leery of people watching such ceremonies for fear they would be ridiculed. Ma said it seemed to consist of a repetitive four-note chant and a very understated hula that mimed a fisherman catching something big and throwing it back into the sea. We were later told that some of the family actually carried this further, taking a live dog out in the fishing boat and throwing it into the water about where the shark should have been; the dog disappeared in a flurry of foam, which indicated that the sacrifice had been accepted and all was as before.

School started for both Bee and me in the fall. The first year we were there, the school was on the post and only the children of the post personnel attended it. Unfortunately, although we knew everyone by then, we were not really part of the group. Being different was to be set apart. We had nearly always been taught at home by a governess and we were dumb enough to talk about it; we dressed alike for awhile; we were not allowed to drink Coca Cola, or chew gum, or eat ice cream sodas; and we weren't, admittedly, interested in boys. If we went to the movies either Georgie or Ma, or both, took us. This was also a problem, as if it was a war movie—and it often was in those days—Georgie would walk out if the uniforms were incorrect, or the weapons were of the wrong period, so often we didn't get to see the end of the movie.

This didn't worry me too much, as at ten or eleven years old I was in the taxidermy stage, and also made candles by the dipping method. However, being different did bother Bee to the extent that one day she took Ma's shears into her closet and cut in half all her dresses that matched mine. Ma was terribly upset, but Georgie told her that it was a perfectly normal thing for Bee to have done, and that Ma should have realized long ago that Bee was growing up. Georgie got to thinking about that, too, and one day at lunch he said to Ma, "Beatrice Ayer Patton, how did a beautiful woman like yourself ever have two such ugly daughters?"

This upset Ma even more than the dress destruction, because she suddenly felt that she had been neglecting the finer things in life. To our despair—at least, my despair—Ma enrolled us in tap dancing classes and ballet classes, and started thinking about boarding school for Bee. This last upheaval was brought about because boys had started carrying Bee's books home from school, and Ma thought that she was "too young."

Growing up on Army posts, where the population is about 96 percent men, we were early taught the facts of life that were necessary for us to know. Ma believed in answering in detail any questions we asked, but to wait until the question was asked and to not go out of our depth by rushing ahead. Bee and I had been warned not to accept candy or car rides from strangers, and were both warned about "being careful." As we both had pets from the time we were old enough to take care of them, the mysteries of conception and birth were everyday affairs to us. I don't remember when we first found out the facts of life, but they were certainly no shock to us. Where Bee was indifferent to the male sex, and more interested in piano and dancing, I had begun to find boys perfectly fascinating. As I was as wide as I was high at that point, boys, fortunately, did not find me fascinating, so I was allowed to go my way pretty much as I liked. I had decided years before that I was going to grow up to be a boy anyhow, because they certainly had more freedom and more fun, and didn't have to worry about clothes or go to dancing school.

Among Ma's other worries was what she considered the decadent influence of the continued love stories in the evening edition of the *Honolulu Advertiser*. Bee and I would rush for the paper when we got back from school and devour the scenes of sultry passion within its still damp pages. We had been asked not to read trash, but this was so tempting—and all the other kids read it! Georgie devised an ingenious check for this. He said we could read the stories, and welcome—but if we did we would have to memorize the first three paragraphs of each night's serial and recite it to him when he got home. Memorizing came easily to us, as we had had to memorize a poem a week all the time we were growing up—a brain exercise, he called it—so we agreed. We were angry with him, however, because we knew he was doing this to somehow turn us against the *Honolulu Advertiser*. We memorized valiantly for about a week, but it got embarrassing, and my final chapter had in it a paragraph I have never forgotten: "Her eyes glowed like hot coals behind her fluttering lashes. 'SIR!' she said." "Now," said Georgie, "see if you can do that!" I fluttered my lashes with such success that everyone had hysterics, and I decided that it wasn't worth being laughed at. After that, Georgie paid us to read things that he chose. I got through all of Plutarch's *Lives* at ten cents a page, but was too bad a sport to admit at the time that I enjoyed it. It certainly beat the *Honolulu Advertiser*.

We went on memorizing poems, and I memorized one of Georgie's own poems that made a lot of trouble for me at school. It was one of his better ones, called "A Mercenary 1000 A.D.":

> I am no callow Christian,
> No fat faced prelate, I
> I hope not for salvation,
> Nor fear the day I'll die
> In wantonness of appetite,
> In women, wine and war,
> In fire and blood and rapine
> In these my pleasures are.

I love the smell of horse dung,
The sight of corpse strewn mud,
The sound of steel on armor
The feel of clotting blood;
The women I have ravished,
The infants I have slain,
The priests and nuns I've roasted,
They haunt me not again.

Priests talk of soul's salvation
And shining lights afar
But give me harlot's laughter
And the battle flash of war
Priests talk of soul's damnation
The white hot pits of hell;
I fear more wounds that fester
And gape and rot and smell

Then here's to blood and blasphemy
And here's to whores and drink
In life you know you're living
But in death you only stink.

This I recited at school to make the other kids, who called us "sissies," notice me. The teacher was informed that I was using bad language, so I had to recite it to her. She took me in to the poor bedeviled headmaster, Mr. Clowes, and I had to recite it to him. By now I knew I was in trouble. Mr. Clowes was horrified, and even more so when I told him my father had written it. He said he was sure that I didn't know what the words meant, and I assured him that I did indeed. I was sent home with a note, and Ma was terribly distressed, but Georgie thought it was funny. He said he had always thought it was one of his best poems, and it certainly appeared to be effective. Ma then tried to explain to me that some people were not "as frank and open with their children" as she and Georgie were with us, and that if it occurred to me to share some of the books we had read and the stories we had heard with the other members of Leilehua School, I had better check them out with her. Of course, this put a mighty weapon in my hands that I have used the rest of my life: the incredible success of shock tactics.

Another effort on Ma's part to ready us for the give-and-take of society more or less backfired about that time. She told Georgie that it was terrible that we had no "graces." All we knew how to do was ride horses and swim, and she thought we should take up tennis. Ma had never played anything but polite lawn tennis, but real tennis had been a big game in California when Georgie was growing up, and he agreed with her that we should get right after it. So, he bought us each a racquet and a can of six balls, and took us out to the practice court, which was up in the 19th Infantry area and near where he exercised his polo ponies. There was a backboard on that court—and I can see it now—battle-ship gray with a white line the height of a net. Georgie told us to get in there and practice hitting the balls above the white line. He took us there during the lunch hour, as he didn't want us to interfere with any real players. So, Bee and I, in the boiling sun, hit ball after ball at the backboard. Georgie would usually be riding nearby, circling and practicing polo shots, and if we stopped even for a minute, he would gallop up and yell at us to keep going. After a few weeks of this, my sister Bee and I wrote a paper which vowed that we would never play tennis as long as we lived, and we pricked our fingers and signed it in our own blood. I still have the paper. We never did play tennis.

Ma was still agitating about boarding schools, and, although she had always thought her sister-in-law, Theodora Ayer, was rather worldly, she admired her two daughters, Theo and Anne, who were a little bit older than Bee. The Ayer girls had gone to Foxcroft School in Virginia, so Ma wrote to Aunt Theodora to inquire about it. Aunt Theodora replied by return mail, and said that Ma could not find a better school. However, it was rather hard to get into, and as no one had ever heard of the Pattons—*in the Army, my dear*—Aunt Theodora would have to visit the headmistress, Miss Charlotte Noland, and tell her about Bee and about "who she was." This last remark made Ma mad. She had always maintained that wherever she was, that was SOCIETY, as it was the society of the people she cared about and respected: the rest of the world could follow fickle fashion. But Ma wanted the best for Bee, and so she let Aunt Theodora have her way. If Ma could have looked into the future she would have left Bee right there at Leilehua High School, but she was doing what she thought best for her beloved eldest daughter, and Foxcroft was THE place at the time.

When the dreaded parting came, Ma took Bee back east with her, and left me with Georgie and Alice Holmes and little George. Georgie picked me up at school every day for lunch and took me back. There was a bus in the morning and afternoon, but Ma was not happy with the school lunches. By our second year at Schofield, school had moved off the post and became a public school, open to all of the children of the cane and pineapple workers, and the people who lived nearby. From Wahiawa, the Japanese kids brought dried fish and balls of rice with a pickle in the center; the Hawaiian children brought hard poi, or squid tentacles, and there was always a length of sugar cane to chew, and sunflower seeds to nibble on and spread across the floor and desks. One pair of little brothers was very interesting. They were about ten months apart in age, but the older one looked after the younger one and at lunchtime he would chew up his little brother's lunch and carefully spit it into his mouth, just like a mother bird. Ma thought I was making this up when I told her about it, and came one day to observe for herself. After she had seen the scene, she hugged me and said something about walking with crowds and keeping my virtue, and walking with kings and not losing the common touch. In a way, I think she almost envied me my varied fare of humanity.

I preferred the Hawaiian and Japanese and Chinese girls to the post girls, who were very clique-y, and still thought I was "different." The native kids didn't seem to care. I had four close friends, a Hawaiian girl, a Japanese girl, a Portuguese-Hawaiian mixture, and a beautiful Eurasian child. They were a world away from me in sophistication and knowledge of the world, but they were always laughing and happy, and went from boyfriend to boyfriend, and were a lot of fun. Ma had me take hula lessons, but my friends really taught me the hula, which came to them as naturally as walking. They did not only the Hawaiian hula but also Tahitian hulas, which were a lot more vigorous and noisy.

One day I will never forget. We all went to the lavatory during our milk-and-crackers break, and Agnes, one of the big girls, was standing at the door as we came in. She took some of us aside and said, "Now, all you little haole kids mess around and if teacher comes in, keep her busy and ask her questions or something." As an afterthought: "Jennie is having her baby." Jennie was my Hawaiian friend. Most of the post girls scrambled out, but I stayed right near the door so that I could presumably distract any entering teacher, but really because I was so curious. Jennie lay down on the floor and the big girls—the fourteen- and fifteen-year-olds—drew around her so no one could really see anything. Presently, Agnes stood up with a little bundle wrapped in paper towels, and went into the toilet stall with two of the big girls. Agnes came out of the toilet and shoved the little bundle deep into the paper waste can, under the towels. I asked her what would happen if a teacher found it. Agnes gave me a hard look and said, "Mr. Mahoe (Jennie's uncle, the janitor)—he know what happen. He fix ever'thing. Don't worry your head. This baby no good—Jennie didn't want it. Fader no good."

I couldn't wait to get home to tell Ma about it. She took it like a lady, but it must have been traumatic for her. She did not say anything to anyone; she would have to discuss it with Georgie. After dinner they took me into the living room and very solemnly questioned me. Had I seen the baby? Had it cried or made any noise? The answer was "no" on both counts. Then Ma explained to me how the ancient Hawaiians had felt about unwanted children. Ma had read in the missionary diaries how the Hawaiians had happily given their children away, or buried them under the floor in extreme cases, and how the chiefesses (the Hawaiians used the Salic Law, where the inheritance came through the mother's line) were allowed to have lovers after they had borne heirs, but how the babies of such unions had their heads dashed against the doorpost of the birthing hut right after birth. She said that, of course, we didn't feel that way, that no baby was unwanted in our society, but that other people had their customs, and that it would be unfair to Jennie if I ever mentioned this to anyone as she might have to leave school. I was much impressed at being talked to in such a grown-up way and swore myself to secrecy.

Looking back on it, I suppose the baby was aborted. The Hawaiians had a store of herbal knowledge, and Jennie or her family may have taken care of this little inconvenience. Ma and Georgie must have taken this into consideration, as my story could have led to a murder charge, and all sorts of unpleasantness with wide implications. But what a woman Ma was: with her background, to be able to make this really horrendous experience into something ethnic, and not give me a trauma or a sense of guilt!

I saw Jennie all the time I was at school, and then I saw her again, about forty years later. Our eldest son, serving in Vietnam, came back for his rest and recreation furlough to Hawaii, and our daughter-in-law invited me to go as far as Hawaii with her and their infant son to meet him. I only stayed a few days on the Islands and rented a car so that I could revisit some of the fun places we had seen in the old days. I was driving along the coast near Kamuela Bay and saw a hukilau going on. This is a fishing party where the fish are driven into a large net, each end of which is fastened on the shore. When the fish are schooling inside the perimeter of the net, it is raised and everyone joins in hauling it ashore. It's a lot of fun to watch. I got out of the car to see better, and after a while a perfectly enormous Hawaiian woman came billowing up to me. Her hair was done in a twist on top of her head with a hibiscus blossom in its folds, and her eyes were gleaming above her teeth. She grabbed me around the neck and embraced me, saying, "Hello, Ruthie Patton—here we are again! I'm Jennie, six kids and three husbands later. Leilehua! Aloha!" "Lest auld acquaintance be forgot and never brought to mind."

While Ma and Bee were gone to settle Bee at Foxcroft, I had another memorable experience. Georgie, as a child, had never been made to eat anything he didn't want to. If he was forced to eat, his Aunt Nannie would have hysterics. When he and Ma got married, she was horrified by this habit and told him what a wasteful crime it appeared to a New Englander whose motto was "Use it up, wear it out, make it do, do without." He actually got pretty good about eating what Ma served, with the exception of fish, which he hated. He knew that a clean plate was next to godliness in her eyes. One day our houseman Goto served us breadfruit for lunch. I had never heard of it, and said, with the finicky unreasonableness of a twelve-year-old, that I would not, could not, eat it. Georgie, trying to enforce discipline with Ma away, told me to either eat it or "take a licking." I chose, to his consternation, to take a licking. He told me to go out in the lanai and pick out the whip he was going to lick me with. Scared to death, and mad as hell, I picked out what I thought was the worst whip on the rack. It was a hunting whip with a long thong with a red cracker on the end of it. Actually, it was a poor choice for him, as a quirt would have hurt me a lot worse. I took the hunting whip back to the dining room, and nonplussed, he cracked it and then laid it along my fat legs four times. When he had finished, I said as haughtily as I could: "THAT didn't hurt!"

George and Alice sat at a separate table in the dining room, and I can still see the look of woe on George's little face. I finished the rest of my lunch sans breadfruit, swollen with rage and self-pity, and was delighted to see on returning to school that there were four small welts on my legs. I told my friends all about the awful thing that had happened to me, and they were rather "ho-hum" about it. They liked breadfruit—it was good.

Ma told me years after that Georgie wrote her all about the incident and offered to let her divorce him for maltreating her child.

Ma had asked two of her friends to "help Georgie keep an eye on things," and they were always around while she was gone: Miriam and Eleanor. Their husbands were friends of Georgie's. I think they both had crushes on Georgie but he gave them no encouragement. I sensed this last because while they were ostensibly coming to keep an eye on me, they never said much to me but sat around the living room trying to fascinate Georgie the way Miss Dennett had used to do. It was all a bunch of foolishness to me. They were OLD, and old people couldn't have much in the way of feelings, and who wanted Georgie around anyhow? However, one of them turned out to be a great comfort to me when I had another misadventure.

One of Georgie's hunting friends had given him a red and white pointer bitch named "Jujube," and he gave her to me to keep me from missing Ma too much. I was thrilled—she was my first personal dog—and I religiously walked her for miles every day. One day I was walking 'Jube up near the Artillery post when a high school boy who had been driving his car round and round the block stopped his car and propositioned me. He didn't put it in so many words, but I knew what he meant all right, and my scorn and fury knew no bounds. Didn't this clod realize that somehow I was going to grow up to be a boy? (I certainly did not look as if I would, being a mass of undulating curves of baby fat with a budding bosom that made my dresses stick out in front—humiliating!)

I told this boy off with some inelegant Hawaiian phrases I had picked up at school, stalked home and told Ma's friend Miriam, who happened to be in the living room. Miriam's children were some years younger than I was, and I think this situation was a real poser for her. She started telling me about the birds and the bees, but I assured her that Ma had already told me all that stuff, and that I had just wanted to tell someone what had happened because I was very mad—and a little scared. I had just sense enough not to tell her his name.

She must have told Georgie right away because he tried to get me to tell him the boy's name too, and spoke dourly of horse-whipping. This would not have been at all the thing. The villain of the piece was Leilehua High School's number one football player. Finally, I was told I could take no more walks alone. Another feather clipped by the rapidly approaching threat of being a girl! I was disgusted.

Ma was east longer than she had anticipated. She had been fox-hunting with Myopia, riding one of her brother Fred's horses, and had had a terrible fall in which she was nearly killed. Ma wrote this poem about her fall:

> Why must you drag me back?
> Death would have been so sweet!
> I gallop through the orchard pied with sunlight
> My blood fast racing.
> The hoofs of all the field pounding accompaniment,
> And then, swift as a lightning flash, the fall—
> And waken in God's arms.
> What's this? No, I do not remember—
> Oh, my death!
> Please, doctor, let me die—don't bring me back.
> Yes, I am winning though—broken, you say?
> What matters it, so long as I can live to feel your arms about me;
> Never to hear his little feet come pounding down the hall,
> Never to feel your lips on mine again—
> Dear God, be merciful and grant my prayer;
> Grant me a few more years of life!
>
> November 13, 1926

She was not very reassured on her return by a play-by-play description of Georgie's time alone with a nubile daughter. She summoned her inner forces to take me to the Japanese dressmaker, where she had two party dresses made for me, after which she enrolled me in the ballroom dancing class some other anxious mothers had started. My dresses were awful—they would have been correct in Boston at the turn of the century. Of course, no one danced with me unless I threatened to beat them up.

Oh, how I envied the new girl who had just arrived! Her name was Virginia Cane. Virginia had a boyish bob; her skirts were above her knees. She said wonderful things like "Get hot!" and "Where's the action at?" She had an orange dress for dancing class (which she despised as being for little kids) and the dress had silk fringe down both sides that swished when she walked. She chewed gum with her mouth open, and snapped her fingers a lot, and did the Charleston, and sang in a husky voice "Bye Bye Blackbird" and "Sleepy Time Gal." I told Kent all about her, and Kent said that she sounded cheap to him, but—all the boys danced with Virginia. Her younger sister Mary, who wore thick glasses and braces on her teeth, said that Virginia was a big fake. I wished I could have believed her. Ma and Georgie didn't know the Canes. Instinct, and Kent, decided me that Ma would not like Virginia.

About this time I reached the first nadir of existence. There have been a few since, but the first one is always the worst one. In the language of today, I was "trying to find myself." In the language of that day, especially Georgie's, I was "so goddam adolescent it hurt." Nature had finally proven beyond the shadow of a doubt that I was going to grow up a female, and on top of that physical insult, I had been forbidden to play on the second football team at Leilehua in case I might get cancer if someone hit me on the chest. ("Breast" was a dirty word except in sentimental songs.) I had at one time "put on the gloves" with the smallest boy in the eighth grade, and he had either bent or broken my nose. I was ashamed to tell Ma about that, not only because I had been licked in a fair fight, but because it would have upset her.

I had skipped seventh grade because of the lessons with Miss Dennett, but I was way out of step as I hadn't a clue about math and grammar. Miss Dennett had taken it for granted that all "young ladies" used good grammar and that someone else balanced their checkbooks, or handled whatever little math they might conceivably require. I was years ahead of the class in history, reading, geography, and music. The teachers at Leilehua had to struggle with every kind of mind—the wily Oriental, the totally undeveloped, or the just plain stupid—and I think they promoted me to get rid of me. So algebra came into my life before I could do long division. I hated it, saw no use in it, and decided to fail it so badly that I wouldn't have to take it any more. The teachers and the parents thought differently.

Ma gave up trying to help me—she wasn't any good at math for the same reasons that I wasn't. She, too, was governess-educated. There was a test next day and Georgie volunteered to help me. He started off being very patient and I suddenly began to understand it. I at once closed my mind, realizing that once I understood it I would have to do it.

It came on to nine o'clock, and I heard the bugle sounding Tattoo, that most beautiful of all the bugle calls. I sat at my desk and doodled. Georgie's voice began to rise. My mind closed tighter and tighter. It seemed a very short time until the bugle sounded Taps, that saddest of all bugle calls. It was eleven o'clock, two hours past my bedtime. Georgie was sweating and shouting, and I started to have hysterics for the first and only time in my life. When I suddenly found out that I could not stop crying, I began to enjoy it. I was standing away from myself watching a poor fat little girl sobbing and crying while her cruel father, nine feet tall, strode up and down the room, cursing and slapping his hands together. All at once he turned and slapped me so hard that I fell right off my chair. I also stopped having hysterics. He strode out of the room banging the door. Having nothing better to do, I started going to bed. After awhile, Ma stuck her head in the door and asked me if I was all right. I wanted to start crying again and tell her that I was not all right and never would be again, but I was too tired to do anything but nod—so she went away. Old Tank, the bull terrier, was sleeping in my room. He had always slept with Bee when she was at home, but when she went away to school, he moved in with me. I pushed him over to the side of his mat and spent the rest of the night sleeping beside him. He was the only person who loved me and he, too, preferred my sister Bee.

Of course, what none of us realized was how much we all missed Bee. She had been my best friend and, sometimes in spite of herself, my constant companion. ("Ma will you please stop 'Lukey' from following me around. She even follows me into the bathroom!") She was the most beautiful and the most talented and the funniest person in the world. We had our own mythology, our own jokes, our own language, and when she went away to school, I was forlorn.

Ma realized this, as she missed Bee too. We talked about her all the time, and lived for her letters. Ma took me with her more and more often on her expeditions into ancient Hawaii and historical jaunts, and I got to see more of her than I ever had before in my life, and she was a lot of fun.

But still, life was a test. My "hui," my group of four friends, was still in seventh grade, and I was the youngest person in the eighth grade, and had nothing in common with any of the kids. They all had boyfriends, and were dating, and talked endlessly about clothes. Mary Cane and Josephine Toshi, a Japanese girl who was an inspired artist, and I were the only "sensible" girls in the eighth grade. We hated clothes. We had no boyfriends. We were the misfits.

My school grades were very bad. The teachers had wised up to me, and wouldn't call on me when I raised my hand to answer questions in a subject in which I was at home. They would only call on me for grammar and math. I re-convinced myself that I was an "unwanted child." (For years when I was little, I was sure I had been adopted and that my real mother had been an Irish princess in a long green velvet gown with an Irish lace collar and long bronze hair to her knees—shades of Deirdre the Beautiful!)

So I decided to commit suicide. Maybe then they would realize how nice I was and how they loved me! Georgie had warned us that the spillway of the reservoir, across the road from our gate, was very dangerous, and that if you fell over the cement lip you would be churned away in the waters below.

One evening just about dark, when the family was out to dinner, and Alice was busy with George, I decided to do it. I started to walk out the gate, and the military policeman on duty there asked me where I was going. He must have been about eighteen years old. I told him who I was and that I was going to cross the road and go and commit suicide over the spillway. He got a terribly worried look on his face and said he really did not know what to do; should he call the officer of the guard or shoot his pistol three times into the air? Or what? There seemed to be nothing in the regulations that covered this situa-tion. We discussed this for a while and then, because he seemed so genuinely distressed—he told me it was his first time on sentry duty—I told him I wouldn't do it that night—that I would go home and maybe try another day. This suited us both.

I don't know if I would have felt any better at the time if I had known that Ma was making regular visits to a psychiatrist in Honolulu to discuss me. She was doing it for me as she didn't want to send me for fear it would "mark me for life."

I have not said much about my brother, George, up until now because he was living in another cycle. He and Alice and Ma had a life of their own, and he was not included in many of our trips, except those to the beach. He had a sandbox and there were quite a few other little children his age, and he and Alice walked over to see the Retreat Ceremony at the flagpole every afternoon and to listen to the band, but aside from his messing up our dollhouses, we saw comparatively little of him.

He lived on a wholesome, loathsome diet of dry milk called "Dryco," various strained fruits and vegetables, and Pablum. When we first got to Schofield there was no tuberculin-tested dairy, so he kept on with the Dryco for some time.

Eventually, a dairy was started on the island that Ma thought was safe. The milk was terribly expensive, but she invested in it daily, and everyone was thrilled with it except little George. He wouldn't touch it.

Ma planned a picnic just for him at Haleiwa, and she and Alice and George and I went one fine day with sandwiches and fruit and a thermos of the fabulous real milk. We started to eat our lunch after a happy morning of paddling and digging, and Ma took a big drink of the milk. Suddenly, she seemed to go crazy. She jumped around, and waved her arms, and staggered and laughed, and kept saying: "The wild milk! I'm going wild! The wild milk!" George was fascinated, he followed her up and down the beach, studying her, and then he asked Alice for some of the "wild milk" too, and he went careening around the beach like a bat. After that it was no problem to get him to drink his milk, except for a day or two when every time he had a glass of milk he had to go crazy. But his "Dryco" days were over.

George's first big family outing was to the Big Island, Hawaii. Georgie was ordered to go over to the Parker Ranch and buy about one hundred horses for the Field Artillery units. The Army had been buying horses in bulk for years from the Parker Ranch, and as Georgie was the leading expert on horseflesh in the command, he got the job. The ranch raised very sturdy quarterhorses and racehorses and some thoroughbreds, and sold them to the Army at the government price of a little more than one hundred dollars apiece.

Ma had been dying to visit the Big Island to see the volcano and the black sand beaches. So she laid out a family trip that included Alice and George and me. She booked rooms at the Volcano House, which was a military rest area, and the Kona Inn, and was told there would be rooms for us at the very small guest house on the Parker Ranch.

In those days one went to Hawaii on the interisland steamer—an overnight trip. The channel between the islands was called (in Hawaiian) the "channel of crying children," and it is well named. Ma, as usual, made friends with everyone and got into every cranny of the ship. She made a great hit with the skipper, an elderly Scot with hair growing out of his ears, because of her sea-going background. There were no deck chairs on the steamer, just benches fastened to the cabin walls. We sat on these to see the islands going past, and the flying fish, and the sunset, and to keep out of the rather stuffy little cabins.

After we left Honolulu, the skipper came and sat with us for awhile. He told one story that we never forgot. In fact, Ma wrote a very fine short story about it. It was the story of a beautiful part-Hawaiian heiress, who had been to school in the States, and had come home to see her dying father. She insisted on sailing for the Big Island as soon as she got off the steamer in Honolulu, although it was a bad, stormy night, and she had been advised to wait.

She was to be put ashore on a dock on her father's property on the coast. When they reached the spot, the skipper saw that landing there would be too tricky—the seas were too wild. The old skipper (our friend had been the second mate in those days) told her he would not set her ashore, he would take the ship around to Hilo Harbor. The girl made a terrible scene, saying that her father was dying and that her family were there waiting for her, and that her father owned the steamship line, and that he would take the skipper's papers if she was not allowed to land. So the skipper, against his will, had to agree. A huge Hawaiian sailor volunteered to row her to the dock, and the two of them were lowered in the lifeboat. The man rowed mightily, but just before they reached the landing, the boat broached and started to sink. The big Hawaiian grabbed the girl and managed to stay off the rocks until a huge wave lifted him up and he could reach the hook on the crane used for loading and unloading sugar on the dock. The Hawaiian hung there by one hand over the raging sea that reached up to snatch him down to death until the skipper could signal to the shore with flares. The crane was wheeled in and the Hawaiian sailor and the girl were lowered to the dock in safety. Ma asked what happened then, and the old skipper replied, "Oh, the girl was dead—from the shock, maybe. The Hawaiian had his hand cut through to the bone, but after it was stitched up by the plantation doctor, he came back to sea with us."

We had our car with us on the steamer, and the next morning we docked in Hilo and drove along the coast toward the Parker Ranch. The beauty of that drive is beyond description. It was even awe-inspiring to an eleven-year-old. Ma was beside herself with pleasure. The great snow-crowned Mauna Kea (White Mountain) loomed over all as we drove through rain forests and across desolate lava flows that went from the mountain to the sea. Where the flows reached the sea, the mighty waves broke and shattered over them, sending up rainbows.

We finally got to the Parker Ranch and were directed to the guest house, where we settled in and unpacked. Georgie went to the office of the ranch to notify the manager, Alfred Carter, of his arrival. Mr. Carter was ready for him. The horses from which the Army remounts were to be chosen had been driven in from their mountain paddocks to the main pens, and would be ready for inspection the next morning. Georgie did not meet Mr. Carter, who was off doing ranch business, but he was told all this by the secretary.

The next morning, Georgie and Ma went to the selling paddock with me tagging along. The Hawaiian cowboys, "paniolas," brought in the horses one at a time. The Hawaiian word for cowboy came from the Spanish "Espaniola," as the first cowmen to come to the Islands were Spaniards. The paniolas wore regular American cowboy clothes—chaps, high-heeled boots, neckerchiefs, and five- or ten-gallon hats. Around each hat was a lei of fresh flowers.

Georgie was much impressed with both the unbroken horses and their handlers. The horses were bold and in high spirits, and seemed to have no fear of the men. Georgie started separating the horses into three groups: "impossible," "possible," and "probable." The rejects were turned out and the others were put into two pens for further consideration.

Among the Hawaiian and Japanese and mixed-blood paniolas there was an old white gentleman with a white mustache and a hat with a lei around it, working the horses and seemingly in a position of authority. Ma and I sat on the fence and Georgie went over each prospective government purchase, checking their teeth, jaws, nostrils, eyes, legs, looking under their tails, and giving each one a complete physical exam. The old gentleman with the mustache joined him, and they talked, and Georgie gave his reasons for picking one horse above another.

That evening, when we got back to the guest house, we found that we had been moved into a really nice vacant house that had been built for the visiting nurse of the district. The old gentleman with the mustache was Mr. Carter himself, and he was so impressed with Georgie's knowledge of horseflesh that he had decided that they were to be friends. After that, when we went to the Parker Ranch we stayed with the Carters in their own house.

The day after choosing the Army remounts, Mr. Carter had some horses of another color brought down. These were Mr. Carter's beloved thoroughbreds. This kind of horse breeding was a sideline with him, but it was one of his hobbies and he knew each horse personally—its bloodlines, family history, races won or lost by its ancestors and siblings, the victories and defeats of the past hundred years. Georgie and Ma had not come to Hawaii with the thought of buying any horses for themselves, but they were so impressed with the quality of the animals that they bought two of them on the spot. Mr. Carter was very pleased—he said that they had chosen the two that he would have bought himself.

Ma was not very interested in horse breeding, but she was always interested in people—she would say "interested people are interesting." Mr. Carter, who was a very withdrawn and quiet man, took a great liking to Ma. She drew him out on his interests, and on his life, and I think he told her things that most people never knew about himself and the Islands.

Alfred Carter was a legend in his own time. He was from Honolulu and he had been in the post office there, knowing nothing whatsoever about ranching. The Parker Ranch, when Mr. Carter was first connected with it, was a vast conglomeration of fields, hills, mountains, lava flows, streams, and valleys, and belonged to various members of the Parker family. The original Parker had come to Hawaii on a whaling ship, and had married a chiefess: the ranch was her family holding.

In ancient Hawaii, all property came down on the mother's side, as did rank and privilege. The half-breed children of this match were a wild and cheerful lot, accustomed to power and wealth and privilege. They had given away or gambled away some of the land and most of the water rights, and the borders and boundaries were in confusion. The Parkers lived high, wide, and handsome in their houses in Honolulu, or in the great house right in the middle of the ranch—a house called "Mana." This is an ambiguous word that stands for spiritual power, or possession, and it has a rather uncanny feeling to it. The house, which had been closed for many years when we saw it, was all on one story with many rooms leading one into the other, with vast beds—the Hawaiians called them "hikiaas"—that could accommodate a dozen people. There was a spooky feeling of passing laughter and people moving about. In back of Mana stood old Parker's own house, a New England farmhouse, built of the local stone, but still shouting "New England" from its chimney and its shingled roof and uncompromising upstairs-downstairs shuttered windows. Old Parker had loved his wife, but his half-Hawaiian children and their ways were too much for his Yankee soul.

Near Mana stood the family cemetery, a ghostly place with great ironwood trees sweeping their fringes over little tomb houses.

The last Parker had been a fragile girl, married to an American. Her trustees, some Hawaiian and some American, felt that the ranch, which was all she had left, was going downhill fast. The cattle were screws, of no particular breeding; the horses were cayuses; the cowboys were a motley lot—many of them illegitimate cousins. It was what was called a "luau ranch"—and a luau is a long, long party. When, in the old days, the Parkers had come to stay at Mana, they brought with them cases of wine and champagne—as well as all the pretty girls in Honolulu that could be persuaded to come—and had one long luau until it was time to go home. They spent the money as fast as it came in, and the money was running out.

The trustees of the ranch decided that the only really trustworthy man they knew was Alfred Carter, and they asked him to take on the ranch, which he finally did. He made sweeping changes that brought on a ranch war and ill feelings that still existed, but he was honest and just, and he was the boss. The first rule he made was that there would be no liquor on the ranch and anyone who drank would lose his job. This, at first, cost Mr. Carter some of his best hands and one of his oldest friends, but he had made the rule and he stuck with it. The ranch war came when he tried to get back the water rights. At one point he sat at his desk for more than forty-eight hours. The Hawaiians believed that the man at the desk was the man in charge. After he got the water and the land somewhat straightened out, he had to clear the titles, some of which went back more than one hundred years. Finally, he had to get good breeding stock and kill off the maverick cattle and horses.

When we met him, he had run the ranch for half a lifetime, and had made it a paying proposition. It was an extraordinary feat. The ranch was totally self-sufficient, except for sugar, tea, coffee, flour, and a very few items like that. There was meat and vegetables for all. They raised their own hay and grain; there were experimental farms and tracts, as well as working land. The ranch supplied all of the Islands with meat. Mr. Carter's thoroughbreds were bought as racehorses and handled by his brother-in-law, Mr. Hartwell, and raced all over the United States. Every paddock on the huge ranch was named and numbered, its soil content on record, and the horses born and raised on it were known and numbered. The cowboys who worked that particular area would stay with the stock from birth to sale.

Georgie bought a beautiful chestnut gelding who had been raised in one of the paddocks near the border of the ranch. This paddock had a sign on the road that said, "No Trespassing, By Order of the Manager, Alfred Carter, Trustee" in both English and Hawaiian. The Hawaiian word for trustee is "konokiki," so he named the horse that.

Mr. Carter was always testing and experimenting. He put some of his thoroughbred mares in paddocks where there were old lava flows, as he felt that running among the rocks would make the foals more sure-footed. He tested the soil to see what minerals were released by the oxidizing lava, and what effect they had on the horse's well-being. All these records were kept at his office.

Getting the cattle off the island to the butchers on the other islands was another project. Several times a year the cattle that were ready were driven from the ranch to the shore at Kawaihae. They took the cattle very slowly, so they would keep their weight, and it took a full day. The steamer would be waiting off-shore, and the long boats would be in at the beach. The cattle were driven into the water, a lasso put around their horns, and they would be towed out to the steamer this way, protesting loudly and in vain. The steamer would haul them aboard in slings.

All the paniolas and the ship's crew would get very wet and have a wonderful time.

The Parker ranch was on the mighty slope of Mauna Loa, the volcanic mountain opposite the Carters' house. A misleading distance away was a small cinder cone called "Holoholoku," which means "running around standing still." The name comes from the fact that whichever side of the cone you saw, it appeared to be the same. One of the paniolas told Ma that when he was a little child, one of his great-grandfathers had died, and the family took him into the hollow cone for burial. There, by the light of torches, the little boy saw his ancestors, mummified by the airless dark, wrapped in their feather capes, and lying in their great canoes. The paniola told Ma that the bodies were of very tall men—giants. Ma was dying to see this, but the cowboy told her that no one knew any more where the entrance to the cinder cone was. The people were afraid that strangers would enter the sacred place and vandalize it. They had hidden the tunnel.

Mr. Carter was very interested when Ma told him this story. He said he had known about it for forty years, but had never known any of his Hawaiians to tell a stranger. However, he did know of a burial cave that she could see that might interest her, and he arranged to have us taken there by a part-Hawaiian friend of his named Mr. White. Mr. White was very interested in the history of his people and was delighted to find someone else who shared his passion, so he took us to the Grave of the Common Dead near Hoonaunau. This cave was a broken lava tube, halfway up a crumbling lava flow, similar to a cliff. We had to get there by climbing a rope ladder.

At the front of the cave, in the light, were recent burials—many in coffins, and a few wrapped in tapa cloth like their ancestors. Some of the coffins were open, and we were fascinated by the skeletons, dressed in their crumbling best with their little personal belongings with them. One lady wore a red wig and held an ivory-backed hairbrush in her bony hand. One man had a fishing rod and some pearl shell hooks. One person had a music box. I could have stayed there all day, but Mr. White wanted us to come inside. He had a lantern with him, and we saw an extraordinary sight. The lava tube was larger as you got away from the sunlit entrance, and on the floor were seemingly numberless skeletons laid out nearly side by side. The ones toward the front were about normal size, but toward the back of the cave they got bigger and taller. Mr. White took out a tape measure and, walking carefully around the bones, measured one fairly complete skeleton to show that it was more than seven feet tall. He said the ancient Hawaiians had been a race of giants.

Then to turn us back toward mortality, he led us into a lesser tube that branched from the cave to the left. This tube sloped slightly downward and was filled with a beautiful hushing murmur. When we got to the end of it, we were looking down into the sea, blue-green and shining as it moved softly against the base of the cliff, sending an aquamarine light into the roof of the cave.

Mr. White was so enthused by Ma's interest that he told her a lot of stories about the past. When he was a little boy, some Hawaiian fishermen took him to another lava tube, just like the one we had visited, which ended at a great pool of water roofed over by the rock. There was an entrance into the sea and, as the waves washed in and out, perfectly enormous sharks came in and out with them and swam around the cave. These sharks were bigger than any he had ever seen. The Hawaiians told him that he must not be afraid, that this cave was the home of the giant sharks and that they were his relatives and would not hurt him. He told Ma he had never been there again and that he didn't know where it was. Ma said that she thought he did, but didn't want to be asked to show it.

Ma's ever-growing enthusiasm brought her many such stories. As soon as people discovered she was genuinely interested, they came to see her, or took her to visit with their "old aunties." She met people that were certainly not included in any social set, although all the people like Mr. Carter and the Dillinghams knew and respected them. The Hawaiians had a great sense of their own history and legend, and their seventh sense also told them that they were a disappearing race.

The ancient Hawaiians had been prevented from overpopulation by several things. One thing was that nature had adjusted them to be not very prolific. Then, their whole lifestyle and religion taught them to have no concern with death. The great Hawaiian sports were all blood sports. They swung from the cliffs on ropes braided from vines or slid down the mountains on sleds with one runner that fitted into slots cut into the smooth lava and oiled with kukui nut oil.

The shock of hitting water on these sleds, going at who knows how many g's, must have taken quite a toll. One of their games was for a man to stand, oiled and naked, and try to catch the spears thrown at him by his friends with intent to kill. They had constant wars and seemed to enjoy them. A man who died a hero's death went to Pali Uli, the blue cliffs of the gods.

The other traditional home of the gods was Ulukaa, the Rolling Island. This was handy for the gods: they used it as a home and for transportation. From there the gods ruled the universe, drank the divine "awa," and played their mighty, god-like games. From there they sometimes came and walked the earth. Sometimes this island was under the ocean, sometimes visible to a favored few "in the red light of the sunset." Ma's friend Edith Rice saw the island in an empty sea beyond the island of Niihau, and pointed it out to Francis Gay, another ethnological friend. "Don't point," he told her. "It is not for mortals to point to the Islands of the Blest."

The souls of the undistinguished dead went to a nether world ruled by the god Milu. Their rather unhappy spirits wander forever in the twilight, subsisting on moths and butterflies. Why these spirits must go to Milu never seems fully explained. There was one leaping-off place of the dead on every island. Sometimes the spirits were guided there by a child to a tree from which it was to leap. The spirits found a tree where they crowded onto one branch until it got so heavy that it broke off and carried them down to Milu. Sometimes the ghost simply leaped from a rock into limbo. One of the explanations for this sad fate is that these poor spirits were caught while absent from their sleeping bodies. Obviously, a hero's death and Pali Uli was preferable to the land of Milu.

For many years, Hawaii and the Hawaiians were what Ma "was about." She became a profound student of the old days and ways, and was greatly respected by Hawaiians and scholars alike. Her secret was her enthusiasm—she was totally sincere. When she said "Tell me more!" she *meant* it. So they did.

Ma was pretty much interested in the missionaries. Of course, she came to the Islands with all their journals and memoirs and statistics, and I think she thought that was what was going to be the object of her explorations. But in spite of her final conclusions about missionaries (as the Hawaiians say, "they came to the islands to do good, and they made a good thing out of it"), she always stood up for them. She said that they were brave and true and dedicated, and stuck to their beliefs, but they made it terribly hard for each other. A favorite story concerned the Reverend Dr. Asa Thurston, who had his house built so that its windows faced neither the mountains nor the sea. He was afraid that Mrs. Thurston would be tempted by the devil to look out at all the sinful beauty and get slack with the housework. I think it was this same man who, on the ship that brought him to Hawaii with his bride, knelt down and prayed every night before he made love to her that he would not enjoy it too much.

The Hawaiian servants worried Dr. Thurston a lot. They were faithful and loving and wonderful with children, but they were so easily distracted by the devil! When the missionaries got to the Islands, the Hawaiians had only their primitive chants on a four-note scale, although they had loads of rhythm. The hymns of the church opened up a world of glory for them and they went music-mad. They all seem to have glorious voices, and they love to sing. Different from us, their voices do not seem to crack or diminish with age. They sing like children—all out—all their lives.

Dr. Thurston was delighted with their interest in hymns, and was much pleased by one particular hymn his people often sang at work. He didn't understand the words, but it seemed to be a very holy tune. He couldn't understand why it made them laugh. When he asked, the servants assured him it was a very moral song "from the Bible," about a pitcher that went too often to the well and finally got broken. He approved of that. Of course, he missed the Hawaiian gift and love of the double entendre, and the fact that one of the maids, though unmarried, was pregnant. Being Hawaiian, she enjoyed the song as much as anyone else.

Poor Dr. Thurston fought the devil mightily all his life, and he was against sin, but he didn't have it all his way. He saw many of his children die, and many of his converts too, and he saw some of them slip back into the bad old pagan ways no matter how he tried. When he was dying, he was obsessed with the idea that the Lord was letting the Kingdom of Heaven down to him on a string, but every time he almost grabbed and reached it, the Lord would jerk it away, as if playing a big fish. Dr. Thurston probably got to his Kingdom of Heaven eventually, but you can be sure it was nothing like the one his Hawaiians had waiting for them.

The missionary diaries affected Ma a lot. One story always made her cry. One old missionary lady sat with her daughter—also married to a missionary—and watched her baby granddaughter die of diphtheria. Her little grandson contracted the disease. There was no doctor and no cure, so the grandmother took the little boy in her arms and sang to him, "There is a Happy Land, far far away." She told him that his baby sister had gone to the "Happy Land" and that he would be going there soon and would see her, that she knew he wanted to go to the "Happy Land" to be with his sister and gentle Jesus. She sat there dry eyed, singing to the little boy, till he died in her arms.

Of course, hundreds and thousands of Hawaiians died from imported diseases, like diphtheria and measles and mumps. They had no immunity at all, and no one to take care of them, so when they were burning with fever they crowded into the cool sea and then crawled out on the beaches and died—and there was no one to bury them.

Some Navy cousins of Georgie's had a beach cottage at Kailua, below the Pali, and I used to spend weekends there with their daughter, Clifford. We used to rent horses and ride along the beach, where we would see half-covered human bones in the sand, bleached white by salt and sun.

Ma actually worked up quite a case against the missionaries and their works in her mind. Although she had some inner struggles, having been brought up a Congregationalist, turning Episcopalian only to make it simpler to go to church with Georgie, she never had the immensely strong religious leanings that he had, although she had a perfect faith in God. But the missionaries always stuck in her craw, and I want to tell one of her most cogent stories in her own words:

Kauileaouli, who became Kamehameha III, was the first royal fruit of missionary teaching. He and his sister Nahienaena were the children of Kamehameha's I's tabu queen, Keopuolani, and after their mother's death, the regent Kaahumanu gave the children to the missionaries to educate. A word here about Kaahumanu. She was Kamehameha's favorite wife, but she was barren. Their married life and association was stormy; she was a strong-minded woman and of a higher caste than he was, but he loved and trusted her and left his kingdom in her hands. Little *Kauileaouli's* portrait as a child prince shows the face of a baffled, wistful little boy, dressed in the ponderous feather cape of royalty and holding a bow and arrow (for shooting mice—this was the only thing for which the ancient Hawaiians used the bow and arrow). The child's life was a battlefield over which raged the warring tabus of his own race and the laws of his adopted religion.

When he was twenty, he declared himself king. In 1839 at his missionary teacher's request, he divided the land into thirds; one-third for the chiefs, and one-third for the common people who heretofore had never owned land. In 1840 he gave up his absolute power and put it into the House of Nobles. He died a young man, confused, unhappy, yet faithful to the teaching which had brought his people out of savagery into that fringe of civilization that is the limbo of all primitive races.

The story of Pohakuloa is typical of the opposing forces that beset his short troubled life.

Pohakuloa was a giant boulder representing the goddess of maternity. Ever since the Islands had been fished from the sea by Maui's giant hook, she had stood in Manoa valley and the children conceived in her shadow were said to be born without pain to the mother. One can imagine the scenes which so shocked the missionary ladies and irritated their husbands, so that they finally decided to move the goddess away and break her up into little pieces. No one could be prevailed upon to do it. She was too sacred. At last it was settled that she could be moved if the king ordered it. The missionaries persuaded him to do this and, so, dressed in his black coat and striped trousers, he climbed up on her back and sat there, drinking champagne, while the rollers were put under her and she was pushed down the hill, broken up, and put into the wall of the new missionary school at Punahou where today the children of all classes and races mingle.

Years after the breaking up, the Japanese consul asked King Kalakaua's queen, Kapiolani, if he might have a certain nobby stone from the wall as an ornament for his garden. The queen, not realizing it was Pohakuloa's head, gave it to him (or, did he know?). The consulate was royal property, and she eventually gave it to the City of Honolulu for a maternity home.

Hawaiians declare that every part of the boulder has the power of the head.

"Do they still conceive their children up by the wall at Punahou?" I asked. My friend's eyes veiled.

"I wonder. You know, the night-blooming cereus the missionaries planted along the wall is covered with thorns."

(The night-blooming cereus at Punahou is one of the sights of Honolulu during the blossoming season.)

Poor Kauileaouli! According to custom, the chiefs intended to marry him to his full sister, Nahienaena, but it was against the laws of the Christian church. Nahienaena bore a child, and when she refused to name the father, she was put out of the congregation and died, defiant and unrepentant, soon after.

The king married a woman of lower rank against the will of the chiefs. Her two babies sickened and died. (Can the prick of a brass pin in a diaper cause death?) This beautiful wife, Kalama (the torch), was unfaithful to him with his closest friend, handsome John, son of Kamehameha's bosun-governor, John Young.

In the "time before Jesus came," Kalama could have loved both men and no one would have been unhappy, but to the missionary-taught king adultery was a sin and, while he did not denounce the lover to his teachers because of the public punishment and disgrace that would be involved, he could not afford to ignore the situation and be laughed at behind his back. He chose an occasion when there was a large gathering of chiefs to take them into his confidence and, while asking neither their advice nor their pity, he turned the culprit over to his peers by stepping delicately out of the picture. He did this by giving them the following "mele," or chant.

The lehua, house of the bird, has been stripped by the battleaxe
Even to its smallest petal, the tree trembles.
A fog, a bleak bitter rain is in the mountains and dark are the wild woods
Bruising is the bite of the wind that blows, sways, swirls,
rejoicing at the driving rain that leaves the ground all glistening.
The sun is cut off and sails away. That is always the way of the pelting rain that droops the hala blossoms until the wreath droops like a piece of folded tapa—the pretty wreath that is shrunk into a ball and lies still.
Alas, for my land of Hala in the upland! How I regret the field of lehua that I first wandered on!
The Bird has become wild and shy and flits away. That is the end of it all.
A salty sea that sweeps over a man and makes him bitter.
So be it, my love!
A robber has stripped my tree of its blossoms
His black deed has darkened my life
Gossips smack their lips over the scandal of this shameless love, while I stand blinded with sorrow.
I gave on the beloved who once was mine. How I regret my lovely flower!
Now wild and shy, I flit away, for my despair engulfs me—a tidal wave of tears.

The Hawaiian language was rich in many ways, and it was a sustained "double entendre" both for comedy and tragedy. In this case of the king's chant, when he referred to the "lehua" he referred to a blossom native to the Islands (ohia lehua, metrosideros collina var, polymorpha) which was called the "flower of love," but also was used as a poetic referral to the pubic hair of a woman as the blossom itself is pink and fuzzy and soft to the touch, sweetly scented.

The chiefs did not need this euphemistic chant to catch the king's meaning. "Who has betrayed our king?" they demanded, and Handsome John was found guilty. (Contemporary memoirs say that although Handsome John could barely read and write, he was the "loveliest and most beautiful man ever bred in the eight islands.")

The chiefs sentenced Handsome John to the Law of the Sea, sentencing him to swim to Tahiti, 2,100 miles away.

On the day when the punishment was to be fulfilled, the chiefs gathered at the beach and Handsome John strode out of his prison and stepped into the ocean. There was a shriek, and the queen, followed by every woman of her court, broke through the rings of judges and plunged in after him while astonished husbands were left clutching the empty dresses of the wives they had tried to detain who preferred to die with Handsome John rather than to live without him.

The whole party was rescued in canoes; the women were restored to their husbands and the judges declared that the culprit should stand at the flagpole with his eyes on the sun until he died. Fortunately, for Handsome John, some of the husbands thought to hasten his death by stoning him. At the sight of the blood streaming from his friend's head, the king himself ran to the flagpole and baring his own sacred head, he put his arm around Handsome John's shoulder as a sign of forgiveness. Thus, the punishment was ended.

Poor child of warring tabus. His life held little happiness though he tried to be a good king according to his dual loyalties. In public Kalama posed as his wife, but in private she was Handsome John's. Sometimes the king took comfort with the Jesuit fathers at Aihuimanu (gathering place of the birds), visits to which monastery the missionaries thought it best to close their eyes, since once they had tried and failed to put the Catholic order out of the Islands. When the king was too unhappy, he got drunk.*

(A sidelight to the Hawaiian love of life: there was no word for prostitute in the language until after the sailors came to the Islands, and then the word was Hawaiianized from "Hey! Come here!" to "Hookamemkame.")*

Ma had a full life with Georgie above and beyond her Hawaiian studies. Georgie was a great polo player. He had been on the official Army team for years and carried a big handicap. Polo was a great sport in the Islands, and Georgie organized an Army polo team at Schofield Barracks. West Point cadets had polo among the Academy sports, so there were some potentially great players there among the officers.

The Inter-Island Tournament was THE social event of the year. The islands of Oahu, Maui, and Kauai each had teams, and the games lasted all week. House parties, beach parties, dances, and everything glorious happened in polo week. Our whole family went into Honolulu and took a cottage at the Halekulani ("House in Favor of Heaven"—and indeed it was) for a week, right on Waikiki Beach. The horses were stabled at the Dillinghams—just the other side of Kapiolani Park. Early in the morning we would go up to the stables, ride the horses down across the park, and swim them off Waikiki Beach before the tourists even woke up. Swimming is the best and quickest way to get a horse in shape, and the horses loved it.

Of course, my sister and I did not go to most of the parties, but the two boys whose father owned the hotel were about our age and they were very nice to us.

We used to hunt for lizard eggs in the bark of the great hau trees that shaded the court and take them to our rooms to hatch, and we would sit out of sight and listen to the music at night. One day the boys took us for a day picnic to the Blowhole, around the point of Diamond Head. In those days there wasn't a real road there and it was quite a trip. The blowhole was a hole in a leaf of lava that stuck out into the sea. The big waves would strike the rock, there would be an unearthly sucking sound and a roar, and a column of water as high as a house would shoot up into the air, and then crash down on the rock and rush back into the sea. The boys told us that they knew of some murdered bodies that had been disposed of in the blowhole. This made it even better.

George and Ma soon knew everyone in Honolulu and most of the people from the other islands. Ma loved the parties, the music, the hula dancing, the singing, the flowers, and the stories. Georgie was a good party drinker and could hold his own in any company. On the other hand, Ma couldn't drink at all. Hard liquor put her to sleep. She had a fine palate and enjoyed a glass of good wine with a meal, but anything stronger than Dubonnet put her out for the count. Not being able to drink herself, she had no patience with people who drank too much. In fact, she was a little afraid of liquor and so she made fun of it.

Ma and Georgie had sailing friends as well as horsey ones, and one day Georgie came home from a sail with the story of a new drink that had been invented by his sailing friend, Teddy Cook. It had been christened "Sabbath Calm" and he would not tell Ma what was in it, but he teased her into having one before Sunday dinner. Ma liked it very much, said she couldn't taste much alcohol in it, and drank it down. If I remember correctly, it was made of brandy, cream, honey, and coconut milk. Right in the middle of lunch, when we were well into the usual alternate meal of roast beef, mashed potatoes, and peas, we heard a little sigh and looked up to see Ma, with the sweetest imaginable smile, put her head down on her mashed potatoes and fall asleep. She had achieved Sabbath Calm.

Then there was the great day when Ma discovered the Hawaiian temple, or heiau. She was riding with Georgie out on the Artillery ground after a range fire, and the great stone platform was exposed. A Hawaiian temple consisted of a platform made of many stones, and in the old days it had had a superstructure of matting and poles of sandalwood and great grimacing admonitory idols around the edges. The holy of holies was always an empty hut in the center of the structure—a hut for the god.

Ma and Georgie dismounted and gave the horses to the groom: after they climbed up on the platform, they could see it really was a heiau, and a big one.

We went back out the next day with machetes and spent hours on the platform, clearing and poking around. We found the holes where the idols had stood on their posts, and in one hole we found a tooth that later proved to be human, and some fragments of still-fragrant sandalwood. People from the museum came out and confirmed Ma's conclusion that it was an important heiau, and she was in seventh heaven.

Chapter 10

Legendes Hawaiiennes

About this time, Emma Ahuena Taylor came into our lives to stay. Emma was one of the most interesting and extraordinary people I have ever known. She was oueha Hawaiian—the most important part—and part English. She was probably in her seventies, a queenly woman, dressed always in a black holoku with real feather leis around her neck, leis of extinct birds that should have been in the museum and now are. She wore enormous hats and lots of makeup around her dark and flashing eyes. Emma was justly and loudly proud of her Hawaiian blood. She was of the "alii," the Hawaiian aristocrats, who could chant their genealogies back a thousand years and were related to more birds and beasts than the lesser folk. This was from her mother. Her English ancestor had come to the Islands with Admiral Vancouver. He was the younger son of a title in England, a friend of the great Kamehameha and the builder of Hawaii's first fleet. Emma was the widow of Albert Taylor, who had been keeper of the Archives, but she had buried him long before we had met, apparently with no regrets.

Everyone on the eight islands knew Emma and she knew them all, their histories printable or otherwise, and who their families were. She and Ma were meant for each other. As soon as Emma found out for herself that Ma was genuinely interested in Hawaiian antiquities, she was in and out of our house all the time, calling on the phone frequently to tell Ma something she had forgotten. She said that she was growing old and had to get it all recorded by someone who didn't laugh at the old ways, as Mr. Taylor had done.

Emma claimed to be descended from the red-tailed Koai bird and the Moo, the giant lizard. She was also descended from several noteworthy sharks. Emma and Georgie got along very well after she told him about her sister's death and ceremonial burial.

Ma made a special trip to the Big Island to see a volcanic eruption. When she came back she told Emma and her friend, Mrs. Sylvester, that it was said there that Pele the fire goddess had been seen the day before the eruption riding on the clouds with her flaming hair streaming and whipping in the wind. Mrs. Sylvester was at that time engaged in making an imitation feather cloak for little George, a copy of the cloak worn by the half-god Kamohoalii, Lord of Steam. Mrs. Sylvester had been chosen to do this by Emma because she was not only descended from the ancient class of feather weavers who were so highly esteemed that they were exempt from military service but also kin to the goddess Pele herself. Her name, Keahi Luahine, meant "fires of the old woman."

When Ma told them Pele had been seen, Mrs. Sylvester said she had seen Pele that way often. She asked if Ma had made a suitable offering to Pele when she got to the firepit to see the eruption. Ma, that good Episcopalian, said that she had made one with Pele's favorite ohelo berries (vaccinium pendulformis var. reticulatum) but that one branch of her offering had blown back from the edge of the crater and landed at her feet. Emma and Mrs. Sylvester discussed this at length in Hawaiian and then Emma said: "It is clear that Pele wants to share with you. I am glad of this eruption for it shows that Pele has come home. She has homes everywhere, Pere, Fere, but Hawaii is home. Pele is the heart of the world and every one of my family has some part of them buried with her. There in her fire my people are revived and live again." (Emma really talked like that when she got started. One had the feeling she was translating her thoughts from Hawaiian to English.)

"My sister, Rose Davison, was the first humane officer in Hawaii. When she died as a leper on Molokai, the death foam from her mouth was saved in a handkerchief, and a lock of her hair was saved to be given to Pele. Later, I went on a pilgrimage to Kilauea [the volcano]. All the way through the lehua forest I picked the lehua blossoms and laid them on stones whenever the driver would stop, and walking down from the Volcano House to Halemauma ['house of everlasting fire,' the fire pit]. I made offerings everywhere. Then, I came out onto the lava. A mist rose and all at once I was caught up in a rainbow that swooped down and lifted me from the ground. There, all around me, were the chiefs in feather capes, and I knew they were my people alive in Pele, crowding around me to show me the way. There were no faces visible, only the capes, tier on tier, hundreds upon hundreds. The wind from the swirling capes was cold in my ears, and the swish of their marching feet."

This story is what won Georgie over to a real friendship and respect for Emma. He remembered his experience of seeing his ancestors in World War I. Until this time, Georgie had been a little bit standoffish with Ma's Hawaiian friends because of the color of their skins. He had been brought up to believe that in the world people came in four colors: white, red, yellow, and black—and in that order. But when Georgie became a friend, he came with a whole heart and no reservations, and the Hawaiians who knew him all loved and treated him with both laughter and respect. He even had a special hula made for him during our second tour in the Islands, when he sailed from San Francisco in the schooner *Arcturus*. This was a very graphic hula about a little boat with one mast that sailed into a close little harbor—always the same little harbor. Typically Hawaiian, it was loaded with "naughty Polynesian fun" and always brought down the house. Yes, a faithful husband deserved a special hula!

Emma lived in the Alexander Young Hotel in the middle of Honolulu. She also had a tiny cottage at Kawela Bay on the windward side of the island. We had a standing invitation to visit her there, and we loved going because there, in the presence of some of her ancestors, she would "get going." Just outside the door of her cottage was a pool of water in the lava rock, and in the pool were two stone shapes that she said were two of her lizard ancestors. The way she referred to them made it all seem very matter of fact. Emma was not only related to everybody, she was related to everything.

She would also tell us about her late husband, Mr. Taylor. "And when I woke up last night, there was Mr. Taylor sitting in the Liholiho chair just wasting his time looking at me. So, I said 'Enough of this' and I called my niece, Mary Anne, and gave her the chair. He can sit there in her house if he wants to, and cease to trouble me."

Mr. Taylor turned up quite often. Apparently, his ghostly desire was to make Emma speak to him. When she did this, she said she knew she would die and she was not yet ready to go, especially since she had met Ma and Ma was taking all these notes. One day she came to call, and told Ma that she had had a very poor night. Every time she woke up, she saw Mr. Taylor standing in the bathroom doorway, "jingling the keys in his pocket in a way he knew I so disliked. I was not going to speak to him about it, though—not *this* time."

Emma's friendship with Ma, and all her stories, came to blossom in Ma's novel, *Blood of the Shark*, which she wrote between 1928 and 1936. It was published in Honolulu and was a great success. In fact, it became required reading for senior English at the University of Hawaii. The book was Emma's family history, slightly romanticized. It is a fascinating book, quite erudite in a way that sneaks up on you, with a very touching love story of a high-ranking Hawaiian chiefess and a young officer from Vancouver's flagship. It deals with the blending and the warring of two utterly dissimilar cultures, and the true love that underlies the protagonists' lives and caused some triumph and much tragedy. The book was published shortly before we left Hawaii, at the end of our second tour. Emma died a few months after we left. I have always supposed that in getting her story told she had achieved her life's purpose, and that she finally succumbed to Mr. Taylor's importunities and spoke to him.

Ma wrote another book during our first tour in the Islands. Some of her Honolulu friends had started brushing up on their schoolgirl French with a very intelligent and literate French lady, Mme. Riviere. Ma spoke every bit as well as the teacher, but she thought a refresher course would be fun, and she wanted to translate some Hawaiian legends into French as an exercise. Ma worked on her book of legends for two years. It was eventually published in Paris, exquisitely illustrated by a local artist.

Mme. Riviere was a character. I remember hearing that she was in Honolulu "on her uppers," and was a "Madame" by courtesy, having either been dumped by a sharp French gambler or having survived a liaison with a native—the whole bit being quite scandalous. For some reason, the Honolulu ladies wanted to help Mme. Riviere to survive.

We often spent weekends at the Halekulani Hotel. Among the buildings there was a huge open lanai, called "the house without a key," where many of the local people entertained. There was a party there the night I remember, and it went on into the small hours, and everyone decided to go swimming. Georgie, who didn't like swimming, must have had a drink or two, because he joined them. When he got into the water he found he was being pursued by Mme. Riviere, who was swimming after him in the nude. Her plan, according to his explanation to Ma, was that they would seduce one another on a large flat channel buoy fairly near the beach. The idea so terrified Georgie that he broke all records swimming back to the beach and came panting into our cottage practically begging Ma to save him. I was in the next room, still awake because I had been listening to the music at the party, and I heard the whole thing, including Ma nearly choking with laughter.

I could hardly wait to see Mme. Riviere again! When she came for Ma's next lesson, I saw a lean and scrawny woman of "a certain age," stylishly dressed and nicely put together, but old! So old! I was appalled at the thought that anyone who appeared so juiceless could be contemplating the magic of love—and in the nude! Georgie never came home when Mme. Riviere was giving Ma a lesson, although she would always tarry over her tea and keep looking at the front door.

Prohibition complicated Georgie's official life. His commanding officer, a totally humorless man named Colonel Lowbar, was dead set against drinking.

At one point, he ordered Georgie to bore a hole through the wall of Major So-and-so's house and peek through it to see if they were serving liquor at their New Year's party. Georgie said that he would resign his commission first, but before he did, he would report Colonel Lowbar to the commanding general for acts unsuitable to an officer and a gentleman. The colonel withdrew his order for the hole-boring, but after that he rode Georgie to death on little things until the colonel left the post. Ma managed to keep the peace, although Mrs. Lowbar was very condescending and patronizing to her. Then the Lowbars got their orders to the base in Boston, and Mrs. Lowbar said to Ma that she understood that Ma was from the Boston area, and that it would be very nice to go there with some letters of introduction. Ma told Mrs. Lowbar that her family were all country people who lived outside of Boston in the farming area, and Mrs. Lowbar said that in that case, she didn't think she and the colonel would be interested in meeting them as, after all, they would have nothing in common. Ma agreed.

Georgie, who really didn't know the birds from the flowers, had decided to have the last word with Lowbar, so he consulted with Ma about poisonous plants, saying he was worried about little George getting poisoned by something in the yard. Ma, not tumbling to his fell design, said that she thought the only thing in the yard that might be troublesome was the beautiful oleander, whose flowers and leaves exuded a milky sap that was highly irritating to the skin. Georgie put on some gloves and very painstakingly made a lei of oleander blossoms which he took to the transport when he went to see the Lowbars off. Ma would not go—she said it would be hypocritical. Georgie threw the lei over Colonel Lowbar's shoulders, and to his horror that worthy burst into tears: "Oh, Georgie, I didn't know you cared!" Georgie came home that night with mixed feelings.

Ma was fascinated by one of the mysteries of the Hawaiian people: their apparent ability to die at will. If the setting was right, it was as easy for a Hawaiian to die in our time as it had been "before Jesus came." Pueo, the rusty owl, is always the messenger of danger unto death to a Hawaiian, and he is the messenger of the "Nameless One." There were many gods in the Polynesian pantheon. Some of the oldest were not only represented by an amulet, an odd-shaped stone, or a leaf braided into an intricate pattern, but the oldest one of all had no earthly symbol. The indication of this "Nameless One's" presence or possession was the prefix "mea." Most Hawaiian place names are associated with extreme beauty or danger, or a god. Any place that had the syllables "mea" was more or less tabu because it was "someone's" beach, "someone's" undertow, "someone's" waterfall—it belonged to "someone," the life-taker. We were told by a Hawaiian friend never to swim on a beach that had "mea" in its Hawaiian name.

While we were in Hawaii, a pueo, attracted by the light in the unscreened general men's ward in the Queen's Hospital, flew down the length of the ward and out again. There were no patients in the ward at the time on the critical list, but next morning seven of the eleven Hawaiian patients in the ward were dead.

In one of Ma's unpublished essays, she quotes another example:

> An old lady asked my daughter, Ruth Ellen, then an Occupational Therapist at the Queen's Hospital [this was 1937] to teach her to feather stitch in pink and blue. Ruth Ellen picked up the garment to look at it and the old lady laughed, and said, "No, it isn't for a baby; this is my shroud. I am sick to death of living with my stepchildren, and as soon as I can get this shroud done, I will die." She did and was buried in the shroud that Ruth Ellen had helped her to decorate.

I well remember that occasion, and also that Ma was quite exercised about it and called her friend, Dr. Hubert Woods, to ask about it. He told her the following story.

> On my first job as a plantation doctor at Libbyville years ago, I was sitting in the manager's office one Saturday morning when a Hawaiian came in and asked for some planks to make a coffin for his wife. "I'm sorry, I didn't even know she was sick," said my friend. The Hawaiian answered, "Oh, she's not sick at all, but she is to die on Monday at five. She says that yesterday she was out crabbing and she saw her grandfather standing on the bluff and beckoning to her, just as he used to when he was alive. He has told her that he needs her and she has promised to go to him at five on Monday." "But are you going to allow that?" "I have begged her to stay, but she only says, "You can easily get another wife, and the children are grown and don't need me any more, and grandfather must need me, or he would never have sent for me."
>
> The manager gave him an order for the planks, and he left the office.
>
> "That woman will die as surely as five o'clock strikes" he said to me. "Better go and see for yourself."
>
> Monday found me jogging toward Libbyville. The road was full of people in holiday garb and, as I neared the plantation village, they grew more and more numerous. I offered a pretty girl a lift and as she climbed into the buggy, she said, "Are you going to the luau?" "What luau?" I asked. "Mileka's. She and her husband are having a big luau because she is to die at five."
>
> Over the hills kanakas were streaming; men in purple shirts and girls in ruffled starched holokus with guitars and ukuleles. We drew up to the house. Long fern-covered tables were set out in front and Mileka, herself, dressed in a muumuu [undergarment to a holoku] was going busily back and forth preparing the feast. In the Hawaiian way of hospitality, I was invited at once and a gayer luau I never saw. At ten minutes to five, Mileka rose quietly from the table and went

into the house, followed by her sister and a cousin. I followed as soon as I could and placed myself so that I could see in the window.

On the big bed, with its red patchwork quilt and mosquito bar, dressed in a fresh holoku, lay Mileka, and I could see marks of the soles of her new shoes— she had been barefoot at the party. Her sister sat beside her and held her hand, and her cousin stood at the other side slowly waving a kahili. As my watch pointed to five o'clock, Mileka's hand dropped to the coverlet and the wailing for the dead began. I went into the room and looked at her, but there was no need to take her pulse, she was gone.

Ma's notes continue: "Death often comes this way to the Hawaiians. I asked my friend Emma Ahuena Taylor if she could explain it. She said: 'It's a gift. We just let go.'"

Our darling grandfather Bamps spent his last Christmas with us in Hawaii. Bamps and Bamma and Nita Patton came over. Aunt Nannie Wilson would not come because she was deathly afraid of leprosy. It was no use explaining to her that leprosy was almost totally arrested in Hawaii, that all the remaining lepers were on Molokai, and, anyhow, that it was a very hard disease to catch, the spirochete of leprosy being unable to stand sunlight for any length of time. Aunt Nannie knew all about Molokai and Father Damien, and it was not the scene for her.

Tinta had a wonderful time. A very nice Army officer fell in love with her and really showed her off and around. The grandparents were happy being with us, "the boy," and Ma, whom they truly loved. They had a wonderful time with little George, the grandson who would carry on The Name. It was altogether a happy time.

It was during this visit that Bamps told Ma something that she always considered the finest compliment a husband had ever given his wife. He told Ma that before he had retired, he would spend all day in Los Angeles or Wilmington, dealing with the land scrambles and mixed-up business affairs of the Shorbs and the Bannings and the rest of the feckless members of the family, and that getting home in the evening to Lake Vineyard and Bamma was "like plunging into a warm, quiet pool where all tensions and troubles washed away, and there was peace and I could see the stars."

Georgie was in Hawaii when Bamps died, and he took the next boat home. He was absolutely undone. He blamed himself for not having been at Bamps's bedside when he died; for not having been there when Bamps needed him; and for having spent so much of his life away from home: for all the little things he might have done for his father. Ma was most supportive, and reminded him that he had written home every single week of his life, that he had always kept in touch in every possible way, that she and the children had spent many months with the Pattons, and that they had enjoyed us for a visit in every station that Georgie had had, but he was still inconsolable.

My sister was on her way west from school as soon as she got her telegram. She got to Lake Vineyard before Georgie did. From what she later told me, it is just as well that Georgie missed his father's funeral.

There was a real wake with Bamps laid out in his open coffin in front of the huge fireplace in the living room, candled at the head and feet. Bee, Tinta, Bamma, and various aunts and cousins were all in the room at one time or another, so that Bamps was never left alone without his family for three days. He was much loved. Many of the mourners were Mexicans and Mexican-Indians whose families had worked for his father-in-law, Don Benito Wilson, and whose children had worked for him. From the back of the house came the constant awful keening for the dead from Mary Scally, Georgie's nurse, and her friends in the Irish community, and many of the Mexicans to whom such wailing was part of the leave-taking ceremonies.

Bee said it was really awful but the worst part of all was Aunt Nannie, upstairs in her bedroom. She had apparently lost or abandoned all control, and was screaming and calling for George to come and take her with him, and that she knew that it was she he had always loved, and not Ruth, whom he had married. She screamed that Georgie should have been her son. In fact, some of the things she screamed, Bee never told me; she said that they were "just too awful."

Aunt Nannie had been drifting toward the comfort of the bottle for years, although this was kept a "graveyard secret" in the family so that even Ma didn't know. Remarks were always being made about "poor Miss Wilson's appetite, her health, her spells, etc." I realize now that the poor soul was really a refined alcoholic. They were always "tempting her appetite" with rich custards, paper-thin slices of Virginia ham, Bristol Cream Sherry, and the like—all pure poison to the liver. So I should imagine that at Bamps's funeral she was on a real crying jag and living up to the "in vino veritas."

My sister was overcome by the whole experience. None of us had had any idea of this undercurrent in what had always been our second home. She told me that through it all, Bamma and Tinta remained calm and collected, and apparently deaf to the keening and screaming. In all the emotion that was let loose in those sad days, I don't remember that anyone but Ma ever thought of the strain on Bamma and Tinta. Everybody else was shaking their heads and talking about "poor Georgie."

Georgie got home to Lake Vineyard several days after the funeral and stayed several weeks. Ma remained in Hawaii with little George and me. She felt with her great delicacy that Georgie should be alone with his mother and sister and Aunt Nannie. But Ma was devastated too. She had known the Pattons her whole life long and was deeply devoted to them. Ma never had the traditional "in-law" relationship with them—they were her other parents.

Georgie had two of his psychic experiences there at Lake Vineyard at that time, and they brought him some comfort. He told Ma about them when he got back to Hawaii. The first one happened when he was sitting at his father's desk in his private office in the basement. The office was a large room with a fireplace, lined with bookshelves filled with law books, text books from his long-ago days at VMI, and leather-bound classics in Greek and Latin—both languages as familiar to Bamps as English. Where there were no books, there were dozens of photographs, groups of VMI cadets, horses, and dogs, but mostly of "the boy" in his many stages. There was an adjoining lavatory with a well-stocked liquor cabinet, and there were two huge safes full of family memorabilia.

Georgie had been going through the contents of the safes: he had found the toy grenadier guards that Aunt Nannie had brought him from Paris; his toy engine that she had driven all the way to Los Angeles to buy for him when he had had the earache; his grandmother Wilson's mourning brooch with twists of Don Benito's hair, and the curls of her dead children, twisted into curlicues behind the heavy crystal front. He had found the gold piece that had kept a Yankee bullet from killing his grandfather Patton, deeply dented where the Minié ball had struck it and driven it into the flesh on his side, and the shell fragment, wrapped in the blood-stained shirttail, that had given the same grandfather his mortal wound at Cedar Creek. He had found his step-grandfather Smith's flint and steel, given to him for his eleventh birthday, and Don Benito's carved gold pipe stem—a host of family treasures.

The door into the office opened into a big straw-matted hall in the cellar where all the larger trophies hung: the shell of a giant sea turtle he had once harpooned, his first swordfish, the saddle of the Mexican bandit he had killed, the German helmet and body armor pierced by shell fire. In a way, he was sitting in a shrine dedicated to himself.

At the far end of the basement, opposite the door, were the stairs going up to the front hall. He told Ma that he was sitting at the desk, the tears running down his cheeks, thinking how he had failed his father in so many little ways, when something made him look up and there stood his father in the door, frowning at him and shaking his head. Georgie felt a clear, distinct message that "all was well; he was not to mourn." He said that his mind seemed to answer: "I understand. Alright, Poppa." At that, his father gave him his radiant smile and turned and walked to the stairs; only when Georgie saw the trousered legs disappearing up to the door into the front hall did he remember that the Honorable George S. Patton had been dead and in his grave for five days.

A few days later, he was in the cemetery at the Church of Our Savior in San Gabriel, the church built by Don Benito Wilson for Georgie's grandmother, Margaret Hereford Wilson. He was in the family burial plot near the ostentatious red obelisk put up for Don Benito, with the other graves grouped worshipfully around its base, and he was again feeling very low and lonely. He looked up and saw his father walking down the pathway between the plots, his soft fedora worn dashingly, as always, on the side of his head, carrying his cane. Georgie always said that his father carried a cane the way a knight carried a sword. Bamps was slashing off the heads of the flowers along the way with the cane. As he passed Georgie, he looked at him with his warm smile and a twinkle in his eye, and continued on down the path. Georgie said that at that moment he knew his father was all right, and that all the things his father had ever taught him about the life that continues after death were true. Georgie never felt badly again about his father.

Bee came back to Hawaii with Georgie and we had a wonderful summer, partly on the Parker Ranch, and partly on the post, riding, exploring, swimming, and avoiding tennis as much as possible. Bee went to quite a few parties, but it was the awkward age where the boys stand in groups in one side of the room, poised for flight, and the girls stand on the other in agony, wondering if they will be asked to dance and, if so, will they be able to keep from making fools of themselves. So, although I envied her, and Ma encouraged her, she didn't have a very good time.

One of the things Ma loved to do was to "dress up." No matter where we went, the costume trunk came with us. Every occasion was one for putting on a costume and what was more, acting the part while you were in it. Ma was a member of every post dramatic society, and that summer she had one of the leading parts in *Captain Applejack,* the society's offering for the year. (The year before it had been a Bach Cantata, and Ma had been in the front line.) Bee and I went through a stage that summer of rewriting plays and putting them on. Our audience was Ma, little George, Alice Holmes, Kani, Goto, and sometimes Georgie, but we gave our all.

There was one play I will never forget about bandits in Italy, a kidnapped heiress and a corpse that dripped blood (watercolor paint) when its murderer approached. Bee got to be the kidnapped heiress because she was the prettiest, and I got to be all the bandits. George wore his pirate costume and banged a drum.

Bee and I combined this with our own adaptation of Byron's "Lala Roukh," and at the end we sang, to the tune of "The Old Oaken Bucket," the Peri's Lament, which goes:

> Farewell, oh farewell to thee, Araby's daughter
> Thus warbled a peri beneath the green sea
> No pearl ever lay under Oman's green water
> As pure in its shell as thy spirit in thee

We were peris, dressed in a lot of veils and old curtains, and one of the larger dolls was Araby's drowned daughter.

Unfortunately, the play was ready for production the night that Ma and Georgie were unexpectedly invited to a party for the Crown Prince and Princess of Sweden. The Crown Prince's aide was one of the Swedish officers who had competed in the Olympics with Georgie, and when he had found out the Pattons were in Hawaii, he had asked that they be included in the party. He came all the way to Schofield Barracks to fetch them. Bee and I raised a howl because we were being set aside when they had promised to watch us, so the aide and Ma and Georgie had to sit through a shortened version of our production because Ma said she never broke a promise to her children. I can see them now—sitting in the living room watching us do our act in the lanai, Georgie and the colonel in their dress blues with all their medals, and Ma wearing Ellie's diamond and aquamarine tiara and long white gloves; and the aide's wife, who was a countess, in her diamond tiara. Fortunately, Georgie was always able to produce drinks even in the midst of Prohibition. I am sure they needed them.

We spent one summer of that first tour in Hawaii in the rented house of a friend of a friend on the mysterious island of Maui, sharing the house with the Aleshires (Eleanor Aleshire's mother was the unforgettable Carol Vidmer). It was a wonderful summer. All the sporting crowd—what would now be called "the beautiful people"—were on Maui that summer, including Mr. and Mrs. Jay Gould and their daughters. The daughters were far more sophisticated than were Bee and me or the three Aleshire girls, but they did not know where babies came from and this gave us a tremendous advantage, as the Gould girls had a lot of things we didn't have including permanent waves. But we knew the facts of life!

We met the von Tempskis on that trip. Old Mr. von Tempski had been the foreman of the Baldwins' Ulapalakua ("the ripe bread fruit of the gods") Ranch. It was the biggest ranch on Maui. He had died from being gored by a bull, but he had had time to suffer a lot and to utter a number of memorable last words. Three of his children lived in their father's house and helped run the ranch. Armine, the eldest, was a tiny little woman with bright red hair who wore movie-cowboy clothes and wrote passionate novels. Her greatest work was *Hula*, which became a sensational movie and starred Clara Bow. The next daughter, Lorna, worked as a cowboy, as did the younger brother, Errol. The von Tempskis were the most romantic people that I had ever encountered. They took in a few boarders in a refined way—references required. At the end of their main room in the dining area, there was a pond with running water and goldfish in it; it also contained frogs, who hopped out and joined the guests. During one of my vacations I was sent there with my cousin, Clifford Watson, as a boarder: we had the time of our lives. Armine was in the middle of a love scene for one of her novels, and my job was to keep the Victrola playing romantic music while she "created." "Moonlight and Roses," "Melancholy Baby," "Roses are Blooming in Picardy," and other deathless classics ground out her literary struggles. I took this job very seriously, and felt unspeakable thrills and immortal longings at being so close to a Genius at Work. She used to read bits aloud to us: they certainly beat any of the continued stories we had read in the *Honolulu Advertiser*. I remember when I got home I burbled interminably about the von Tempskis, and I once heard Georgie mutter to Ma: "I guess it couldn't have done her any *real* harm."

Ma joined us at the ranch for a four-day pack trip over the edge of the great dead volcano Haleakala, "house of the everlasting sun." There was only a horse trail in those days that we followed up past the tree line into the sky. We slept in a crummy guest house on the edge of the crater. It was from there that we saw the Brocken—our own shadows on the sky, enormous, rainbow-edged. We slept one night in another guest house in the crater and then rode out the other end where the mountain had long ago exploded and cast one side into the sea. From there we rode to a Chinese store for one night and the next night we spent at the house of an old retired Hawaiian cowboy who had worked all his life at Ulupalakua. All this time Ma was busy taking notes and writing down the stories and songs that the old people told her. Everything was grist to her mill. She had the most enormous zest and curiosity about all phases of life.

Our tour in Hawaii was growing short. It was at this time that Georgie and Ma took a giant step and bought the first and only house they ever owned, "Green Meadows," in South Hamilton, Massachusetts. They bought it by telegram. Neither of them had ever been upstairs in the house.

Georgie had a lifelong conviction that he would die and be buried in a foreign land. He talked about it, quoting Napoleon: "The boundaries of an empire are the graves of her soldiers." He was convinced that we would soon be at war with the Japanese Empire and he wanted Ma settled somewhere before he took off. After Bamps's death, California did not call him as home. His own inclination was toward Virginia, the land of his ancestors, which had grown in his mind into the Land of Cockaigne, with its fox-hunting and pseudo-plantation society, and the soft elegance of diction he associated with his family. But Ma was one of seven brothers and sisters—all grouped around Boston—and Georgie wanted to leave her amongst her own.

After the senior Ayers died, the house at 395 Commonwealth Avenue in Boston had been sold. The summer home, Avalon, was deliberated over for some time and then the six shares of the brothers and sisters were sold to Kay and Keith Merrill. Every Ayer had a home except Beatrice Patton. Ellen, Chilly, and Fred lived on the North Shore; Louise had a farm in Lincoln, near Boston. The oldest Ayer brother, Jamie, had headquarters in New York City, but spent a lot of time on his yacht off Marblehead.

Green Meadows was right in the middle of the Myopia hunting country in Hamilton. It had been bought and restored at the turn of the century by Mr. and Mrs. George Burroughs, and both Ma and Georgie had been there for hunt breakfasts. Mrs. Burroughs had been from Georgia, and had installed Venetian blinds, a veranda, and a garden with a clipped ornamental hedge; otherwise, the house was straight eighteenth-century New England, with the original four rooms upstairs and downstairs and added ells. When the Burroughses died, the neighbors, including Freddy and Chilly Ayer, had bought the place to keep it from being subdivided, and they offered it to Ma and Georgie for what they had paid, plus taxes. Ma had always loved it, and it seemed an answer to a prayer for Georgie, so they bought it by telegram.

We came back to the mainland in 1928, via California, and went to Massachusetts for the summer, which we spent with the Fred Ayers, while Ma had glorious hours with builders and contractors restoring and refurbishing her first real home. There was not a great deal to do, except to put in electricity and modernize the plumbing and scrape the red flock wallpaper off the walls. The carpenter talked Ma out of replacing the toilet seat in the third-floor bathroom. He said it was "the finest solid cherry seat in Essex County," so she left it where it was.

Georgie's heart's home was the stable—a truly magnificent English-novel building with every convenience and room for carriages, carts, and six horses. We moved into Green Meadows, using it as our summer home until Georgie died in 1945, when it became Ma's year-round home: she died there in 1953.

Georgie went for station to Washington, D.C. There he rented a marvelous old house called Woodley, near the Cathedral. It had a large wood lot, a garden, stable, and squash-racket court and was loaded with history. It had once been a summer White House, but I don't remember for which president.

Bee was in her last year at Foxcroft and by the help of luck and a long-handled spoon they got me into Miss Madeira's School on Dupont Circle. The years at Leilehua had done a lot for everything but my formal education. I knew no algebra or grammar. All the summer before we went to Washington, I was tutored daily in both subjects with no success. Finally, Georgie took me aside and told me not to try to figure out the subjects, just to memorize both textbooks and pass the exam. He said that was how he had gotten through West Point. It worked for me too.

It was this summer that Aunt Theodora, Uncle Chilly's wife, decided to be a dea ex machina and help Ma plan Bee's social life and future. She reminded a slightly bristling Ma that she had been away from the haut monde for some time while she, Theodora, had succeeded in bringing out and marrying off two lovely daughters most successfully. Ma adored Uncle Chilly, so she agreed when Bee and I were asked to come to tea alone at their beautiful house nearby. We both said that we thought it was a terrible idea, but Ma made us put on our good clothes and go, driven by our new chauffeur, Reggie Maidment. Reggie was newly married and looking for a life job, which he got. He was one of our dearest friends.

Aunt Theodora's redoubtable butler, Herne, met us at the door and asked us to leave our hats in the coat room. We were then escorted into the before-dinner living-room, all white and rose with vases of delphinium and lilies. Aunt Theodora was there behind the tea set in a white chiffon tea gown, trimmed with marabou, and looking frighteningly pretty and assured. We were given tea with lemon slices, into which were stuck whole cloves, and dainty watercress sandwiches. As soon as we were settled, we were subjected to some pretty searching questions: Did we know who we were? Did we know how much money we had? Did we know what would be expected of us socially? And so on and on.

No one had ever talked like that to us before because, of course, we knew who we were, and it was not "done" to talk about money. As for society, Ma had always told us "we were society—other people want to be with us."

Finally, Aunt Theodora got a firm but kind expression on her face and asked if we realized that "fond as we all are of Georgie" that Ma had "married beneath her," that a lot would be expected of us and that we would be looked at very critically as marriage prospects by the fond "mammas" of Boston.

At this point, Bee rose to her feet and said: "Come on, Lukie, let's go home." Aunt Theodora protested that she was not yet finished and that Reggie was not to come for us for at least another half-hour. Bee replied, "Come on, Lukie, let's get our hats and go home." Which we did. We started off down the driveway to be shortly followed by Aunt Theodora in her Rolls, driven by Herne, leaning out the window and begging us, ordering us, pleading with us to come back—she hadn't finished and, at any rate, we were not to repeat anything she had said to Ma.

Bee kept on walking. When we had got to Myopia, we cut across the golf course so that the Rolls could not follow us. We walked all the way home in our good patent leather shoes, not speaking, just walking.

The minute we got home Bee went and found Ma. She told Ma everything Aunt Theodora had said, then burst into tears. Ma, when she could catch her breath, started laughing and laughing. "Poor Fedy!" she cried. "What a wasp's nest she bumped into! Don't worry, girls, she's just gotten her priorities a little mixed up. She and your Uncle Chilly are really devoted to your father!"

The first winter I was at Madeira's, Ma and I had an extraordinary meeting with an extraordinary woman—the mother of the chief of staff, General Douglas MacArthur.

General MacArthur was between wives, so his mother was keeping house for him in Quarters 1 at Fort Myer. A notice appeared in the *Daily Bulletin* that Mrs. MacArthur would not receive callers. This worried Ma a lot and finally one day, when I had been home from school for a week with a cold, Ma said she thought it would be nice to go to Fort Myer and leave cards on the Great Lady, to show that at least we knew what was proper.

Ma turned down the proper corner of her card to show she had delivered it in person, and we went up on the porch and rang the doorbell and were effusively welcomed by a Filipino houseboy who didn't seem to speak any English except "Come light in, radies, come light in!" Ma assured him that she knew we were not welcome and that she only wanted to leave her card, but he kept trying to draw us in and all of a sudden this deep voice from the dark hall called out, "Since you are already within, you may remain," and there we saw this tremendous figure descending the stairs, like a storm cloud. Mrs. MacArthur was all in black, with a net collar that supported her throat—very fashionable in the 1890s: she was the first person we ever saw wearing dark glasses in the house.

She urged us into the living room, asking Ma who she was. Ma said, "I'm Mrs. Georgie Patton, Mrs. MacArthur, my husband is a major serving here on the general's staff." Mrs. MacArthur peered darkly at Ma and said, "Patton? George Patton? Oh yes, Twenty-second Virginia, fell at Cedar Creek in 1864; very distinguished officer." Ma said that yes, that was Georgie's grandfather, and so we sat down. Then Mrs. MacArthur told the houseboy to fetch her jewel box. While he was gone, she leaned over and gave my cheek a firm pinch and asked me how old I was. I think she was trying to be gracious.

The boy returned with a box about the size of a child's coffin and set it down on the table by Mrs. MacArthur, who opened it and drew out a brooch, set with a single white stone. "Young woman, do you know what this is?" I said I didn't and she replied, with relish, "Well, it is a piece of my brother's skull, he was wounded at Antietam and seven pieces were shot out of his skull. He brought them home and presented them to his sisters, and we had brooches made from them!"

After we left, Ma laughed, "No wonder Douglas is the kind of man he is! Dragon's seed!"

While we were stationed in Washington, Ma took us to a Patton family reunion at Dogwood Farm somewhere in Virginia. Bamps's first cousin, Sadie Patton Hutchinson, was back from California and she insisted that we come. The farmhouse was old and had an old smell. I can remember the smell even if I can't remember the town. Ma was in her element with people, and Aunt Sadie was a high-born lady, and the conversation was a montage of family stories, pedigrees, and mish-mash. At one point the lady I was sitting close to said to Aunt Sadie something about the fact that Ma was a Yankee, and Aunt Sadie replied in her piercing whisper, "Of course, my dear, but she has some quite good southern connections!" When I told Ma about this, she said that it was all right, the Yankees thought she had fallen from grace by marrying a southerner even if he was from southern California, and the southerners thought that Georgie had blotted his copy book by marrying a Yankee, but that maybe someday the Civil War would be over and Johnny would come marching home.

The summer following our move to Washington, Bamma died. She was on her way east with Tinta to visit us at Woodley, and she died on the train at Albuquerque. Ma and Georgie and Bee went west for her funeral, leaving George and me with Alice Holmes. Bamma had been in poor health for years, and after Bamps died she didn't feel she had much reason to go on. Aunt Nannie had moved out of Lake Vineyard into her own house after Bamps's death. Tinta was Bamma's favorite child. Bamma told Ma that Georgie had been given everything, and that Nita had had to take second best all her life, but Bamma knew that Tinta had inherited her tremendous strength of character and her total integrity and that Tinta could get along without her. Georgie turned over his entire share of the California estate to his sister so that she could live at Lake Vineyard in comfort for life.

It was soon after Bamma's death that Tinta had her psychic experience. She had adored her mother as much as Georgie had adored Bamps, and she felt very lonely and lost. She awoke one night to the exquisite scent of Parma violets—the only scent that Bamma always wore—and felt someone rise from the edge of her bed and a hand pass across her cheek, and with that she felt a sense of profound happiness and peace that she never lost.

My sister, Bee, had always been a misfit at Foxcroft. Georgie was not rich enough or famous enough then to give her an entrée into Miss Charlotte's inner circle. Bee was lovely to look at, but not stylish or beautiful; she was gifted but far from a genius; she was gentle, sensitive, and humble. When she first went to Foxcroft, Ma had written to Anne Steward, Chilly and Theodora's younger daughter, who had graduated from Foxcroft just before her marriage, to ask her if there was anything about the school that Ma should know. Anne wrote back that everything about the school was just peachy except for one teacher, Miss Alice, who was bad news. Anne didn't say what kind of bad news.

To Ma's confusion, Bee's next letter was all about Miss Alice, and how kind she was, letting Bee cool her horse, shine her shoes, and do all the little chores that Bee said the girls were standing in line to perform for Miss Alice. Ma was innocent but nonplussed. Bee's last year, the whole pot came a-boiling. There was a scandal involving Miss Alice and some of the girls, and Bee, being relatively unimportant and having no social clout, was the scapegoat. Bee was always an innocent, and I don't think she even knew what people were talking about, but she was blamed and shunned and started running a temperature of 100 degrees, at which point she was put into the school infirmary. From there, the assistant headmistress, who was a fine uncompromising Scot, removed her, gave her a diploma, and told Ma to take Bee to Europe. The assistant headmistress then resigned, after Miss Alice was fired.

Ma took Bee to Europe and Tinta came east and kept house for Georgie, little George, and me. The whole affair was only a nine-days wonder, shushed up by Miss Charlotte and her guilty cohorts, but Bee's soul never recovered from the perfidy of her so-called friends, and she let this worm in the bud feed on her damask cheek.

In the fall of 1929 Bee made her debut. The Merrills gave her a big summer ball at Avalon and she went to the parties that were still marvelous in spite of the shadow of depression. Aunt Theodora had bought a fabulous trousseau in Paris for Anne, the use of which Anne confounded by getting pregnant as soon as she got married. So, Ma, very happily, accepted Anne's trousseau for Bee's debut, and I will never forget the marvelous clothes, some of which I inherited in my turn. It was the year of the dipping skirt. There was one dress of white taffeta ruffles, each ruffle edged with leaf-green ribbon, at the waistline of which was a bunch of green and white taffeta grapes. There was a dress of cut velvet, colored velvet flowers on a cream background, edged with a brown velvet ruffle; there was a very best dress of yards and yards of red satin ribbon of graded colors, sewn onto red chiffon. Oh, they were all so lovely, and looked so luscious on my sister. Bee had the most exquisite figure, and dressing her was a joy. She had fairy-tale princess golden brown hair, slightly curly; big blue eyes; a peach complexion with a dusting of freckles like cinnamon on cream. One of my favorite dresses was a romantic long-sleeved dress of a color called elephant's breath. With it she wore a Juliet cap of golden cords, threaded with golden topaz. She always had loads of beaux, but she was shy.

Ma and Daddy wanted her to have a good time, and to get to know lots of young men and date at West Point, as Ma had done. When Georgie went to his twentieth reunion at West Point in the spring of 1929, he wrote to the cadet hostess, Mrs. Harriett Rogers, an old friend and the wife of an old friend, and asked them to pick a cadet to squire Bee around. The Rogerses produced the young man they considered to be the outstanding cadet in the Academy, a second-year man from Baltimore named John Knight Waters. He was everything there was, and from that weekend for the rest of her life, there was no one else for Bee but Johnnie Waters. However, he had three more years at the Academy, so she had three years to try her wings, which she did. As she got used to a less sheltered life, she lost most of her shyness, became outgoing, and gave everyone a wonderful time.

We only lived in beautiful Woodley for a year, and then it was sold to Secretary of State and Mrs. Henry Stimson. We then moved to a modern manor on Cleveland Avenue called White Oaks. It didn't have Woodley's charm, but it had a ballroom for Bee's debutante ball, which was to come that winter. There was no stable at White Oaks, so we kept the horses at the Riding and Hunt Club on P Street. From there we rode daily for miles and miles on Rock Creek Park. Those were the days before crime, and the park was for everyone.

White Oaks was a grand house, very convenient and very new and very definitely haunted. The family never saw the ghost, but our deaf old Tank, who had extrasensory abilities, saw the ghost every evening. We always sat in a small living room near the front door. Georgie had his leather armchair by the fireplace there, right where the master's chair ought to be, and every evening about 5:30 p.m. Tank would station himself by the front door and wait. Something would apparently come in because Tank would follow It, tail wagging and eyes lifted up as It came into the room, and then he would lie down at the foot of the chair and look lovingly upward toward the One no one could see but himself. Whoever It was, It must have been friendly.

We were told that the owner-builder had gotten so in debt building this, his dream house, that he had committed suicide.

There were six large bedrooms on the second floor, and three on the third floor, and we had a lot of parties and a lot of company. Many of the Massachusetts family came south for the fox hunting in Virginia that went on all winter. One day two very proper cold-roast-Boston maiden ladies, Miss Mary Curtis and Miss Katherine Wellman, came to visit. The door of Georgie's dressing room opened onto the balconied upstairs hall right opposite the front door, and just as the ladies entered, Georgie emerged from his dressing room as naked as a jaybird on his way to the closet in Bee's bedroom where he kept his electric exercising machine, known as the belly shaker. The front door opened, Georgie stopped to see who it was, the two ladies looked up to see who was looking at them, and that was a moment frozen forever in time. Then, very calmly the ladies turned and walked back out the front door, closing it. Georgie fled back into his dressing room. The front doorbell rang, and the ladies reentered and were shown to their third-floor rooms as planned.

Ma and Georgie were in an environment they could understand and appreciate. The only cloud on the horizon was Georgie's career. There was no actual war in sight, and no one was getting promoted. One night Georgie remarked that "General so-and-so died today, and every colonel in Washington is like a wolf bitch in heat, waiting to see who will step up into his slot." That was the way promotion went in those days; top of the ladder had to tumble off before the bottom could go up one step—a sort of human Parcheesi.

But in the interim, there was polo, fox hunting, steeple chasing, horse shows, and a tremendous and sometimes interesting social life. The Henry Stimsons were very fond of the family, and through them Georgie and Ma met a great many people who would be prominent in the war to come.

Georgie and Ma had a friend from Massachusetts who was a real character. His name was Francis Colby. He was a colonel in the Army and somehow he managed to go off to Africa on safari a good deal of the time, but he was one of those permanent fixtures in life. He had gone to dancing school with Ma and had played squash and hunted and showed and raced with Georgie and, while he was as real a phoney as ever lived, he was also a friend. One night the phone rang and this tremendously cultivated Harvard accent inquired for Major Patton. Georgie ran to the phone and said happily, "Why Francis, you damned old nigger lover! What the hell are you doing in Washington, and who the hell let you out of jail?" The beautifully cultivated voice on the other end hesitated a moment: "I think you have made a mistake in identity. This is the secretary of state. I called to see if Major Patton would care to come over to Woodley for a game of squash rackets and a drink."

When Georgie rented White Oaks, which he did while Ma and the rest of us were in Massachusetts, he was having one of his rare twinges of conscience about having taken Ma away from her native heath to a frontier sort-of-life. White Oaks required a minimum of nine servants to run, and Georgie told Ma he had rented it for her because he thought it would remind her of Avalon. If it did, she never mentioned it. She told Bee and me that nine servants were nine times more trouble than one or two because they were more specialized; the boots didn't get cleaned on the boot boy's day off, and the waitress wouldn't make the beds on the chambermaid's day off, and the kitchen maid couldn't cook on the cook's day off, and that Georgie didn't realize that Mama had Mamie Ryan and his mother had Mary Scally to do the actual overseeing.

The servants came and went. I remember one in particular named Jennie. She was the upstairs maid. She had a goiter and a pompadour. She refused to enter my room because I had a flying squirrel that launched himself from the curtain rods onto any passing shoulder, and a kangaroo rat who kept his hoarded dinner under a corner of the rug waiting for the hard times that never came, and a long-haired guinea pig named King Lear, and a crow. But Jennie made one immortal remark. I had just read *Dracula* by Bram Stoker, and was in quite a state about vampires. I liked Jennie, so I loaned her my well-worn copy of the book to read. When she had read it and brought it back to me, her only comment was, "Well, Miss, 'twas an unlikely tale."

Young George and Alice and I lived in a three-room suite over the ballroom and poor Alice had to clean up after me but, most fortunately, she and George both liked my pets.

To my everlasting woe, I was sent to the Masters School at Dobbs Ferry, New York, the fall before Bee's great ball. Miss Madeira and Ma and the rest of them had had enough of me, and it was time I went into the cocoon to reappear, they hoped, as a butterfly. I was given a choice between Dobbs, where Kay Merrill had been a star pupil, and Miss Spence in New York, where Hilda Ayer had been a star pupil. I chose Dobbs, inwardly and outwardly kicking and screaming because it was in the country. Dobbs and I went to the mat and stayed there for three tiresome years. I was deeply resentful that all the fun was going on at home while I was in durance vile, being finished. I particularly hated missing Bee's debut, which had grown in my mind into a Cinderella affair of a lifetime.

Coming out in Washington, D.C., was a real commercial enterprise. There were three professional hostesses—ladies from the *Social Register* who had fallen on hard times—who ran the balls, owned the lists of eligible men, planned the dates, chose the orchestra, and picked the caterer. Loads of government people brought their daughters to Washington for the season, and there were brunches, luncheons, teas and tea dances, as well as huge subscription balls and cotillions, and private parties. Rich parents tried to one-up each other on the novelty and expense of the parties, and the official hostesses reaped rich rewards.

The lists of men were strictly graded by cost: the most expensive listed the bachelor diplomats, the rising young politicians, a few of the cave dwellers (slang for native Washingtonians) and, usually, the young service officers, plus a few enterprising fortune hunters who paid the hostesses to include their names. The young men listed were assumed to all own their own tuxedos.

Ma had no doubts at all about her daughter's debut. This was a party in which you introduced your daughter to your personal friends, their children, and such young people you knew as friends or potential friends from similar backgrounds. A debut, in Ma's eyes, was not about putting your daughter on the auction block.

Several months before Bee's debut, one of the official hostesses called Ma and said that she understood that Ma was planning a ball. She knew Ma slightly, socially, and asked her what hostess she was employing. Ma said she was handling the party herself. The would-be dictator of Washington's social life told Ma in no uncertain terms that this was an impossibility; that it would not only set a bad precedent but also ensure a bad party because Ma had not checked out the dates, the orchestra, or the caterer with the bureau. Ma said that she hoped it would not upset them all too much, as she had planned on doing it her way, at which the hostess snarled that she and the other hostesses would get together and schedule several grand balls on the night of Bee's party so that no one would come.

Ma went ahead with her plans and, of course, it was the party of the year. She invited her old friends. Secretary of State and Mrs. Stimson came, as did General Pershing, and loads of historic personages and legends who would never have bothered with other parties but came because they loved Ma and Georgie. Of course, there were no photographers, but at least one of the guests must have been an underground reporter as Bee's party was on the front page of the Society Section the following Sunday.

The next three years I was away from home at Dobbs for nine months of the year and, to my mind, I missed a lot. Poor Aunt Nannie Wilson died in 1931 after a lifetime of frustration. Georgie remarked that he had never realized what a strong face Aunt Nannie had until he saw her on her bier.

Georgie and Ma spent a good deal of every fall and winter fox hunting in Virginia. Ma, who was half-blind—and always had been, but was too proud to wear glasses except for reading—simply got on her horse and followed Georgie wherever he went in the hunting field. She got the reputation of being a bruising rider, although she rarely saw what she was jumping. Georgie got her fine horses: Popcorn, Nutmeg, Memorial, Quicksilver—all handsome and probably the safest mounts in Virginia—and because Ma loved, she was fearless.

~

Several years later, after we got back from Hawaii in 1938, Georgie bought a motor cruiser that he named the *Moku,* the Hawaiian word for boat. He kept it on the Potomac River, and we went cruising on it on fine weekends. Bee and I hated and despised it, as Georgie kept us busy shining brass and holystoning the deck, so we couldn't look like the girls in the advertisements, who lay on the decks of motor cruisers in brief bathing suits with flowing hair. The Potomac is a lovely river for cruising, and with the help of a great book called *Potomac Landings,* we explored a lot of the creeks and inlets where the grand old houses of colonial times lay drowsing and decaying, wrapped in their memories of when the river had been the only access road to their hospitality.

Ma always went ashore and scouted around, and dug up bulbs from the ruined gardens, and transplanted bushes she found there. The garden at Green Meadows is still beautiful with daffodils from Belvoir, Lord Baltimore's Virginia estate.

The nadir of this cruising bug came when Georgie finally decided to take the *Moku* to Massachusetts via the inland waterways. Ma, Bee, George, and I were the crew with occasional friends getting on for a day or an hour. Ma had always been crazy about the water—any water—so she thought it was great fun and was charmed with the locks and drawbridges, but even she had second thoughts when we finally reached Massachusetts Bay and the sea.

Ma was a sailboat woman and Georgie was a sailor. Sails are dependable— you can always think of something to do with them. Motors are not dependable. After a thrill-packed ride up the coast toward the home port of Manchester, the *Moku*'s motor broke down right near Marblehead Light on that rocky and treacherous coast where every rock is named for a maritime disaster. Memory draws a kindly veil over how we got home. We were to visit the Merrills at Avalon. Georgie put the *Moku* up for sale the next day, and, although we didn't know it at the time, he started dreaming larger dreams with bigger sails on them.

The hunting was much more fun than the boating, although Ma had racing sailboats for us for the summers we spent at Green Meadows. We started off in Manchester in a Manchester fifteen-footer, and over the ensuing years graduated to a seventeen-footer, and eventually, to an International. Ma was one helluva sailor. The minute she got at the tiller, she became a different person. Captain Bligh could have taken a lesson! In fact, Georgie refused to crew for her! We crewed for her for years and learned a great deal. After every race we would get out the books and the model sailboats and rerace the race and see what we had done wrong. Ma, having been brought up in Marblehead Harbor and Massachusetts Bay, knew local secrets, such as the fact that when the wind died down, if you sailed close to the islands, the warm rocks would create a draft that might carry you past your opponent; that halfway rock was almost impossible to pass if the tide was coming in and the wind was from a certain direction: all sorts of things that she tried to impart to us. Bee was better at it than I was and, also, she got to handle the main sail, and I was always on the jib sail. But we learned a lot and even represented Manchester Yacht Club in the Women's International Races one year.

That was quite an experience. We were invited to stay in the huge hotel that had been bought by Mrs. Charles Francis Adams's father back in the 1890s to house his growing family in the summer. It was a Gothic building and all the various families had a wing, but ate in the hotel dining room where their own servants, brought down for the summer, fixed their separate meals. Mr. Charlie Adams was secretary of the Navy at that time, but at the Glades he was just another sea-going Yankee in salt-whitened trousers with a little white hat lined with green—which is what everyone wore in those days. Mrs. Adams, a queenly figure with a pompadour and a no-nonsense air about her, went through her personal wing killing flies and urging people to sweep up the sand they had tracked in. No one thought or talked about anything but boats and everyone looked as if they slept underwater and only came up for meals.

The competition was fierce and we did not win, but it wasn't from not trying. Ma loved every minute of it. These were *her* people at their best. The famous Minot Light was just off the rocks there, and it always seemed ironic to me that it flashes 1–4–3 endlessly, which means, of course, I love you, on that harsh and dangerous coast—almost a siren song to the passing ships.

The boat racing filled another purpose in that it kept us apart during the polio season. The minute the first case of polio was published in the local paper, all parties and gatherings of the young ceased—no movies, dances, picnics, or sing-songs from then until after the first couple of frosts. But Ma didn't see how anyone could catch polio sailing a boat, so we sailed and sailed. We actually raced five times a week, some of the races in Manchester and some in Marblehead. Ma stayed with us at Green Meadows all summer, except for a very occasional visit to Washington, and Georgie came up for most weekends on the train. He would arrive Saturday morning early and leave Sunday night after dinner.

About this time in his career, Georgie made what he considered his great sacrifice for his daughters. Ma once told us about it when we were complaining about him and said we must always remember that he had given up his dream of a lifetime because of us. He was told that he had been assigned to the office of Military Attaché to Great Britain. This job would have meant that he would have had a chance to hunt with all the great packs of foxhounds, ride in the International Horse Shows, and play polo with all the greats: it was the Premier Horse World, about which he had read and dreamed all of his adult life.

After due thought, he requested that he not be given the assignment. Ma was amazed. She would have adored to live in London, or the country, in the Europe she knew so well, for a few years, but Georgie told her this: "We have two marriageable daughters who aren't bad looking and will be rich someday. If we got to London it stands to reason that one or both of them will marry an Englishman. Englishmen, well-bred Englishmen, are the most attractive bastards in the world, and they always need all the money they can lay their hands on to keep up the castle, or the grouse moor, or the stud farm, or whatever it is they have inherited. I served with the British in the war, and I heard their talk. They are men's men, and they are totally inconsiderate of their wives and daughters; everything goes to their sons, nothing to the girls. I just can't see Little Bee or Ruth Ellen in that role. Someday, just tell them what I did for them and maybe they won't think I'm such an old bastard after all."

It was during this time that I particularly remember another incident with Georgie—maybe it was soon after he had made his great sacrifice. Bee and I were in the third floor in our rooms and Ma came upstairs, very distressed, and said that Georgie was lying in the hammock on the porch and was feeling very low and depressed because he said that we didn't love him, that we never talked to him or told him what we were thinking. She said that one or both of us had to go down to the porch right then and there and talk to our father nicely.

Bee and I were appalled. I said that I couldn't think of anything to talk to him about and she said that she couldn't either, so finally we drew lots and I lost.

I went down onto the porch and I can see it now. He was lying in the hammock, looking out over the green meadow that lay between the house and the pond, and the sun was making a very dramatic setting. He looked as if he had been crying—we all cried very easily so that was no surprise. I said "Hello," and he said "Hello," but he didn't look at me—just kept on looking at the sunset. In desperation I suggested that I hadn't heard him recite any Kipling lately and there was one about—

I dreamed to wait my pleasure, unchanged my spring would bide,
Therefore to wait my pleasure, I put my spring aside.

This galvanized him somewhat, as it was one of his favorites that he often quoted when he wanted to do something and didn't want to put it off. It's one of Kipling's best poems, "The Song of Diego Valdez," and very dramatic.

He got so involved that he started reciting it: he was still going strong at the cocktail time, at which that time Ma and Bee and George had all come down to listen—Georgie really did recite poetry better than any actor I have ever heard. At dinner he said to Ma that he and I had had a very interesting conversation and that I knew a lot more than he had thought I did.

Georgie, Master of Fox Hounds, Cobbler Hunt, Virginia, 1934.

Arcturus, 1936.

Bee aboard the *Arcturus*, 1935.

Bee's Star Boat the *Abba Dabba*.

Louise Ayer—Ellie's "Rose Friend."

Quarters 92A, Fort Sheridan, Illinois, 1911.

Ceiling at Villa Guardabassi. Foreground, left to right: the Yankee secretary (with baba-in-arms), Junio, Diddah, Mario, Frederico.

Bee on Popcorn, National Horse Show, 1930.

Beatrice Ayer Patton (Little Bea) at her debut, Avalon, 1929.

Lieutenant Colonel and Mrs. John K. Waters (Little Bea), Green Meadows, 1934.

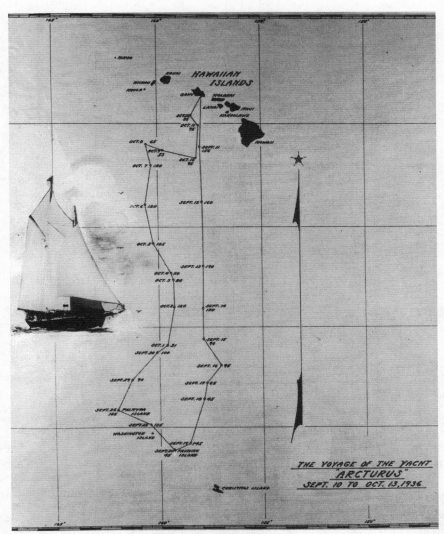

Voyage of the *Arcturus*, 1936.

Cobbler Hunt, 1934.

The Pattons, Hawaii, 1927. Left to right: Ana, Ruth Ellen,
Bee, George, Alice Holmes, Goto, Georgie.

Bee, 1930.

Riding trophies, 1930. Left to right: George, Ruth Ellen, Bee, Little Bea.

Family Class, Myopia Horse Show, 1935. Left to right:
George, Ruth Ellen, Little Bea, Bee, Georgie.

Mario Guardabassi.

Christmas 1939, Fort Myer, Virginia. Left to right:
Georgie, Ajax, Briseis, Bee, Bea Waters (Little Bea), and Butch.

Christmas 1939, Fort Myer, Virginia. Left to right: Ruth Ellen, Butch, Little Bea.

Georgie and Bee, 49er party, Fort Myer, Virginia, 1939.

Bee on the *When and If*, 1950.

James W. Totten.

George S. Patton IV, USMA, 1946.

Ruth Ellen on Quicksilver, 1st Cavalry Division Horse Show, Fort Bliss, Texas, 1938.

Bee on Quicksilver, 1st Cavalry Division Horse Show, Fort Bliss, 1938.
Quicksilver campaigned well into the 1950s and taught another generation
of Pattons to ride before he died. He is buried at Green Meadows.

Kent, Ruth Ellen's friend and adviser, 1938.

Georgie on Konohiki, Fort Clark, 1938.

On board the *Arcturus,* Hawaii, 1937. Bee, Ruth Ellen, Joe Eckeland.

Kalili, 1936.

Rosemary Merrill and Fletcher Cole at the Gone With the Wind Party, Fort Myer, 1940. This is the uniform that scared the sentinel at Arlington Cemetery, when Fletcher Cole, the officer of the day, went to check the guard on the way to the party.

George Meeks and Butch, Fort Myer, 1940.

With Cousin Mario's
affectionate wishes for great happiness
July 6 – 1940

Mario's portrait of Ruth Ellen painted while
she was recovering from a broken leg, 1937.

Ruth Ellen and Jimmie Totten at the Gone With the Wind party.
They hadn't announced their engagement.

Bee with grandson, James Patton Totten, Panama, 1949.

The Tottens, 1952. Left to right: Jamie, Mike, Ruth Ellen, Jimmie, Bea.

Ruth Ellen, June 1941, Ellie's wedding dress.

Chapter 11
"The Debutante Racket"

During the years between the two tours in Hawaii lots of exciting things happened, and one of them was the marriage of Ma's niece, Rosalind Wood, daughter of Ma's oldest half-sister. Rosalind was very bright, very scatty, and had been engaged to somebody or other for years, but this time the engagement took. The groom's name was Francesco Maria Guardabassi. Rosalind, known to the family as Diddah, met him in New York where he was part owner of a very chic restaurant. Mario was a huge man, a real presence, and not typical of a restaurateur. He came from a very old family of Perugia, an enchanting town near Assisi, and had been in his time a student priest, an opera singer, an officer in the Italian Army, and a portrait painter. Rosalind, who was about forty at the time of her marriage, did not make any announcements or bring Mario home to be looked over. She simply announced that she was getting married. Aunt Ellen rallied to her daughter and summoned all the family to the rites. The two older brothers, Uncle Jamie and Uncle Chilly, were very dubious. Jamie said to Chilly before the wedding, "I'm glad that the Governor won't know his oldest grandchild is marrying an Italian adventurer." Chilly solemnly agreed. After the wedding and attendant festivities, Chilly said to Jamie, "If that young niece of ours does anything to annoy that fine Italian gentleman who has given her his hand in marriage, she will most certainly hear about it from me." And Uncle Jamie agreed.

Mario was one of the most delightful persons who ever joined the family. He swept into the Ayer clan like a breeze from the Mediterranean; swept his fragile little mother-in-law off her feet, and charmed the ladies and delighted the men. At the wedding reception, when he met Ma and Aunty Kay for the first time, he turned to his bride and cried, "Darleeng, do you have any more little old aunties?"

He was some fifteen years older than either of them, but always called them his tzietas, which he said meant little old auntie. He never lost his zest for life: he was music personified. Galli-Curci, Rosa Ponselle, Heifetz, and a score of others came to the wedding and sang off and on during the reception. At one point Mario left Rosalind's side and they all sang the sextette from *Lucia*. Mario was slightly off key, but it didn't bother anyone, especially Mario. He had partially lost his hearing when he was in the Italian Army in the Great War.

His story was that he had stopped a rout of Italian soldiers by standing on a narrow bridge and hitting them on the head with his frying pan as they tried to run away. He was highly decorated, for this or some other derring-do. After the war, he had to give up opera, so he became a portrait painter, painting all the fashionable beauties in Rome—also making love to them—he said it made them more paintable. He was loaded with talent. His lady portraits were very attractive, but his later portraits of his two sons and of his mother-in-law, and several of the older ladies of the family, had an amazing delicacy and tenderness that Mario always found in the very old and the very young.

Mario thoroughly enjoyed spending money and had marvelous taste. They ended up with a superb villa in Perugia, built around a medieval watchtower, called "Torre de Pila." Upon this dream place Mario lavished his artistic talents and his native shrewdness. Rosalind was always jealous of Mario because no matter what she did, she could never possess him completely—no one could or had or did. Ma really loved Mario and understood him; she asked him to paint my portrait, for which she would pay him in cash. I had had a bad horse accident that summer and was in a cast from the hip to the ankle of my right leg, so posing was no problem. Rosalind had forbidden him to paint any portraits of younger ladies for fear of dalliance, but I was fat and homely in my teens, and no menace. Mario was to be driven over every day to Green Meadows by one of Rosalind's trusted hirelings and returned intact. Sometimes he stayed for lunch, especially if Georgie was there.

Mario and Ma and I had a perfectly wonderful time during that portrait. I got glimpses of a life I had never dreamed of—a world that had passed by with the war—filled with glamorous opera stars, their temper-tantrums, their clothes, their oddities, their lives and loves (expurgated for my tender ears). Mario hummed and sang when he was painting and Ma would often join in. She was an opera buff, and knew the scores of dozens of operas by heart.

One day Mario arrived weeping lima-bean-sized tears. He always wore his smock and a large beret when he was painting, but this day his costume had lost its jaunty look. He was disconsolate. Ma asked him what was wrong and he burst into lamentations. "Ah, Tzieta, you do not know what a burden my life has become! I had to fight with darling Diddah this morning, and she has flushed all her priceless jewels into the water closet, including my sainted mother's engagement ring, a beautiful turquoise surrounded by diamonds—a family heirloom . . ."

Ma knew Rosalind well, and told Mario to wait a minute and compose himself: she would be right back. In a short time Ma returned, beaming, "I just reached Diddah's secretary on the telephone and everything is in order. Diddah has the plumber locked into the bathroom. She has a list of every piece of jewelry she flushed down the toilet, and is holding a gun on him. She has told him that if he doesn't produce every single item from the trap, she will shoot him through the door." Predictably, everything turned up and all was well.

In 1932, Georgie was given command of a unit at Fort Myer, and we moved from White Oaks to a house in Rosslyn, Virginia, just outside the gate of the post. We rented the house from a wonderful woman named Bessie Christian. The thing I most admired about that house was the all-black bathroom: that seemed to me the ultimate in sophistication (but it was almost impossible to clean).

It was during this time that the World War I soldiers made the Bonus March on Washington, and Georgie led the troops against them when the march turned into a riot. We were in Massachusetts when it happened, but it was terribly upsetting to both Georgie and Ma, and to all the regular servicemen who had to discipline the Bonus Marchers, once their comrades in battle. The worst part of it for Georgie was that Joe Angelo, the man who had saved his life in the first war, was among the marchers. Somehow or other, Joe ended up in Walter Reed Hospital, and we were taken to see him. He was a sad little man—all eyes—and we wondered how he could have dragged Georgie into the shell hole and saved him.

To pass the time in Rosslyn, Georgie built a boat in the garage. He called it the *Menehune,* for the Hawaiian fairy-people—the tribe that would undertake any job they could complete in a single night. It was not an appropriate name, as it took more than a year to build the boat, and it was never much good. But Georgie loved it—he did it all from a plan he had bought—and Ma helped him build it. She could not drive a nail straight, but she fetched and carried and sat on boards to keep them from moving, and they had a lot of fun. Georgie could do anything with his hands; he had a delicate touch with tools, as well as with horses.

While he had been in the office of the chief of Cavalry, when we lived at White Oaks, he had made a most interesting friend, a Colonel Latrobe. Colonel

Latrobe had been Calvin Coolidge's military aide, but other than that, I don't know what he did, except he had a fascinating fund of true stories and a Cuban wife who was a legend in her own time. Colonel Latrobe looked just like a gunfighter in an early western movie. He had a long mustache, light blue killer's eyes, and a soft, pleasing southern voice. There is no accent on earth more appealing than that of a well-bred southerner. He was very courtly and very silent around Ma, but Georgie would come home with wild tales the colonel told him. He had been fighting in Cuba with Teddy Roosevelt's men when he saw the fiery Maria, later to become Mrs. Latrobe. As she was a well-bred Spanish lady, he never got to speak to her, but he saw her in church and somehow it came about—I don't think the details were ever revealed—that she decided to elope with Colonel Latrobe.

In order to get her, he had to hitch his Cavalry charger to the iron bars of her window, rip the whole thing off the wall, and flee into the night to the waiting priest with her wrathful family in pursuit. When we knew Maria, she was of a certain age, but her eyes were black and flashing. She had beautiful tapered hands, and came to dinner parties dressed in a Spanish shawl that was somehow secured so as to leave one shoulder bare, and looked as if the slightest breath would dislodge it still further. She had her eye on my sister for one of her sons, and would pinch Bee's chin between her scarlet-tipped fingers, remarking that a certain tonic she knew, made with lemon juice and some kind of acid, could remove Bee's freckles permanently. Bee was scared to death of her, and so was Colonel Latrobe. He never left the office without first calling home to tell her where he was going. Georgie said the voice he used to Maria was not the official voice he used while issuing orders.

His military life was only referred to in snatches. He turned to Georgie one day and murmured, "Jawge, have you evah looted a town?" When Georgie replied that he hadn't yet had that opportunity, he noted, "Jawge, you would ENJOY looting a town." He had another story about his father, who had been an officer in the Confederate Army. The story went on and on about how his father had been riding along and a likely young fellow had come up and ridden along beside him for awhile, and they had had some elegant conversation, and then his father had pulled his pistol and shot that likely young fellow dead— right between the eyes. When Georgie asked why, Colonel Latrobe said, "Well, you see, my papa had been studying on this likely young fellow and he felt surely there was something wrong and, sure enough, he finally noticed that this young fellow had a Yankee bridle on his horse, and the US was right-side up, and when any of us captured a Yankee bridle we always turned the US upside-down, so my papa decided that this young fellow was a Yankee spy and, do you know, when he went through that likely young fellow's pockets, he found out that that was just what he was!"

Another story about Colonel Latrobe's papa we loved was about how, after the Civil War, the old gentleman went back into the hills to look up some farmer that had rescued him while he was wounded and nursed him back to health while hidden in the loft of his barn. Old Mr. Latrobe found the place all right, but when he asked for his benefactor, one of the children told him, "He's daid. Some officer fella come along during the war and taught grandpa to drink greens with his licker, and it kilt him; and the whole family been lookin' for that feller every since."

Old Mr. Latrobe withdrew without giving his name. He had introduced his farmer friend to the delights of the mint julep while he was convalescing.

Colonel Latrobe died hard—it may have been cancer—but I don't think I was ever told. However, Georgie told Ma that the colonel sought solace from his pain in drink, and that Maria was against it, and so she had fixed a series of mirrors throughout their apartment so that she could keep an eye on him in every room, and see that he was not drinking. When he finally got so sick he had to go to Walter Reed, he asked his boys to smuggle in his pistol so that he could kill himself. I think they were quite willing, but Maria didn't believe in that either, so she stood guard over their visits until he died.

It was in the house in Rosslyn that Bee did her final courting. Johnnie Waters had graduated from West Point in 1931. The depression had taken its toll of all, and John's father had been one of the losers, but Mr. Waters was not a quitter. He sold his beautiful place, Fairlea, went back to work in a smaller office, and his three sons pitched in to help him pay off his investors. The eldest son, who was getting an advanced degree in college, took a job as night watchman in the Carroll mansion in Baltimore. Johnnie taught fencing at a girls' school and played semi-pro hockey in Baltimore; he had been the goalie on the West Point team. The youngest son, still an undergraduate, took a job in a dairy. Johnnie didn't feel that he was in a position to ask for Bee's hand in marriage at this point, although he knew she loved him—and so did all the family.

Bee, who had thought that Johnnie would propose to her the minute he graduated from West Point, was upset by the delay. She was a real belle, and went to parties constantly, broke hearts right and left, and cried herself to sleep every night.

Finally, Johnnie felt that he could honorably propose, and he did so. I was at home on vacation when this glorious occasion took place, packing to go back to school and stagnation. Ma was in my room, helping me pack when Bee came in and said, "I'm going to marry Johnnie Waters!" To our complete amazement, Ma burst into tears, jumped up, slapped Bee's face, crying, "You can't! You're much too young!" and rushed out of the room, slamming the door.

Bee ran weeping to her room, Ma ran weeping to find Georgie, and I sat weeping on my suitcase. I suppose that Ma had never really realized that she was old enough to have a marriageable daughter! Georgie had exhorted her for so many years to stay young with him, and to never grow old—and then, suddenly—

The rest of the year went like lightning. Bee was getting married; I was graduating from Dobbs; and there was not enough time. Graduation was eminently forgettable. There were much more exciting things to look forward to. I was very touched because Georgie came with Ma to my graduation. He caused quite a flutter in the hen coop. I suppose it is difficult for a child to think of a parent as sexually attractive, and it was disgusting to me when my friends all said how thrilling Georgie was, how handsome, etc., etc., etc. I was proud, but embarrassed.

We thought we knew him so well. We knew when he was showing off in front of company and when he was really doing his stuff, which was great. To hear him recite "The Ballad of the Fleet"—

Sink me the ship, Master Gunner! Sink her, split her in twain!

Fall into the hands of God, not into the hands of Spain!

—was a spine-tingling experience. He put us right there on the deck of the *Little Revenge,* salt-soaked and gun-powdered to the eyes. And we could feel the loathing of Obadiah-Bind-their-kings-in-chains-and-their-nobles-in-links-of-iron, the Sergeant in Ireton's regiment as he declaimed at the Battle of Naseby in 1645:

> Oh, evil was the root, and bitter was the fruit
> And crimson was the juice of the vintage that we trod,
> For we trampled on the throne of the haughty and the strong
> Who sate in the high places and slew the saints of God
> It was about the noon of a glorious day of June
> That we saw their banners dance and their cutlasses shine
> And the Man of Blood was there, with his long perfumed hair
> And Astley, and Sir Marmaduke, and Rupert of the Rhine!

Actually, I am sure that Georgie's sympathies were with the Cavaliers and not with Cromwell's Roundheads, as many of his sacred ancestors had been Jacobites, but he could give equal time to both sides, and did.

But my school friends acting up to Georgie startled me, and at that point in my life, Ma embarrassed me. She was so enthusiastic and uninhibited about anything to do with the theatre and its by-products. She was not what I considered sophisticated, as were the mothers of my friends. The other mothers had long polished nails, and had their hair done every week, and talked about the same things. Ma had short nails—she played the piano—and her hair, which was long, she washed herself. She was capable of talking trivia, but it was an act with her. She liked interesting conversations and could keep up her end with anyone. She was different; there was no doubt about that. She was also a great lady. There was no doubt about that either.

Ma had a lot of what she called maxims. She gave us each a little book at one time, called *The Maxims of the Duc de la Rochefoucauld.* They were full of things like "He who laughs last, laughs best," and rather ordinary thoughts, but we were fascinated because she said the duc had written this book while he was waiting for the duchesse to finish dressing. Ma's maxims were much more applicable to the times. Some she got from Ellie and some, I am sure, she got the hard way, but they are unforgettable. She observed: "When in doubt about what to do, the kind thing is usually the right thing." She quoted Lord Chesterfield in saying, "A gentleman is one who never hurts anyone's feelings by mistake." Also, "A lady is a woman who behaves like a gentleman." Ma's puritan ethic underlay a lot of her maxims: make it last, wear it out, use it up, do without. She adored dressing up, especially for fancy dress parties, and deplored the ladies who came to such parties dressed as maids: "Dress like a servant, and you'll end up acting like one." Ma always wore becoming clothes, and she kept them for years whether they were in style or not: "If you feel pretty, you'll look pretty." She went to all kinds of trouble to make costumes, or to have them made, for our school plays, and she insisted on authenticity even when it was uncomfortable. If we dressed as gypsies, we had to have dirty feet and dirty faces.

One of Ma's many talents was palmistry. She would always have a booth at church fairs, or carnivals, to make money for Army Relief. She would get so dressed up that her friends actually wouldn't recognize her, and she was a frighteningly good fortune teller. She had studied it for years, and she said there were many ways of doing it: you could be honest and do a technically correct job or, when you wanted to make money, you could watch the subject's face, especially the eyes, and ask leading questions that your subject would answer automatically. She taught Bee and me to read palms. She said it was an invaluable way to break the ice at parties. We were warned about the murderer's thumb, the suicide line, and to watch for the boys whose palms had a big soft mound of Venus. At fairs she would dress me up as a gypsy brat and have me circulate, selling tickets. I was not to tell my name, and I could rattle a tambourine. I would sell tickets for Ma's booth and then listen to the people who came to mock and remained to pray. It was a real education. It stood me well all my life.

To get back to Ma's individual way of dressing—about once a year Kay Merrill would make a ceremonial visit to Ma's closet and go through her clothes, asking, "How long is it since you wore that, Bee?" If it had not been worn for over year, Aunty Kay would firmly remove it for giving away, although I saw Ma put up some pretty stirring battles for some of her evening gowns and tea gowns. Aunty Kay was always perfectly dressed to the smallest detail. Ma had lovely clothes, but she didn't really care about them unless they were for an occasion. She always dressed for dinner in a long gown, and Georgie always wore a tux with a soft collar, and my sister Bee and I also dressed in long dresses. Dinner was the time we sat at ease and had light and elegant conversation, and Ma felt that we should dress for it.

Clothes were not really Ma's subject, but I have one more story I love to tell on her. During World War II, all the men had gone to the war or to the defense plants, and most of the able women joined them. My sister was living in Hamilton with two small boys under five years old, young George was at West Point, and I was living with Ma with two children under two years old. There were some aged relics still cooking and serving in the house, but no men in the garden. So Ma worked in the garden as if her life and sanity depended on it, and perhaps it did, as we were not at all sure we were going to win that war. One day one of Ma's marginal friends who always seemed to have meat on the table and gasoline in the car remarked how beautiful the garden at Green Meadows was looking and how lucky Ma was to have help. Ma asked her what she meant by help and the lady replied, "Oh, every time I drive by Green Meadows I see a little old man in blue overalls and a red bandanna weeding away there. How do you manage to keep him?" Ma, with never a twinkle, said, "He's a friend of mine. I have known him all my life and, although he would really like to, he's too old to go into the service." Of course, the little old man was Ma in her gardening costume—she referred to it as her petit costume du mal.

But the war was still just a shadow on the mind in 1934, and I am reminded of two dear friends of Ma's and Georgie's who also loved to dress up. One of them was the divine Mario Guardabassi, Rosalind's long-suffering husband. Whenever you saw him, you knew by his costume what role he was playing that day. When he was painting, he wore a paint-stained smock and a beret; when he was feeling operatic, he wore a shirt with an open collar and a bright scarf; when he was superintending his estate in Italy, or bird shooting there, he wore gaiters, a coat of poison-green tweed, and a little German hat with a badger tail in the band; when he was the bon vivant and raconteur, he wore a vast overcoat lined with sable, and a derby hat, over some other appropriate costume.

The other dear friend did not have the scope that Mario did, but he had the imagination! This friend was De Russy Hoyle, only son of Ma's Mrs. Hoyle, and an Army officer like his father. When he was a bachelor, he once went to a fancy dress hop dressed as a gardener and sprinkled all the wall flowers with a little green watering can. Another time, at a post hop, a little old lady in deep mourning with a cross face sat in the ladies' room all evening. She was so grumpy that no one talked to her; they just assumed that she was not having a good time and had come into the ladies' room to brood about it. Actually, the old lady was horrid De Russy in one of his sisters' dresses, and everyone on the post steered clear of him for months, wondering just what he had heard as the ladies exchanged combs and confidences.

De Russy was also notable for answering the cable that informed him of the arrival of twins with a laconic, "Quit your kidding."

But his greatest coup happened after his father died. Mrs. Hoyle, all three hundred pounds of her, was inconsolable and took to what everyone thought was her final bed. She kept the shades drawn, and the windows closed, and re-fused to see anyone but her daughters. A few days after the funeral, a lady in deepest mourning came to the door and demanded to see Mrs. Hoyle in a voice shaking with emotion. The lady's face was veiled and her hand shook as she reached her hanky up under it to wipe her presumably streaming eyes. She made such a point of seeing Mrs. Hoyle that the daughter on duty braved the closed door and told her Mama that she simply HAD to see this person. Mrs. Hoyle tottered out, and was at once overwhelmed by a torrent of heart-broken reminiscences and family intimacies so secret that Mrs. Hoyle rose from the torpor of grief to alertness and, finally, went into a blasting rage. SO! General Hoyle had been keeping another woman all those years! As she rose to her full height of about five feet to blast this breaker of widows' hearts and stealers of husbands' loves, the nameless hussy threw back her veil, and it was De Russy. He said he had just come around to see if he could take Mama out of her self. Mrs. Hoyle decided not to go back to bed again, and so rejoined the human race.

Ma's last meeting with her idol was at a tea at the Chevy Chase Club outside Washington. Ma was pouring tea (Georgie was only a major and coffee ranks tea when you invite the ladies to pour), and Mrs. Hoyle tituped up behind her, not a pound lighter, nor a twinkle less. Ma asked her how she would have her tea, and Mrs. Hoyle in her glorious contralto replied, "Sugar and cream, my dear, until the end."

In March of 1934, George was finally promoted to lieutenant colonel after fourteen years as a major. I finally graduated from school, and we went to Green Meadows to prepare for Bee's wedding. She was to be married in the church where Ma and Georgie had been married, twenty-four years before. Their wedding had been the first military wedding on the North Shore since the Civil War, and Bee's and Johnnie's was the second. This suggests the way the North Shore viewed the Regular Army.

The wedding was on June 27, and, as they had at Ma's wedding, the choir marched down the aisle ahead of the bridal party, singing the wedding march from "Lohengrin." I will never forget Georgie's face as he led Bee down the aisle to Johnnie. He looked just like a child who is having his favorite toy taken away. All his determination to remain forever young was being undermined by having a daughter getting married. He was forty-eight years old, and he still had not won a war or kept his part of his bargain with Granfer Ayer about winning the glory. He looked stricken to the heart.

I was too young and too interested in the beating of my own heart to realize this, but Ma did. Perhaps that was why she had slapped Bee's face: Bee was finally taking Georgie's youth away from him.

The summer that followed was fun but not the same. Our triumphant racing triumvirate was broken up by marriage and, although Ma and I tried to race, it wasn't as much fun. We had both been dependent on Bee.

Autumn took us back to Rosslyn, the Cobbler Hunt, and my debut. Before we left Massachusetts my aunt by marriage, and godmother, Hilda Ayer, had wanted to give a ball for me in Boston, but we talked her out of that and so instead she gave me a fabulous Forty-Niner Party that was the talk of the town. Everyone came in suitable costume. There was a slot machine and a nude over the bar. No one on the North Shore had ever done anything like that for a debut, and it was great.

I went to several balls in New York with a favorite cousin, Martha Proctor, who was also making her debut. They were a terrible strain as neither Martha nor I knew any of the boys. She was all right because she was related to most of the raisins in the upper crust of New York Society, but I was a country cousin and, what is more, my father was one of the brutal and licentious mercenary group, and no one had ever heard of the Pattons.

I fell back on Ma's maxims: If the boys and the girls are standing in separate groups, it's usually because the boys are shy. Leave the girls and go and stand with the boys, and when the other boys see you are surrounded, they will want to know why. Be different; ask a boy what his interests are and then LISTEN as if your life depended on it; make him feel interesting and important. Don't smoke or drink just because the other girls are doing it; read a few palms, that will break the ice. Above all, make your partner comfortable; make him feel good even if you have to bend your knees a little; look UP at him. Don't fuss with your hair or face; when you leave the mirror in the powder room, forget it. I put all Ma's maxims to work at once and then added my own idea of developing a southern accent. It all worked like a charm. I got danced with. I didn't get stuck, but, oh, what a lot of work it was!

That fall I hunted at least twice a week with the Cobbler Hunt, of which Ma and Georgie were co-masters. In addition to that, we were planning my debut. It was to be at the Sulgrave Club, just off Dupont Circle, the same place where Ma, years before, had decked Georgie's armchair colonel. This had been the town house of the Wadsworths, a family legendary for horses and oddballs, but it was more like a grand residence than a club. The reigning hostess-for-hire called Ma and gave her the same threats she had given her when Bee made her debut. This time Ma was prepared and said, coolly, "That will be perfectly all right; I doubt very much that the same people would care to go to both parties as we will be having our own friends."

My ball is still a glowing memory. Bee came all the way back from Fort Riley, Kansas, for the party. Her dress was a form-fitting gold tissue mermaid sheath with a split train. Johnnie Waters could not get away, but he sent me a dozen American Beauty roses with three-foot stems. There were so many flowers sent that there had to be a table beside the receiving line for the extra bouquets and corsages. My dress was white taffeta, shot with rosy metallic thread that looked like city windows reflecting the sunset, and I carried an old-fashioned bouquet with a lace frill around it, and a rose in the center, set off by sweet peas and forget-me-nots. I don't remember what Ma wore, but I do remember that she had the time of her life—she just loved parties. Georgie wore his dress blues, and all the pretty girls and their mothers came and made a fuss over him and he loved that.

The members of the Cobbler Hunt came in their pink coats and black shoes and canary-colored waistcoats. One of the huntsmen, James Gibson, had never been to a ball before, and he was on cloud nine. The waiters kept filling his glass with champagne, which he called Heaven's ginger ale. Of all the balls I went to that winter, I really think mine was the most lovely. It was a gathering of friends and comrades, and everyone looked well and acted like ladies and gentlemen. Unlike other balls, we all knew our guests and they knew us.

Ma made one hard and fast rule: I could not go to a ball and then go fox hunting the next day; it was physically impossible. We had to get up at about 4 a.m. to get to Cobbler Country to start the hunt. I usually did not get in before 3 a.m. My dates were not allowed to drive me home, so I had to call poor Reggie Maidment to come and get me or, usually, I had a prearranged time with Reggie to be there, but Ma was adamant about enough sleep and the right food. She said that most debs looked all washed out and ready for the rest home by the end of their season, and she would have none of that.

As the winter went on, I went to fewer and fewer balls and went hunting more and more often. I am sure this was a relief to Ma. It certainly was a lot more fun for me.

General Henry, the chief of Cavalry, had given Georgie official permission to be the Master of Foxhounds for the Cobbler Hunt and to count it as time on duty, on condition that he mount at least two Cavalry or Artillery officers for each hunt so as to give them cross-country riding experience for the next war. This gave me plenty of beautiful young men to flirt with and, of course, there were some very attractive landholders hunting with us also.

At this point Georgie owned twelve horses who boarded at Cobbler with the huntsman, Tom. Ma usually rode Quicksilver or Memorial, and Georgie had Ho'okupuu, the huge Hawaiian thoroughbred that Ma had given him. Ho'o-kupuu, in Hawaiian, means a present to the chief, but he was generally referred to as that damned Hook. The great chestnut was always ready to roll, and if things took too long getting started, he would walk around on his hind legs like a curious horse looking terribly dangerous. Georgie won the Hunter Trials over the Maryland Gold Cup course on Hook, which proves what a goer he was. I rode different horses, depending on the needs of our guests. We had no bad horses; some of them were just more fun than others.

The Hunt breakfasts, which were any meal you had after hunting, were generally impromptu affairs at the homes of the landowners, and were simply glorious. There was always a Virginia ham in various stages of use, hot bread, homemade preserves, farm eggs any style, corn pone; maybe everything tasted so good because we were all so hungry, but it seemed to me that in those lovely falling-down Colonial houses we ate the food of the gods of field and woods.

The houses were fabulous and, as I said, falling down. Antiques were not kept in museum shape—they were used and battered and patched—and everything had that good old smell of ancient leather, cats, closed rooms, food that had been eaten a hundred years ago, wood fires, horse smells, saddle oil, gun oil, kerosene, boot polish, and boxwood hedges. Nothing was new and nobody cared. William Alexander Carruthers said it for all of them—that generous, fox-hunting, wine drinking, dueling and reckless race of men which gives so distinct a character to Virginians wherever they may be found.

Even Ma, who always kept a trace of her Yankee hard shell, felt it and loved them.

Two of the local landholders that we particularly liked were Mr. and Mrs. Gaddis. Mrs. Gaddis was the daughter of a wealthy middle-westerner, and she was an enthusiastic horse lover. Her father sent her to Virginia to buy herself the horse of her choice, and she got not only the horses but the horse dealer as well. They lived in a hand-to-mouth and happy situation for years with a number of charming children in a delightful decaying mansion—lots of land and no cash. They trained and sold hunters, and had a hard and joyous life. Fate finally caught up with them, and the fascinating husband was killed in a horse accident. Mrs. Gaddis buried him between the in-and-out of a double jump, so that he could hear the galloping over his head. She coped alone for some years, and then Mr. Gaddis, who had always known and loved her, came from the Middle West and married her and raised her children. He was a darling man.

One day out hunting, Mrs. Gaddis's horse veered to the right over a split-rail fence and caught her a terrible crack on the head from an overhanging branch, pulling her off her sidesaddle onto the frozen ground. As she passed out, she said something about not stopping the hunt. We all waited until a car came to pick her up and take her to the hospital, and then went on hunting, although our hearts were not in it.

Georgie had cast the hounds around for an hour or so when, coming back by the fence where Mrs. Gaddis had taken her fall, the hounds took up the scent of a fox and were off and away on one of the best runs we ever had in Cobbler Country. The fox went to earth just at sunset.

On the long hack back to the stables, Georgie was very silent. When we reached the stable, he went right to the telephone and called the hospital. When he came out of the room, he was sweating hard. Ma asked him what was wrong, and he told her that he simply could not believe that Mrs. Gaddis was still alive. He had been sure that she was dead, and that when the hounds picked up her scent near the jump, he thought it was Mrs. Gaddis's ghost come back to give us that fabulous run, because all during the run he had never once seen the fox.

Ma told her about this after she got well, and Mrs. Gaddis was very pleased. She said that if she had been killed, that was just what she would have done— she would have given them that great run to remember her by.

In the spring Georgie and Ma gave a great barbecue for all the Cobbler people. Georgie brought the troops from Fort Myer and they had a real pit barbecue with a whole steer and two sheep. The Cobbler Hunt put on a tournament for the event, something never to be forgotten. Tournaments were a rapidly disappearing memory of the old days. Three gallows-like erections were put in line, and from each would hang a string with a ring suspended from it. The young bloods—who practiced for months beforehand—would gallop down the line as fast as they could, carrying barless spears at porte and trying to spear as many rings as possible. The winner got to crown the Queen of Love and Beauty. Georgie knew all about this custom, and had me make three crowns, copied from an illustration in the "Costume Book." I made them from artificial flowers—one of white apple blossoms tied with white velvet ribbon, one of pink apple blossoms tied with pink velvet, and one of blue.

All the ladies from doe-eyed teenagers to large fat wives were at the tournament cheering on their champions. Ed Strother won the tournament. He could not crown his sweetheart publicly as she was not his wife but his leman. I think she was a Langhorne. James Gibson, he of the Heaven ginger ale, was second and he crowned me with the pink crown! I am sure it was for political and polite reasons, as I saw a weeping maiden being led away by her mother, acting as one who should have had the crown. But, nevertheless, I have never been so pleased in my life! I still have that crown in our costume trunk.

It was at this barbecue that Georgie's famous bull terrier, Willy, as yet unborn, got his name. Georgie was checking on everything and he saw a little colored boy writhing on the ground under a tree and making loud sounds. Georgie was afraid the youngster had eaten something bad, or had appendicitis, or something had bit him. When he got close enough to hear the sounds, he heard: "L'il Willy Whiffle, you belly full for the first time in yo life—you got a FULL belly—boy, don't it feel good! L'il Willy Whiffle, you is got all the ribs and racks you kin hol' an' that big white man done done that fo you, an' he don' even know yo name, but you name is L'il Willy Whiffle an' you is happy an you is full as a TICK!"

By spring I was sick and tired of the debutante racket. All the girls of my year were getting engaged to the boys at the balls, and it was old hat. I was not allowed to date, except at West Point or Annapolis, although I could go to the movies or to horse shows with a favored few. This was pretty extreme for 1934–1935, but it was the way Ma had been brought up, and it had worked out for her. She also felt that times were so wild compared to her deb days that I needed all the protection and home backing I could get. This had made me different, but in a way, it had been an asset. Of course, there were a few very nice and attractive civilian men in the debutante crowd, and they made pretty good friends, but I had made up my mind at an early age that I wanted to marry into the service, so I didn't pay too much attention to the party beaux.

All winter long the mounted troops at Fort Myer gave exhibition rides every Friday in the riding hall on the old troop horses. These demonstration rides had started off with horse-and-man gymnastics, and had grown to include regular jumping exhibitions with the band playing, and it culminated in the Society Circus, where the Army daughters and the local debutantes were included in acts that were especially tailored to their abilities. This encouraged their parents to buy box seats. The Washington girls simply loved it, and so did the young officers on duty at Fort Myer. For about eight weeks in January and February it was one big party. This was a grand finale for the Patton family, as Georgie had been ordered to duty in Hawaii, and we were, in Sir Richard Francis Burton's immortal words to his wife, Isabel, getting ready to pack, pay, and follow.

Ma was absolutely thrilled with the orders—she had been working on her book about ancient Hawaii all the time we had been gone. Georgie decided that his life was turning into something flat, stale, dull, and unprofitable, so he decided to test his luck again, as he had so many years before on the rifle butts at Fort Sheridan. He kept it in mind that before Napoleon awarded a promotion, he always inquired of the man to be considered, "Is he lucky?" Pasteur had said, "Chance favors the prepared mind," and General Allenby, one of Georgie's heroes that he had met while serving with the British in the First World War, told him a story about himself that reinforced all of Georgie's instincts.

Allenby, a subaltern in the British Army, had requested a shooting leave. He was on duty in India at the time, and his commanding officer decided to kill two birds with one stone, giving Allenby leave with the provision that he go and hunt in a district where there were two well-known ivory poachers at work. Allenby was ordered to capture them, if possible. The three hunters caught up with each other; one of the poachers had a double-barreled shotgun, and the other one had a revolver. They directed both weapons at the young subaltern for final results. The shotgun shells were damp and did not detonate, and the revolver jammed. Allenby captured both men and took them back to the law. He said that he knew at that moment that he was destined for a great military career.

Allenby elaborated on his theory and told Georgie that for every Napoleon, Alexander, and Jesus Christ who made history there were several born. Only the lucky ones made it to the summit. He felt that in every age and time, men were born ready to serve their country and their god, but sometimes were not needed; you had to be at the right place at the right time—you had to be lucky.

So, Georgie, tired of being behind the hump and tired of the inaction of the last fourteen odd years, decided to give his luck a supreme test and buy a schooner to sail to Hawaii. He told Ma that he would rather be dead than be nobody. He drove to Annapolis several nights a week and took a course in celestial navigation. Mathematics had always been his Achilles' heel, so he was a little uncertain about getting from San Diego to Hawaii, but he had made up his mind that he would. The schooner they bought, the *Arcturus,* was shipped by rail from the Potomac River, where he had had it for nearly a year, to San Diego.

Ma said that she would not let Georgie go and drown without her. She was not strong enough to handle the big sails, so she signed on this fantastic voyage as ship's cook. She had never cooked in her life, so she went to visit Bee, in order to learn the art. Bee didn't know very much about cooking, as she had a good maid, but somehow between the three of them, Ma picked up the essentials. She did her cooking standing on a board balanced on the side of a No. 2 can, so that she had to do a balancing act to keep on her feet while cooking; she thought cooking in a ship's galley would require this skill.

With the help of her brother, Fred Ayer, who was a notable cruising man, she wrote out long lists of necessary supplies to buy in California. In May of 1935, Ma and Georgie, Gordon and Anna Prince from South Hamilton, and Francis "Doc" Graves (who was married to Georgie's first cousin, Kash Banning), plus the immortal Joe Ekeland, sailed for Hawaii.

Chapter 12

Hawaii Revisited

Fortunately for everyone, Doc Graves was a gourmet cook, and Joe Ekeland, who had apprenticed as a young boy on a Norwegian square-rigger, could also cook. Ma, who had raced sail boats all her life, found out that, like Admiral Nelson, she was continually seasick. Dramamine had not yet been invented, and so she slept most all of the way to Hawaii.

Georgie made their lives difficult by using the main cabin for his navigation, so they could never cook or clean when they wanted to, but only when he was satisfied that they were headed in the right direction. It was at this point in their lives they started keeping a notebook on a schooner that they hoped some day to build. The notebook was entitled "When and If We Ever Build a Boat."

Georgie made his landfall on the white peak of Mauna Kea within hours of his plan time, and they landed first in Hilo and then came onto Honolulu where they were met by Alice Holmes and young George and me and lots of friends from the former tour—all laden with leis and drinks and invitations—and with a band in the background playing Hawaiian music, and girls in hula skirts dancing on the dock.

Georgie had been assigned to the general staff, so we had quarters at Fort Shafter, just outside of Honolulu, and right across the golf course from the Moanalua Gardens, a part of the old Damon estate that had been turned into a park. None of us played golf, but it gave us lots of lovely open space as the parade ground, surrounded with royal palms, was in front of us.

There is an old saying that goes, "There is the right way, the wrong way, and the Army way." This last bit applied to the quarters at Fort Shafter. These had been built about the time the United States sent permanent troops to Alaska, and, so, the quarters were built on the newest plans of that day—the Alaska plans. This allowed the whole house to be heated from a central furnace that also heated the water. Over the years, various commanding officers and engineers had adjusted the plans and made alterations, but the houses at Fort Shafter never ceased to be out-of-date monstrosities. Downstairs, there was a life-saving porch on two sides of the house that made a narrow outdoor living room. There was a huge front hall that went up two stories, and a small living room, smaller dining room, and tiny pantry, kitchen maids' quarters, and storage room—these last two added at a later date. On the second floor, there were three bedrooms: a big one, a small one, and a tiny one, and two bathrooms. Georgie turned the large attic on the third floor into a commodious bedroom with bathroom for George and Alice. Georgie also had a lavatory built under the front stairs. As I think back, it seems to me that everywhere we went, the family added a bathroom to their quarters. A lot of people should be grateful to us!

Next door, to the right, was the commanding general's quarters. The CG was Major General Hugh A. Drum. His only child, Peaches, was exactly my age, but as she had been a general's daughter since birth, she wasn't a whole lot of fun. Her mother was a saint, and her mother's sister, Miss Shug (short for Sugar) Reaume, was right out of a Deep South novel. It was a strange two-and-a-half-year association.

General Drum was jealous of Georgie, although I don't think he realized it. Georgie had everything—youth, good looks, money, a beautiful wife, a lot of eye and ear appeal, and, hardest of all to bear, important social connections on the Island. General Drum was invited to parties because he was the commanding general; Georgie and Ma were invited because everyone loved them. Mrs. Drum, a wonderful person with a soul of great sensitivity, realized all of this and went out of her way to smooth the paths and round off the corners. Miss Shug was a sublimated tiger mother, and her main interest in life was seeing to it that Little Peach had everything the other girls had and more, as befitted her Daddy's rank. Peaches and I more or less tried to keep out of each other's way, as we were definitely not on the same wavelength. She was very, very bright, and was going to college. I was not very bright, and I was going to have a good time, which I did.

Ma had brought up the subject of going to college when I graduated from Dobbs. She had never been to school herself, except for two short years at Miss Carroll's in Boston, but she saw all the other girls my age going off to college, and she thought it might be nice. I climbed right up the wall when she suggested it. Of course, in my family's book, there was no such thing as a co-ed college for a decent girl; as for me, I had seen all I ever wanted to see of other females for the rest of my life. Ma was not hard to persuade. She really loved her children, and wanted to keep her family together, and her children with her, and she was glad I wasn't yet ready to leave home. Also, I suppose she wanted to keep an eye on me. We were very close, and had much the same hobbies, but my attitude toward boys and the fleshpots was beyond her experience, and she literally didn't know quite what to do with me. In Boston, and more or less in Washington, it was all planned out: you graduated from school, made your debut, and if you were not engaged or married at the end of your season you went to Europe, then you came back and did something useful. Also, you gradually crept onto the shelf if you weren't at least spoken for by the time you were twenty-five. My sister, Bee, had been spoken for, so all she had to do was fill in the time between Foxcroft and her wedding day, but here I was, twenty years old and out on the town.

The first thing Ma said after we got settled was that I had to do something useful. Fortunately, Aunt Kay Merrill's close Dobbs' friend, Laura Judd, had married an enchanting islander, Herbert Dowsett, who was part missionary and part Hawaiian. I had roomed with their daughter, Joan, at Dobbs. Laura Dowsett was an enormous wheel in the Junior League of Honolulu, particularly interested in the occupational therapy department at the Queen's Hospital. So I was taken into the occupational therapy workshop at Queen's and put right to work—one of the luckiest things that ever happened to me. I had no friends in Honolulu except Joan Dowsett, so Ma made me join the Little Theatre Group in Honolulu and that was marvelous. I was a quick study; loved showing off; and had long yellow hair that fell below my waist, blue eyes, and a snub lose. I loved comedy—so I was a built-in ingenue. The first play the group did that season was *The Bishop Misbehaves.* At the end, I had to kiss the hero, and this presented an unusual problem. I didn't want to make a fool of myself, so I finally came right out and asked the director how to do it. I will never forget the stunned look on his face when he asked me to repeat what I had just said: "Mr. Fulmer, I have never kissed a boy and I don't know how. Will you show me?" A slow look of delighted comprehension came into his eyes, and he said: "Miss Patton, that's the best news I've heard since I became director of the Little Theatre Group. There is THE kiss; then there is the STAGE kiss; you have nothing to unlearn, thank God. Come here and I will show you how the movie stars kiss without smearing their makeup."

I did and he did. And I can do it to this day. It comes in very handy.

This particular blank spot in my career came from a secret promise I made to myself when I was about fourteen. When I was twelve, Bee looked me over thoroughly and told me, "R.E., you are never going to be pretty, so you had better learn to be funny." From that day, I had concentrated my efforts on that goal, and then decided I was going to be funny and popular. That's what every girl in that generation wanted above all. Ma had always exhorted us to be different, so I decided, as a real challenge, to see if I could be popular without kissing boys. It went without saying—the evidence was all about us—that if you let boys kiss you, you would be popular, but then, the rumor had it, from kissing you slipped to going all the way, and then you were damaged goods and no one would marry you. Hadn't Ellie told Ma that when you went to Franklin Simons to buy a pair of white gloves, you never bought a soiled pair? And hadn't Georgie said, when backing up Ma's little talks on morality, "What man would want to blow his nose in another man's dirty handkerchief?" Other girls might have mightier ambitions than I did, but the only ambition I ever had, after I outgrew my desire to be a Red Cross nurse, was to get married and have babies, and I wanted to marry the right person and be his first and only true love. There was a verse in a hymn by Rudyard Kipling that we sang at Dobbs that expressed my feelings:

> Teach us to keep ourselves away
> Controlled and cleanly, night and day
> That we may bring, if need arise
> No maimed or worthless sacrifice.

Bee and I both had the same aspiration. I suppose we were considered prudes. In all fairness to the boys, they were not standing in line to kiss me, but that didn't worry me. I had made up my mind that I would not be kissed on the mouth by a boy till I was twenty-one, and I made it! (I wish I had told Ma my feelings on the subject. I think it would have relieved her mind.) I was also quite popular, and against what I considered heavy odds. The family, very intelligently, did not allow us to date a boy until he had had dinner with them, and it was not just every boy one would submit to their eagle gaze.

When we got to Honolulu in '35, I was officially out, so I had more liberty. We had no chauffeur, so I had a car and I was allowed to go places with boys. Of course, there was a deadline for returning from parties. The family had to know where I was going and with whom and, of course, it was out of the question to eat a meal with a boy—that would be compromising. One of the reasons Bee and I were sought after is because we were placed by the family in a position where a boy couldn't spend money on us; even the gifts we could receive were listed. A boy could give you flowers, books, candy, or anything perishable, but a boy could NOT give you clothing, jewelry, or anything like that, although you could accept handkerchiefs. (I will never forget my embarrassment and despair when I was made to return an inexpensive silver and turquoise bracelet the current love of my life sent me for Christmas when I was sixteen.)

Looking back, my social life in Honolulu must have been a great burden to Ma and Georgie, who loved what privacy they could save from a full and demanding social life, official and unofficial. Strange young men were brought into dinner all the time. Ma was better at this than Georgie because she had a gift for drawing people out and making them feel interesting, but Georgie always wanted to talk shop, and talking shop with a terrified lieutenant was not much fun for either of them. He was really awful to the Army officers because he knew what they were supposed to know, and he had thirty-odd years on them. He was much nicer to the naval ensigns and the Air Corps youths, and he used to complain to Ma that all the best types were being grabbed by the Navy and Air Corps. Ma would say, "You like them, Georgie, because you don't know what they are talking about, and you don't keep correcting them." That made him mad.

Another stricture of Ma's was that I was not to have dates with the same man more than two times in one week because, according to Ma, "After awhile, if you see that much of them, you run out of conversation, and then what—?" This was another part of being different, as all my friends went steady with the inevitable result that they either married the man after six months or had a horrendous breaking-up, and then went undated until a bunch of new lieutenants came on the scene.

Although I did not appreciate it at the time, this idea of Ma's was very helpful. The young men realized that I was not trying to get married, and, also, if they could stand the gaff, they got a lot of free meals. This eased their budgets. There was a free post hop on each post every Saturday night. It only cost $1.50 per couple to go dancing at the Alexander Young Hotel where there was a floor show. It was a little more at the Royal Hawaiian, but, of course, it was more glamorous. Another thing that helped was that I did not drink. We had been allowed to drink beer, wine, and, later, cocktails at home from a very tender age. Georgie said that we had better learn to drink at home and take it for granted than to start off in strange company and make fools of ourselves. Ma had been brought up with wine on the table. I don't think either of them ever worried much about us taking to drink, because it was simply a part of life. I didn't drink, partly because I liked being different—for the same reason that I didn't smoke—and, partly, because I wanted to be independent.

I am sure neither Ma nor Georgie guessed how often I had to drive people home from the parties. The fact that I was not allowed to go steady opened up a lot of doors for me, as Ma must have known it would. When the fleet came in, and the ensigns were looking for female company, they could take me out without trespassing on their friend's preserves. My best friend, Miss Anne Magruder, and I got around a lot more than most of our other friends. This is not to say that Miss Anne and I were not always madly in love, because we were. I was in love with some of the nicest and best-looking men that ever lived. But Ma's rules were Ma's rules and there was no way around them. I did have one funny experience initiated by these rules that set her back on her heels a bit.

I occasionally went to parties in town with a nonservice group of nice young people. Most of the young men worked in some capacity on the sugar and pineapple plantations and my childhood friend, Kingi Kimball, usually took me. Everyone except Miss Anne and I belonged to the all-service group, so going out with this group, many of them slightly older, was fun and interesting. They talked about civilian things and had a different slant. One of the girls in this group, the daughter of an Army officer, was a well-known model. She was home on vacation and all the older officers (the old gentlemen, aged twenty-seven or twenty-eight) were mad about her. She was perfectly gorgeous and just as nice as she was beautiful. Her older brother, equally handsome, belonged to this same crowd. One night he, who had never noticed me before, took me aside and said he wanted to talk to me seriously, for my own good. The gist of his conversation was that he had been observing me for some time, and he could not understand where I had gotten the reputation of being so fast—that I really had a shocking reputation! I was appalled. No one knew better than I that I was as pure as driven snow, still waiting for the Robert E. Lee. When I collected my wits, I told him that in all fairness, he should tell me what people were saying about me. He said that it was a well-known fact that Ma and Georgie belonged to the polo and drinking set, the fastest set in Honolulu, and that I went out with a different man nearly every night, which, somehow, indicated that I was a regular Messalina and just as fast as my parents were!

I could not wait to get home that night and tell Ma. It really took her aback— just as it had taken me. I am sure she knew far better than I did just how fast the Honolulu polo group was, but she and Georgie had never settled into its warm and oozy depth. After thinking a minute, she started to laugh and insisted that I repeat the whole conversation to Georgie. It was after midnight, but he was still sitting in his big black leather chair, reading his endless military books, as he did every night. When he heard me out, he started saying, "Well, I'll be goddamned! I *will* be goddamned!" I said that the young man had only been trying to be helpful and set me right, but what should I do now? There was quite a family discussion and, finally, Ma said, "I think that we must consider that, helpful as he was trying to be, he has what your father and I think of as a middle-class attitude. We know that only the servant class 'goes steady' and that a young lady goes out with many different beaux until she has made her choice, and then she never goes out with anyone else again, except a member of her family."

Georgie, never at a loss for a tag-line, told me to remember the quotation from Stephen Vincent Benet's *John Brown's Body,* a family Bible of sorts, where Benet is describing Mary Lou Wingate, the heroine of the southern portion of the book:

> Always, always to have the charm
> That makes the gentleman take your arm
> But never that bright unseemly spell
> That makes strange gentlemen love too well
> Once you are married and settled down
> With a suitable gentleman of your own.

Forty years later, I was to hear this quoted back to me by one of my own children, who were strongly criticizing me for my attitude about social customs. I was told, "The trouble with you, Ma, is that you've spent your whole life trying to live like Mary Lou Wingate!" Do you know? I could have done a lot worse.

Georgie was working very hard as chief intelligence officer of the Hawaiian Department. He was also organizing another crack polo team at Schofield Barracks, looking for a chance to be invited to play again in the Inter-Island Matches. Of course, he was ten years older, but so were the captains of the other island teams, and they had all urged Georgie to get the Army involved again.

Ma was deep into Polynesian ethnology, polishing up her novel, *The Blood of the Shark,* and meeting all the fascinating people in the museum crowd. One of her great friends and advisers was Dr. Peter Buck (Te Rangi Heroa). His father had been an Irish doctor in New Zealand, and his mother had been one of the highest chiefesses of the Maori people—she had a tattooed chin. Peter Buck was a cultivated and delightful man, a truly great gentleman and a scholar. It was a thrill to hear his beautiful deep voice speaking flawless Oxford English from a totally Maori face, with its hooked and flattened nose and idol's eyes. He gave Ma a small job in the Bishop Museum, and she was in her element. She was put to classifying fishhooks! The scientists could trace the various migrations of the Hawaiians from Polynesia and Melanesia by the shapes and sizes of their pearl shellfish hooks. This gave Ma an entrée behind the green baize curtain, and she reveled in it.

The eminent Professor J. F. G. Stokes was head of the museum, or at least of the part of it where Ma worked. He was a mild little man who had given his whole life to the ethnology of the Pacific peoples. He had a mild little wife and a nice little boy, the fruit of their middle years. Professor Stokes worked in a crowded office in the back part of the museum, and we only saw him emerge when we all went on the monthly hikes of the Piko Club, a hiking club of enthusiastic islanders who took us all over mountains and the trails only the native-born knew. Most of us carried sandwiches, but Professor and Mrs. Stokes usually shared a can of baby octopus or a few dried sea cucumbers.

Ma used to take me into the back parts of the museum with her (the best part of any museum is the part the public never sees), and there was one room that had us both hysterical with laughter. This was the idol room, full of idols of all shapes and sizes from all over the Pacific world. Most of them were phallic idols and, believe me, a Polynesian phallic idol is about as phallic as you can get. The sex organs of both sexes are grossly exaggerated with a kind of exuberant innocence; there is absolutely no mistaking which is which. In this room every idol wore a neat white ruffled apron—just like the one Grandma wore on Sunday—all made by Mrs. Stokes so that the Professor would not be distracted from his work. It was a glory of incongruity to see the bold carven faces, deeply cicatrized, the huge pearl-shell eyes madly into space, the mouths, set with dog's teeth, hideously gaping—and then the white aprons.

Ma's interest in ethnology was well known, and she met all kinds of people who told her legends, and asked her to write down the music of their old songs. One night Kingi Kimball asked me if Ma would be interested in going with us to a luau that an old friend of his was giving to celebrate the tenth anniversary of his first wife's death. It would be just an ordinary luau, Kingi said, except for one thing: one of the dead wife's relatives was the last of the Oahu tribe of the chanters of genealogies, and she was coming. In the days before Jesus came there was a tribe on each island whose life service was to know the genealogy of every chiefly family, and to be able to chant it at any grand occasion. Since writing had been brought to the islands, the custom had died out and this old woman was probably the last of the line.

Ma was delighted, and came with us armed with notebook and pencil and great expectations. Our Hawaiian host was a dignified gentleman in his sixties, and he and his present wife made a big fuss over Ma and showed her to a seat near the head of the table. At the head of the table, in the place of honor, was a life-size photograph of the first wife in her coffin. This was customary on such occasions.

Many of Ma's Hawaiian friends were there. The food was authentic, the music mostly of the older and more harmonious songs, and there were some very fine formal hulas. Then the chanter was brought in. She was an old, old woman, shrunk down to doll size. Her holoku was of a dark tapa print; she had the family heirloom feather leis around her neck, and her still-black hair hung down over her shrunken shoulders. She was carried to the head of the table, near the photograph of her relative, and squatted there on the ground. One of

Ma's friends, sotto voce, explained that the chanter was supposed to chant the genealogy of the dead woman, but that she was so very old, you could not depend on her to remember what she was supposed to do, so she would probably just chant what came to the forefront of her mind.

There was a polite silence, and after awhile the old woman began to sway, and in a reedy, whispery voice, she began to chant in endless strings of four-note liquid Hawaiian words and syllables. The older guests began to sway with her, and an occasional *a-u-we*—would break from them, the Hawaiian word for *alas—it is gone* . . . Then, as suddenly as she had begun, the old woman stopped and seemed to sink into a sort of trance. Her grandchildren and great-grandchildren, who had brought her, went and picked her up and, saying polite alohas to everyone, they left. It had been an eerie experience, a glimpse into the past no longer there and we left shortly afterwards.

Ma was terribly elated and begged Kingi to tell her what the old woman had said, but Kingi said that he hadn't caught all of it but that Aunt Emma Taylor would probably know. Kingi and I had planned to go on to a political meeting (he was running for some office; he said it was over head sewers for Honolulu, which made all the Hawaiians laugh inordinately and vote for him)—so we left Ma at the quarters at Fort Shafter and went back. When we got to the post gate, Kingi drove over to the side of the road and stopped the car, and I saw that he was laughing so hard, the tears were running down his face. When he finally pulled himself together, he said: "Eee-ah, that was a terribly close thing! I just couldn't tell your mother what that old wahine was chanting about! I maybe shouldn't even tell you!" I begged and pleaded with him and after he made me promise not to tell Ma (I did, and I did) he said that the woman was so old that she had no mind control any more and she had just chanted what was on the top of her head, and the chant tonight had been a total and vivid description of the sex organs of all the Kamehamehas, their capabilities, possibilities, and probabilities. He shook his head and said that never in his life had he heard anything like it, that it was incredible and, then, sadly, ". . . and she'll probably never be able to do it again because she won't remember." I asked him why all the old ladies had been chanting *A-u-we* and he said: "All that beauty gone! All that fun gone! You would say, 'alas' too, if you knew what you had missed!"

When I told Ma, she was fascinated, and she asked Emma Taylor about it, but Emma said that she, herself, had never heard anything like that either, and it was too bad that no one had taken notes, but that that would have been impolite.

Emma was often with us. The Damon mansion was on the other side of the golf course in back of us, and the Damons were friends and distant connections of Emma's. The dowager Mrs. Damon, a McAdam originally from Scotland, lived in the mansion and was a great friend of Ma's. Emma had a lot to say about the Damons. When the original Dr. Damon, a missionary of the first emigration, acquired the Moanalua tract, he pulled down the local chief's house, which was built of human bones and, then, not caring too much for that site, planned his house for a higher part of the land. When his plans became known, a deputation of elder Hawaiians came to him and asked him not to build there. They said that in the valley below, where his house drains would empty, were the sacrosanct Graves of the Dead. In times long past, a war party from Oahu had captured and kidnapped a group of soothsayers and magicians from the Island of Maui. These had lived at Moana Loa and died and been buried there, and they would resent human waste near their graves. The Reverend Damon said that that was heathen nonsense and that Jesus would not allow anything like that to happen, and built his house where he had planned. The Hawaiians warned him that in building there, he had brought a curse on the heads of his family. Strangely enough (or was it so strange?), almost all the Damons were affected in some way in their heads. Ma's friend, the living Mrs. Damon, had married two brothers. Her first husband was driving home from Honolulu one night and saw a workman removing a lantern from an excavation in the road. He stopped his horse to reprimand the workman, who hotheadedly stabbed Mr. Damon in the face, penetrating his eye and piercing his brain. Mrs. Damon heard the horse drive up and stop by the front door, and when her husband did not come in, she went to see what was wrong, and found him slumped dead in the seat. Some years later she married his brother. The second Mr. Damon had a disabling malady, and went everywhere in a wheelchair. One day she left him sitting in his chair by one of the ornamental ponds in the garden. When she came back for him, he had tumbled from his chair into the pond, either dead or unconscious, and the crabs had eaten off his face.

She raised her children alone. I don't remember how many she had, but she told Ma that there was an equal number of her dear ones alive and dead, and that sometimes, when she heard her children calling her, she didn't know from which world their voices came.

The third Damon brother never married. He lived by himself, a recluse, although he was very fond of his sister-in-law, and she of him. One night she dreamed that a crowd of Hawaiians came to her, wailing for the dead, and carrying with them a package wrapped in leaves. This was the ancient way in which the Hawaiians wrapped the bones of the dead, after they had boiled the flesh away and fed it to the totem animal associated with the dead person. The Hawaiians, in Mrs. Damon's dream, gave her the package and told her she would know what to do with it. She woke up in the morning, knowing that her brother-in-law was dead. Sometime late in the day the news was brought to her that he had died in the night of some injury to his head, and had been found by his servant. She buried him with his brothers.

Emma used to visit the Damons a lot and, when they were away, she would stay in their house to watch it. One night she telephoned Ma to tell her that she must come right over to the Damons, that there was something making big, wet footprints on the porch! Ma was about to take off across the golf course to see what was going on, but Georgie wouldn't let her, and she had to wait until morning. The next morning she went over to the Damons bright and early, and Emma had quite a tale to tell. She said that since she had been sleeping at the Damons', she had not had one single good night's rest; something kept twitching the covers off her bed, and whispering to her, but she couldn't understand what was said, except that somebody wanted her to do something for them. She told Ma that she was going to take the house apart and see what was amiss.

A few days later, Emma arrived at our quarters in triumph. She had been through every closet and drawer in the Damon's house, and had finally found on the top shelf of a storage closet three human skulls. She waited until Mr. Damon, the present owner, returned from his trip and then asked him where he had gotten them. He said he had not thought of them for years, but that when he and his brother were kids they had found them in a burial cave away up on top of the mountain overlooking Moana Loa, and had brought them home for trophies. Emma said to me, "That explained everything. In the old days, a chief owned land that went from the knife edge of the mountain ridge in a strip right down to the sea and out to include any islands there. This strip where Henry found the skulls belonged to my ancestors, and naturally, when they recognized me, they wanted me to take them back to their grave, so, without further ado, I insisted that we take the skulls right back up the mountain. So Henry got us mules, and I rode up with him, and he put the skulls right back where he had found them. I went into the cave with him to see that everything was in order, and we returned. After that I slept like an angel in that bed."

Ma was dying to go back to the cave with Emma and see it, but Emma said that it was not the time, that it would take the skulls awhile to settle down again after all that excitement. Ma guessed that Emma's Hawaiian blood did not want Ma to enter the secret place even though they were such great friends. Emma never mentioned the cave or the skulls again.

Ma was deeply involved in her ethnological studies and her book, but, in spite of being back in her beloved Hawaii, this was not a very happy time for her. Georgie was frustrated at every turn by General Drum's refusal to back him up in the things he discovered about the Japanese underground; by his lack of promotion; and by being in the frightening fifties when you realize you haven't done all the things you planned to do—haven't written the Great American Novel—haven't looted a town, as Colonel Latrobe had suggested—haven't found the end of the rainbow—and Time's winged chariot is audible in the distance. Caesar and Alexander the Great, and Napoleon, and a lot of Georgie's other heroes, had all made their pile by the time they were in their thirties and forties, and all Georgie had left to emulate was the Duke of Wellington. Georgie was worrying about getting old; he deviled Ma about her gray hair; he was worried that my sister, Bee, might get pregnant and make him a grandfather; and he was extremely disagreeable. Ma bought a book called *Change of Life in Men,* which simply infuriated him, although it made pretty good sense to me when I read it—he burned it in the alley. He started to seek the company of younger people than himself and Ma, and let himself be flattered by the eternal harpies who are always standing in the wings of successful marriages, hoping the wife will falter and the man will be there for them to feast on.

He was also drinking too much. This is not just the way it sounds: he did not take to drink, and he did not drink any more than usual, but he had a very bad fall playing polo, which affected his drinking capacity for the rest of his life.

I remember that day only too well. We were all out at Schofield Barracks. It was one of the big games prior to the Inter-Island games. There was a scrimmage and Georgie was thrown heavily from his pony. He landed on his head, and he just lay there, letting go of the reins, which was a sign it was a bad fall as one of the fundamental rules of riding is "never let go of the reins." I had seen him take plenty of falls, but that was the only time I ever saw him let go. The other players jumped off their horses and Ma started to run out on the field, but he got groggily to his feet and yelled at everyone to get out of the way and get on with the game, which they did. Thank goodness, it was nearly over. From there we went to a cocktail party for the team, and then we went to Pearl Harbor and spent the night on the *Arcturus,* preparatory to a weekend sail.

Saturday and Sunday all seemed as usual, but late Sunday afternoon, on our way back to the anchorage, Georgie, who was steering, suddenly looked at Ma and asked, "Where the hell am I? The last thing I remember is seeing the ground come up and hit my face!"

Ma was worried and took him to the doctor the next day. After examining him, Dr. Withington told Ma that Georgie had had a slight concussion and told her to keep him out of the sun and away from alcohol for a week or so. This was, of course, two days too late. Whatever happened to his head, it cut down on his capacity to carry alcohol; whereas, before, he had never shown his liquor in his whole life, now just a couple of drinks made him quite tight. This upset

Ma no end. She had a thing about drinking anyhow, and she told him so. Ma had never criticized Georgie in his life, and that upset him and made him very disagreeable. Sometimes he would take an extra drink while she was looking at him, just to show her. This all embarrassed me terribly because he did not appear well when he was tight: he got tearful and sentimental, recited poetry out of place and context, and picked on Ma.

Chapter 13
Trouble in Paradise

At this point the serpent, with his or her well-known sense of timing, saw fit to enter our uncertain Eden. My first cousin, Jean Gordon—one of my oldest, dearest, and closest (I thought) friends—came through Hawaii on her way to the Orient with an elderly cousin, Florence Hatheway, as chaperone. They stayed at the Halekulani Hotel, but they might just as well have stayed in our quarters. Jean was there daily, with offerings of flowers and tasteful gifts for Ma and little George, invitations for me, and lots of splendid ideas for fun and unusual things to do. She was a quiet but witty girl, highly intelligent and beautiful. Looking back on it all, I can see that she had started making a play for Georgie as far back as Bee's wedding. But at that time, it was highly unlikely that I could have thought my best friend, exactly my age, could ever see anything in my father, an old, old man—nearly into his fifties!

There was gradually no doubt in our minds that she was after just one thing, and she had timed it all perfectly. Georgie was mad at Ma for ceasing to be his adoring public, which she had been for thirty-odd years; he was scared of getting old and dissatisfied with his static career. To have an unusually attractive girl, his own daughter's age, make a play for him was just what his starved ego needed. He made a damned fool of himself. I was stunned. The only solution I could think of was to get her dates with all my beaux, which I did, but none of them ever dated her more than once. I finally asked a beau who was also a very good friend why this should be, and he said he guessed it was because she acted as if she wasn't a bit interested.

I can only imagine, vividly, because I loved her very much, how Ma suffered, for she did not discuss her inner feelings. The only thing she ever said was when we watched the liner bearing the fair deceiver away from Hawaii toward

Japan; the lady was smothered in jasmine and orchid leis that Georgie had put around her neck, and Georgie was standing at the end of the dock waving madly: "You know, it's lucky for us that I don't have a mother because, if I did, I'd pack up and go home to her now, and your father needs me. He doesn't know it right now, but he needs me. In fact, right now he needs me more than I need him."

Ma looked away, and then turned back to me with tears in her eyes, and continued: "Perhaps there is a reason for all of this. I want you to remember this; that even the best and truest of men can be bedazzled and make fools of themselves. So, if your husband ever does this to you, you can remember that I didn't leave your father. I stuck with him because I am all that he really has, and I love him; and he loves me."

Several days later, she was playing the piano. The piece had a haunting tune, and I asked her what it was. She replied that she was just putting a tune to some words of a poem she hadn't thought of for years:

> Regarde, Narcisse,
> Regarde dans l'eau
> Regarde, Narcisse, que tu est beau
> Il n'y au monde
> Que la beaute
> Et la Jeunesse
> He-las et la Jeunesse
> Regarde, Narcisse,
> Regarde dans l'eau.

Not long after this incident, Ma repeated (this time to more hearing ears) her little sermon on marriage that she had given Bee and me, and which I have since passed on to many people.

> A marriage is like a tree; sometimes it is in bud; sometimes in blossom; sometimes in leaf, sometimes in fruit, and then; sometimes the leaves will all fall off and it will look dead, but if you keep on cultivating the roots, always cultivating the roots, it will come alive again.

At this time she also wrote:

> Not long ago a friend found the image of the fish god, Luula, under the floor of her house. "I didn't want it in the house," she explained, "and I didn't know what to do with it, nor what to give it to eat, so Brother took it to the place where

he works at the Navy Yard, and a man died the very next day. When he brought it home I got so nervous of it, that I just took it to Peter Buck at the Museum. No one interfered with it there."

Ma went on in her notes to say:

> A similarly discontented idol was given to me with the explanation that he was a soldier idol, and would be happier in a military family. He was a small helmeted head and had probably been somebody's personal fetish. My friend gave me minute directions as to his installation, saying, "When you unpack him, make him a lei and give him a little okelehau, but only do it once. He will know then that you have aloha for him, but he must not be spoiled." I had the idol for several years, but during a period of unrest in my family, I got angry with him and threw him into the pond. Later, I retrieved him and since then he has made a splendid record for himself, having assisted a British Commando on my husband's staff [in World War II, then to come] in several invasions.

The okelehau that Ma gave the idol is a native liquor distilled from the root of the ti plant (cordyline terminalis) and it is one of the most powerful drinks there is. During prohibition everyone on the Islands drank it. It has the potency of the best brandy, and can be lethal in large quantities; "terminalis" is a good indication.

This second tour in Hawaii, from 1935 to 1937, was great fun. We went to the other islands to visit, and we had visitors from the mainland. Georgie was always experimenting and trying new things. He built a diving helmet that we took out on the boat to try. It was a huge thing that balanced on one's shoulders, and air was supplied by a hand pump that put air through a hole into the helmet. A rope was lowered for the diver to use to signal. The first time we took it out to try it, Bee was visiting us. We went to the leeward side of the island, and the only volunteer for the first dive was Ma, so the helmet was lowered until the edge was in the water and Ma dove: the whole ponderous machine was lowered until we could see that she had her feet on the bottom. The water was very clear and about twelve feet deep. My sister was pumping away on the air pump, and the bubbles were coming up in bunches, and Georgie was very pleased with his invention, and went below to change as he thought he would go down next. The signal rope jerked a few times and then was still. When Georgie came up from below, he asked if everything was all right, and Bee said that it seemed to be, but that there weren't any bubbles coming up anymore. He asked if she was pumping, and she obviously was, so he jerked the signal rope and there was no reply. He looked around, and suddenly it appeared that young George, in enthusiastic observation, was standing on the air hose. We got Ma up just in time! The helmet had filled up with water when the air stopped pumping in, and she couldn't get out. Georgie said to us: "Your mother is a fearless woman!" No one else used the helmet that day. He said that it needed some modification.

Two favorite cousins came to visit for a month or so during the summer of 1935. They were Fred and Anne Ayer, Ma's brother Fred's children. They were accustomed to the stately halls of the North Shore of Boston, and were somewhat appalled by our quarters, which were far from grand and very crowded. Anne slept in the guest room, and Fred slept in a section of the downstairs porch that had been walled off as a small den for Georgie.

The Ayers were much taken with the civilian crowd—grandsons and great-grandsons of the militant missionaries, many of whom were very rich, and most of whom went east to school to the silver-spoon preparatory schools and the Ivy League colleges. These young people were a lot of fun up to a point, but they did in Hawaii just what you could do in Palm Beach or Monterey, or on the North Shore—tennis, waterskiing, sunning, swimming, and all-night parties. Ma and Georgie had brought us up to do the things of the country in which we lived. We took Anne and Fred to the Parker Ranch—a real privilege, as Mr. and Mrs. Carter did not open their doors to the world and his wife. The Ayers were bored to death with it. They resented having to learn to ride Western style. They had ridden before they could walk: first in baskets on old retired ponies, and then in English saddles on slightly larger ponies—and they said that just nobody rode Western.

Ma's pride in showing them the ancient places and telling them the matching tales also bored them. Fred's comment, after he was shown one of the largest and most sacred of the ancient temple ruins on Hawaii, was, "My goodness, Auntie Bee, Ethan [his younger brother] and I could have piled up a pile of rocks like that in one afternoon." Granted, all that was left of the heiau was a vast square base of lava rock. Ma could mentally invest it with its idols, grass huts, sandalwood posts, and pits for the human sacrifices, but to the cousins it was and always would be a pile of rocks.

The Ayers didn't care much for the service crowd either as most of the men were West Point or Annapolis graduates from all walks of life, and the girls were very different from New England debutantes who, as Ma always said, thought they had made their contribution to the party when they left the mirror. The cowboys at the Parker Ranch had a good laugh at Fred's expense, as they sensed he was down-grading them. One day, while we were there, we stopped for lunch in the middle of a day of calf branding. One of the cowboys, about Fred's age, brought him a sandwich, saying, "This all is kinda what you eat in

Bost-awn." Fred bit into it—a pair of calf testicles, still warm. He was a good sport and didn't throw up, and the Hawaiians laughed until they cried. It was their kind of naughty Polynesian fun.

Just before Fred and Anne left to go back to the mainland, Ma told them they would have to have a party to repay their social debts. She offered to have it at our quarters, or on the *Arcturus,* but Fred and Anne wanted it to be very grand. They got a splendid table at the Alexander Young Hotel, right on the dance floor. The guest list was a bit of a problem, as they just wanted to have the stylish crowd, but the service people had included them in all their parties, and Ma insisted that they were to be invited. However, they were most particular to include the son and daughter of the ranking admiral. This particular admiral had been a devoted beau of Ma's and, better still, his wife was from Boston. The admiral had been voted the handsomest man in his class at the Naval Academy, and was still absolutely stunning in his fifties. His son and daughter were most attractive, though not service minded, and his visiting niece was one of the most delectable creatures anyone had ever seen. Her name was Barbara, and she looked like a chocolate-box nymph. Before the party, I overheard Ma and the admiral talking about Barbara, and gathered that she had been sent to spend the summer because she had gotten into some kind of mess at home, and her parents thought the change would do her good. As the admiral left, he said to Ma, "Don't worry too much about what I have told you, Beatrice; my children will keep an eye on her."

The Ayers' party was a huge success, and we did not leave until the band started to pack. As we were assembling our wraps and bags, the admiral's son appeared with startling eyes, asking, "Has anyone seen Barbara?" I said that I understood that he was supposed to be keeping an eye on her. He said, "Omygod," and grabbing the naval officer who was my date, he rushed out of the ballroom and down the stairs to the lobby with his sister and me hot on his heels. There, under the streetlight on the corner, stood Barbara, smiling mysteriously, while an earnest young sailor was carefully undoing all the tiny buttons on the back of her dress, under which she was as naked as Eve. The rest of the party came downstairs in time to take in the whole performance. My date, who was in uniform, went up to the sailor who had a friend with him and suggested that they beat it, which they did with bad grace when he threatened to call the shore police. As they left, one of them said, plaintively, "But, Loo-tenint, sir, *we* didn't pick her up, she picked *us* up!"

Ma was waiting up for us. Fred and Anne had not yet arrived as they were dropping off some of the guests, so I was able to tell Ma the whole story. She shook her head mournfully, and kept saying, "Oh, the poor things!" and then she told me that the trouble that Barbara had gotten into at home was the same: she was not very bright and a nymphomaniac, and her widowed mother had thought that a visit to her uncle would solve their problem. We never saw Barbara again, but I see her still in my mind's eye, looking so pleased and so anticipatory under the streetlight.

My brother, George, was growing up fast, and was the prototype of the younger brother with strong leanings toward brat as far as I was concerned. I was genuinely fond of him in his place, and I think he loved me, but I never stopped complaining to Ma about how he followed me around, hiding under the hikiai (a huge square sofa) on the porch, or lying flat on the stair landing when my beaux came to call. Ma said that all he wanted was to be included in the fun, and why didn't I take him with me to some of the picnics and outings I went on. I thought this was a perfectly terrible idea, but it grew on Ma with promptings from young George, and while he embarrassed me to death, some of my beaux had kid brothers of their own and didn't seem to mind his tagging along, asking a question a minute.

One disastrous occasion occurred when the fleet was in. All the midshipmen I had dated while we were stationed in Washington were now ensigns, and I had a glorious time with our quarters constantly full of nice young men, making it a home away from home, and always ready for food and entertainment. Ma loved it—she was always at her best with men of any age—and Georgie liked it as he was the soul of hospitality and loved to entertain. On the occasion I shudder to remember, the destroyer upon which one of my beaux served was having an open house and everyone was invited. Ma shamed me into taking George along: "You wouldn't deprive your little brother of the only chance he may ever have to see the insides of a destroyer, would you?"

We went out from the dock in a ship's boat and were piped aboard. My date was waiting, and he took us all over the cleaned and dusted parts of the ship, but that was not enough for George. With glittering eyes, he demanded to be taken to the bridge, the signal deck, the engine room—in short, the works. My date, with the look of a wounded deer, left me in the ward room with friends and was gone with George for nearly an hour. When he returned his immaculate whites were white no longer; he looked as if he had been drawn backwards through a keyhole. George, however, was as fresh as a daisy. He had some further suggestions, such as a visit to the crow's nest, but was forestalled by my date's suggestion that we all have a drink. Liquor, of course, was not served on naval vessels, but George didn't know this, and he drew himself up in front of the poor startled young man: "My sister is not allowed by my parents to partake of spirituous liquors." That night when I stormed in to complain to Ma, she laughed and laughed and said that she doubted if the incident would ruin my social life, that men always had more respect for girls who had a brother to protect them, and she burst into her brother Chilly's song: "...and you wouldn't dare insult me, sir, if Brother Jack were here!"

I thought her most unfeeling.

Because I was a free agent and not going steady, I knew nearly every bachelor on the island. One evening the phone rang and an Air Corps lieutenant, whom I knew only because he danced with me sometimes at the post hops, called and asked if I could do him a favor: he wanted to bring a girl to call on Ma the next afternoon, and he wanted permission to do so. Ma said that she supposed it was all right, although she could not imagine why he wanted to see her.

The next day, at fifteen hundred hours sharp, Lieutenant Smith arrived, leading by the hand the prettiest young girl you could dream of. She had naturally curly brown hair, big blue eyes, rosy cheeks, and looked as if she had just taken off her kitchen apron and brushed the flour from her hands. Ma greeted them and Lieutenant Smith asked if they could talk to her in private. The three of them went into the living room. In a few minutes he came out, saying he would be back in an hour. At the end of the hour, he was back, and Ma led the girl out onto the porch, kissed her cheek, saying, "God bless you both," and to Lieutenant Smith, "You are a very lucky young man." The girl had been crying: her eyes looked just like the eyes of the heroine in the book where it describes them as drenched with dew.

After they left, Ma began to cry, telling me, "I have never been so touched in all my life. I feel unworthy. I am going to tell your father all about this, and I am going to tell you right now in case there is any talk. If there is, I want you to scotch it. You can tell anyone who asks that Miss Jones is a friend of mine."

The story Ma told is one of the Seven Original Plots. Lieutenant Smith had met Miss Jones in the biggest and most high-class whore house in Honolulu. They had licensed prostitution in those days, which made excellent sense. Miss Jones was one of the new girls who had just arrived from the source of supply in San Francisco. She had gotten into trouble in her hometown in the Southwest, and had been thrown out by her Salt Water Baptist family. A kind lady had taken her in and helped her until her little daughter was born. Then the kind lady took the little child to an adoption agency and introduced Miss Jones to a kind man who had promised her a good job in San Francisco. She had only been in Honolulu a few days when she met Lieutenant Smith. He fell in love with her, bought her time-book from the Madam who was a well-known and respected figure in Honolulu, and intended to marry her. He had brought Miss Jones to Ma to be checked out, as he told Ma that she was the greatest lady he had ever met, and he wanted Ma's seal of approval on Miss Jones. Ma had questioned the girl gently for an hour, and said that she was one of those people from whom sin departed like water off a duck's back: she was sweet, innocent, probably a little stupid, but Ma thought she would make an excellent wife for Lieutenant Smith. Ma repeated again what she had often told us, that there were only two kinds of women in the world—the potential mother and the potential whore—and that sometimes the potential mother made the best whore, and vice versa.

Lieutenant Smith and Miss Jones were married quietly soon after their call. There was talk, and I did what Ma had told me to do. The years passed by and Lieutenant Smith became a lieutenant general in the Air Force; his wife was an asset to him, they had four beautiful children, and I saw them many times. I doubt if Mrs. Smith ever remembered the first time we met.

Working for the Junior League in the Queen's Hospital, doing both occupational therapy and filling in with the library cart, I got to know most of the registered whores in Honolulu. They all came in on Monday morning for their anti-luetic shots, and sometimes some of them needed rest and repairs. They were a cheerful group of girls, always passing around the flowers and candy their boyfriends had given them, making jokes and loaning each other makeup and stockings and hair ornaments. I told Ma once how generous they were and she replied, darkly, "Yes, indeed, and that's how they got into that business in the first place." I know Ma worried herself sick about some of the things I saw and lots of the things I did, but she felt—and rightly so—that if I told her about it openly, I couldn't be in any real trouble. I know she worried a lot about our virginity and the hanging onto thereof, but she need not have. Bee and I were absolutely convinced on that subject. Ma had told us for as long as I can remember that a woman's only truly personal possessions are her reputation and her virginity; you inherit your maiden name from your father; your husband trusts you with his family name when you marry; but your virginity is yours and yours alone to give to whom you choose, and if you give it away for nothing you get nothing in return. She said that virginity was a physical fact and that chastity was spiritual virginity and it was to be handled with equal care. After Bee and I resented being different we started to glory in it, and keeping ourselves for Prince Charming in his golden cloak was very real. Bee's Prince Charming, in the guise of Johnnie Waters, had appeared, but mine was still to come.

I must say I saw a lot of cloaks that looked pretty golden from the distance, but they didn't hold up to close inspection. Also, a lot of my friends were selling out in order to be popular, or to catch themselves a Prince, and they left the charmed circle when they did that, and missed a lot of the fun. In addition to the terribly boring ladies' room talk about how late their periods were, or what they would do if their periods were late, their conversations lacked stimulus and sparkle, and made you feel slightly soiled. It was embarrassing to go back on the dance floor and see them gazing deeply into their partner's eyes after what they had just been confiding about said partner.

I did not stress too much how many of the girls to whom I was a bridesmaid were a teeny-weeny bit pregnant, or thought they were. Ma would have been embarrassed in front of their parents, who were mostly her friends.

Propositions, of course, came thick and fast, but I used my sister's advice, which was to say something funny when a boy started getting that look. You couldn't really move in on a girl if you were laughing. It was excellent advice. Between my slipping and sliding friends and the jolly whores, I was pretty safe.

During the inter-island polo matches, the Maui team, consisting of Mr. Baldwin and three of his sons, would come to Honolulu for extended visits. They came to the Army horse shows at Schofield Barracks and were anxious to try the typical horse show events themselves, to increase the scope of their horse activities. Georgie volunteered to go to Maui, where he and Ma and I would give some exhibition jumping performances, and he would try to start the Baldwins out on training jumpers. We were all looking forward to this expedition very much. Georgie would be in his element; Ma had the names of a lot of Emma's relatives who would show her some of the ethnic sights of Maui; and I thought all the Baldwin boys were just gorgeous. Then Ma got a terrible case of bronchitis on the eve of our departure. I was torn, as I thought I should stay— she was very sick—but she insisted that I go, saying that Alice Holmes would keep an eye on her, and that Emma Taylor was bringing a friend who was a gifted masseuse and an herb specialist. So I went. But before I go into that adventure, I want to quote Ma's notes on her treatment while we were gone. Whatever happened to Ma, she got something out of it.

> During a bout of bronchitis in 1936, a friend sent me a well-known Hawaiian masseuse, a devout Catholic, and a descendant of those skillful priests who had done so much for the old-time travelers. She [the masseuse] had gone into the hills at dawn to pick the noni leaves (morinda citrifolia) for my chest, while the dew was still upon them, and she arrived with the leaves in one hand, and an electric extension cord with a light bulb on it in the other. She laid the leaves on me and heated them by passing the 100-watt light bulb back and forth over them while I lay, and coughed, and reflected on the blend of old and new that is Hawaii as we know it. Then she kneaded me all over with mashed kukui nuts, squeezed into a cloth, and, as she worked she talked: "One must always pray before you pick, that the strength may go into the leaves. This uhalo (aleurites muluccana) now is for you to gargle. This, boiled in the whiskey bottle, is for you to take the sore cough away. It will come up in your throat in foam, and you will spit it out with the cough. Now, I shall pray, and each time I say your name, Beatrice, you will say, Amen. You must not think this is Kahuna stuff, so I will tell you the prayers. The first two will be formal prayers, the Our Father and the Hail

Mary. The second two are the real prayers, to Ku and Hina. When I breathe on
your spine, that is the strength of the prayers flowing over you. Then, I will ask
you five times, thus: Beatrice, do you wish to be healed? Answer then, yes, and
have faith. Hina will heal even a broken bone if you have the right prayer. No, I
am not a doctor, but I know many herbs; pounded ohia bark for strains, and
pounded noni for diabetes—it washes the kidneys and bladder. The juice of five
kukui nuts, swabbed on a baby's tongue, will take away the white coat, and it is
nicer than swabbing it with urine as some people do. There is a little leaf too that
grows on the beach that is good, but it is very strong, and as I am not a doctor, I
do not use it. What is it, I wonder? Kukui is stronger than castor oil. Ape leaves
(alocacia macrorhiza) heated and laid over the kidneys ease pain. Noni leaves,
bound over the breast of a new mother, dry up the milk, and, if she does not
want another child, she must bury the afterbirth with a prayer. In my childhood,
the doctor could tap the belly and tell us the sickness and what was the herb
needed. Sometimes he gave us a whole bowl full of herbs, good for everything."

The Baldwins owned the Ulupalakua Ranch, a sumptuous place. Of course I
had never seen the old Lake Vineyard Ranch where Georgie had been born and
raised, but in my mind's eye, it was just like Ulupalakua. The Baldwins were
fun people and the ranch was not run austerely, as was the Parker Ranch. We
were to give a jumping demonstration, and our horses had been shipped over
to Maui a week in advance so they could get used to a strange stable. Georgie
and I went in the *Arcturus,* which was about a long day's cruise. I was thrilled
by the whole scene, as I was madly in love with the youngest Baldwin at the
time; the fact that he had never noticed me didn't bother me in the least. I had
seen him play polo, which he did very dashingly, and among my secret fancies
was a dream of being the wife of a large ranch owner in the Islands. I think it
was the ranch I wanted more than the owner.

The evening we got there, we were met at the dock by the Baldwins and
taken up the mountain to the ranch where there was a great party going on with
lots of food and drink and handsome men and beautiful women and a cowboy
orchestra, and everyone getting up and doing the hula when the spirit moved
him or her. Actually, many of the men were better hula dancers than the ladies.
Georgie and I were installed in the guest house on the lawn. The party broke
up at all hours. Georgie told me to leave the door from the bathroom between
our rooms open. He was going to leave his open, too, and if I heard him call
out in the night I was to come into his room as fast as possible. I couldn't imagine what it was all about and, as the moon was shining into my window, I
couldn't get to sleep, so when he yelled out, I tore into his room, just in time to
see our hostess scuttling out the door. She was clearly visible in the silvery light
and was not overdressed. Georgie sat there in his bed and laughed until the

tears ran down the face. Then he said, "All right, you can go back to bed now, but leave your door open just in case." Next morning we went into breakfast about 6:30 a.m. I was charmed to find a glass of okelehau beside each tumbler of orange juice, and was about to scoff mine up to study the effect of drinking pure alcohol before breakfast, but Georgie shook his head at me, so I put my glass down and ate my breakfast. The men took off horse-wards, and I was alone when our hostess finally came in. She glared at me, drank her oke, then drank mine: "What a hell of a little spoil-sport you turned out to be! There must be enough tail there to go around!"

I had never heard a lady talk like that before, and I was sincerely shaken up—but I wasn't so dumb that I didn't realize that THAT WOMAN had been after MY FATHER for NO GOOD PURPOSE. I thought it was perfectly disgusting. They were both so *old*.

I told Ma about it after we got home and she got her thoughtful look and then she laughed. "Well, good for Georgie! He doesn't have to come all over the old Adam and say the woman tempted me and I did eat." I had to figure that one out too.

After about five days of steady riding and partying, we had to get back to Oahu. The sail back was awful. Not for nothing was that piece of water called "the channel of screaming children." However, this time instead of huge swells, we hit the doldrums; the engine went on the blink, and we seemed to be sailing backwards most of the time. Joe and Georgie went down into the engine cuddy to play with the machinery and I stayed aboveboard, as the smell of gasoline did nothing for me in the cabin, and I was polishing brass. Georgie could not bear to see one idle on a ship, boat, or yacht (his definition of a yacht was any boat that had a toilet on it), and I was thinking long, disagreeable thoughts when right off our starboard bow, a submarine surfaced! It had the same effect as a sudden appearance of the Kraken! However, Georgie came aloft and, after a certain number of ahoys and now hear this's, it turned out that Ma had gotten exercised because the *Arcturus* was forty-eight hours overdue, and had called a friend in the Navy Yard to see if there were any submarines in the channel that would take a look around for us.

Whatever was done to her, Ma was cured when we came back from Maui. This experience started her on a course of experimentation in native herbs and foods. Ma really liked the native food: baked pig, all kinds of fish, taro root (baked like a potato before being turned into poi), coconut pudding, some green stuff that looked and tasted like spinach, lomi-lomi, raw salmon with onions. All this was very well, but in her enthusiasm she went one step too far. At a very high-toned luau, she ate a very special ancient Hawaiian treat, a raw dog's liver. From this, she got a case of galloping dysentery that nearly carried her off.

Georgie said that it served her right, that anyone who ate dog's liver would eat their own children, like Cronos. Ma replied weakly from her bed of pain that she had really never cared for dogs anyhow, and that this disaster proved her point. Ma was not a real dog-o-phile like the rest of us. Her family had always had outdoor dogs; Georgie's family shared bed and board, mud and fleas, joy and sorrow with their dogs. Ma put up with it all of her married life because she loved Georgie, and dogs loved Ma. She once said sadly that there was never a dog so sick that he couldn't make it to her feet before he vomited.

Ma's ethnological fun and games got her into some other funny situations besides the dysentery. We were staying at the beautiful Kona Inn on Hawaii one time and Ma was exploring the back parts of town. We came across a deserted old house, obviously once a house of importance, but gradually decaying with dignity back into the lush jungle garden that surrounded it. The doors were locked with padlocks, which was a little unusual in the free and easy Islands. The windows were uncurtained, so Ma peered in. I was right beside her and we saw the expected mess, but among the trash was a lovely sort of Madame Recamier daybed and some old tapa cloth strewn around. Most people, when they think of tapa cloth, think of that awful stiff black and white stuff from the curio shops. The real Hawaiian tapa was quite different. It was soft and of many colors—pink, green, blue—small or large patterns. It is made from the inner bark of the mulberry tree, which is pounded out to a material suitable for anything. The Hawaiians wore it in every way it was useful.

Ma had never seen any of the real tapa anywhere except in the museum, so she was all agog to get some and quickly persuaded herself that, as the house was empty and falling down, no one would care if she liberated a few samples. She had one of us break the lock on the front door, which was easy as the wood was old and termite-ridden, and into the house she went—and all over it. After getting a sketch of the daybed, which was too full of dry rot to even move, she collected some large samples of the pink and blue tapa and we retreated, putting the door back together as well as we could. Emma Taylor had told Ma that the real tapa often had the symbol or the totem of the family it belonged to beaten into the material, so Ma was eager to show the stuff to Emma when we got home and find out if she knew the signs.

That night Ma asked the lady manager of the inn, who was Hawaiian and a friend of Emma's, who the old house under the big hau tree just by the ford on the stream had belonged to. The lady knew all about it, and told Ma that it had been the final home of two old sisters of royal blood who were lepers, and who had locked themselves into the house and put a tabu on it to keep the doctors from taking them to the leper colony on Molokai. As they were royal, and were also very private, they were allowed to stay there until they died. Their family came and took the bodies and locked up the house and no one had been in it since—maybe for forty years. Ma was absolutely horrified! She didn't dare tell the lady that she had been in the house that afternoon, handling everything she saw and, while she knew, technically, that leprosy is not very catching, especially after forty years, most human beings have an atavistic fear of the disease—just as they do of snakes. For years and years after that incident, whenever Georgie wanted to tease Ma, he would ask her if she had noticed that her eyebrows were getting heavier, or that her hands were slightly swollen, and she fell for it every time! One of the signs of incipient leprosy is a facial disfiguration called the lion's brow where the swelling of the tissue above the eyes and nose thickens on the face, and, of course, the hands and feet swell grotesquely in some cases of the disease.

Another time when we were on Hawaii, we were prowling around a beach where there had been a historic battle between soldiers of the different islands. Ma was always looking for artifacts and actually had a nice collection of things she had found, including a skull with a stone axe in it. We all thought this was terrific, and hunted happily for bones and stones wherever we were. Young George had strayed away from us, and suddenly we heard him shouting and calling, and we ran to where he was, on a hill above the beach standing by a large hole. He was wildly excited and told Ma that he had found her a whole lot of bones—human bones—down in the hole! There are no snakes in Hawaii, but even if there had been, Ma would have gone down that hole from sheer curiosity. Bee and I stood on the lip above and listened to her shouting up at us. She had never seen so many bones in her life! Her shouts grew further and further apart and pretty soon she said that there was something funny about this place—it was too neat. Georgie had come up from the beach and stood beside us: "There certainly is; Beatrice, you are in a whited sepulchre, full of dead men's bones—dammit, come out of there and go around front and look. You're in somebody's family vault!" And that she was! Young George had approached it from the rear, where the roof had caved in. On the beach side there was an iron door with chains and locks and somebody's name on it. Ma crawled out, very dusty and looking sort of ashamed. She did not have any artifacts in her hands that time.

Although we were animal lovers, none of us liked cats very much. Among our neighbors at Fort Shafter were Colonel and Mrs. Paine. He looked like a dedicated bloodhound; Mrs. Paine called him "lover." Mrs. Paine was a Rubens woman of a certain age, and she was an artist. She painted with a brush six feet long that she supported on the crook of her left arm like a crossbow. She was from Louisiana, and her first name was LeGrande. She was much taken with

Georgie and his gallant southern ways. (The more Georgie disliked a person, the more gallant and southern he became! Sometimes it was almost unbearable.)

The Paines went home on leave and before they left, LeGrande asked Georgie to feed her cats. She said he was so simpatico that he was the only one she would trust to feed her darlings. She was in the habit of picking up wild kittens on the side of the road and bringing them home. Mrs. Paine had rescued twenty-four of them.

Georgie accepted her charge with southern charm and spent the month the Paines were gone in shooting her cats with his air gun. About the time the Paines were expected back, Ma asked him how he was going to explain the cases of canned milk unopened on the Paines' back porch. Georgie gave the cases of milk to the orphan asylum the very next day. I don't know how he explained the absence of the cats to Le Grande, but every evening for weeks you could hear her melodious contralto keening Kitty—Kitty—Kitty up and down the back line. Ma asked him if it didn't smite his conscience. He said that it did not.

Georgie named his highly recommended and impeccably bred hunting dog Lover after Colonel Paine. He said that they were look-alikes. Lover was quite mad. He had slipped a cog in his brain somewhere and he would assume the most perfect classical pointing position toward anything that smelled—orange peels, an oily wrench, a dead bird, gym shoes—anything. What's more, he would hold the point until he dropped. So every evening, if Lover wasn't home by dark, we would have to hunt for him and take him off the point so that he could come home. Naturally, he was useless for hunting, but he was very handsome, and he followed Georgie like his shadow and lay under his desk at the office, which irritated General Drum, but to no effect because he couldn't find anything in Army regulations that said it was against the rules to have a pointer lying under your desk. Georgie said that it made him feel like a crusader whose carven dog lay always under his carven feet on his tomb.

Another neighbor down the block was the chief of staff, Colonel Ulio. He was a jolly bachelor and greatly in demand at parties. Ma didn't like him because she thought he encouraged Georgie's drinking. When Ma was so very sick with bronchitis, our Japanese cook, Goto, brought her a well-known Japanese cure-all that was terrible to contemplate. It was a glass flask of pale golden rice wine in which a black and yellow viper was suspended. Goto called it viper juice, and said it would give her strength. Ma put it with the other drinkables on the bar and asked Goto to get her another bottle for emergencies. I must add that Ma, in her fearless ethnic pursuit, tasted it.

In the usual friendly exchange of Christmas token gifts at the post Christmas tree party, Ma gave Jimmie Ulio a well-wrapped present. He did not get around to opening it until New Year's Day, although it was clearly marked "The

Hair of the Dog for Jimmie from Beatrice." New Year's morning we heard a terrible yelling and screaming from Jimmie Ulio's quarters. Georgie thought something desperate had happened, and started running up the street, meeting Jimmie's cook, Suzuki, who was running down to get him. Together they entered Jimmie's quarters. Georgie came home about a half-an-hour later. He looked very thoughtful. He told Ma that Jimmie had had a terrific time at a New Year's party the night before, and when he had surfaced that morning, he had reached for the hair of the dog and being a little short on hair, he had remembered Ma's Christmas present and opened it. A bottled snake was not what he had expected. Georgie said, "Beatrice, did you *really* send that awful thing to Jimmie?" Ma replied, firmly, "Yes, I did. I thought it was just what he needed in his condition."

It was a troublous time in 1935. Georgie had his fiftieth birthday on November 11, and when he woke up that morning he refused to get up because he said his life was over. He turned his face to the wall and refused to eat breakfast. It took Ma several hours to persuade him that he had been fifty for a whole year and was going into his fifty-first year. He finally got out of bed, but he wasn't much comforted. I must have been thinking about all of this when I wrote in my thought book on January 2, 1937. It is all pretty ponderous stuff, but, then, I was a green twenty-one.

There is no real happiness in getting unless you get in order to give, or unless what you receive gives happiness to the donor. Work brings happiness because in working you give part of yourself, and yet it is selfish to do all the giving if it robs the other of happiness. Deep love and true friendship come from an equality of interchange . . . I can see how people fall into that fallacy of living where they do not create—these are the restless ones, who travel aimlessly, drink too much, go to movies, play bridge, always waiting for something to happen—always looking for happiness. Ma has been so happy here, because she has created her book, and given herself to it without sparing, and done everything else too that she always did. Daddy has been unhappy because he has lost energy and where before he gave himself unsparingly, now he has no extra to give and misses it without knowing why. If he realized this, he would make the effort and be happy again. But men who live on action seldom stop to realize why they do things and, as they grow older, gates of activity, which their energy held open like a spring, shut as the spring slackens and they are trapped by a lack of understanding of themselves which causes fear. No man will be happy if his wife does all the giving, or vice versa. It makes him crave opposition so he can give, and when he doesn't get it, he doesn't realize what he's missing—he merely thinks his wife is spineless and seeks further afield for spirit and opposition.

Georgie was the military intelligence officer—the G-2—of the staff, and he and Ma shared some interesting experiences. One night the doorbell rang well into the small hours. My bedroom was over the front door, so I heard the bell and went down and answered it. A strange-looking man was standing there. He wanted to see the colonel right away. I woke up the parents, and Georgie went down in his nightshirt—he never wore pajamas. He listened to the man for a minute and then gestured to me, fiercely, to get lost. I heard them go out the front door. It was a still night; I heard the sentry at the gate challenge them, and then no more until Georgie stormed back in the front door, cursing and muttering to Ma. Next morning it came out that this character out of the night was one of the fringes of the intelligence system—very fringy—and he had come to tell Georgie that he had seen a Japanese submarine signaling from the entrance of the harbor. He said that he had left his car just outside the post gate and would run Georgie down to see the submarine. On the way to the car, under questioning, the man said that it was very clearly enemy signals—there was a red blinking on the left and green light blinking on the right. Of course, the man had seen the lighted buoys at the harbor entrance. Georgie said that it was part of the price one paid for hiring bums.

Georgie's growing frustration with General Drum, and the whole scene, which he felt was one of blind inactivity, made him decide to see if his luck still held. He planned a cruise to Fanning and Palmyra Islands, two small dots in the southern Pacific. Ma was enchanted with the idea, not only because he was showing some enthusiasm but also because one of her relatives was the Captain James Fanning for whom the atoll was named. She loved cruising, and she loved getting Georgie off to herself. The crew for this voyage consisted of young George, a Lieutenant Levenick who was a West Point classmate of Johnnie Waters, and Jimmie Wilder, a descendant of missionaries and son of a great local ethnologist—and a good friend. They took Jimmie Ulio's Suzuki along as cook (Jimmie had returned to the States) and, of course, Joe Ekeland.

Joe lived on board the *Arcturus* while we were stationed in Hawaii. He had a wife in Sweden and a son whom he had named Kelvin after the Kelvin, White Company because they made the best compasses. Mrs. Ekeland had also borne twins, but they had died shortly after birth. Joe carried a snapshot of them in their coffin, along with snapshots of Kelvin and, when anyone asked him if he had any children, he always said that he had three. Ma said it reminded her of that dreary poem by Wordsworth: "We are seven." Joe also had a spectacular dragon named Mu-Fat tattooed all over his back and shoulders. Mu-Fat's tail started where Joe's would have been had he had a tail. Joe was one of young George's heroes—and also one of mine.

They went off on their cruise, leaving me in charge of dear Alice Holmes, which must have been a real burden for her. I was given strict orders not to give Alice any trouble, and to be home by 1 a.m., my regular curfew. Actually, this curfew made good sense as all my beaux were in the service, and had to keep early hours, but I felt terribly abused. Here I was, twenty-one years old and still having to be home at a reasonable hour. Ma said that boys respected a girl whose parents showed that they cared for her, but I was not on Ma's wavelength at the time. The truth was that in spite of young George's fevered hopes, and probably the hopes of some of my young men, I didn't *do* anything. I drank only beer, and not much of that, as beer drinking leads inevitably to the bathroom, and in those days we were a little shy of saying that we had to go. Bamma had always allowed that real ladies were so refined that no one ever knew when they had to go to the bathroom. These types were known as angels, because angels, obviously, never had to go—if they did, you know what it would be like down here on the earth.

Of course, I had kissed a few boys that I liked, but that was as far as it went. I saw too much of where that garden path led: to the altar or to the shelf. But I don't think the parents ever quite trusted me. During my deb season, there had been a very popular musician at all of the big parties, who walked from table to table and played the theme song he had chosen for each debutante, and mine was, to my distress, "Stay as sweet as you are, don't let a thing ever change you." The other girls got "You're devastating" or "Miss Otis regrets" or "I wanna be bad," but there I was, stuck with staying as sweet as I was and not letting a thing ever change me—and, I think, Ma went along with that all the way.

Ma had never ever had as much freedom as I had, and Bee had been a post-debutante back in the manageable United States where the three months of the year we spent in New England were spent racing boats, riding horses, beagling, and occasionally going into Boston to hear the Pops. The rest of the year was spent in Washington with fox hunting, Junior League, teaching riding classes to Girl Scouts, going to the post hops, and some few dates in town when the young men could afford it. Ma always knew where Bee was and, helpfully, she got engaged at twenty-two and married at twenty-three.

I not only had the parents worrying about me, but I had my problems next door too. Mrs. Drum's sister, Miss Shug, was very interested in everything that Little Peach and I did. I will never forget one night when I got home—just at the 1 a.m. deadline. I had had a first date with a perfectly gorgeous Naval aviator, an older man of at least thirty. I had worn my gray lace dress and, as he was old and rich, we had gone to the Royal Hawaiian and danced all the lovely evening, and there seemed a prospect of future dates. This paragon had rented a car, as he was only in Honolulu for temporary duty. The round ball on the gear shift was missing, and my full skirt got caught on the exposed screw-top. I was trying to unwind it without tearing it. As I sat there struggling, the lights on the Drums' porch went on and Miss Shug's deep contralto rang out into the shimmering tropic night: "Young man, what are you doing to that nice young Patton girl?" As if by signal, the lights went on on our front porch, and Georgie appeared in his nightshirt, and in his hand the pistol he always kept in the table beside his bed. I tore my dress leaping out of the car. The young man didn't even get out. With a hurried "Good night" he took off and I never saw him again. Ma thought it was terribly funny—I was cut to the quick. I truly felt that I was protected to the nth-degree more than I really cared to be!

Dear Mrs. Drum! She spent her life trying to make up for the things that her family perpetrated. The day the parents and George were to take off on this cruise, she got herself driven down to the harbor, and went aboard the *Arcturus,* and nailed a St. Jude medal on the mast. She knew we were not of the Catholic faith, but she assured Ma that St. Jude would not care as he had been a Roman slave and knew that we all needed help and he was the saint of hopeless cases and desperate situations. Georgie was much touched by this. He agreed that he needed all the help he could get.

The cruise to the South Pacific was a success. The family had all sorts of adventures, saw many wonders, and—thanks possibly to St. Jude—got back in one piece. Georgie's faith in his luck was restored, and Ma was all rested up and ready for the next act. Neither of them knew it, thank goodness, but they had only nine more years.

The inter-island polo matches were the big season in Honolulu, and everyone came from all the Islands. There were house parties and balls and new and old scandals and liaisons, cocktail parties, luaus—and no one went to bed. The ladies all dressed as for a tropical Dublin Horseshow, and it was glorious. After two tours in the Islands and innumerable horse shows, polo games, and boat races, Ma and Georgie knew everybody and everybody knew them. The last season we were there was the greatest. Movie stars came from the coast. Bing Crosby was there with his wife, Dixie Lee. They were very young and attractive, and were invited to a lot of the parties as guests—not entertainers. Everyone wore flower leis, and nearly everyone was slightly tight most of the time, but it was a season of lights.

Georgie had suffered all his life from having a very light, high voice that did not carry and which he did not think suited him, so he made up for its lack of carrying quality by yelling at the top of his lungs. Near the end of the tournament, the Army was playing Oahu. The Oahu team was Walter Dillingham, his son, Lowell, and Jack and Dick Walter—four of the most beautiful men I have ever seen. There was a great scrimmage along the sideboards at the edge of the polo field with the horses squealing and farting, hoofs drumming, mallets making savage thwacks at the ball, and the players grunting and gasping. Georgie's voice rose high like a kite's, screaming a string of meaningless and rather colorless profanity at Walter Dillingham, who was riding him off. As in the case of another such incident in the hunting field long ago, it was just Anglo-Saxon sporting terms, such as one sportsman uses to another, but General Drum, who was not a sporting character, was outraged. I don't know what got into him. Perhaps he really did object to the goddammits and sunnuvabitches, or perhaps he was quite unconsciously jealous that an obscure lieutenant colonel on his staff was asked to all the parties, slapped on the back by all the big ranch owners, and first-named and kissed by all their pretty ladies, while he, the highest-ranking officer on the island, was only invited to the token affairs, and had never been one of the inner circle, a mysterious group that only exists in the imaginations of the people who don't think they are in it. Anyhow, General Drum got up in his important flag-draped box, signaled for the game to stop, and called for Georgie to come to his box.

It was an unprecedented departure for the sport, but the game stopped more or less in midair, and Georgie rode up, dismounted in front of General Drum, and was in front of God and everybody sternly reprimanded for foul language and conduct unbecoming to a gentleman, and relieved forthwith of the captaincy of the Army team. There was a stunned silence. All you could hear were people and horses breathing. Georgie came to attention, saluted, said, "Yes Sir," and started to lead his horse off the field.

Walter Dillingham, captain of the Oahu team, and Mr. Baldwin, captain of the Maui team (who was a spectator during that game between Army and Oahu), withdrew and conferred right in the middle of the field—Walter still on his horse. Then, Walter rode up to General Drum, who was still standing, and said loudly so that everyone heard him, that if Colonel Patton was relieved of his position on the Army team, the game would not be finished, and the rest of the tournament would be unfinished. There was quite a moment there when two strong men stood face to face, but Walter won the staring down. General Drum recalled Georgie, warned him to watch his language, and, turning around, gathered Mrs. Drum and Miss Shug and Peaches with a gesture of his head, got into his official car, and drove off. The game continued. General Drum never forgave Georgie.

The longer we stayed on the island, the more parties we went to, and there is one I often remember. The Mormons, over on the windward side of the island, had a huge party for some visiting elders of the church from Salt Lake City, and we were all invited by Kalili to go with him. Georgie had known a lot of Mormons when he was with Pershing in the Villa campaign, so he was interested to see them again. Ma, being a very special friend of Kalili's, was seated near the head of the table next to a very sour-looking elder who had no small talk. Undaunted, Ma tried him on every subject, and, finally, seeing his name on his placecard, she said brightly, "Are you by any chance related to that nice Bishop Crow and his lovely wives that Colonel Patton escorted out of Mexican territory in 1914 when we were having trouble with Pancho Villa?" The elder gave her a Grant Wood look, and replied, "He was my father, Madam, but Bishop Crow is now one of the Twelve Apostles." Ma was vastly entertained by that. When Georgie, who had studied the Book of Mormon during the evacuation, tried to explain the Mormon church to her, she just waved him away and said that she didn't want to hear any of the boring facts, that it would spoil the sense of history she had from sitting next to the son of one of the Twelve Apostles.

It is plain to see from all of this that I took both parents for granted. It is only in the course of being a parent and a grandparent myself that I have come to realize how very many adjustments Ma had had to make in manners, customs, lifestyles, and moral judgments, and how gracefully she handled them. Her reactions to some of our predicaments were extraordinarily sensible, although we must have been a sore trial to her when her own personal life was not going as smoothly as it could have been.

One situation that I did not see as such at the time, but that must have really startled her, was a reckoning with one of my beaux. He was a civilian, son and grandson of Island people of the missionary stock, and his parents were good friends of my parents. We had known each other since our first tour in 1925. He finally stopped propositioning me and proposed honorable marriage. I had not mentioned the propositions to Ma as they were not (I thought) in her frame of reference. She would immediately have concluded that I had been asking for trouble as it would have been impossible for her to realize that nice people you knew did that—either offered or accepted propositions. The proposal was quite unorthodox as it was. He took me off for a day's picnic, as he had long promised to do, to show me his various projects, which included grazing cattle on resting pineapple land, which he rented very cheaply as the cattle were supposed to enrich the land, and to a slaughterhouse he had built for slaughtering those same cattle to save butchering bills. We went in his truck, which he had bought cheaply by becoming a salesman for the truck company. That afternoon we visited all of his establishments, including the homes of his five illegitimate children, and their mothers, and their mothers' husbands, who were all terribly glad to see him and broke out the okelehao. He explained to me that it was customary to give each child eighteen dollars a month until the child was old enough to go to work, and there was no onus attached to this agreement as everyone loved everybody, and it was all naughty Polynesian fun. I was very fond of this young man—and still am—but I had not yet met anyone I wanted to marry and told him so. He took this in good part and said that if I didn't find anyone I wanted to marry to keep him in mind, as he thought we would have a very good time together. He stuck to his part of the idea. He announced his engagement to a darling girl about a month after my wedding.

I was so interested in this manifestation of Hawaiian love that I couldn't wait to tell Ma. Instead of getting mad, she said that she thought it was interesting too, especially in an ethnic way. Georgie got very mad. He thought I had been insulted, but Ma calmed him down, saying that she thought my friend had done the honorable thing: how would it have been if I had found out afterwards? She mentioned, darkly, that Georgie knew WHO she was talking about. Of course, there was always gossip about some of the old Island families and their look-alikes among godsons and children of friends. Ma said that it would be hard to be moral in such a lovely climate.

However, Ma's reaction to my really frightening brush with the facts of life was quite different. It was one of the few times I ever ran into a total lack of sympathy from her, which made me pretty bitter at the time because, for once, this mess I got into was not my own fault, and I thought she should have instinctively known it.

It happened near the end of our tour in 1937. Nearly all of my friends had gotten married. I had been a bridesmaid five times; wedding bells were breaking up that old gang of mine, and the new crop of bachelors didn't seem as much fun as the ones that were there when we got there. I was invited to a dinner dance out at Schofield Barracks and, because I had told everyone many times that I would not ever call a boy and ask him to take me to a party, my hostess delegated one of her husband's young lieutenants to be my date. I had hardly met him but my friend, Miss Anne, whose father was stationed at Schofield, said he had a rotten reputation and to be careful.

The young officer came to pick me up dressed in his nice white uniform—a giant of a man with a mean, hillbilly face. The Army takes all kinds and they become officers and gentlemen by Acts of Congress. This character's father was in the government in Washington, a backwoods politician equally at home with a whip and Bible.

It was a typical evening of dance and eating and drinking, and when my deadline for being at home (still 1 a.m.) was approaching, I told my date we had better get started as we had a forty-five-minute drive. I should have had premonitions, as the creature had gotten quieter and quieter, and had had more and more to drink as the evening wore on, but in spite of the fact that I had seen a good deal of so-called life, and had heard a great deal more, and had been propositioned quite often, I didn't really believe that people like us did things like that. The people who went around with their virginity missing were whores, fringies and some of my friends who were desperate to get married, and had played their ultimate card.

My date was perfectly agreeable about leaving, but when we went out the post gate, instead of turning toward Honolulu, he went in the opposite direction. I said that we had better start for home, and he said nothing, but turned off the road into a cane field through which I had often ridden the horses, and one that I knew well. It had in its center a fenced-in oasis of large stones, bushes, and several huge old palm trees. It was Kuhniloko, the sacred spot where the ancient Hawaiian chiefesses were brought to deliver their babies, which they did there in the open, surrounded by witnesses of high chiefs and priests so that there could be no substitutions.

The young man stopped the car right beside the sacred spot and, without further ado, tried to rape me. I had never been so surprised in my life, but my mind had never worked faster. To shorten the scene, I managed to get out of the car and, using my weakness as my strength as Georgie had taught Bee and me to do, I kneed him in the groin with the desired effect, but not before he had torn my dress, pulled down my hair, lost my hairpins, and given me the making of a black eye. I had to think fast. My first thought was, of course, to leave him writhing on the ground, and let him try to explain it to the military police when they found him. Then I reminded myself that he was the only son of a powerful politician who could ruin Georgie's career. Then I realized that if Georgie found out this fine young officer had tried to rape me, he, Georgie, would follow his code of honor and kill him. It was a Hobson's choice.

Somehow I got this total wreck (I was a very strong woman, used to riding large, active horses, and my knees and back were in great shape) into the back of his car, and then drove back to Fort Shafter. All of this had taken some time. As I drove up—leaving the car some way from the house—I could see that all the lights were on in our quarters, and in General Drum's quarters as well, which meant that Miss Shug had concerned herself. I pulled myself together as well as I could, and walked in the front door, scared as hell and, therefore, mad as hell, plus beginning to feel the effects of shock—and I caught hell. The latter is quite understandable—I *looked* like hell! Georgie and Ma new something had happened, and they put pressure on me in every way they knew, including cutting off my allowance, but I would not tell them what had happened, although I knew they suspected the worst. I knew very well the offending officer would never tell.

Fortunately, I was riding in a horse show the next day, and my faithful steed,

Keanakkolu (the only thing left on earth that loved me), took a header over a jump and I broke my arm among other things, so that all my battling bruises, which were beginning to show, had a reason to exist.

Years later, after I was married, I told Ma and Georgie the whole story. Georgie gave a sentimental sniff, put his arm around me and hugged me, and said, "You did the right thing, R-E, I would have had to kill the son-of-a-bitch, and it would have wrecked my career." Ma got a very thoughtful look: "Imagine his turning into that sacred birthing place, of all places! I wonder what put that into his head? Could there be any significance, or psychic influence, connected with that?"

During our first tour on the Islands in 1926, there was a tremendous eruption of the volcano on Mauna Loa, and the village of Hoopuloa was blotted out. Dr. Jagger, the famous volcanologist, told Ma that, shortly after the eruption, he and Mrs. Jagger were driving to their mountain home when they met a crowd of people on the road—men, women, and children—carrying bundles of food and goods, and helping their aged relatives along the way. It seemed to be a whole village on the move. A few miles farther along he met the bus and asked the driver, who was only part Hawaiian, what it was all about. The driver snorted, "Those natives! Yes, those are the people of Hoopuloa moving. They have been three days on the road. They are on their way to throw themselves into Halemaumau [the fire pit]." Dr. Jagger discovered that a girl of the village had dreamed for three nights in a row that the whole island of Hawaii was to be destroyed, and that when she told her dream to the village kahuna, the native priest, he interpreted it to mean that all the inhabitants of Hoopuloa would have to sacrifice themselves to save the island.

Dr. Jagger told the bus driver to go after them and tell them that he had intervened with the goddess, Pele, and that their willingness to be sacrificed had been accepted as a sacrifice, and that they were to go home.

The Hawaiians believed this because they thought Dr. Jagger was in the confidence of Pele. He had harnessed some of the steam vents in the lava flows for heat and power, and he walked fearlessly over the bleak territory she had marked for her own.

In 1936 Mauna Loa erupted again, and the waterworks of the city of Hilo were threatened. Once before, during a crisis of this kind, Princess Ruth, then the governor of Hawaii, had thrown a lock of the hair of Kamehameha the Great into the oncoming lava and this had stopped it, but times had changed and the government decided to bomb the flowing lava and see if that would alter its course. Three Army bombers dropped their bombs near the source of the lava flow, and the flow ceased. No one could prove the bombs were responsible, but everyone knew that Pele was furious, for she immediately destroyed two cities in South America with earthquakes and caused the deaths of two elderly part-Hawaiian ladies who lived in California. The Hawaiians all said that Pele would punish the three bomber pilots also.

The first flight these men made after the bombing of the volcano their planes collided with another plane in mid-air and one officer was killed outright. The second officer jumped, but his parachute failed to open. His chute tangled in the guy wires of a gasoline storage tank and his life was saved, but his legs were badly injured. Some time later, the wife of the third pilot drank a bottle of drain cleaner and died in agony. Pele was avenged.

A month or so after all of this, we took some touristing friends to the Hawaiian Village for an evening of native food and dance. One of Ma's Hawaiian friends was with us, and I had invited the second bomber pilot—the one who had hurt his legs—as an escort for one of the visiting girls. At the end of the evening, the Hawaiian dancers performed a very special hula for Pele. There was a lot of scenery involved with red flames in the background. In the middle of the performance, the pilot, who had been easing his pain with the bottle, called out loudly, "Phooey on Pele! They said I should give her a pig, but I gave her a bomb—that's what I did—I gave her a bomb!" One of the Hawaiian girls waiting on our table whispered to Ma, "This is your friend? Better you push black pig into Halemaumau for him, and put his name on it. Then, mebbe OK."

We all tried to shut the young man up, but he was quite tight and probably still somewhat in shock from all he had been through, so he kept on making offensive remarks, and we left the village. The dancers, as well as the other guests, had heard what he was saying, and the Hawaiians looked very serious.

There were always old women selling flower leis outside the Hawaiian Village, and one very old lady with red eyes put a lei around Ma's neck and one around mine. She leaned over and touched Ma's cheek with her cheek. Then she drew back and began to very softly wail for the dead. The pilot did not catch on, but the rest of us did.

He was routinely transferred back to the States some months later and we never heard for sure what became of him, but I was told by another officer, after the war, that he died in a flameout over Germany.

The high point of our second tour was for Ma the publication of her book, *The Blood of the Shark*. The newspapers were very complimentary about it:

Beatrice Ayer Patton's *Blood of the Shark* (Paradise of the Pacific Press) is a classic. Many have written concerning the Hawaiians and their deeds of prowess in a land of glamour, beauty and ancient beliefs, but Mrs. Patton achieves the peak.

Beatrice Patton, wife of Colonel George S. Patton, Jr. is a Bostonian whose early loves were the sea and ships. She is a skilled navigator and her knowledge shows in her meticulous use of nautical terms. She is a linguist of the romance languages; she speaks the Hawaiian language perfectly [this was not quite true]. She loves Hawaii, its lore, legends and people. This great affection is the warp and woof of *Blood of the Shark*. Mrs. Patton dipped her pen into brilliant flowing colors and produced paintings of old Hawaii to which one returns again and again to discover new beauty—the ultimate end of writing. Mrs. Patton spent seven years of intensive study before writing [the book].

Blood of the Shark is a journey of bewilderment and non-understanding for Adam Gordon, English Midshipman under the famed navigator Captain Vancouver who came to the Islands at the beginning of the Nineteenth Century. The novel is a story of adventure. It is also psychological in its dramatic narrative concerning the courageous and faithful Kilohana, daughter of the High Chief, Kaha, and his wife, Ahia, and of the Aawini Clan, who believed they were the offspring of the Shark.

Mrs. Patton's novel rings true to the times of Kamehameha and the life of that period. There is a concentrated intensity that is felt throughout. It has a panoramic richness as one goes from Honolulu to Kohala, to Madam Pele's home, and on the brig, Lucy, when Adam, Kilohana and their daughter sail to Monterey, California. The pace never lets down and over all the main characters is always the shadow of the shark. The detail is vivid, the quality of imagery is rare, and the novel marks Mrs. Patton as a writer who can recreate the legends of the past and make them come alive.

Emma Ahuena Taylor, descendant of the high chiefs and chiefesses of Hawaii, many who form the character-bases of the story, has written an appreciative criticism of Mrs. Patton's book . . .

Actually, Adam Gordon (which is a fictional name) was Emma's ancestor, as was the Kilohana of the book, whose real name was Ahia.

The night before the publication of Ma's book, she was given a party by her Hawaiian friends. The food, specially chosen as suitable ceremonial fare, was cooked in earth ovens and brought to our quarters. Before we sat down to eat, Dr. Peter Buck—Te Rangi Hiroa—who was the author of the foreword, sprinkled the four corners of the area with sea water, and Emma Taylor offered a prayer in Hawaiian that translates as:

Oh, Io, Oh, Io
Thy servant calls thee to the very housetops
No other god can ascend thy mountain-like tabus
Thou art Iolani, the eyes of gracious eternity
Eternity that sees the righteous, eternity that sees the wrong-doer
Father of those who hearken, think and propagate

Father whose eyes are everywhere
Have mercy on thine offspring, Beatrice Patton
Give her ever more knowledge, skill and power
And to the chieftain sitting at this board of love offering tonight
Give all the benefits, for he is our prop and our witness
Here is the hog that Beatrice has placed before you
Here is the red kumu, symbol of the sacredness of God
Here is the white hog of the ocean, a mullet, Ainaholo
Here is the squid, symbol of the war god who melts away all obstacles
Here is the breadfruit, symbol of growth; let this book succeed and grow
As, with Thy help, the knowledge of Hawaii-nei grows within her
Give love and success to Colonel Patton, her husband, and their children
And all of us gathered at this board to partake of this offering to you
So be it. The prayer is free.

As Ma had said, Emma Taylor was an Episcopalian, but she believed in rendering unto Caesar—

Later, to Ma, who was simply overwhelmed with the success of her book, Emma said, "It could not fail. The prayer was completed."

I should add that this prayer is almost word for word in its main substance the prayer of Kamehameha the Great. It is said that he was a priest of Io, god of light, and that his family belonged to the Order of Powerful Lips, so no prayer of his could really ever fail.

The family sailed the *Arcturus* back to California. Their departure was dramatic and traumatic. They took young George with them. He was annoyed with them. I did not want to go and, most fortunately, there was not room for me on the schooner, but he accused me of getting out of it just because I had a broken arm and he thought that most unfair.

Alice Holmes and I went back to the mainland by steamer, and were much more comfortable. The *Arcturus* had a wicked trip. They were in one storm where they had to lie to for a couple of days. But we were all down on the dock in San Diego when they made their landfall.

The family left the *Arcturus* in San Diego to be sold; Joe Ekeland stayed with her. Someone found out about the voyage and about Joe and, as a publicity gimmick, Greta Garbo went down to see the boat and meet Joe. He told me, "Oh, she was a very nice lady, all right; and ven she smiled her mouth vas all pink and healthy, yoost like a nice dog."

Ma and Georgie and George and Alice went back to Massachusetts so that Georgie could have a long leave at Green Meadows. I stayed on in California for a visit with my Aunt Tinta. Georgie had orders to report for duty at Fort Riley, Kansas. During his leave at the farm, he was out riding with Ma and Johnnie Waters, and the one thing I am sure he had never believed could happen to him did happen to him. He was, by his own admission, riding in the danger zone—his horse's head even with Ma's stirrup. He had warned us, and even punished us, about riding in this position, and he had been right, because it was fly time and Ma's horse, Memorial, lashed out at a horsefly and broke Georgie's leg with a sound like a dry stick snapping. He ended up in the good local Beverly Hospital, which was the dream-child of Fred Ayer, and which was doctored by some of Georgie's and Ma's best friends. The broken leg assumed the complication of phlebitis, and he was in a bad way. Phlebitis was treated more with immobility than with drugs in those days, and there was a constant fear of further complication. This was the bottom of the barrel for Georgie. His frenetic tour under General Drum, his growing discouragement with lack of promotion, and his ever-present worry that he would never have his war piled up on him, and he was suicidally depressed. To pile Ossa on Pelion, the Army sent a medical board out from Boston to find out if he had been under the influence of drugs or drinking when the horse kicked him. Of course, he was cleared and the accident was decided to be in the line of duty, but Georgie thought it was a direct sign from the Goddess Fortuna that she was through with him.

Georgie ran a regular night club in his hospital room—he called it the Hula Hula Night Club and the room was decorated with streams of colored toilet paper among other things. He had a steady stream of visitors, and all the nurses fell in love with him, but beneath it all he was the victim of a deepening depression that was sensed by few but Ma.

All the time the family had had the *Arcturus,* they had talked about the boat they wanted to build when and if Georgie retired. Ma at this time had the inspiration to get hold of John Alden, the world-famous boat designer, and also a friend of many friends, and ask him to collaborate with Georgie on designing their dream schooner in which they would sail around the world when Georgie retired from active duty. Mr. Alden was immensely impressed by all of Georgie's and Ma's ideas, and between them they designed a boat that was later christened *When and If,* and which gave years of pleasure to the whole family. This occupation was the only thing that kept Georgie, like Christian, from sinking into the Slough of Despond.

When Georgie finally got home, Ma had had a bathroom built off the playroom on the ground floor, and he was installed there—right next to the front door and the dining room—where he was the center of attention. As soon as he could hobble on sticks, he went down to the stable and beat Memorial with his crutch and threatened to shoot him dead. Ma did not take kindly to this, and told Georgie to stop being so dramatic, that he knew very well it was his own fault that he had been kicked, and it was childish to take it out on a dumb animal. This made Georgie very huffy and he accused her of denying him one of the few pleasures he had left, the killing of the horse that had ruined his career.

The six months he stayed home and convalesced were hard on everyone, especially Ma. She always said that in every marriage, each partner always thought that they were doing 60 percent of the getting-along, but during those months she was *really* doing everything. She tried to keep up Georgie's morale—which he always referred to as a dirty French word—kept people coming to see him, and encouraged his plans for the *When and If.* To get out of the house, she rode every day, and raced her boat in Manchester and Marblehead in the twice-weekly series, but her absences were deeply resented by Georgie. Something always seemed to go wrong the minute she stepped out of the house, and one day, she said, exasperated, "Georgie, you sound more and more like your father when he used to talk to your mother about walking hand in hand into the sunset!"

Georgie did his doctor-exercises with religious zeal and improved much faster than his doctors had thought possible, but nothing helped his state of mind. One day when my sister was home on a visit that was supposed to cheer him up, we were gossiping in our third-floor eyrie when Ma came upstairs and said, "For goodness' sake, one or both of you girls go down and talk to your father! He's lying brooding in the hammock about not knowing his children and the fact that no one loves him, and he's very depressed; I can't do another thing with him!"

Bee and I drew lots, as we had done years before, and I lost again, so I went downstairs to the brick-floored porch in the back of the dining room where he was, indeed, lying in the hammock with his leg propped up, and an expression of deepest woe on his face. I couldn't think of a thing to say! Finally, in desperation, remembering that it had worked before, I remarked that I hadn't heard him recite Bind-their-kings-in-chains-and-their-nobles-with-links-of-iron for a long time, and I certainly would like to hear it again because he did it so well. With a little encouragement, he continued with part of his vast repertoire. By the time it was the cocktail hour, he was back to normal, and as he got up to go and dress, he squeezed me affectionately, and said, "My, I certainly did enjoy our talk. I don't see enough of you girls!" History repeats itself all right.

Chapter 14
Europe Before the War

After the Christmas of 1937, Georgie was well enough to take off for Fort Riley. Bee and Johnnie Waters had been stationed there since their marriage in 1934, but Johnnie got orders to the Military Academy at West Point, which was a real disappointment to us as it would have been such fun to be stationed together, although it would have probably been very hard on Johnnie.

When we went to Hawaii in 1935, Georgie had more or less dumped the older hunters (the ones he did not think would survive the long boat trip to and from the Islands) on the Waterses, so we had some of our old horses waiting for us at Fort Riley in addition to the ones we brought with us from Massachusetts. The dumping of the hunters had not been an unmixed blessing for Johnnie Waters. As a first-year student in the Cavalry School, he was assigned a trained horse to ride, and a young remount to train, so Bee had to keep our old horses exercised; that was all she did. Bee was an outstanding rider. She looked better on a horse than any woman I have ever seen. The whole life at Fort Riley was centered around King Horse—care, feeding, sickness, breeding, their quirks and habits, their infinitely various shoeing—and the Waterses were well-mounted and able to compete, and it was a life that was one long competition. There was a horse show every Friday, and the winners of the Friday horse show were qualified to compete in the Saturday horse show. Bee turned in perfect performance after perfect performance, but never got into the ribbons. We had been taught by Ma and Georgie never to complain or question the judge's decision; that to be a good sport was as important as being a good Christian and far more important than just winning—but sometimes her heart was sore.

One night, however, she got a clue to her dilemma. The Waterses were at the usual cocktail party after the horse show, and Colonel C. L. Scott, a close friend of Georgie's and one of the vertebrae of the backbone of the U.S. Cavalry, came up to Bee, quite tight, and said, "Well, Little Bee, I guess you know you won that last class." Bee, who had not even been called in, murmured something about how she did not think her horse had put in a good performance, and Scotty replied, "Well, you damn well won it, and I want to tell you here and now how we just love to give you the gate—you riding your goddam father's goddam thousand-dollar horses against these flea-bitten remounts! It just does us good to show up Georgie's goddam thoroughbreds with him off in Hawaii where he can't do a goddam thing about it!"

Bee didn't feel it worthwhile to tell Scotty that the horse she had been riding was a $170 horse from the Parker Ranch, but she said that she felt a lot better, knowing that spite and not incompetence was keeping her out of the ribbons.

Colonel Scott was just a symptom of the times. Georgie was not the only officer suffering from a lack of purpose. The other colonels his age were just as frustrated as he was. There they were at the height of their powers, trained all their military lives to a fine point; knowledgeable, dedicated men of patriotism and vision with nothing to do but wait and wait, and while waiting, risking their necks over hurdles in the riding ring, or trying to kill each other on the polo fields—Scott, Chaffee, Wainwright, Herr, Henry, Patton, Richardson, Van Voohris, and Lear—they would, within five years, become the builders and leaders of the greatest armored force the world has ever seen. In 1937, they were at Riley and Bliss and Leavenworth and Clark, wasting their sweetness on the desert air—ready to go with no place to go.

Bee and Johnnie were leaving behind them a very good cook named Vergie, whom they thought would be just right for Ma and Georgie. However, Bee felt she had to explain to Ma about Vergie's private life. Vergie was married, but not to Private George Meeks, who lived with her in the maids' quarters of the Waters' quarters. Private Meeks was very quiet and unobtrusive and they seldom saw him, but he *was* living there. Ma said that she certainly would like to have Vergie as her cook, but it would have to be as Vergie Meeks with marriage lines. Ma had her standards.

By the time we got to Fort Riley all of this had been taken care of, and that is how George Meeks came into our lives. At first we never saw him, but then Ma found that Georgie's immaculate uniforms were being processed without her supervision; his brass took on the appearance of solid gold; his boots were as mirrors; his woven belts were soaked in the proper solution of Clorox and water that gave them the necessary faded look that went with working khaki; his uniforms, which had been her responsibility all of their married life, with the aid of various orderlies, were being slowly but surely taken out of Ma's hands by the hands of a master. The night Ma found Georgie's tuxedo laid out on the bed with the studs in the shirt, and the cufflinks already installed, she decided to just be thankful and ask no questions.

Gradually, George Meeks emerged as a definite character. He was a man of few words and some mystery. He either did not know or would not say how old he was, but he did mention once that he had been with the U.S. troops in Archangel. That did not and still does not mean a thing to me, but Georgie said that it meant Meeks was a lot older than he looked. Meeks was very black with a beautiful rare smile which showed a mouth full of perfect teeth that looked as if they had been filed to points. He shaved his head. He said something once to the effect that he did so that the gray wool wouldn't show. He could neither read nor write, except for his name, rank, and serial number. He had been in the Army goodness knows how long; had always been a private; and was carried on the Army lists as a cook.

George Meeks was always there in the background waiting. He was wonderful with the dogs, who loved him. What it was that he discovered in Georgie, only George Meeks and God will know, but what Georgie found in him was Man Friday, the loyal and true. They were together from then on until Georgie died.

After the war, George Meeks disappeared, except for times when someone in the family was stationed in Washington, D.C. Then, if any one of us was having a party, George Meeks would appear in his white coat and black trousers, and wait on the table, mix drinks, and speak politely in a monotone to the many officers who had known him when Georgie was alive. He would never take money for his services, although he would accept a bottle of Johnnie Walker Black Label Scotch. We found out that he kept track of us through a laundress we always used when we were in Washington—a wonderful little woman named Fanny Hardin. He would not communicate with us, and Fanny said that she didn't know where he lived; he left a locked trunk in her house, and she rarely saw him. Bee asked him once at one of her parties if there was anything the family could do for him, and he said, "No, Miss Bee. I is taken care of. The Army got to doctor me and bury me. The General he see to it I got all I need before he die."

George Meeks closed his eyes for the last time in the Old Soldiers Home in the 1960s. He really died on December 21, 1945.

Fort Riley was a wonderful station and we all loved it, especially Ma. She had a lot of old friends and acquaintances there. Our quarters were next door to the Bachelor Officers' Quarters and across the street from the chapel. There is an old saying that all good Field Artillerymen go to Fort Sill, Oklahoma, when they die. The Cavalry had a song about a place called Fiddler's Green, which

was halfway down the road to hell and where old Cavalrymen were supposed
to meet. I think it was old Fort Riley.

Ma rode horseback every day, gardened madly as soon as the weather permitted, joined the Choral Society and the Dramatic Club, and enjoyed most of
all the fact that Georgie was back in the Cavalry with his peers, and not on some
general staff with a mixed bag of infantrymen, engineers, and God-knows-
what-all. We all rode in the horse shows and chased jackrabbits across the
prairies. We had a sordid sort of pack at the time—a greyhound given to me in
California by one of the Callahans; a large Siamese cat named Dinah, who
could keep up with horses when she felt like it; the pointer, Lover; and an elderly police dog named Samson. Old Sam was descended from a dog Georgie
had brought back from World War I. He had found that dog, which he named
Wolf, half starved, guarding the decomposing body of a German soldier on the
battlefield. We always had a couple of his descendants. Georgie hated cats, but
made an exception of Dinah because as a kitten at Green Meadows, when he
was convalescing from his broken leg, she had bitten him on the toe when he
struck at her with his crutch, and even after he started beating her, she had
hung on, growling. He said she was a werecat.

Ma was so happy to see Georgie out of the dumps and megrims, and writing
manuals and articles, and being like his old self, that she said it was really too
good to be true and couldn't last.

Meanwhile at West Point, Bee, finally freed from exercising all those horses,
started exercising her rights and privileges, and got pregnant, and Ma went east
in April of 1938 to assist in the arrival of her first grandchild. I stayed on and
kept house for Georgie and George, when he was home, but the complexities
of my social life, which included flying (literally) visits from some of my Air
Corps beaux who were stationed nearby, decided Ma and Georgie to send me
off for the summer to England and France with Cousin Florence Hatheway.

Mostly my never-to-be-forgotten trip was due to some kind of family con-
ference that Ma and Georgie had about me. I knew that they did not care for
the particular officer I said that I was in love with at the time, although he was
a dear. At one point, when they were trying to talk some sense into my head,
Georgie remarked testily that he was glad the bastard was in the Air Corps because he would probably die young and set me free. Anyhow, that is when they
decided to use the time-tested Victorian remedy for an unsuitable affair and
send me to Europe. I really hadn't planned it that way, but I would have pretended to be in love with Caliban to have gotten a trip to Europe!

Auntie Florence and I embarked on the German ocean liner *Europa,* and
stayed for a month at the Hotel Wagram in Paris. This was an enchanting family

hotel opposite the main entrance to the Tuileries. Auntie was a wonderful companion. She never appeared until lunch time, but she had a lot of French friends who took me on exhausting tours of the city. Mostly she let me wander around Paris by myself, with a copy of a Dumas novel in one hand and a guidebook in the other. I spoke good workable French, and managed not to get my bottom pinched too often. Every night we dined together; the rest of the time was mine and I walked all over Paris, spending whole days in the Louvre.

As soon as George's school was out, we went to London and met Ma and Georgie and there Auntie turned me over to Ma, fading from the scene.

Ma adored Europe, and she was ready to roll! She wanted to show George and me the whole thing in six weeks!

Her first act was to get in touch with Colonel Horace Fuller who was with the U.S. embassy in Paris and an old friend. She wanted to see the battlefields of World War I where Georgie had fought, and she wanted a good guide. Colonel Fuller produced one of the most interesting, mysterious, and enchanting characters that ever came into our lives—M. Vsevolod Aglaimoff, who was with the embassy in some capacity, and whom Colonel Fuller considered an expert on World War I. M. Vsevolod was a White Russian. He had been in one of the regiments that was sponsored by one of the grand duchesses, and after we got to know him well, he showed us his photograph albums. What a different M. Vsevolod he had been in those days! Plump, laughing, surrounded by joyous fellow officers, and the grand duchess, so pretty in her hat-crowned pompadour, passing out honors to her own regiment! But the Revolution had been the great equalizer. M. Vsevolod's brother, a Naval officer, and other of his classmates had been fed alive into the boilers of the ships they had commanded by the communist crews. M. Vsevolod himself had been wounded, and he never spoke of this period in his life. The man who took us through the battlefields was a walking skeleton with waxen white skin, high-stretched cheekbones, and the darkly hooded eyes of his Tartar inheritance. He never smiled, but he was very gentle.

Our tour of the war zone was ruthless. No detail of any spot where Georgie had been was overlooked. We photographed each other standing on the little bridge over the Rupt de Mad, where Georgie had walked to see if it was mined; we searched in vain for the exact spot where he had been wounded, a little plain between two hills. We roamed the streets of Langres, and Ma was sure she had located the ancient chateau where he had been billeted although no one answered the bell when she pulled it. We did find the little cathedral with its Roman capital snitched from some local long-gone pagan temple where Georgie and his friends had killed the wild pig.

Nearby were the remains of one of the camps of Attila the Hun, who ravaged

Gaul in around 451 AD. Georgie had loved that site. We also saw Champlieu, near the river Oise, where Georgie had his déjà vu experience of having camped there with Caesar's armies. The ruin had been much excavated and restored since 1917–1918. Ma was in her element. All the guides everywhere fell for her dynamic enthusiasm and her excellent French. They told her things and showed her things they didn't usually take time to demonstrate to the other tourists and Ma, in her time, told them a lot of things they didn't know. She was a walking encyclopedia of World War I, so the old veterans would talk to her also. The amount of ground that we covered between June 16, when Ma and George arrived in London, and June 30, when we left for Italy, has to be a record!

The visit to Italy had been the big question on our itinerary ever since we had gotten to Europe. Cousin Mario was dying for us to come to visit, but Ma said that she would not go if her niece, Diddah, was in residence; Diddah had so many wild ideas and revolutionary projects that Ma said that she would spoil our holiday. Finally, Mario wired us that Diddah had decided to go back to her mother in Massachusetts for a month, and he was alone with the two little boys in Perugia, so Ma wired back that we were on our way rejoicing. Cousin Mario met us at the Rome airport with much emotion and a huge bunch of gladioli. Nothing would do but that we should see the sights of Rome before we went to the hotel, so we drove all over Rome with Mario giving a dramatic, running dialogue all mixed together about which Caesar had done what in such and such a place, and what he, Mario, had also done there. Mario spoke excellent English when he wanted to, but when he was excited, he spoke Italian, so George and I missed most of the best parts, but Ma was in whoops. Her spoken Italian was a bit rusty, but she understood every word.

Mario took us that night to a very romantic restaurant about which he had many happy memories. We ate under the stars among fireflies, and for dessert he peeled for each of us a perfect peach—sent for and inspected in detail—each one of which he set into a tall glass of champagne where the little bubbles made the peach bob up and down. I was overcome by the storybook atmosphere.

Next day we set off for Perugia in their expensive Italian car, driven by a speed-freak named Luigi, who wore a uniform, carried a gun, and doubled as a chauffeur, bodyguard, and goodness knows what else. We hurtled through walled towns where the sides of the car brushed the sides of the gates and made it through by centimeters. The lovely time-mellowed walls of the little towns were covered with Mussolini's slogans, which Mario translated for us exuberantly. Cousin Mario had to stop every half hour or so to relieve himself, but this he did with unself-conscious cheer, and always came back to the car with a bunch of flowers that he had picked while peeing. The gladioli had the place of honor on the jump seat, but the rest of the car soon filled up with fragrant carnations, wild mint, and anemones. Mario had stories about every town and ruin we passed. It was a fascinating ride into a past full of emperors and marching legions, and a more recent past where the galantes of Mario's heyday sported in the fields of clover and bucolic females.

In the afternoon we reached Pila, an ancient town near Assisi. The town was small in size but huge in history. For centuries it had been the home base of two families, the Oddi and the Balleoni. These families were rivals in all things, and when the Balleoni were in the driver's seat, the Oddi left town and went and soldiered as condottierri until they had gotten together enough bully boys to go back to Pila and oust the Balleoni, who would leave town and repeat the scene. The town was also famous for a rock fight that took place each year when the neighbors pelted each other with rocks—the bigger the better—and the side with the fewer casualties was the winner.

The townspeople had other ways of pacifying each other. Cousin Mario pointed out two crudely man-shaped iron cages hanging rusting on the walls of the large palazzi, and told us that his ancestors (I was never sure whether he was an Oddi or a Balleoni) hung their enemies alive in these cages until they died of hunger and exposure and that, when he was a little boy, there were still some human bones on one of the cages. My brother was charmed by this.

The nearby lake of Trasimene was inhabited by a certain fish called tilapia gallilie, which was considered a great delicacy. During the Renaissance, one of the popes decided that he would fancy a dish of fish from Trasimene, and ordered it to be produced. The people of Pila had never really acknowledged the pope, their idea being that if he didn't bother them, they wouldn't bother him. They sent one of the most important people in Pila to the pope with the fish. They had the tilapia caught and strung into a necklace, which the messenger wore around his neck as he walked to Rome where he presented the rotting fish in person to the pope. Ma was so pleased with this story that she asked Mario if he could have some served to her. Several nights later there was fish for dinner, a whole fish, uncleaned, fried in olive oil, full of bones as a pincushion. Mario complained loudly that these were not tilapia, and the waiter, Georgio, allowed that that was indeed the truth, but that no one had felt like fishing that morning, and that as we were strangers, we would never know the difference. (Ma understood the conversation—the servants never quite realized that she understood Italian.) Mario seized the dish of fish, and going over to the dumbwaiter behind his chair, he shouted challenges to the cook below and dropped the plate, fish and all, down the dumbwaiter where there was a horrid crash, and a stunned silence for a short time. We eventually got our genuine tilapia, and they were very like smelt, but more tasteless, being a freshwater fish.

Mario's and Diddah's home, Torre de Pila, was old and lovely and full of surprises. Mario had designed it. It was an old manor built around a fourteenth century watchtower. There was a fountain with falling water on the stair landings so the house was always full of the sound of moving water. A huge hall on the main floor divided the house into two sections. Every window in the house was double-screened, as Diddah had a loathing of bugs and germs, but the huge double doors at each end of the hall stood open night and day with fishnets draped across them, hung with bunches of herbs and dried flowers tied artistically on the nets, a sure way to keep out the flies according to the local customs; the flies had not heard about this so the house was full of them. Mario spent all day swatting at them, calling out dramatically, "Morte a mosca! Mosca infama!"

The food was full of flies, the wine was full of flies, and when Georgio, the apprentice butler, found out that Ma had a distaste for flies in her food, he stood behind her chair at meals. From time to time, his huge hand would dart down over her shoulder to remove a fly from her food or drink, and then he would lean over her, smiling winningly, and show her the fly, which had been squished between his fingers: "Mosca, signora!"

Georgio was a beautiful Etruscan with classic curls, classic features, and gray eyes with long lashes. He was the footman when Diddah was in residence, but when she went on trips all the upper servants took a much-needed break and the second team came in—all except Porcorossi, the be-all, do-all, and end-all. Porcorossi was Mario's factotum, a small, violent man with fierce energy and a sense of drama. When he was serving the wine, he wore his wine steward's costume with a silver taster on a chain around his neck; when he was the game keeper, he wore a Robin Hood hat with a long pheasant feather in it. Mario, being of a certain age, did not sleep well and all night long you could hear his bellow: "Porcorossi!"

The other unsleeping pillar of the house was Philomena, who did everything that Porcarossi didn't have time to do. I think she was the housekeeper. The kitchen was under the dining room, and all the food came up on the dumbwaiter. If Mario was not pleased with what came up, he would stand over the dumbwaiter and shriek down at the cook, as with the tilapia, and the cook would shriek back. Once in a while, he would pick up our full dishes of food and drop them down the hole. Then he would start worrying about what Diddah would say when she got home and counted the china and glass. Ma, who thoroughly enjoyed the whole scene, suggested that, as he had the second-team servants working, he could blame it all on their clumsiness and give them a few lira to keep them quiet. Mario told Ma that she thought just like an Italian!

Cousin Mario was hell-bent to give us a good time, and the day would start with, "Well, darleeengs, w'at shall we do on this buon giorno? Be-a-triz, would you lak to deeg up a naice Roman temple today?" Of course, Ma always was ready to dig up a temple of any kind, so we would repair to the last place where Mario had seen a temple, and it would usually have been plowed for corn. We always went in style, and before we left there always had to be a picnic basket full of wine, fruit, and cheese, to keep our strength up. This basket he oversaw himself so whenever we finally got someplace, it was usually time to turn around and go home.

However, the day we went to dig up the temple, the peasants plowing the fields agreed with the Count that, indeed, there was a temple—but where? So we wandered around, Count and peasant and George and me, and eventually we found some broken roof tiles, jug handles, and shards of iridescent glass that George and I prayerfully collected and which we have to this day.

Another day Cousin Mario said they would have a fox hunt—just as they did at Myopia—because the foxes were killing his baby pheasants. George and I—Ma had too much sense—eagerly joined the hunt. It consisted of all the workmen on the place, led by Cousin Mario and Porcarossi, running wildly through the woods, carrying cocked and loaded shotguns, and shouting for the infama volpone to come out and show himself. There were shots and cries and screams, and George and I threw ourselves down under a bush and lay there as flat as we could until the hunt was over. There were frantic armed Italians in funny hats running in every direction, and all that was needed was one case of mistaken identity, or one awkward stumble. George said it must be like being in a war, pinned down by enemy fire.

We found out later that the leader of the beaters was a neighbor, the Marchese Spinola. The Marchese usually led the beaters during game hunts, because he had discovered years ago that his wife had been unfaithful to him, and he, therefore, hoped to die honorably in the hunting field to make her feel badly. Her maiden name had been Graffanetta Balleoni, so I don't suppose she would have cared.

Another time Mario took us to see the famous tomb of the Volumna family, who, he said, were his ancestors. It is the most famous of underground Etruscan tombs carved from the tufa, shaped like a room, with couches built along the walls and paintings of torches, dancers, fauns, nymphs, garlands, and cooking equipment on the walls.

Mario also had several parties, culminating in a dance for us. The first party was an inaugurazione de la piscina—in other words, they filled the swimming pool and invited people over to swim. All Mario's friends and relatives came, plus a few carefully chosen officers from a nearby air base, so that I would have plenty of beaux. In uniform, these were a bunch of young Roman gods. In bathing suits they all had little paunches, which Ma blamed on their diet of pasta. What a bunch of fast workers they were!

The dance was unforgettable. Philomena decorated the whole house with flowers; everything was sumptuous. During the afternoon Ma overheard a violent altercation between Philomena and Mario; then she heard water running, and Philomena complaining loudly about American plumbing. Ma went to see what was going on and found Philomena trying to poke the whole dining room centerpiece of gladioli, to which Mario had objected, down the lavatory toilet with a poker. Ma tried to explain that the toilet was not really for flower disposal, and Philomena asked what use was it, then?

The fantastic dance had all ages dancing apart and together to the sometimes eerie music of the hometown band. As Ma had predicted, most of the young Air Force officers proposed to me as a matter of honor. She had told me that the combination of blonde hair and money would prove irresistible. Mario and I had a wonderful time, and so did Ma, and even George, who felt the lack of the language deeply. He finally got up his courage and danced with some of the younger girl cousins who had been looking at him with their great doe-eyes all evening, positively willing him to dance. He was blond and rich, too.

The next day Mario said that he and I must have a serious talk. This boiled down to the fact that here I was twenty-three and still unmarried and, therefore, I was ripening on the branch, ready for plucking. He wanted me to know that all of his unmarried cousins were available, but that he had also been very careful in choosing the young officers he had invited to the house; they were all Medici or Borgia or d'Este or Buoncompagnia of impeccable lineage, and he thought that the ideal situation would be that I marry one of them and settle down in Italy, where I would be good company for Diddah. Of course, after I had borne the requisite number of sons, I could entertain whomever I pleased and enjoy lovers by the score and, my husband, the lucky devil, could go and do likewise. I hastily assured Mario that I was touched by his concern and friendship, but that I was madly in love with someone in the U.S.A., and my engagement was about to be announced. He was very philosophical about it all, and said that his offer would hold, although I would have gotten a better choice of husband if I had come as a virgin and not as a divorcée.

Diddah had obviously filled the requirement of having the requisite number of sons. Their two little boys, Frederico and Giunio, were at Pila with governesses and nannies, and were the apples of Mario's eyes. The boys were small and dark and very bright and very dear. Frederico was around all the time, but

Giunio was still in the nursery. Diddah's secretary had been left behind to deal with Diddah's endless correspondence. She was very nice, very much from New England—a typical rockbound coast type. If you had met her naked in Eden, you would have known she was a Yankee.

Diddah had a finger in every pie, and the letters to prove it. Some of her activities were upsetting to Mario. He told Ma that Diddah had really caused a lot of ill feeling when she walked up to a group of nuns on the street in Pila and called out "Priests' whores!" Mario said that some of these nuns were his old cousins and relatives who had been too poor to have dowries, or too ugly to be married, and their feelings were hurt. Diddah also collected stray dogs and kept them in a modern heated kennel and fed them meat. When she was away, the help ate the meat. She also fancied peacocks on the lawn, and that was all right except on cold nights they roosted on top of the chimneys, which made the fireplaces smoke. But all in all, Mario was very fond of Diddah, and he loved his house. One of his treasures was the painted ceiling in the grand salon done by an artist friend. It depicted an idyllic farm scene with hay makers, wagons, farmers and their wives—all portraits of Mario's servitors, and on the back of the main wagon an unmistakable portrait of Mussolini, bare to the waist, loading grain. Mario and Diddah stood looking noble, holding onto the heads of two horses with the little boys by their knees wearing black shirts. In the distance was Assisi with St. Francis shooting out of it like a Roman candle. Mario had begged Diddah's secretary to pose so that she, too, would be immortalized and, although she was shy, he talked her into it. The artist was a man of talent and humor. When the picture was at last unveiled at a huge party, every portrait was recognizable, including the secretary, whose nice New England head was attached to the voluptuous body of a peasant mother nursing an enormous baby from an enormous breast. The secretary refused to ever enter the room again!

The bathrooms in Torre de Pila were Mario's pièces de résistance. Diddah's bath had a mosaic of Botticelli's Venus in her cockleshell, and the hot and cold water came out of her breasts. Mario had satyrs for the faucets on his tub. Ma had the room that was designed for Diddah's mother, Aunt Ellen Wood, and it had everything. The light fixtures in her bathroom were Venetian glass bouquets, and the taps were silverplated swans. I was in the tower room, at the very top of the fourteenth-century tower. Mario thought this was a romantic idea. This room was reached by a winding stair and an elevator. Mario warned me to keep both doors locked at all times as Italians were very hot-blooded.

Being a natural blonde in Italy in the thirties was very heady stuff. I took Mario's advice. Georgio, on his free time, would run the elevator and knock on the door with nods and wreathed smiles, asking to be let in, and sometimes bringing a friend to admire through the locked door.

My bathroom was lovely, too, with a splendid view of Assisi in the distance, but only the hot water worked. However, the incredible bed made up for it. Mario had had it in his studio in Rome, and he said that Diddah would not allow it downstairs—it was a bed of magnificent memories. It was also a bed of peril. It was three-sided, made of wrought iron, with nymphs and satyrs either chasing each other with one thing in mind, or locked in imaginative embraces among grapevines, fruited, leafed, and tendriled. You had to sleep on the outside edge, hanging over the floor, to keep from being gouged by a grape leaf or a hoof or things too fierce to mention.

There was something about that room all right, because it was there that I had my sole far back memory of another life, the only one I ever had, and, as Georgie said, you only remember the horrible, unforgettable things that even death cannot erase.

We went back to Rome after a glorious week. Just before we left, Ma told Mario that she wanted to give the house a memento of our happy visit. He was terribly pleased, and took her to a shop that sold garden statues and fountains. The one thing he longed for was a fountain, a column rising from a fluted bowl and crowned with three lovely female torsos. The water for the fountain, as might have been expected, either dripped, trickled, or squirted from their six breasts, according to the water pressure. None of us had ever seen anything quite so awful, but Ma bought it for Mario and paid to have it installed because she said that Mario really wanted it and it would infuriate Diddah.

Luigi outdid himself on the way back to Rome and Ma, who had been feeling a little under the weather, began to get queasy. She finally persuaded Mario to stop, although he would not stop until he found a house where he knew there was a toilet. Ma really was past caring by this time, but finally Luigi slammed on the brakes at a tall house in one of the towns and Mario bellowed explanations out of the car window, and we were escorted to the rooftop where there was, indeed, a toilet, an American toilet. It sat proudly on the flat roof, surrounded by boxes of blooming flowers. The buildings on each side were taller than our building, so there was an admiring and sympathetic throng to watch and encourage Ma, who attended to her problems with dignity and calm.

I was so embarrassed for her I thought I would die, but she said, "It can't be the first time they've seen this toilet used. It smells as if it was very popular." And indeed it did.

We left Rome for England, where we stayed until August 6. On reaching the hotel in London, Ma found a wire from Georgie saying he had been ordered to Fort Clark, Texas, to command the 5th Cavalry Regiment. Ma wrestled with her angel all night as to whether she should rush back to be with him. George and I prevailed, saying that if she went, we would have to go with her, and it would be a shame as it was George's first trip to Europe—so she stayed. As I remember it, we never sat down. I think we went to every abbey and cathedral in England, and saw everything there was to see, and some things we didn't even know were there to be seen. It took me years, actually, to absorb what I did see that summer. Ma was a wonderful traveler, and an even better guide—and she loved every minute of it. She would talk to everyone she met.

There is a family legend that she even went up and started a conversation with the wax policeman at Madame Tussaud's, and that he answered her! People told Ma things, and took her down back alleys, and showed her things, and it was all because she had such zest. She really was interested! I once heard that if you are interested, you are interesting, and that was Ma. Of all the people I ever met, she best fitted the quotation, "To love her was a liberal education." She spoke to everyone in their own language, which was part of her charm. Her French was impeccable, her German was schoolgirl, her Italian was deplorable, and her Spanish was a mixture of Castilian and Mexican border—which Georgie spoke, having been raised with the Californios—but her heart was international!

Chapter 15

Visiting Firemen

During our trip, Georgie had undertaken to move the furniture from Fort Riley to Fort Clark, and was very proud of himself. However, when we got there, the books had not yet been unpacked, and the pictures were still on the picture wires that had been the right length at Riley but were much too short for the high ceilings of the quarters at Clark. The pictures were always going to be re-hung but, alas, the Clark tour ended suddenly in December of 1938, before Ma really had a chance to get going.

We had four perfectly wonderful months there, and we all loved it. Ma loved it as much as any post she had ever lived on. Fort Clark was a genuine frontier post. It had been built to guard an extraordinary artesian well that boiled up out of the desert, giving thousands and thousands of gallons of pure water per minute. In the old days, the Indians had kept scouts on a nearby strange geo-logical formation called Lookout Mountain, and when they saw a wagon train coming across the plains to water at the well, they would attack and kill the wagoners and steal the stock. The post cemetery was filled with graves marked Unknown Civilian, and there was one grave with an epitaph that read:

> Oh, stranger, remember to pray for the soldier
> That rode o'er the prairie for many a year,
> He chased the Comanches away from your ranches
> And harried them far o'er the distant frontier.

Robert E. Lee and J. E. B. Stuart had served there as lieutenants, as had many of our Army heroes. The regiment owned a silver punchbowl, and its silver cups were engraved with the names of the donors—an old military custom—and this was kept in the safe for use at official parties. It was a thrill to read who had given the cup one was drinking out of—a touch from the finger of history.

Clark was a one-regiment post, so it was like being in a family. At night the sentries rode patrol on horseback. You could hear the horses' hoofs ringing on the hard baked roads, and hear the soldiers call out the All clear! The bugle calls that marked off the serviceman's day in sections were blown by a bugler and not played on a recording. The bugler was traditionally the colonel's orderly. However, as we had George Meeks in the house, the bugler just helped Kent with the horses. This bugler was a tiny little man with a terrible temper. He had never left his hometown of Brackettville (the town just outside the post), except for one trip to San Antonio, 130 miles away.

Georgie had his king-size chestnut gelding with him, Hoo'kupu, and when Hook reared up and tossed his head, the bugler would be swished back and forth like a flag—but he never let go. Ma, as was her wont, got to know everyone on post and off, including all the enlisted men's wives. One day she mentioned to Georgie that the bugler's wife appeared to be in the last stages of pregnancy, so Georgie, in the old military tradition, had a small silver cup engraved Baby Smith, and gave it to the bugler with good wishes for all. Several days later Kent came over to the quarters, nearly dead with laughing. He told Ma that he had been having a beer at the Bucket of Blood, the saloon in Brackettville, and the bugler was there, roaring drunk, making everyone that came in drink with him out of the little silver baby cup, saying, with the tears running down his cheeks: "What the hell do you know! The old man really loves me! He really appreciates me! He calls me Baby!" Apparently, the bugler's wife was not pregnant—she just looked that way, and the bugler thought the cup was a token of esteem for him.

Georgie made friends with all the ranchers in the neighborhood, so we not only got to ride over their land, but they came to all the post hops and extended their hospitality to us—the first time this had happened in many years. They really enjoyed us, and we them. Aside from San Antonio, there were only two towns in the vicinity, Piedras Negras to the west and Del Rio to the north. Del Rio was the home of a dubious doctor who restored virility by grafting goat glands onto elderly men—or so the story went with many sly asides.

One night, Georgie took us to the famous Mexican restaurant in Piedra Negras. A number of Mexican Army officers were dining there, and one of them kept looking at us in a rather pointed way. When the time came to pay our bill, the Mexicans had gone. The proprietor came over to say that he hoped everything had been muy bueno. Georgie said that it had been and that he would like the check. The proprietor said that there was no check, that the Mexican general who had been here said that our dinner was our pleasure. He was the commander of the Coahuila district, and he wanted to be remembered to the Teniete Patton, whom he had last seen under somewhat different circumstances in 1915. Georgie slapped his leg and cried out, "I *knew* I had seen that man before! He was one of Pancho Villa's officers! That goddam Yaqui shot at me and nearly winged me!"

We had another memorable experience at Fort Clark that was as funny as it was frightful. The Friday after Thanksgiving, I had a date with one of the two bachelor lieutenants on the post. I went out with them alternately as I was the only single girl on the post. One was Angel Eyes, and the other was Dowlin' Chowlie (darling Charlie). Of the two, Dowlin' Chowlie was the more dashing.

Dowlin' Chowlie, Angel Eyes, a girl named Gladys, and I went to Del Rio for Mexican food, beer and music, and an evening of good clean fun. (No one had any money at the end of the month, so it was beer and chili, and not the flesh-pots of Ol' San Antone.) We got back to Clark about midnight, as the next morning there was the traditional dress parade that came before the traditional club party, where the Army-Navy football game would be broadcast and played on a blackboard by two ex-Army team members—a ceremony that takes place on every post all over the world every year.

Ma was, as always, awake when I came in, but I didn't need to knock on her door to give her that all-clear as the nights at Clark were so still you could hear the horses stomping in the stable half a mile away. I went into the bathroom to brush my teeth and drink a glass of water. The water bounced! It didn't even get all the way down! I tried it again, and with the same results. At this point Ma, who could hear everything, came and stood in the bathroom door glaring at me while I tried it again—ditto. Ma hissed at me to go to bed and she would *speak* to me in the morning! I was undone! It *had* been a night of good clean fun, and we had not taken over much beer because of the parade the next day, but Ma was against drinking in any form, and very suspicious of the charms of Dowlin' Chowlie. I didn't sleep very much. Every so often I would try to drink a little water as I was getting terribly thirsty, but always with the same horrid results. Next morning Ma came into my room bright and early with a grim expression and a cup of strong tea, saying, "You had better see if you can keep *this* down, and you are *not* coming to the parade!"

I was terribly disappointed, but I was also scared of Ma, so I meekly drank the tea, which strangely enough stayed down. Pretty soon I felt better and got up and got dressed. I was sitting in the living room, drinking more tea and wondering if it would be better for everyone if I left home and disappeared so as to be a burden no longer, when Ma burst in the front door, wiping tears of laughter from her eyes, and came over and kissed me.

The whole glorious 5th Cavalry Regiment had been out on the parade ground in full dress: horses' coats agleam; hoofs oiled and shiny; boots ashimmer; brass glowing—the works—when suddenly ranks broke and everyone went scooting for the bushes, including the glorious colonel of the regiment, Saber George, himself! Then some of the ladies in the audience rushed off. There was chaos! The post medical officer, when he had sufficiently recovered from the general malaise, staggered off to discover the cause of the mass poisoning. It was all very simple. The recruit who had been put in charge of the post water supply had decided for himself that it was a waste of time to put in the required chlorine a little at a time over the week, and had dumped the whole week's supply into the waterworks the night before. I had a drink of practically pure chlorine at midnight and the rest of the post had had it in some form or another at breakfast, though by then it was somewhat diluted. The reason my tea had stayed down and the reason that Ma hadn't gotten sick was because she had drunk tea also—she was not a plain water drinker—and, as the tea was made with boiling water, the chlorine had boiled off. Coffee, percolated, does not boil so strongly, so the whole 5th Cavalry, and dependents, had had a dose of chlorine poisoning.

Nothing further was said about Ma's terrible suspicions of the night before, and I went to dinner at the club in a glow of rosy health, which is more than can be said for those who were later afflicted. To this day I can't drink chlorinated water.

That autumn at Fort Clark was one of the best of our lives. We sightsaw all over that part of Texas: old Fort Davis, haunted by the ghost of the Indian maiden who had been shot and killed by a sentry while waiting for her lover; Judge Roy Bean's office in Langtry, named for the Jersey Lily he never saw; roundups and barbecues; dove hunting at dawn and at dusk when the doves fly to the water holes—life like it must have been in the "Old Army" without, of course, the Indians to worry about.

We took the horses up to Fort Bliss for the horse show, staying with Mrs. Vidmer's daughter and her husband, and Ma won several ribbons in the hunter classes on her faithful Quicksilver. There was a party every night, and lots of memories revived, old reputations reshredded or regilded, and old songs sung. The towns of El Paso, just outside Fort Bliss, and San Antonio are known as the mothers-in-law of the Army, so there were kissin' kin everywhere, and all doors were open. Ma's piano playing and Georgie's tall tales were part of it all and, of course, there was always the underlying preoccupation among the officers of their preparations and predictions for the war they knew was coming.

The whole autumn was wonderful because Georgie was happy and occupied and when he was, Ma was.

In December the blow fell. The chief of Cavalry, General John Herr, telephoned Georgie, personally, in our quarters, and told him he was to be assigned to the 3rd Cavalry at Fort Myer, replacing Colonel Jonathan Wainwright. General Herr minced no words. He told Georgie that he had done a splendid job at Fort Clark, but that Fort Myer took priority due to its proximity to Washington, D.C. The many duties at Fort Myer were too much for anyone without an outside income to handle socially; and socially, Myer was of the utmost importance because it was the showcase for Congress and for visiting firemen; the home base for all important government funerals, and a place where all the military attachés from the other countries came to make notes.

This rebroke Georgie's heart, and in the heat of the moment he told Ma that her money had done a terrible thing to him. It had put him in line for a phoney job of bear-leading, taking him away from real soldiering with the 5th Cavalry. He said it would be the death knell of his career. At Fort Clark, he was fulfilling himself as a soldier; at Fort Myer he would simply be glad-handing the succubi from Congress and the lobbies. A lot of very fancy language got thrown around as we packed, and Ma got her feelings hurt. She had been crazy about Fort Clark, too.

We drove east in the car, rather tensely and unpleasantly. On reaching Washington, we found that the Wainwrights were having the quarters at Fort Myer painted, so we couldn't move right away. Aunt Kay and Uncle Keith Merrill invited all of us—Ma, Georgie, young George, and myself—to stay with them over Christmas with their usual inclusive and warm hospitality. Georgie, who had placed a large chip on his shoulder, and was striding around waiting for someone to knock it off, was very angry with the Wainwrights, and said that they had done it on purpose. Ma asked him what they had done on purpose, and he said that he didn't know, but whatever it was, they had done it on purpose to make him look badly.

We moved into the quarters right after Christmas. They were at the end of the front line at Fort Myer, and faced across the little plain where the flagpole stood, with a remarkable view over the city of Washington. Ma looked out over the lights of the town one night and said, Thine everlasting cities gleam, undimmed by human tears, and that said it.

Our quarters were well built, but badly designed—very Gay-Nineties-ish, with scrollwork around the fireplaces and little mirrors set into odd corners. Various occupants had nibbled away at the house for years without making much headway or improvement. Downstairs there was an overlarge hall with the stairs going up to the right, and a tiny den under the stairs. To the left was an awkward living room, and an overcrowded dining room that opened onto a very narrow porch running along three sides of the house but enclosed next to the living room. Ma used this for a plant room. Upstairs there were five bedrooms—all too small—with two bathrooms set side by side over the kitchen.

The guest room had a wash basin in it that looked perfectly awful, but did take the strain off the bathrooms. Halfway up the back stairs was a huge walk-in linen closet, and on the third floor was a room and bath for George and Vergie Meeks. It was a terrible house for entertaining, but there we were, and that was what we were supposed to do.

I remembered the house when Colonel and Mrs. Rivers had lived there, and there was a memento of another colonel on the porch railing. Years before, when Colonel and Mrs. Harry Cootes had lived in that set of quarters, Mrs. Cootes had come downstairs to answer the doorbell and found a large family setting up a picnic on the porch, ringing her bell to request the use of her bathroom for the children. Mrs. Cootes, a high-spirited Confederate lady, said that she was sorry to be disobliging, but she was expecting company. Would the family kindly get off her porch and use the public bathroom at headquarters? The father said that he would not; that the quarters were the property of the American people who paid taxes and also paid Colonel Cootes's salary. Mrs. Cootes went into the kitchen and came back out with a large knife (she told Ma that at that point the family started to pack up the picnic hastily) and cut off a splinter from the porch railing, which she handed the man: "That is what you paid for. Take it and get out." He got.

The first event for which Georgie had to gird up his loins fulfilled his meanest expectations of being a bear-leader. This was the dread ordeal of ten luncheons on the ten successive Fridays in January and February for the various congressional committees and lobbies that most affected the Armed Services. The prospect of the luncheons on top of the move from Fort Clark, Georgie's disappointment at the assignment, and all the various nerve-wracking strains finally got to Ma, and it was one of the few times in her life she ever got sick enough to take to her bed. She got something the post doctor called kidney colic, and she was utterly miserable. When Ma got sick, Georgie fell to pieces. Ma always said that all men fell to pieces when their wives got sick because it threatened their comfort and security. But Georgie really did fall apart this time, and we were fortunate that the post doctor at the time was wonderful Colonel Albert Kenner, who was not only a good doctor but also a fine psychologist. Of the two of them, Georgie was the worse patient.

Vergie and I tried to cope and get the house settled and Ma taken care of while attending to all of the details—pictures hung, curtains up, linen stacked, silver polished—because the luncheons were about to begin.

There was a horse show at the riding hall the first Friday we were in quarters and Georgie was obliged to go as certain foreign military men of might were going to be there. I planned to stay home, but Ma told me that I looked awful and that I should go and forget about it for awhile: Vergie would be there if she needed anything. I was dying to get out of the house and when I saw Georgie all duded up in his blue uniform with his swirling cape lined in Cavalry yellow, I put my best foot forward. I will never forget my dress: it was of violet crepe with a long, sculptured skirt, a very low neck, and a jeweled belt that is still in the costume trunk in my cellar, and has been used to gird on the wooden sword of many a youthful knight in the past forty years. My evening wrap was a black tweed cape with red enamel buttons, and a hood lined with red velvet.

Georgie and I got to the horse show, and were shown into the commanding officer's box by an enlisted man in a blue uniform. It was a very dressy night. Loads of old friends were there, and they came out of their seats and into the box to see us. We had only been on the post a week and Georgie had been busy, and I had been at home. The most beautiful girl in the Army, Helen Herr Holbrook, was there with her husband. She was the granddaughter of Ma's beloved Mrs. Hoyle, and her father was the chief of Cavalry who had so summarily ordered Georgie to Myer. She later—much later—became young George's mother-in-law. Helen came lilting down the stand, kissed both of us, and said, "Darlin', I want you to meet little Jim Totten. He's Max Murray's aide, and he just this minute got here to Washington and doesn't know a soul—Jimmie, here is Ruth Ellen."

An officer in a blue uniform with his cape lined in Artillery crimson, who had been standing in front of us, seating General and Mrs. Murray, turned around when Helen called his name and came up the steps to shake hands. It's only supposed to happen in fairy tales, but it happened to me right there in the riding hall at Fort Myer, Virginia. I had been madly in love ever since I was old enough to be read aloud to: Sigfried, Roland, Richard Coeur de Lion, Tom Mix, the bronze boy on the tomb in Arlington, Heathcliff, Gary Cooper—innumerable cadets and midshipmen and lieutenants in all three of the Armed Services. This time I fell in love for the last time—then, now, and always. I can't imagine why nobody noticed it but me.

That winter at Fort Myer was a madhouse winter. Ma worked out menus for the Friday luncheons, and had them on alternate Fridays; she ran a roster on all the officers on the post so that they and their wives, and a few of the bachelors, came in turn to each luncheon. Ma said that the younger officers should have the opportunity to meet congressmen, foreign attachés, and the big wheels that came so that they would feel at ease and learn how to cope when they got to be high-ranking themselves.

All day Thursdays we spent getting ready for Fridays. We had to move most of the furniture out of the downstairs to make room for the tables. Ma would not serve buffet meals on these occasions as she said that foreign guests did not understand the custom, and Georgie loathed buffet meals anyhow. She said that certain things were expected of her and of Georgie in this assignment, and she was going to do him proud if it killed her. It came close.

There were many incidents, but the one that made her the most angry happened when a Mrs. Congressman Schultz cornered Ma after one of the luncheons and remarked that she certainly was living high off the hog with all her silver and linen marked with her initials and paid for by the poor taxpayers. Ma said coldly that the silver and linen were hers, gifts from her family. Mrs. Schultz replied, "I beg to differ with you, Mrs. Patton. I happen to know everything in this house is the property of the United States Government. The congressman so informed me." She then wanted to know why some of the doors upstairs were locked. She also wanted to know how many unmarried officers there were on the post, and why some of them had not been sent to take out her daughter, Carla. After she left, Ma went upstairs to the linen closet and found that the lady had gone through it thoroughly and had taken some embroidered guest towels as souvenirs. (The congressman was a big gun on the Military Appropriations Committee—very frustrating!)

In addition to the luncheons, Ma had to give a lot of dinner parties and, of course, attend even more of them.

The shadows of the coming war were growing longer and darker. There was a lot of coming and going among the big brass, most of whom were friends or classmates of Georgie's, and all of whom Ma entertained and, frequently, had as house guests. The fact that many of them had been promoted to general did not help Georgie's morale, and he really strained his mirthless smile trying to show that he was glad for them.

Ma made a schedule for herself that she called her sanity plan. This included a brisk ride every morning, except Fridays. On rainy days we all rode in the riding hall, which was terribly boring, although good for man and beast. Everyone had to ride in the same direction until the ranking officer in the hall decided it was time to change directions. The people walking their horses rode on the inside, the trotting horses took the middle circle, and the gallopers went around the outside. At a certain time, late in the afternoon, jumps would be brought in and set up, and those who wished to school over jumps would stay on. On nice days we rode outside, and in those days there were many places to ride. One of the nicest rides was around the wall of Arlington Cemetery. We would also ride in what was then the Experimental Farm—it is now part of the freeway to Alexandria and the airport. In fact, you could ride all the way to Alexandria on bridlepaths that ran beside the highway.

Another lady with a sanity plan was Mrs. Franklin D. Roosevelt. She kept her horse at Fort Myer and rode as often as she could, usually accompanied by one of the White House aides. One day the aide with Mrs. Roosevelt recognized Ma from all the Friday luncheons and introduced her to Mrs. Roosevelt. Ma and Georgie had met the Roosevelts at the usual receptions and parties at the White House, but only as one of the throng. However, Ma and the president's lady soon became friends, riding together often; sometimes Ma would bring her home for lunch. The two ladies had a lot in common—background, up-bringing, education, and dedicated and demanding husbands. Ma said that Mrs. Roosevelt had the finest eyes she had ever seen in a woman's face.

Georgie asked Ma what they talked about when they were riding, and Ma said, "Oh, just ordinary things—the children, you and the president, books— she has some very good ideas." Ma added that she thought Mrs. Roosevelt was very shy and very lonely.

Georgie still kept up his interest in the Civil War, and we visited the battle-fields, referring to some of the new books on the war that were coming out all the time. Georgie said that the truth was never known about a war until every-one that had fought in it was dead and, of course, that time was coming closer. The German military attaché, General von Boetticher, a friend of long stand-ing, was a great student of our Civil War. He had been von Mackensen's chief of staff in World War I, and he and Georgie would have long discussions on both wars, about which armies were better led, and why the winners won.

We had a very interesting experience visiting the Battle of the Wilderness site with General von Boetticher during that time. Georgie had us all lined up and assigned each of us a position, as was his custom. Ma, as usual, had to be the Union forces, and young George and I were somebody's troops. General von Boetticher was allowed to be the timekeeper and the critic. While we were lin-ing up and receiving our orders, we noticed a group of tourists with a guide. Georgie was gesticulating and explaining the battle, and one old gentleman with pork chop whiskers was getting farther and farther from the guide, and closer and closer to our group, obviously intrigued. Georgie finished his speech by saying that he was General Early and would be with his aides on a nearby rise of ground. General von Boetticher, who had the book they were using, pointed out that General Early had been in another part of the battlefield, and he and Georgie began to discuss it. The old gentleman could stand it no longer and broke in: "The young gentleman is quite right. General Early was on the nearby rise. I was in that battle, gentlemen, with the —rd New York Regiment and, gentlemen, we ran like hell!" Georgie looked at him and calmly replied, "Of course General Early was on that rise; I saw him there myself." General von Boetticher methodically corrected the text of the book with his pen.

Then one night when the von Boettichers were at the house for dinner, the one thing that every hostess thinks can't possibly happen to her—prays can't possibly happen to her—happened to Ma. She had a small dinner for some visiting VIPs, and invited the von Bs and the parents of one of my roommates from school: a couple who were very cultivated, charming, wealthy—and he just happened to be a Jew. Fran von Boetticher had told Ma that they were not asked out as often as they had been before Hitler, and Ma had thought that the quality of the guests would raise the conversation to unmilitant levels. But during dinner, my roommate's father kept bringing up the Hitler situation, and his conversation became more and more provocative and offensive. The von Boettichers, schooled in diplomacy, did everything they could to change the subject to one of general interest, but it was of no use. The man became so vituperative that he inflamed himself and, finally, gathering his speechless wife up, so to speak, under his arm, he stalked out the front door, cursing Germany and Hitler. The dinner party broke up very soon after.

The next day Ma received a hand-delivered letter from General von Boetticher in which he apologized for having been the underlying cause for such an embarrassment and saying that, while nothing would ever change his and Frau von Boetticher's gratitude for the friendship and consideration that Ma and Georgie had shown for them, they felt that it would be better if they did not come to our house anymore as their presence might hurt Georgie's career.

Sometime later Ma saw Frau von Boetticher at an embassy party and went up to speak to her where she was standing most conspicuously alone. Ma asked her very quietly how she and the general, who were members of the old German aristocracy, could stomach Hitler and his outrages. Frau von Boetticher answered very sadly, "My husband is an officer in the German Army, and no matter what happens, he is a German. The Fatherland is still our Fatherland."

The family went out nearly every night, and so did I. I knew all the service bachelors in Washington and environs, but I waited for Jim Totten to ask me out more and more often, and he did. Several of my friends warned me against him, which made it all the more exciting. He was said to have left a string of broken hearts behind him wherever he went. I set mine up for next in line!

Ma got exercised about my doing nothing useful, so I started teaching Sunday School in the post chapel. I got so attached to the children that I started a daily nursery school—also in the post chapel. That took up five mornings a week, and the rest of the time was given over to exercising horses and going to parties. It should have been fun, but being in love is never fun, and I was miserable except when I was with Jim. I paid little attention to what went on at home. When I did sit up and take notice from time to time, I saw what I now realize was a very unhappy and frustrated man, striking out in all directions, and a woman who felt quite powerless to help him. I finally told Ma that I thought Georgie was being terribly childish, and that he made me mad and that I didn't see why he was always yelling at her and being so disagreeable. Ma said that men always struck out at the thing they loved best when they were unhappy, and that was what Oscar Wilde had been trying to say in the "Ballad of Reading Gaol" when he wrote:

> Yet each man kills the thing he loves, by each let this be heard;
> Some do it with a loving look, some with a flattering word,
> The coward does it with a kiss, and the brave man with a sword.
> Mighty cold comfort, that.

But Georgie was impossible: he had Vergie in tears because he kept sending the food back to the kitchen because it wasn't cooked right, or it was too hot or too cold. He had Ma in tears because when dinner was announced, and she went in and sat down, he would pour himself another martini and drink it in the living room. He said that he would not carry a drink to the table, while Ma had a built-in conviction that the servants would leave if one did not sit down to dinner when it was announced. Ma would call from the dining room and remind him of this fact, and he would shout back saying that goddammit, let them go then, and get some others who were more reasonable; that his mother had never had that problem. He was not drinking over much—just drinking inconveniently.

Georgie criticized everyone at this time, even the blacksmith. He went so far as to take the hammer out of that worthy's hand and show him how to shoe a horse. The tough thing for the farrier was that Georgie really did know how to shoe a horse. It had been part of the course at Fort Riley when he was a lieutenant. Georgie took a passionate dislike to all my beaux, particularly to Jim Totten. He said that he was fresh. It was a tense and disagreeable time. More and more of Georgie's friends got promoted and he didn't. He took it out on Fort Myer, as well as on us, and the place ran like a clock with spit and polish to spare.

Finally, fate took a hand, as she always does, and Georgie broke his leg again. The *When and If* was being built and he went to inspect it, and stepped on what he thought was the hatch cover, but found out, after he fell through clear down into the cabin, that it was just a piece of canvas stretched tight.

Georgie had been taking out a lot of his tensions in riding the spring horse show circuit all over the East. We had three splendid chestnut geldings—Hoo'-kupu, Kohohiki, and Artifact—and the bay colt Keanakolu. We were really cleaning up in all of the shows. I lost heart about going alone, but Georgie, who had the horses in top condition, volunteered for Jim Totten to go along and ride his entries as he said that Jim, in spite of being a Field Artilleryman, had a good seat on a horse and good hands. So, driven by Kent, Jim and I and the horses went to all the shows and did our courting between classes. We also won a lot of ribbons.

Eventually, eight months after we met, Jim proposed to me and I accepted him, but I told him it would have to be tentative until he got the family's permission. He thought that was a terrible idea, but he agreed, after some persuading that that was the way it was done. I was busting to get it over with, but he took his own sweet time. Of course, Reggie and Kent and Bee had been informed, and they all approved, but everyone was waiting for it to be official.

Finally, one Sunday when Ma was at West Point for the weekend visiting Bee and Johnnie and her handsome grandson, Little John, I tackled Georgie. We had been riding most of the morning, had shot a few rounds of skeet, and were home waiting for lunch. I didn't know just how to bring it up, so I jumped in with both feet, and said, "What do you think Ma will do when I tell her I'm going to marry Jimmie Totten?" Georgie looked up at me with absolute incomprehension. He had been sitting back in his big leather chair, but he snapped to attention, and cried, "Goddammit, you can't marry *him!* He's too short, he's a field Artilleryman, and he's a Catholic!" Then Georgie looked me up and down, adding, "Go and make us a pitcher of martinis, and don't put any vermouth in them. I know you're serious, because if you were still just thinking about it, you would have told your mother first."

I made us a pitcher of gin and ice cubes, and he sat there and gave me a talk on being married to a man of small stature. (Jim was five feet, five and a half inches, and weighed about 135 pounds soaking wet.) His lecture was a most invaluable piece of advice that sustained me in my almost twenty-seven years of marriage. He said that a small man had to leave his house every morning like a rooster leaving his own dunghill, crowing and flapping his wings and shouting to every rooster within hearing distance that he was ready for all comers; such a man must have a wife whose love and loyalty are unquestionable; he must be the head man in his own home. Georgie said that Napoleon and Alexander the Great, and Caesar and Jesus and Hannibal, were all small men (I don't know where he picked that up, but I never questioned him); that a good small man was usually better than a good big man because their reactions were quicker—the nerve impulses didn't have so far to travel—and, also, they didn't have so far to fall, and didn't hit so hard when they landed; a small man had to be dead sure of himself, and when he was, he was usually meaner than hell, which made him a good Army officer.

When Ma got back from West Point, Georgie and I told her together. She was, naturally, quite upset. She didn't think we had known each other long enough, and she thought the difference in our religions might prove to be a drawback. I got so frantic that I took off for California to stay with my darling Aunt Nita Patton and to consult with the Reverend Atwill, who had baptized me and confirmed me and whose word I considered the ultimate on things religious. Nita Patton, having been exposed to our Shorb cousins, both good and bad, far more than Georgie ever had been, took the dimmest possible view of my marrying a Catholic. The Reverend Atwill, on the other hand, said that it was the man who mattered, and not the religion. The last night I was there, Nita Patton gave me such a talking to that I had all my flags at half mast, and my feathers drooping. I said to her, in tears, "Well, then, I guess that I will never marry, I'll just stay home and take care of Ma." Nita gave me the most terrible look, and there was a moment of ringing silence, and then she fairly shouted, "What! And be like me? One sacrifice on the altar of family loyalty is enough. Go home and marry your young man, and God help us both. I'll come to your wedding!"

So I went home and announced to the family that I was going to marry Jim. Of course, he still had not formally asked for my hand. Shortly after I got back, Jim came to take me out one night, and Ma asked him to take off his coat and come into the living room. He was surprised, but he had lovely manners, so he did. Georgie was sitting there, and when Jim walked in, Georgie gave Ma a questioning look, and she gave him an imperceptible nod, both looking very grim. Then Georgie got up, and without speaking put on his coat and his muffler and his black fedora hat, and went out the front door. Ma, very pale, proceeded to sit down and give Jim a long talk on the evils of Catholicism, and how he really ought to be an Episcopalian. What she lacked in knowledge, she made up in drama. I was so paralyzed by the whole scene that for once, I didn't say a word. After about half an hour, she came to a halt: "Well, Mr. Totten, what about it?" Jim got up and went over to her very politely and said, "Mrs. Patton, what do you think of turncoats?" Ma replied, "I don't approve of them." Jim said, "Neither do I. Goodnight." Then, he put on his hat and coat and walked out. Ma gave me a despairing look: "I don't know what has become of your father. I told him I was going to this, and he said that if I did, he would walk out of the house and might never come back. But I just had to try, didn't I?" And she burst into tears; so did I. I thought Jim would never come back either. About an hour later, Georgie came in the front door and found us both weeping. He asked, "Is it over?" and Ma answered that, yes, it was, but that he wouldn't change. Georgie said that he hadn't ever thought that he would.

It turned out that Georgie had been to the post movie and sat through it three times. They went upstairs together, but I sat and wept on in the living room and wondered what would happen in my life, and finally decided that I would be a wonderful aunt like Nita, and go early to the grave, deeply mourned by all of Bee's and George's children.

Several days later, Jim told me that he was going to brave the lion in his den and ask for my hand in marriage, and would I see that the coast was clear. I told the parents, and we all three sat solemnly in the living room until the doorbell rang, and then Ma made me come upstairs with her. She said that it was between Georgie and Jim, and it wouldn't be fair for us to listen. Jim stayed about fifteen minutes. Then, we heard the front door close, and we rushed downstairs. Georgie said, "It's all over." He kissed me and then he kissed Ma, and then we started to plan the wedding. When I asked Jim about it later, he could never remember what they said to each other. I wish I could say that they became great friends, but they never did. However, they developed a real respect for each other during World War II, and Georgie was gracious enough to write me all the good things he heard about Jim, and Jim always stood up for Georgie during all the sturm und drang of the press, the official rebukes, the slings and arrows of outrageous fortune. They were both great gentlemen. God rest their gallant souls.

My twenty-fifth birthday was on February 28, 1940, and Ma and Georgie planned accordingly. We simply loved costume parties, and this was to be a "Gone With the Wind" party. The year before we had had a Forty-Niner party. Ma always had costumes made for the parties, as she and Georgie liked to be historically correct in costume, dress, food, music, and all the details that the other guests might not notice, but the effect of which was always different and striking. Most of the young officers either rented Confederate costumes or fixed up their dress blues to resemble Yankee uniforms. Of course, the dresses of the occasion ran from Mrs. O'Hara's severe elegance to Belle Watling's whorish splendor, so the ladies had a great time. Colonel Carey Crane, the Artillery commander at Fort Myer, fixed up a photographer's booth and took flash pictures of everyone, posing them as for daguerreotypes.

My engagement to Jim was as yet unannounced, so I went to the party with Lieutenant Fletcher Cole, a classmate of Johnnie Waters, and a dear friend of the family. The party was in the hop room at headquarters, and the whole post had been invited. We had a dinner at the house for about twenty-five people, and Ma and Georgie went over to the hop room to see that all was ready.

Fletcher was officer of the day, so he decided he had time to inspect the guard before we went to the party, and I went along with him. He had on a rented Confederate uniform, and I had on hoop skirts, and the proper hair-do—everything as 1863 as it could be. All was well until we got to the final guard post at the post gate of Arlington Cemetery, next to the hospital. It was nearly dark, and we walked over to the sentry post quietly. The sentry on duty took one look at us, let out a scream of anguish, fired his pistol into the air three times, and bellowed, "Corporal of the Guard! Turn out the Guard! The dead is rising and the Rebs are coming out of Arlington!" There was some interesting confusion while Fletcher explained to the armed corporal of the guard who he was, and why he was out of uniform.

The party was a howling success—all of Ma's parties were—and lasted until 2 a.m. when Georgie signaled to the musicians to play "Good Night Ladies" and "Army Blue." Jim and I walked back to the quarters and sat up talking about the party until Georgie started dropping his shoes on the floor overhead. This was the family signal. In the quarters at Fort Myer he had to cross the hall from his and Ma's bedroom to the guest room, which was just over the courting room, to drop his shoes. Sometimes he had to drop as many as five.

Next morning, Ma suggested a walk to clear our heads. We walked, as always, in the cemetery. On our way there, we passed the captains' row of quarters, and one of the captains' wives, Jane Jones, came out when she saw us go by to tell us what a great party it had been and what a marvelous time she had had. I can see her now! She was wearing a dark blue serge skirt and a pale blue cashmere sweater, and I remember wondering how she kept the pale fuzz off the dark serge.

We walked for about an hour. There is no place more beautiful than Arlington Cemetery in the spring. Georgie was waiting for us when we came in for lunch. His face was the color of oatmeal. He said, very abruptly, "Where was Jim Totten at half-past two this morning?" I said that he had been in the den with me, and that surely Georgie must remember dropping his shoes. Georgie did not smile. "Well, you may have to swear to that in court. Jane Jones was raped last night, right on the sofa in her living room, and Captain Jones got a glimpse of the offender as he ran off, and says it is one of the officers at this post, and at this point he is filing rape charges against every bachelor at Fort Myer!" Somehow, this mare's nest was kept out of the press. Everyone but Ma and Georgie and me knew who the culprit was, and there was a lot more to the story than ever came out. Captain Jones was prevailed upon to drop charges, and at a not too obvious later date he was given a change of station. Somehow I will never forget Jane's happy expression when she was telling Ma and me what a good time she had had at our party! Different strokes for different folks.

The Jones affair, though silenced, made a lot of waves. One of the bachelors in the bachelor officers' quarters had been keeping his lady love—the daughter of one of the finest families in Northern Virginia, suh—in his quarters. He brought all of her clothes down to Jim and asked him to keep them, as he said that the assistant commandant of the post was inspecting everyone and every place for signs of sin, but Jim would be above suspicion because he was engaged to me. Jim refused, so they dumped her clothes out of the window into the court. She had been at our party, and slept it off for a couple of days.

I happened to be in the BOQ, where I had been forbidden to go by Ma (I went anyhow, figuring that it was all right now that Jim and I were engaged), and we were sitting in Jim's living room—in those opulent days a bachelor had two rooms and a private bathroom—drinking beer and listening to records with some friends, when this rose with a broken stem came wandering in, inadequately draped in an army blanket. She inquired muzzily for her beau and her clothes. Her beau was out on the firing range and her clothes were out in the alley, or had been until the trash was collected, so I had to go home and get her some of mine. It was years before I had the nerve to tell Ma where my blue linen dress had gone. When I finally told her, she said, "I told you not to go into the BOQ. I knew you would have some unpleasant experiences if you did. But who would have thought that of Mary Alice's little daughter? She was the cunningest baby!" I was reminded then, and often in the years to come, of one of Ma's songs that begins:

> Oh, tell me why the pretty little babies
> All grow up to homely men?

Jim's and my engagement was announced finally at a family dinner with the Tottens and ourselves and a girlhood friend of Mrs. Totten's, one of the Booker girls from Norfolk. She had married a New York capitalist and supported the rest of her charming and penniless family, still beggared by the Civil War. The Tottens and the Pattons were instantly friends. Colonel Totten was Army clear back to the Revolution when his ancestor had been George Washington's chief of Engineers. His family had built the Panama Railroad and the prison at Dry Tortugas; all the Fort Tottens in the East were named for them. The Tottens had been Engineers and Coast Artillery. I think my father-in-law was, without exception, the finest man that I have ever known. Mrs. Totten was born Julia Willoughby Walke of Norfolk, Virginia. Her father was a general, an expert in explosives, and a bon vivant and southern gallant of the old school. He was the tenth son of a family who had also been impoverished by the war. His nine older brothers had all gotten into and through the University of Virginia, but when it came to Willoughby, the bottom of the money barrel had been scraped. His brothers were all in the law or in government, so they got him an appointment to Annapolis and one to West Point. But the Walkes were hard losers. Before he went to West Point, he visited a tattoo parlor in Norfolk and had the stars and bars tattooed over his heart and the stars and stripes tattooed across his bottom. He almost didn't get into the Academy because of the tattoos, but there were some southerners on the staff there, so his advertised loyalties were overlooked. My mother-in-law, Julie Totten, was one of the most enchanting women I have ever met. She was a southern lady right out of the books, beautiful, flirtatious in public but never in private—gay, funny, and beloved by all. She and Ma could not have been more different and yet, they were just alike. They dearly loved each other.

Ma was still a little shaky about my marrying Jim so soon. She said that, after all, she had known Georgie for almost twenty years, and Bee had known Johnnie for at least six, and I had only known Jim for a short two years, and if you married in haste, you repented in leisure. But she got caught up in the excitement of planning the wedding and, except for an occasional weakening of the sinews when she thought about his being a Catholic, she had a splendid time. She was always coming around with things she had just thought of, and bits of good advice. I wrote some of them down.

BAP FOR REP

Live each day to the best of your ability and the future will take care of itself.

We would be spared the pain of misunderstanding if we realized that there is no [more] limit to true understanding than there is to light, for both have no point of starting, no end to development, and both illuminate all; light illuminates the dark places of the world, and understanding illuminates the dark places of the spirit.

Virtues, to us, may be taken for granted by our betters and may even be considered vices by our superiors, and they may also be the ultimate in ideals to those who walk another road; as no man knows his brothers' burdens, he cannot censure him for his pleasures, for what is pleasure but a remedy for pain?

To wish to reform a man is to set yourself above God. Live the best you know, and perhaps one unhappy seeker will see in your behavior the key to his own freedom.

The kind thing is the right thing.

I don't suppose those thoughts are original with Ma, and I don't know where she got them, but they work. One thought that was original with her, and that

I have remembered many times, was her observations on Miss Mulock's song to Douglas. Ma said that it was the saddest song in the world and that whenever I felt in time to come like being mean to my husband, I should sing it to myself:

> Could you come back to me, Douglas, Douglas
> In the old likeness that I knew
> I would be so faithful, so loving, Douglas
> Douglas, Douglas, tender and true.
> Oh, to call back the days that are not!
> Mine eyes were blinded, your words were few,
> Do you know the truth now, up in Heaven?
> Douglas, Douglas, tender and true!

After my return from California with Nita and the Reverend Atwill's blessings, I was sure that I would have to be married in Jim's church. I timidly suggested that we have a double ceremony to quiet my family, but Jim said that he wouldn't dream of taking a pagan like myself into his church: we would be married in the Episcopal church, and this performance would always give him an out, as, in the eyes of his church, he would not be truly married, so if I didn't behave myself, he could always walk out blameless. I spent the next twenty-seven years waiting for him to go.

Ma had firm convictions about a bride being rested, so she announced she was going to remove me from the scene at Fort Myer early in the spring. The wedding was to be on July 6. I had wanted a Fourth of July wedding with fireworks, but that year the Fourth was on a Thursday and none of the officers could get away. So the Washington parties had to be given right away, and there were lots of them, including one memorable shower with far-reaching effects.

Ma's old friends wanted to give us a kitchen shower, and both Ma and I knew they couldn't afford it. No one in the Army ever has money. We could not hurt their feelings by telling them so, so Ma came up with the bright idea that the one thing her friends could give that no one else in the world could produce was a recipe shower. These ladies were some of the finest cooks in the world, having learned the hard way over coal and wood and kerosene stoves on frontier posts. The ladies were thrilled with the idea, although, bless their generous hearts, I don't think any of them realized why we asked for a recipe shower. They gave away their best, family secrets and all. Year later, I wrote a cookbook to sell for the benefit of the Army Distaff Foundation, a home for Army dependents, where the ladies could end their careers among service friends. Most of the recipes in the cookbook came from that shower. The cookbook sold like hotcakes; the bread that the ladies had cast upon the waters in 1940 came back to them as cake in 1960.

The time passed very fast between the announcement of our engagement and the wedding day and lots of the things that happened were very interesting. The most bizarre happening sticks in my memory as one of the many times Ma saved my bacon, even in absentia. We were still at Fort Myer and I was home alone. I answered the doorbell and admitted the officer of the day, who was properly attired for the pursuit of his duties with an armband that was marked O.D., a saber hanging from his belt, and a Colt .45 in his holster. He was an Army brat, one of the ones that had been always carried and covered for by his friends and classmates. At this time, he was no brat but a major with two small daughters, an alcoholic, an all-time loser, and no use to anyone at any time. Georgie always referred to this type as lapsed officers and gentlemen who, with their good inheritance, usually do well in desperate battle and, hopefully, manage to get themselves killed as heroes before they die in the gutter.

This officer's wife had left him some time before, and I had his little girls in my nursery school. Actually, they were better off with an alcoholic father than they would have been with their fly-by-night mother. The gentleman in question was loaded to the gills, but carrying it fairly well, as was his wont, except that he announced that as I was marrying Jim Totten he had come to kill himself in front of me, just to show me! He took out his pistol and cocked it. Words spring unbidden to my tongue, as had Athena sprung from the brow of Zeus, and I remember that I sounded perfectly calm: "You had better not do it here, Dick. That's Ma's Chinese rug, and she has just had it cleaned and she will be furious. You know what bloodstains are! Ma will never forgive you!" Possibly, because he was fond of Ma, this got through to him. He replaced his pistol, burst into tears, said that he didn't know what was going to happen to his two little girls, excused himself, and went back out the front door. He managed to last until World War II, when he died gallantly in action—in the Battle of the Bulge. His sainted mother brought up the two little girls.

After we went to the farm in Massachusetts came the ordeal of buying my trousseau, which was sheer hell. Ma and I met Bee in New York, and they picked out enough clothes for me to outfit a movie star. I was never consulted. It was well known that I had no taste. Ma's mother had had Ma's name embroidered on every bit of Ma's trousseau in Ellie's handwriting, and Ma insisted that Bee and I have the same—our names in Ma's handwriting. Then all the clothes had to be packed and shipped, invitations were sent, wedding presents acknowledged and listed, and the things for our first station at Fort Sill, Oklahoma, packed: although it was all very exciting, one wedding like that is sufficient for a lifetime.

Georgie added a grace note by insisting that the United States was going to march on Mexico about the time of the wedding and that I would end up having to marry Jim's sword. This was an old custom from the Middle Ages, and I really think Georgie would have loved following through on it. If the Middle Ages bridegroom was absent on a Crusade or something, his fiancée would be married to his sword with bell, book, and candle, and the marriage was binding. Which sword she married was never quite clear. Did the groom take his best sword with him and leave her his second best, or vice versa? I was sure Georgie was only teasing, but then Georgie might know something the rest of us did not. When the wedding weekend finally dawned, and Jim turned up with the ushers, and there was no war with Mexico, I was faint with relief.

The ride from Green Meadows to the church in Beverly Farms was slightly traumatic. Georgie was gorgeous in his white uniform with all his decorations, and I was pretty gorgeous myself in my grandmother Ellie's wedding dress. I wasn't allowed to wear any makeup as Ma said that it wasn't suitable, so I was glad the veil would be over my face as I went up the aisle. I had makeup in my little pearl beaded bag, and could fix up on the way home before the reception. During the twenty-minute drive, Georgie and I didn't find much to say to each other. Finally, he said, "I guess you know your mother and George and I will miss you." I said yes and tried not to cry. Then he added, "I hope we gave you a happy childhood." At that, I cried. His last remark was, "If you treat Jim the way your mother has treated me, you will be all right."

We had a wonderful month's honeymoon in Bermuda and came home to Green Meadows to regroup before setting off for Fort Sill. I was bubbling over and Ma was seemingly very happy for us. Just before we left, she asked me the question she had obviously been dying to ask, which was to the effect of how was my love life? I quoted Jim to her. He had said, "It was the most fun you could have without laughing." She gave me a considering look and observed, "Every time your father makes love to me, I consider it a rededication and sanctification of our marriage."

Chapter 16
Long Shadows

Georgie and Ma were still stationed at Fort Myer, but he was soon ordered to Fort Benning, Georgia, to try to pull tanks out of the government's hat. Jim was a student at the Field Artillery School, and so we were parted, each with our own lives to live. Ma was always very faithful about writing, but for a person with so many ideas and so much imagination, she wrote very dull letters, and I had no idea, nor did I care, in that selfish time of new love and new marriage, what she was feeling about things. The coming war was beginning to throw long shadows over us all.

After six months of marriage, Jim suggested that we go ahead and have a baby, as he said that he would like to see his son before he went off to war. We had originally planned to wait a year. I had exactly the same feeling about babies and families that Ma did: the sooner the better, and the more the merrier. As soon as the doctor confirmed our hopes, we called both families and went into high gear. Bee had been pregnant with her second son when she was the matron of honor in our wedding, so grandchildren were not a new thing to Ma, but the Tottens went wild. I could have opened a consultant's office with all the advice that came pouring in by mail and telephone. But it turned out that I didn't need the advice on having a far-from-home baby because the fates decreed that Jim would be on maneuvers from July on, and would then go to a tank destroyer battalion at Fort Knox, Kentucky, so I would have to go home to have the baby.

The summer simply flew, though it started with a row between Ma and me. She had planned everything and had plans to back up the first plans. I was to have the baby in the local Beverly Hospital, the apple of her brother Fred Ayer's eye and, by and large, his creation. I was to have the doctor that delivered all of the Ayer babies. This last threw me. He was a good man and a fine doctor but he had the coldest hands! I stood up and waved my feelers, and said that I would pick my own hospital and my own doctor, and Ma went the whole Great White Way, ending up by weeping and saying that my decision would break poor Fred's heart.

So, I tearfully went to my Uncle Fred and asked him if I was breaking his heart and he said, very cheerfully, that he thought I was a stubborn young fool, but whether I had my baby there or in Timbuktu made no difference to him, except that I was breaking his sister's heart. At this point my own sister came forward and said for me to do whatever I thought was right; after all, it was my baby, and I should pay no attention to all those breaking hearts.

After the necessary bit of drama everything went off well, and Ma actually got very fond of the doctor I picked, Dr. Robert L. DeNormandie, the man who wrote the book on having babies. My sister and her boys came home to stay, as Johnnie and Georgie were slogging around in Louisiana with Jim. Young George was home too. It was a good summer—the last good summer for a long time.

The baby took its own sweet time—it was expected in September, but saw fit to wait until October 4 and then very disobligingly produced complications. I was so relieved when the ball started rolling that I didn't have sense enough to be scared when Dr. DeNormandie announced that I could choose between a forty-eight-hour labor or a Caesarian section. Ma got very pale, and for the only time I ever remember, she was uncertain about what to do and what decision should be made. Being the most uncomfortable person in the room, it was easiest for me to make the decision, and I said that I wanted a C-section. Ma said that she wanted to watch the whole performance, and Dr. DeNormandie, who had dealt with many people in his long life, saw that he had better say yes. What incredible courage she had! She sat through the whole thing without making a sound. I was totally out of the picture, of course, until some hours later when I was presented with an infuriated baby boy with long black hair—like a Japanese doll. After Ma got over the shock of seeing her younger daughter disemboweled before her very eyes, she got a very special feeling about Michael. Ma never admitted to a favorite child, or to a favorite grandchild, but she always had a proprietary feeling toward this one.

Michael was a cause célèbre. Cousin Mario came all the way into Boston with a most elaborate and wildly expensive pink satin outfit from the Grande Maison de Blanc. He had apparently forgiven me for not marrying a Borgia or Medici. Ma was still anxious about Catholics sneaking into the hospital and baptizing Michael on the sly (as had happened to Georgie) and she took a dim view of Mario's visit for that reason, although if there was ever a happy pagan, it was dear Mario. The fact that Monsignor Sheen was recuperating in the next room also upset her. I was having a baby and the Monsignor was having an ulcer, or something like it, and we had some wonderfully interesting talks and discussions when we were pushed out onto the porch. He opened a great many doors that had been unopened in my mind before I met him. But, all in all, Ma was much relieved when she got Mike and me home.

Bee went on a mercy mission from Fort Benning to Elizabethtown, Kentucky, and with great luck found us a house on the Bardstown Road, about thirty miles from Fort Knox. It was the only house in town for rent, and it was a primitive habitation, but thanks to her ever-loving kindness, we would have a roof over our heads when Jim got back from maneuvers. In the days before the war, a lady was supposed to take weeks or even months to get over having a baby, and she was supposed to be cuddled and coddled and done for. When I finally left for Kentucky to settle the house and wait for Jim, I left Mike with Ma and the experienced care of Mary Crowley, who had been with the family since 1918. The arrangement with Miss Crowley was that as soon as I was settled, she would come south with Mike and turn him over to me.

The maneuvers finished, Jim came home to Elizabethtown for a joyous reunion. Two days later I asked Jim's colonel and his wife for Sunday dinner. I was a terrible cook, because the maid that had found me at Fort Sill had done everything, and I was not too far from the fudge and waffle stage, but I was frying chicken and cooking rice and Jim was pouring martinis, and the phone rang. It was Ma calling from Green Meadows, telling me to turn on the radio: the Japs were bombing Pearl Harbor. The world had turned upside down at last.

It was an incredible thing, but not as shocking to us as to the rest of the country. Georgie had tried and tried, while we were in Honolulu, to get it across to General Drum, the War Department, and anyone who would listen that the Japanese were enemies. He had had his wrist slapped repeatedly for rocking the boat and making waves. But the Yellow Peril had finally come.

From the instant of chaos, the clouds cleared away and the roles for which the men of the family had spent their lives preparing were there before them. It meant that Georgie and Johnnie Waters and Jim Totten would go off to war, and if the war lasted long enough, young George, a cadet at West Point, would go, too. All this flashed across my mind as I ran into the living room and told Jim to turn on the radio.

It was outwardly a quiet Christmas for us all. Inwardly, we were all wondering if it was the last Christmas. Georgie came through Fort Knox on a tour of inspection, and he and Jim went out and cut down a scraggly cedar tree for Mike's first Christmas. Jim was gone most of the time. Miss Crowley had to go back to Massachusetts as there was another crisis in the family of some kind, and she was always sent for in a family crisis. Ma moved to Fort Benning with

Georgie, and sent me her cook who had been at Green Meadows with her. This cook was a crisis in herself. She was a marvelous cook, but quite mad and her elephantine search for love and coffee (she was Swedish) added a few light touches to the gathering gloom. The house was heated by an ancient coal furnace fed by a contraption called an iron fireman, which was a motor-run endless belt that fed coal into the furnace by gravity from an enormous pile in the coal bin, which had to be kept just at the right slant. I complained bitterly to Jim that as I was stitched right down my front section, I couldn't heave coal or something might tear loose. Being a practical man, he bought me a small shovel and told me to use it oftener. But nearly every day, when the tanks were rumbling back and forth down the Bardstown road, a tank would overheat near the house and while the driver was fixing it, some soldier or officer would come in and shovel coal! Corporals, captains, even a colonel once, in his pinks and greens, out of a staff car.

In order for Jim to ever get home, he had to have our car, so I was stranded with baby, crazy cook, and a weird nurse from Louisville, and a red coaster wagon that I pulled into town when I went to buy groceries. I also had Jim's beloved bird dog, Derry Walls (Up the Irish! Remember Derry Walls!), but the Bardstown road was a speedway and it wasn't long before Derry was hit by a truck, and I had to haul him to the vet on the wagon and have him put to sleep. The half-witted son of one of the neighbors brought me a big black mutt to be a watchdog.

One spring day Jim came home unexpectedly around dark. When he came in the house he said that he hadn't realized where he was until he saw me. He had a high fever. The local doctor said that it was a stomach upset. By morning I knew it was more than that, and I called the Fort Knox Hospital where dear Colonel Kenner from Fort Myer days was administrative officer. I wept into the telephone, and he said that if I would come and get him, he would take a look at Jim, but that he hadn't practiced for some time, and had no little black kit. I had fired the weird nurse, and the crazy cook was too unstable to take care of Mike, so praying it wasn't the Black Death, I put Mike's bassinet in Jim's room and drove the Death Highway (31W, also known as the "Dixie Dieway" by the soldiers) to Knox. By the time we got back, Jim was delirious and Mike was screaming, so I took Mike off to feed him in the kitchen and Colonel Kenner called downstairs, "You had better bring up three Scotch highballs, Ruth Ellen. I think I have just diagnosed my first case of yellow fever!"

Jim couldn't swallow, and I couldn't stand scotch, so dear Colonel Kenner drank all three and saw Jim into the ambulance when it arrived from Knox, and I called Ma. She was on her way!

I did not appreciate then what a sacrifice that was. Ma had her own war to fight, and her own problems, immeasurably greater than mine, getting Georgie ready for his special war, which had been so long in coming, and being a pillar of strength and wisdom to all the young wives and mothers in his command whom she had taken under her wing as a matter of course. I feel she must have been motivated by something. I remembered again what Georgie's mother had said to Ma years before when Ma asked her if she loved Georgie more than she did Nita. Bamma had replied, "You never have a favorite child until one of them is sick or in trouble, and then you only have one child."

Ma moved right in, took over the cook, Mike, the garden, the dog, and the neighbors. She made friends with them right away, although they had been very standoffish with me. They were bootleggers and made their own whiskey. They confided in Ma that our arrival on the Bardstown Road had been upsetting because they just naturally didn't take to anyone in uniform. Ma didn't drink, but the neighbors admired her so much that she was always finding medicinal bottles of whiskey in the back entry. When she tried to thank them, they would just say that they were just being neighborly. She tasted some one day, and her eyes filled with tears. She said that it must be that White Lightning she had heard about.

I went to see Jim every day, but it was several days before they had any kind of diagnosis, and by the time they did, the soldiers in his outfit were dropping like flies. What they all had was serum hepatitis. Hepatitis was not a common thing then, at least not by that name. It was very scary and no one was quite sure how to treat it. Colonel Kenner asked Ma and me to say that Jim had pneumonia, but he wanted Ma to get word to Georgie right away. All of Jim's division had received the yellow fever inoculation preparatory to going overseas. I have heard since that there were more than four thousand cases of serum hepatitis, and around four hundred fatalities.

Ma stayed until Jim came home from the hospital. Shortly before she left, I came home from visiting him and found Ma digging a grave in the soft shoulder of the road. The same truck that had killed poor Derry had swerved out of its way to kill my watchdog, and Ma was trying to bury him before I got home, so that I wouldn't be upset, but the dog had been too heavy for her to carry or drag, so she decided to bury him where he had died. The neighbor saw her out there and came over and finished digging the grave for her. He said that he liked to see a real lady who was so all-fired neat and tidy that she didn't leave no goddam dog lying by the side of the road for the goddam buzzards. He brought her a big bottle of whiskey as a farewell gift, he said that it was nearly a year old, and he mostly kept it for him and his boys.

The next few months were spent convalescing Jim. His outfit went overseas without him, and he was ordered to a new division at Fort Smith, Arkansas, to the newly activated Camp Chaffee. Getting over hepatitis is miserable. I used to call Ma on the phone and ask her what to feed him and how to put weight on him, and she said to cream all the vegetables, use lots of butter, plenty of eggnogs, light on the sherry. Of course, since that time the treatment for hepatitis is a low-fat diet, no alcohol. So, our tender loving care probably inhibited his recovery, but he survived.

I deeply regret the fact that Ma never got to Fort Smith. We bought a house from the FHA for $250 down and $35 a month, and after we had been there awhile we rented the house next door, as there were five of us, including the crazy cook and my brother George's nanny, Alice Holmes, who, once again, came out of retirement.

Ma would have loved Arkansas. It's one of the most beautiful states in the nation. Also, Fort Smith had history: it was the jumping-off place into Indian territory for many years, and all the bad guys had been through there, including Georgie's grandfather, Don Benito Wilson. It was the home of Hanging Judge Parker and had tornadoes, scorpions, and tarantulas, as well as a citizen who thought he was Abraham Lincoln and who, dressed appropriately, gave the Gettsyburg Address every Saturday on the corner of Parade Street.

But Ma had a full schedule at Fort Benning—and, then, Georgie was ordered to the California desert to train troops for desert warfare.

Ma begged me to come to Benning to say good-bye, so I left Mike with Jim and Alice and the crazy cook and took the train to Georgia. With the war coming on apace, the railroads were all upset, and it was quite a trip, ending abruptly in Phenix City (the sin capital of the South) with my train derailing itself and tipping over on its side. This happened so smoothly that no one was hurt. I was, fortunately, on the up side and managed to hang onto my seat until all the suitcases and things had fallen into the down side. Then, I heard Ma's voice and Bee's voice, and looked up out of the window to see them running back and forth on the embankment by the track, so I got both my suitcases and climbed out with the conductor's help. It was all so surprising that we just stood there and laughed!

The visit was short and sweet. Bee and Johnnie Waters and I planned an old-fashioned *despedida* for Georgie for the day he was to leave for Indio, California. We telephoned everyone and invited them for drinks and snacks at Patton House—the house Georgie had built for himself and Ma out of pine slashings in the Sand Hill area at Fort Benning. Georgie wanted to be right with his troops, and not in the splendid assigned red brick officers' quarters several miles away. Among the many slanders they threw at Georgie later was that he had had the troops build Patton House with government money when they should have been getting ready for the war, but actually Georgie had it built by the lumber company and paid for it himself, and it was later used as an officer's club until it burned down in the sixties.

Georgie, of course, was expecting to be surprised by a *despedida*—he loved parties. He insisted that he would make the drinks. Bee and I had already ordered everything that we thought we would need from the officer's club, but he canceled all the bottle orders and, going through his own liquor cabinet, he assembled all the bottles and half-bottles and bits and pieces, and started to make a gigantic sort of cocktail-punch. Ma was appalled: "Georgie, you can't DO that!" But he assured her that it would be absolutely great, that he would serve it so cold that no one could taste it, and that it would use up all the expensive liquor that might otherwise be wasted, and that she, of all people, with her tradition of New England thrift, should certainly appreciate that fact.

Ma went on about mixed drinks being poison, and how grape and grain should never be combined, but Georgie happily poured Old Crow and Southern Comfort into Johnny Walker's Red Label Scotch and added, at the end, several bottles of California white wine. He fancied himself as an innovator, and had invented a cocktail called the Armored Diesel which he served from oil cans that had been transformed into cocktail goblets by sawing off the bottoms and soldering the can tips onto them. Actually, the diesel fuel would have been more wholesome.

His best friends and worst enemies should have been wise to his *despedida* drinks after that terrible Armored Diesel, the recipe for which I hope has been fortunately lost. Georgie had no taste or smell to speak of. But they all came to the party—those fine upstanding captains and majors and colonels and generals—and they toasted Georgie and Ma in the concoction and slowly came to a standstill, sinking glassy-eyed into chairs, or were taken home by their wives while they could still move. It was a sight never to be forgotten.

Ma was, as always, a perfect hostess, but her face got a bit grim as the ranks shuddered and folded. Bee and Johnnie Waters and Dick Jensen, Georgie's aide, and I stuck to beer. Up until that day, I had always thought that the legendary effect of mixed drinks was an old wives' tale, but, believe me, it is not.

Georgie, himself, high on adrenalin and host-man-ship, was unaffected. He and Ma took off for the desert amid the cheering—and weeping—throngs and I went back to Fort Smith. I didn't see Johnnie Waters again until long after the war was over, and I never saw my childhood friend Dick Jensen again (Johnnie Waters was captured by the Germans at Kasserine Pass and spent the rest of World War II in a POW camp. Dick Jensen was killed in action in North Africa).

Jim assumed command of the 69th Field Artillery at Camp Chaffee. He was the first man in it; he was his own cadre. That year was terrible and memorable for the bitter sweetness of living on the edge of the cliff of war. The division was on what was, literally, a three-day alert for nearly a year. This was hard on wives and mothers, and on all the brides our servicemen collected at Fort Smith. I never saw so many pretty, gracious, attractive girls as the ones they met and married in Arkansas. It was also a region of real hillbillies. The mountainy people from around there were highly inbred and there were quite a few naturals who came into town on Saturdays. My excellent doctor, Wolfermann, told me that the division had done more for the State of Arkansas than anything since the westward migration, that there were several hundred illegitimate babies born since the division had moved in. I thought he was being critical, and made a covert apology about soldiers being soldiers, but he cried, "No, no, Mrs. Totten! I mean what I say. They've brought in new blood! New blood into the hills!"

We brought in a little new blood ourselves. The three-day alert wore me down to the point where I was convinced that I was going to be left a young widow with one son, so I kept hinting around that there might be time to work in another baby before the call to arms. Dr. DeNormandie had told me that I had to wait for two and a half years for the next baby, and Jim was adamant, but one day he came home from camp early and I was in tears. He didn't know that I had just dropped a red-hot iron on my toe, but drew his own conclusion and said comfortingly, "If you want another baby that badly, Ruthie, it's OK by me, if Doctor Wolfermann and Dr. DeNormandie give you the green light." Wasting no time, I wired Dr. DeNormandie and he gave us his blessing on condition that I came home to Massachusetts and let him deliver the baby. He said that wars change rules.

Ma was quite upset by our news, even though I had the doctors' permission. She decided to come and visit. Georgie and Johnnie Waters had gone off to the war and she was alone at Green Meadows. But the word came that Johnnie had been in the battle at Kasserine Pass and was missing in action, so she went to Bee instead.

The Kasserine Pass disaster was a terrible lesson that our army had to learn. Just because America had finally joined the Allies did not mean the war was won. The powers that be sent for Georgie, and the rest of that is oft-written history. I don't think most people know that Georgie went to the battlefield himself, and looked everywhere for some trace of Johnnie Waters, who had fought a hero's battle there. Georgie could find nothing, so he picked up an ammunition clip from a burnt-out American tank to send to Johnnie's boys as a memento of their father in case there was nothing more.

A month before the baby was due, I went home to Ma with Mike, nurse, cook, and bulldog pup. The Arkansas River had flooded, and getting across it to the train in Van Buren was a real adventure. Then, we had to back all the way to St. Louis as the engine turntable was under water, but we made it home and Beatrice Willoughby Totten was born on June 21, 1943. Jim named her for Ma, which was the best compliment he could have given both of them. Ma's own mother, Ellie, had picked the name for her because it means one who blesses. In both cases, it was most appropriate.

When the baby was two weeks old I left her with Ma and Alice Holmes, and went back to Arkansas to see Jim off to his war. For the ones who are left at home, there is no such thing as a good war or a little war. From then until he came home, there was for me only one man and one battalion engaged in fighting the enemy singlehanded. Of course, I helped Ma with the scrapbooks and was aware that Georgie was doing tremendous things, but he was not my major concern.

I sold our FHA home and went to Green Meadows for the duration. Ma spent some of her time in Washington with Bee, who had moved there to be near the Red Cross headquarters where she did wonderful work for the prisoners at the international level. Young George was at West Point where he took the long course, as had Georgie. They both had to spend an extra year at the Military Academy because of mathematics.

We settled down at Green Meadows with red stamps and gasoline coupons, with hens and the vegetable garden. We found an old churn so we made butter, and we lived very well with the help of Ma's older brothers and sisters, who rallied around her as the family always does.

We coped with the problems as they came up and waited for the mail and the news reports.

For the first time in my life I began to know Ma as a person and not just a mother, a teller of tales, a kisser of bumps and cuts, and an ever-present eye. We had more or less the same problems, but the war made an equality of our suffering, even though it was my first and her third. Well-meaning friends would grate us both to the quick by saying, helpfully, "But of course, you're *used to it!*" This was particularly trying if their husbands or sons had staff jobs in Washington. Ma used to recite "The Maid That Binds Her Warrior's Sash" to keep herself calm. In case it is too out-of-date to mean anything, I will give it here, but it lacks something without her drama. It was one of Ellie's pieces.

The maid who binds her warrior's sash
With smile that well her pain dissembles

The while beneath her drooping lash
One starry tear drop hangs and trembles
Though Heaven alone records the tear
And Fame shall never know the story
Her heart has shed a drop as dear
As ere bedewed the field of glory.

The wife who girds her husband's sword
Mid little ones who weep or wonder
And bravely speaks the cheering word
What though her heart be rent asunder
Doomed nightly in her dreams to hear
The bolts of death around him rattle,
Hath shed as sacred blood as e'er
Was poured upon the field of battle!

The mother who conceals her grief
As to her breast her son she presses
Then breathes a few brave words and brief
Kissing the patriot brow she blesses
With no one but her secret God
To know the pain that weighs upon her
Sheds holy blood as e'er the sod
Received on Freedom's field in honor!

That's a real American poem by Thomas Buchanan Read, from *The Wagoner of the Alleghenies,* and Ma liked it better for being home-grown.

Ma got an absolute fixation on using gasoline. She felt very certain that every drop she did not use would go straight to Georgie's tanks, borne on the wings of seraphs, so we almost never used the car. We managed very well, as a beloved cousin down the road, whose husband was too old to go to war, took me to market once a week.

However, Ma wanted very much to go to church, and it finally occurred to us that during good weather we could drive the donkey cart into Hamilton—about four miles away. The donkey cart was a marvelous hand-painted Sicilian cart, with the Holy Family perched on the axle and the Rape of the Sabine Women painted on one side. It had been given to Mike for his second Christmas by the same beloved cousin. It came with an aged and incredibly disagreeable Sicilian donkey named Domenico. Two people could just barely fit into it, and I had to get out and push when we came to the slope, but we made it to church, in our church-going clothes, and no one said anything much. The fourth Sunday, as we came out of the church and started hitching up Domenico for the return trip, Aunt Theodora had her chauffeur bring her Rolls to a sighing halt beside us. She opened the door and leaned out, very beautiful and fragrant, her exquisite little hat tied down under her chin with a spotted veil, and her inevitable bunch of Parma violets pinned to her silver foxes. She looked down at Ma, sitting crosslegged in the cart, and chided, "Beatrice, dear, do you think it is *quite* the thing for an Ayer to be riding to church in that—vehicle?" Ma looked her up and down: "Well, Fedy, if our Lord could enter Jerusalem on the rear end of an ass, I don't see why I can't go to church in a donkey cart." Aunt Theodora closed the door with an aristocratic thump (Ma said it sounded like the door of a vault closing) and purred splendidly away.

Ma's oldest half-sister, Ellen Wood, was a fragile old lady in her early eighties. She had a car and a chauffeur but rarely went abroad. She drove to Boston once a month and had lunch with her old friend, Maud Piper, the famous medium, and that was the extent of her activities. One day, being deeply fond of Ma, and thinking she should do something for Beatrice, she telephoned to say that she was coming to call. This put Ma in a frenzy of tidying. The house looked great to me, considering we had four or five dogs and two tiny children, but Aunt Ellen's house was always squeaky-clean, and Ma wanted to show off.

The great black Cadillac arrived, and Aunt Ellen, who was in perpetual mourning for her two dead children and her deceased husband, was helped into the house by the chauffeur and carefully ensconced on the sofa. Tea was in the offing. I had dressed Mike up in his sailor suit, inherited from Bee's boys, and the baby was in something lacy and old-fashioned that Aunt Ellen had given her when she was born. Mike was terribly impressed by Aunt Ellen. It was for her that he was wearing his best suit. It was a great occasion, and he was very friendly. He gazed at her, sitting on the sofa with her halo of immaculate silver hair, still wearing her black karakul coat, several lengths of black chiffon scarf, and a black fox fur—we kept the heat low because of the oil rationing—and Mike came forward and leaned on her knee. Aunt Ellen and Ma were talking about *les temps passées,* and Ma, with her mind perpetually on Georgie, was not doing too well with the names and dates. Mike jogged Aunt Ellen's elbow, and asked, "Aunt Ellen, would you like a cigarette?" When she murmured that, no, she didn't smoke, he thought awhile. "Then, would you like some chewing gum?" And when she refused that too, very politely, he wrinkled his brow, and said, persuasively, "Then, how about a little gin?" This cracked her up, and after that the conversation went swimmingly.

Mike was a chameleon. He distinguished himself again the day Aunt Theodora came to call. The nurse was having a day off and Ma was trying to dress Beatrice for the audience. Mike was already in his sailor suit, and I was fixing the tea, as we let all the help go on the same day to save gasoline on the trip to the train station.

The doorbell rang twice and, as no one answered it, Aunt Theodora walked in. Beatrice was being slippery, and Ma was pulling on her frilly rubber pants to the usual cries of protest and suddenly, in a moment of silence, Mike, who was dying to go downstairs and see who was there, said loudly, "Don't hurt the baby, Grandma! Don't drag her little arm!" When Ma finally got downstairs, lugging roly-poly Beatrice, Aunt Theodora scrutinized them both at length, looking for the battered child effect.

We were dependent on our chickens for eggs, and Mike was equally dependent on them for entertainment. Ma laid down the law that he was not to go into the chicken house unless accompanied by an adult. She went down one morning to collect the eggs and found her two-year-old grandson just emerging from the chicken house, feathers in hair and egg in hand. He looked up at her growing frown with a heavenly smile, and announced, "Here is this egg, Grandma. I laid it just for you!" Ma told me about it, saying that she couldn't possibly punish the dear, thoughtful little fellow.

We were rigid about blackout-ing, rationing, and all the little useless-seeming things we were asked to do for the war effort. However, one weekend (for reasons I have forgotten), Ma and I went to New York by train. I went to call on Jim's great aunt, Elma Totten, who lived in a mausoleum of an apartment on Park Avenue. She had gone into total mourning when Uncle Rennie Totten died, some twelve years before, and if you did not at once realize that you were in the presence of a completely broken heart, she made it very apparent before you had been with her for ten minutes. World War II meant nothing to her—her world had ended when Rennie died full of the best beef and butter and beer, and in his eighties at that. Ma had never met her and I, who had, did not think the meeting was advisable, but Ma was determined to meet Aunt Elma just because the Totten family held her in such awe. I went to see her about an hour before Ma finished her appointment and arrived. The apartment was all draped in dust sheets, except for Aunt Elma's bedroom and dining room.

Aunt Elma was a formidable old woman, an autocrat and a bully. Ma sensed this the minute they met, and I could see her beginning to bristle, but she was very polite and sympathetic, and listened to the tale of woe of Uncle Rennie's sudden and unexpected death, cut off in the prime of his late eighties. Finally Aunt Elma's nurse brought in a tray with luncheon for Aunt Elma's butterfly Pomeranian, a revolting little dog with runny eyes who had never stopped yapping since we had arrived. The lunch, served on a Sevres plate, consisted of two kidney lamb chops with paper frills on the bones. Ma had practically given up meat (as had I so that the children could use our red ration points), and she looked at the two chops with a rising gorge. Finally she managed to speak, politely: "I do hope these chops are leftovers, Mrs. Totten." Aunt Elma replied haughtily, "Now, why should I feed Juliette leftovers, Mrs. Patton? After all, she is my whole life since Rennie died." Ma stood up, ruffling like a little gamecock, and started out the door, leading me out by the power of her eye. Just as she went out, she turned to Aunt Elma and said the worst thing she could think of: "Mrs. Totten, anyone who could feed their dog lamb chops in the middle of a world war is nothing but a COPPERHEAD!" and stalked out.

Ma went to Washington quite often to visit Bee and the two little boys, John and Pat. When she wasn't in Washington, she was in the brush thickets on the farm doing the work of ten men, cutting out chokecherry and sumac, and weeding and burning. She said that it helped her to get through the day and made her tired enough to sleep at night. We both lived for the mail. Ma had subscribed to a couple of clipping bureaus, and was keeping splendid scrapbooks of all Georgie's doings. When Georgie slapped the soldier and Drew Pearson went out to lunch on it, the clippings she received from friends, relatives, and perfect strangers were absolutely sickening. It seemed as if all those who had enjoyed Georgie as a hero-warrior enjoyed even more pulling him off the pedestal they had built for him and sneering at his feet of clay. Ma got physically sick reading the newspapers, and turned the scrapbooks over to me. She said, "Maybe in the light of history, we will see how unimportant this is, and your father and I will have many a good laugh over them."

At this time, Georgie's almost daily letters to Ma were filled with a monumental quiet despair. He really thought his wanton goddess of luck had deserted him, and he felt his potential would be wasted and thrown away. His pain carried over to Ma, who knew him so well, and it was a very stormy and unhappy time for both of them. Of course, she never lost faith.

Sometimes he had cheerful things to write about, and he often sent Ma clippings and other enclosures. The best one of these was a long letter with several shiny publicity photographs of the notorious striptease artist Faith Bacon. She wrote Georgie that he was her favorite general, and that she hoped she was his favorite artiste. She wrote that, in addition to admiring him very much, she wanted him to know that he was also her cousin, and she included a photocopy of her Colonial Dames papers, which traced her ancestry to a cousin of his grandmother, Margaret Hereford Wilson. The photographs of Miss Bacon were in costume—mostly Bacon, very little costume. There was also a descriptive leaflet about her performances. One was the "Dance of the Living Orchids" in which Miss Bacon came on stage dressed simply in three live orchids, danced to the inhaling and exhaling of the audience plus some percussion instruments and, for a finale, she tossed all three orchids to the palpitating audience. She also performed "L'Aprés Midi d'un Faun" with a real live fawn, and such was her dedication to her art that she had walked down Beacon Street in Boston leading the fawn on a silver chain—the fawn being her only costume. Although she was arrested for this, she continued to dance this masterpiece by request.

There are not very many happy memories for any of us about the war. My sister finally heard from her Johnnie. He had been taken as a prisoner of war by the Germans, first to Germany and then to Poland. He would only be able to write to her at certain times on cards of a certain size, and her replies would also be edited. Bee's preoccupation, aside from her two boys, became working with the International Red Cross and helping the wives of other prisoners of war.

Ma divided her time between her three children, Bee in Washington, me on the farm, and George at West Point. Each of us was working under our own internal stress—Waters a prisoner, Totten in action in Italy, George champing at the bit to get out of West Point and get into the war, and her Georgie, her cor cordium, having finally his war, and with it still the frustrations and the slings and arrows. The newspapers took good care that the world and his wife knew that the controversial General Patton was always at the battlefront, and always risking his life. Ma had expected that, and had known it could not be otherwise, but she never, ever got used to it.

When Ma went to Washington, she often stayed with Keith and Kay Merrill. Her baby sister was an unfailing source of comfort and sustenance to her. I think it was Kay who first suggested to her that she could share in Georgie's war by speaking to the wives of the overseas troops. Ma had always loved acting and had appeared on stage in everything from a Bach chorale to a three-act amateur comedy, and one of our favorite family entertainments was to play charades. But Ma felt very uncertain about addressing a live audience for real with the message she felt so strongly herself.

She had turned her tiger loose and had composed the "Armored Force March" while she and Georgie were still at Fort Benning, and it was and still is a very dramatic and marchable piece for a full band, with the addition of sirens and the firing of the cannon. The Army Band musician had helped her, and also her friend, Peter de Rose, who, with May Singhi Breen, his wife and companion, were the famous radio team whose theme song was "Side by Side." Ma had met them through her usual open-arms approach. May Singhi Breen's daughter, Rita, was married to an officer in the Air Force when we were in Hawaii, and Ma had looked up the ukelele lady on our return to the States and they had become fast friends. Georgie had the march played on all possible occasions, and Ma was justly proud of it. However, public speaking was another matter altogether.

One of Ma's earliest speeches is typical of her approach to speaking—she got better and better as the war continued:

COMMAND PERFORMANCE

A few weeks ago I heard a broadcast called "Command Performance," and because the broadcast is not heard at all on this continent, I want to tell you something about it.

Once a week, "Command Performance" is broadcast from Hollywood to our soldiers, sailors and marines in every corner of the earth, from Iceland to Australia, and the performance itself is planned on the requests received from the men. The program lasted an hour, and was put on by the finest artists in America, who give their time; and before each selection personal letters were read from men of the Armed Forces abroad, written to the stars themselves, asking for their favorite numbers. Soldiers in Libya heard Kay Kyser and Connie Boswell that evening, and sailors in the Aleutians wriggled their toes in their fur boots in time to Larry Adler's harmonica. Wherever our Americans are at war, that broadcast goes—and our Americans are at war *everywhere.*

Most of us have loved ones in some theatre of war, but we older women of the Regular Army have either relatives or friends on every front. I, myself, have friends fighting in the Solomons, in China, in Libya; friends who are prisoners, and friends who are missing; not casual acquaintances nor people I know by name, but folks who have been my neighbors and who call me Bee for short.

This war is everywhere, and every family I know has someone already at the front or going there. Most of the people I know are fine about sending their men to war, who never expected to go, but once in a while I meet people whose conversation runs something like this—"I want my boy to get into defense work. He'll do better in that than in uniform. Anyhow, he never wanted to be a soldier . . ." Or this: "Mrs. Patton, you shouldn't worry about General Patton. His life is too valuable for him to be up in front. Generals direct the job from the rear. They never lead their men."

Well, *my* General does, and wherever he fights, he will be the first man under fire. His men will follow him over the top as they did in France, and, should he fall, he knows that a thousand of the enemy will die to avenge him.

Wars cannot be won by defense. There have been only three successful defensive actions in all history. I looked them up, but I can't remember what they are. Defensive action, rear-guard action, masterly retreat—we read of these camouflaged lickings in the paper very day. Where do they get us?

Do you remember the ballad of "Horatius at the Bridge"? We had it at school. The two armies were facing each other and about to clash. And those in the rear cried, "Forward," while those in the front cried, "Back." Then out stepped brave Horatius. Horatius was not a professional soldier. He was a farmer, like Sergeant York. But someone had to lead out. Someone had to silence those German guns, and it could not be done from the rear.

In these times of peace just passed, some of us have forgotten that anything that's worth keeping is worth fighting for, and the reckoning is now. Ask our soldiers, our Yanks who write to "Command Performance" and sign their names, Jones, Coletti, Slovinski, Noricich—their fathers came to America to gain freedom, and they are fighting for freedom now, paying their interest on their share in America, and paying it in blood, because so far, no one has found any other way.

Life is a struggle and every so many years it grows into a struggle to the death. We are in that struggle now, and it is just as much of a shock to us as though we hadn't seen it coming from the last twenty years.

Compared to this war, World War I was child's play. Then, we fought on a single front with a short supply line against a half-beaten enemy. This time we are fighting enemies who have rolled their victories up like snowballs and who have enslaved entire nations. In spite of their mines and submarines and Stukas, our supply lines circle the world, and our fronts box the compass. American men are fighting on every continent and on every ocean in the world. We women cannot share their glory except by reflected light, but it is for us and our homes and our America that they are fighting.

Our job is a big one, to keep the lines open with beef, and ships and guns and war bonds; and letters of encouragement from home.

Horatius won his battle. So did Sergeant York. Both men believed in themselves.

This is our Command Performance, sent to us from our fighting men all over the world. Believe in them! Tell them so! Don't let them down!

Ma appeared at "The Home Front," a luncheon given by the Women's Press Section of the War Department and sponsored by Mrs. Ada Bailey Allen, a leading American home economist. Mrs. Allen's newsletter gives a flowery description of the scene, and also the menu and several sugar-saving recipes. Ma was the first speaker:

"My husband has fought in three wars," Mrs. Patton said. "When we were first married he was a young lieutenant, stationed at Fort Sheridan, Illinois. The Army was small in those days and had no standing. Add to that, the fact that I was a very young and very green wife. You can well imagine that my induction as an Army wife was difficult. And today, it is perhaps even more difficult for the officers are now selected and the wives are not! In the Army we carry our homes as the turtle carries its shell. I've had twenty-five homes in thirty-two years. And each one of them has been a real home. We hear a great deal about opening up a second front," Mrs. Patton continued; "we have that second front right now—the homes are the second front."

Announcer: Did Mrs. Patton say what women should do to protect that second front?

Woman Commentator: To quote, "Learn to wait cheerfully. Keep in good physical shape. Avoid worry. Be ashamed of it, for worry unfits us. Put on your smile each morning, just as you do your clothes. Lean heavily on prayer. You cannot carry the world on *your* shoulders. Leave everything to the Mercy of God. Write cheerful letters to your men. Remember that furloughs and homecoming are not for family study. Be gay and pretty when your men come home. Remember you have plenty of competition in the pretty hostesses and glamorous movie stars who entertain on the posts. So, hang on to every bit of your charm. As to rumor, kill it—and trust your government. Learn to read the papers with intelligence. Don't stop at headlines—for real news, read the communiques in small print. Look up the names of the cities, villages and countries that you read about, in the encyclopedia—learn something about the places where your men are posted. Be sure to get yourself a war job, if it is only two hours a week. This war is *your* challenge and your opportunity. Keep a brave face, a brave heart, and pray without ceasing."

Announcer: What an inspiring message, and from a woman whose husband has fought in three wars and who, as Mrs. Allen says, is as charming as she is inspiring. The kind of woman one is proud to call friend.

Life magazine quoted one of Ma's talks to an Officers' Wives Club. This talk was one of her pièces de resistance.

There is no career, except that of a minister's wife, in which a woman can be of such a help or such a detriment to her husband as that of an Army wife. She lives practically at his place of business, and sees his associates daily. Her reputation begins at her first post and sticks to her as closely as her skin until she dies. I have known several able officers to be ruined absolutely by malicious gossipy wives.

I joined the Army in 1910—the piping times of peace. But the older women knew. Before my first child was born I had seen my husband's bedding roll at the front door, ready to leave if the regiment went to Mexico. Since then, I have seen him off to three wars. He has led troops in battle, been gravely wounded and has been decorated for extraordinary heroism. Now, I belong to the older generation of Army women who preach, Be happy today. Who knows what tomorrow may hold.

The following is one of Ma's talks that she gave several times. It has the same start as the speech about an Army wife and a minister's wife being sisters under the skin. Then it goes on to say—

The three little monkeys, See No Evil, Hear No Evil, and Speak No Evil should be accompanied by a fourth, Feel No Evil, the key to all the others. It is impossible to live kindly with your neighbors unless you feel kindly toward them. I have told my daughters that there are only two sorts of women in the Army, of one of whom it is said, Mrs. A. is coming to the post. I *know* her and of the other, Mrs. B. is coming to the post. I know *her*.

Army women are drawn from two sources; girls born and reared in the Army, who are supposed to know their stuff, and girls recruited from civil life. Owing to the present emergency, those last outnumber those brought up in the Army tradition, yet the tradition is still so strong that they are shaping up into Army wives as quickly and proudly as their husbands shape up into uniform. All over the United States today women who have never washed a dish or been a hundred miles from home are making homes for their husbands wherever they can unpack a suitcase and pretending it is fun.

During the last year, I have met at least a thousand such and have yet to hear a complaint from one of them.

Many years ago, I, myself, was a recruit from civil life. I came from a family of seven, so devoted to one another that my mother used to accuse us of behaving at parties like birds on a telegraph wire. I must have been a very outgoing young person, for her advice to me when I married was remember, you are going among strangers. Be friends with everyone but confide in no one. I took this seriously. One morning, when I had been several months at my first post, the doorbell rang. I was wearing a dress from my trousseau which no longer met around the middle, so I threw on a shawl and went to the door. My caller was the oldest lady on the post, who came in, sat down, and said, "My dear, the ladies at Fort Sheridan have asked me to call on you as they are very much concerned about you. We have decided you are going to have a baby and since you have not confided in anyone, we wonder if you know it?"

Army life is very like the Gulf Stream which, made of the same watery element as the ocean through which it runs, has no boundaries; yet its temperature and its tempo keep it separate and distinct. It is not only a different color from the rest of the ocean, it supports entirely different fish. Army Officers are highly educated professional men who are content to get along with little of this world's goods, so they must live the life they love; and the women who join them must be of the same sort to be successful and happy, for the lines that prescribe our lives are as definite as the boundaries of the Gulf Stream. An officer must be well dressed; that is part of his job. I know officers' wives who do not only make their own clothes but make their husband's uniform shirts and britches as well as any tailor; and that is not because the men have married tailoresses, but because they have chosen women who are good at anything they put their hands to.

It is an interesting thing to notice that in this common life of ours in which we move about from post to post (I have been married thirty-one years and have had nineteen major moves) we still preserve our local differences within our families, carrying our background with us as a turtle packs its shell. In any Army post, if you go into a row of houses exactly alike on the outside, you will find the Boston people using the broad a and eating fishballs on Sunday morning, while the family from Mississippi next door eat hot bread twice a day in the atmosphere of the deep south.

We are all fish in the great common life of the Gulf Stream, but the dolphins are always dolphins and the amberjacks are amberjacks no matter how often Uncle Sam moves us about. This is because each family unit is a home in a much more concentrated sense than the same family would be in a neighborhood where one had grown up and had all the relatives to fall back on. Wherever we go, whatever background we have goes with us. We must be homemakers in our own right without benefit of our families, and usually with only the sketchiest of local talent to help in the kitchen.

When my oldest daughter was about to be married, I found on her desk a huge blank book labeled "Mother's Thoughts on Marriage." Heavens! What had I said! What pearls had she culled, unknown to me? I opened it. Across the first page was a single entry in her tiny writing; "To see if he is fresh, look in the fish's eye, but feel under the chicken's arm." The rest of the book was blank. I wrote under it, "Recipe for a successful marriage—the Army travels on its stomach," and tucked it in a trunk where she would find it when she reached her first station after her honeymoon.

When I joined the Army, the thing that impressed me most about the older women was their gaiety. According to my ideas, they led terribly serious lives, many of them doing their own work, and pinching and scraping to help with the life insurance, the savings account, and to meet the commissary bill, which must always be settled by the tenth of the month. And the way they figured when they decided to give a party! Coming from a family in very comfortable circumstances, I felt that their lives were pretty hard. There didn't appear to be a great deal in their past, either, to make them so debonair. One woman had lived through a cholera epidemic in the Philippine Islands. Another told me, as if she were telling a story about a perfect stranger, how she once sat on the stern of a tugboat on the Yalu River, watching the corpses float past, and wondering if she could identify her husband's. Gradually, I came to realize what they were doing. These wives of the Old Army were inoculating me little by little with the store of courage which is the legacy of every Army woman and which we hand on from one generation to the next.

I joined the Army in 1910—the piping times of peace. But the older women knew. Before my first child was born, I had seen my husband's bedding roll at the front door, ready to leave if the regiment went to Mexico. Since then, I have seen him off to two wars. He has led troops in battle, been gravely wounded, and been decorated for extraordinary heroism. Now, I belong to the older generation of Army women who preach, Be happy today, who knows what tomorrow may hold?

There is one branch of the service whose wives face this lesson every day—the Air Force. I should like to take you to an Air Force party. It is half-past four in the afternoon and the room sounds like a barnyard. A sudden hush falls; the planes are coming in—one—two—three—four—. The women count them as one counts the beat of a beloved pulse—not missing; not missing—okay, everybody! Once more he is coming home safe. I take my hat off to the Air Force women who do not break under the strain.

This is the Army undercurrent—the thing that colors all our lives. We are reminded of it throughout our waking hours by the uniforms, the drills, and, most of all by the bugle calls; reveille, when the junior officers' wives get up to cook the junior officers' breakfasts; mess call, at noon, when our husbands come home to lunch; retreat, when the flag is hauled down and folded for the night, while the children at play on the parade ground stand at attention in imitation of their father and, last of all, at eleven o'clock, taps, the soldiers' goodnight. We have heard it at West Point, when the lights in the cadet barracks blink out—our sweetheart's light is there somewhere. One day we may be watching our son's light go out in that same window. We hear it filtering through the band music at the hop—time to run home and pick up the baby. And taps is the call that is played over every soldier's grave—the last goodnight.

The bugle calls regulate our lives. We set our watches by them, but they do not sound for us. There will be no taps at the Army wife's funeral.

In my part of the country, domineering women are called Captains. To be a successful Army wife, the only Captain must be the man. And what men they are—a band of hereditary patriots.

A friend of mine who was once engaged to marry an Army officer was urged not to marry him as her informant assured her that in her role of Army wife, she would merely be the tail of the kite. She asked her fiancé if this was true. He answered with another question "How high can a kite soar without its tail?"

Ma always wished that the Ruth of the Old Testament had been sainted as she would have made the perfect patron saint for the service wife. "Whither thou goest, I will go and where thou lodgest, I shall lodge; thy people shall be my people and thy God my God: where thou diest, I will die and there will I be buried: and the Lord do so unto me and more also if ought but death part thee and me."

Ma had started making her speeches for the war effort, and to help sell war bonds. With practice, her speeches got better and better and her audiences got bigger and bigger. It was very good for her; it got her away from her live-in worries; she saw other people; heard other sides of the war, and even had some funny things happen. Also, she was actively engaged in helping Georgie—she was almost fighting at his side. And she was taking her own advice—have a war job.

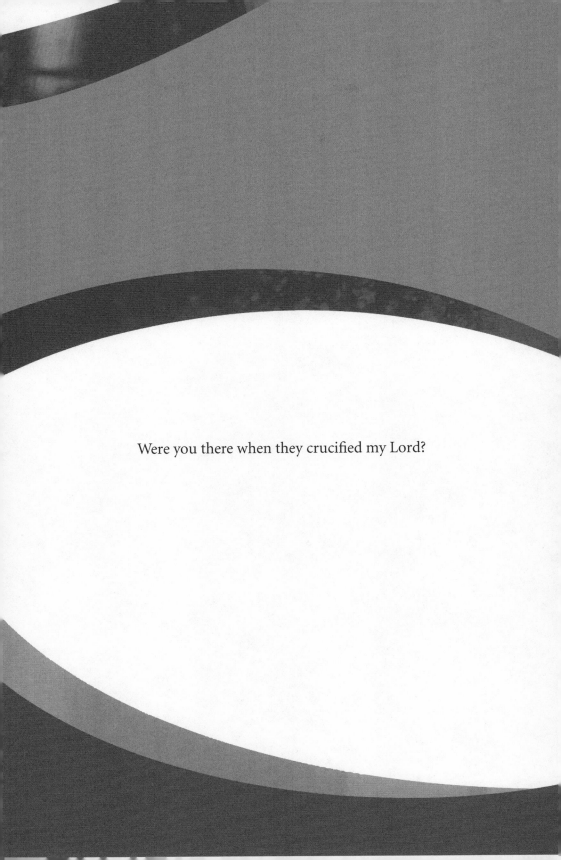

Were you there when they crucified my Lord?

Chapter 17

"A Helluva Way to Die"

There were more lows for Georgie after the slapping incident. He was often pilloried, and this caused Ma hours of suffering. He made his famous remark to an audience of elderly British ladies about the great allies, omitting the Russians, and the newspapers jumped on him like a hen on a june bug. He was a Kipling fanatic, and often quoted Kipling's poem "The Bear That Walks Like a Man"—which is an allegorical poem about Russia, and has really goose-pimply lines in it—

Horrible, hairy, human with paws like hands in prayer
Making his supplication, rose Adam-Zad the Bear
Touched with pity and wonder, I did not fire then
I have looked no more on women, I have walked no more with men
Nearer he tottered, and nearer, with paws like hands that pray
From brow to jaw, that steel-clad paw, it ripped my face away.
Rouse him at noon from the bushes, follow him, press him hard
Not from his ragings and roaring flinch ye from Adam-Zad
——this is the time to fear
When he stands up like a tired man, tottering near and near
When he stands up as pleading, in wavering man-like guise
And he veils the hate and cunning in his little swinish eyes
When he shows as seeking quarter, with paws like hands in prayer
This is the time of peril—that is the Truth of the Bear
Over and over the story, ending as it began
Make ye no truce with Adam-Zad, the Bear that Walks Like a Man!

He also quoted often the Kipling short story called "The Man Who Was," about a British officer who had been a prisoner of the Russians. Georgie did not like or trust the Russians. He did not want them for allies. He understood their devious Oriental minds as few Americans did at that time, and he knew what tremendous fighters they were. History would prove him right.

Another one of his much-referred-to errors was in not sending a strong enough battle group to relieve a POW Camp in Germany where, it turned out later, Johnnie Waters was detained. Georgie honestly thought Johnnie, to whom he was deeply devoted, was dead. The 4th Armored Division took a terrible beating and when it was later discovered that Johnnie was in camp, a lot of people jumped on the newspapers' bandwagon and claimed that Georgie had wasted a lot of lives on personal family business. This hurt Georgie, whose motto was "Duty, Honor, Country." He had never in his life put his family ahead of his duty, or his honor, or his country.

Johnnie Waters came home after more than two years as a POW to Walter Reed Hospital in Washington, D.C. He was in critical condition, having sustained grave wounds at the time his POW camp was recaptured by the Americans. Jim Totten came home, after nearly two years, having spent the last three months of his war in a hospital in Italy with infectious hepatitis, which was little understood in those days. Georgie stayed on in Germany fighting his war, and being crucified by the press and his superiors for telling it like it was, or, at any rate, as he saw it.

Ma went on fighting her war in the only way she could, making speeches, writing letters to the families of the men in the Third Army who wrote to her about their sons and husbands, and exercising one of her greatest gifts, which was the gift of giving. Ma never sent large sums of money to the big charities because she had so many private ones—people who were too proud, or too devastated to ask for help; people who, on the face of things, looked as if they didn't need help. She had a real instinct for trouble and always managed to make the people that she helped feel that they had done her a favor. One of the examples of Ma's gift is that of the wife of a very brave and gallant general who, after losing her only son in battle, gave everything she had, including her insurance, to her widowed daughter-in-law. When the general was killed a few months later, the lady was left with her clothes, her furniture, and two thousand dollars in the bank. She had a real antique paisley Indian shawl—or believed she had—and felt that she had to sell it. It was an 1890 imitation of the real thing, but Ma had it appraised by a friend in the antique business, and bought it for what a real paisley shawl would have cost.

Another friend of hers, the wife of a retired general, needed a very complicated operation on her digestive system to prolong her life. Somehow Ma was able to get her into the best hospital in the district and pay for the five-hour operation by a famous specialist without causing resentful gratitude. However, the general, who had known Ma since she was a bride, and of whom she stood in everlasting awe, said to her in his stiffest manner—and believe me, he was stiff—"Mrs. Patton, I have always called you Mrs. Patton, and you have always called me General Smith, but considering what we have just been through with poor Jane, I shall now call you Beatrice, and you may call me Henry." Ma said that she made herself do it, although it shook her up every time she did, because she insisted, "I still think of him as General Smith."

That same general was a legend in his own time. His children were friends of ours and we went in and out of their house as often as they were in and out of ours. One day I was there for lunch and I saw Mrs. Smith hand the general a small glass of some dark fluid which he drank down at one draught, making a horrible face as he did so. I asked Mrs. Smith what on earth she was giving the general, and she replied in her parade-ground voice, "He is drinking blood, my dear, but don't tell the lieutenants' wives!" It seemed that the general had a slightly anemic condition and she was giving him beef juice.

Ma was always alert to unspoken need, even when she was worrying about Georgie and his war. She heard more confidences than anyone but a priest, but she never divulged them while the confidante was still living, and later, when she told us some of the things she knew, she always changed the names. This does not mean that she was tolerant or permissive. That she was not! Sin was sin to Ma, and she had her special hatreds, which included disloyalty, adultery, divorce, gossip, drink, and coarseness of speech. Georgie will go down through history as a man of vast profanity, but he never used it around Ma—it would not have occurred to him to use strong language in her presence, or, for that matter, in the presence of any lady. She knew all the bad words, of course, but she didn't use them, except very occasionally, for effect. To hear a strong word coming out of Ma's mouth was a real shocker—it shocked even Georgie. I particularly remember one remark that she made one day when Georgie was fussing about some Irish soldiers in his command, how flighty they were, and how they only told him what they thought he wanted to hear. Ma said, "Yes, the Irish have eight faces; one for every day of the week and two for Sunday; and they are really only interested in the three F's." Georgie asked her what the three F's were and without turning a hair, she replied, "Fighting, funerals, and fucking." I have never seen anyone look so shocked as Georgie did!

Ma wrote hundreds of letters during the war to the relatives of the Third Army. She would not keep a secretary, but wrote them all herself by hand. Many people came all the way to South Hamilton to see her. She lived in the constant knowledge that every time the telephone rang it could be the War Department with bad news, but she rose above it and somehow managed to get across to anxious, grief-stricken, apprehensive people that their men were fighting for, or had died for, A CAUSE. *Dulce et decorum est pro patria mori.* She could get it across to them that Georgie was always at the forefront of battle, wearing the panache—the white plume that was worn by Henry of Navarre, who cried to his faltering troops, *Suivez mon panache!* If the cause was not a good one, her Georgie would not be leading the charge.

Our family was under the constant supervision of the press. Several members of the press came out to Hamilton and tried to get jobs either in the house or on the farm, but Ma had an instinct for that kind of imposture and turned them away. She really began to hate the press the same way she hated undertakers. She also got the inevitable hate letters and phone calls. This upset her so much that she finally had me open the mail and answer the telephone; she said that she was afraid she would lose her temper over the phone and make things even harder for Georgie. The worse things got, the harder she gardened. On the very worst days, she would saw down fairly large trees with a handsaw. There was a lot of chokecherry in the part of the bosk that she was reclaiming and this she attacked as if it were the United Press and Hitler combined.

Cousin Mario Guardabassi had been put in a mild sort of detention camp in the Middle West because he had been given his title by Mussolini, and because he was a great friend of Mussolini's son-in-law, Count Ciano. This detention didn't faze Mario in the slightest. He had the sheriff eating out of his hand, and he had a very good time as a man among men, hunting and telling tales. However, Diddah raised total hell, and blamed everything that happened on the Jews. She made so much rumpus that Mario was finally recognized as being as uninterested and uninvolved as he really was, so they sent him home to Prides Crossing. The Guardabassis came over often to call on Ma—gas rationing didn't seem to be part of their problems. Mario would try to cheer Ma up with happy thoughts about how wonderful Georgie was, and how he would win the war singlehanded, if permitted so to do.

The two little boys, Frederico and Guinio, came along with them, their dark eyes glowing with excitement at Ma's tales of the war. Uncle Georgie was their hero, as he was for all of the kids in the family, and they couldn't hear enough or get enough of touching the souvenirs he was always sending Ma. Diddah kept insisting that Georgie was just a pawn of the Jews, and was fighting their battles for them. Mario, quite deaf, would roll his eyes heavenward and shrug his shoulders and complain to the surrounding air: "Now, why she say dat?" Mario was a comfort to Ma, because he would top all her stories of the horrors of World War II with his own stories of his personal horrors in World War I.

Jamie Ayer, Ma's beloved oldest brother, had died before the war, but her other brothers and sisters rallied around and did everything they could for her. One night one of Georgie's horses got the colic, an illness in which the horse has to be kept on his feet until he recovers, because if he ever goes down he will never rise again. We all took turns in walking him, and Ma remembered that Georgie had always dosed this kind of complaint in a horse with whiskey. Liquor was severely rationed, and we didn't have any in the house, so Ma called Uncle Chilly Ayer and asked him if he had any whiskey. Uncle Chilly said, of course, that he did and he would have Herne come right over with a bottle. Herne delivered the goods and somehow, between us all, we managed to drench the horse (the term for administering liquid medicine to a horse) and although he carried on like crazy, he got it down and it did the trick, as he recovered.

Ma called Chilly up several days later to tell him that thanks to him the horse had pulled through. Poor Chilly said, "My God, Beatrice, you never told me it was for a horse! I thought it was for you. I said to myself, 'There's dear little Bee, all alone with Georgie off at the wars and no one to take care of her,' and so I sent Herne over with one of the last bottles of my personal pre–World War I stock! Tell me, did the horse drink the whole bottle?" Ma sadly admitted that he had, and Chilly's deep sigh nearly blew the phone out of her hand.

After a month in the Army hospital at Fort Devens, Massachusetts, and a few weeks at Green Meadows, Jim was ordered to Washington for limited duty at the Pentagon. Limited duty means that they will work you until you either die, retire, or recover. Bee found us a very nice house quite near to hers, and we moved to Washington with dog, children, and an unfortunate nurse-type person who was having a holiday from taking care of mentally retarded children. As Mike and little Bee were far from that, the poor woman had a hard time.

M spent a lot of time in Washington, staying with one or the other of us, and went to West Point to see George whenever it was feasible.

The war was over for the world, but not for Ma and Georgie. He considered that in not being allowed to drive the Russians back to their borders, we had merely achieved a Pyrric victory, and he upset various applecarts by saying so. He was taken away from his Third Army in a series of moves that I think were destined to destroy him if he had lived long enough. He knew too much, and he talked too much: the Army brass could not intimidate him by threatening to take his perks away, as he had an outside income and did not give a damn.

They say. What do they say? Let them say!

Georgie started his own final downfall by assigning ex-Nazis to key jobs in getting Germany back on the tracks. He said that everyone still alive in Germany had been a member of the Nazi party, and he saw no harm in giving the jobs of rehabilitation to qualified personnel. That in the end, it was just a party system—like the Democrats and the Republicans. He made this unfortunate statement in front of a group of newsmen who had been sent in like a pack of jackals to devil the dying lion and make some headlines. Georgie must have realized this, as he said to them, "You boys are out to get me, aren't you?"

One of these jackals made a point of calling on Ma after he was dead and telling her this. He said he was sorry, that it had seemed like a good idea at the time. After he met Georgie and saw what he was like, he realized it was a setup and wanted to back out, but it had gone too far. Ma, who was a good hater, did not give him much comfort.

So much furor ensued—from people who had never heard a shot fired in anger—that General Eisenhower was chivvied into relieving Georgie from his real Third Army, and giving him a paper army to command. Poor Ike, that man of straw, as Georgie called him. He had really tried his best and had been as strong as it was possible for him to be in standing up for Georgie when the going was the toughest and Georgie was needed, but Ike had been told that he was under the magnifying glass for consideration as a presidential candidate, and he was cleaning out his nest. He also had to sweep out his fascinating and clever English chauffeur-confidante, Kay Somersby. In the heat and triumph of battle, he had probably led her to expect more than he meant to deliver, but when General Marshall and President Truman told him he could choose between his liaison and running for the presidency, glory won over glamour.

Ike wired Georgie in code to break the news to Mrs. Somersby that her services would no longer be required. Georgie was furious at being ordered, not requested, to do this. He thought it was an ungentlemanly command. But he followed the order to the letter, and called Mrs. Somersby into his office with several witnesses on hand, to read her Ike's message. He told Ma that he was appalled by her reaction, especially her language, and that her final remark sent shivers up his spine: "Who the hell does he think he is? He can't treat me like this! I'll get even with him if it's the last thing I do, even over my own dead body!"

Ma suffered through all this decline and fall with Georgie, but then the good news came that he was to come home on what was called Operation Eversharp. This was a personal appearance to buck up the war bond sales. Ma said again and again, "I really thought I would never see him again! I really was afraid I would never see him again!"

Bee and Jim and I came north from Washington, and George came from West Point to meet Georgie at the airport. It was a time of great rejoicing. There was a regular Roman triumph, lacking only noble conquered chieftains in chains. The governor and the mayor gave a huge dinner for Georgie and Ma. He had a few days at Green Meadows to see the rest of the family and relax. Then he came to Washington, where it was all repeated. He visited Johnnie

Waters in the hospital and saw his grandchildren. He had met the three little boys, but Beatrice Totten had been born while he was fighting.

Georgie was told that he had to visit Walter Reed Hospital although he hated hospitals. The men in the double-amputation ward, where I worked as an occupational therapist, begged me to have him come to their ward, so I asked him to do it. He came with Ma and a lot of doctors and dignitaries and hovering press men. Georgie was dressed to the nines, all his medals, boots aglow, his trademark swagger stick in his gloved left hand—the whole picture. Just before he entered the ward, he turned to the press and said, "I'll bet you goddam buzzards are just following me in here to see if I'll slap another soldier, aren't you? You're all hoping I will!"

I had worked in that ward for two years, and I guess for my own protection I had ceased to see how truly tragic and horrible it was. The men were all individuals to me, I did not consciously see their afflictions. But that ward was a shock to Ma and Georgie. He strode down to about the center of the row of beds. All of the patients were looking at him with their hearts in their eyes. Suddenly, he whipped out a large white handkerchief and burst into tears: "Goddammit, if I had been a better general, most of you would not be here." He turned on his heel and walked rapidly out the door with the crowd of officials scrambling after him. The men cheered as he went by. One of them said, "Mrs. Totten, did you hear what your father said to *me?*" He had gotten across to them as no one else could have done. They did not want sympathy.

The last time we saw Georgie in the flesh was a day or so later at Bee's house, where we were having lunch. I remember that it was one of the hottest days of the summer. Ma and Georgie were on their way to California to visit the family and his home there and to make some more personal appearances. From there he was to go back to Europe. Ma went upstairs to tidy herself and Georgie said to Bee and me in a most conversational tone, "Well, I guess this is goodbye. I'm not going to see you girls again. Take care of your little brother, and tell John and Jim to take care of you." He paused: "I think I'll see your mother again." We both began to talk at once, exclaiming, What are you talking about? The war is over. You'll be home in a few months for good. Of course, we'll see you again! He replied, "No, my luck has all run out. I've used it up. You're born with a certain amount of luck—it's like money in the bank. A front-line soldier spends it faster than a rear-echelon cook. I've been very lucky, but I've used it all up. The last few shells that fell near me, each one was closer. I've had increasingly narrow escapes. It's too damned bad I wasn't killed before the fighting stopped, but I wasn't. So be it."

He said it all so easily that neither of us could really protest. From the time we could remember, we had heard him predict that he would die on foreign soil, and that he wanted to be buried where he fell. He often quoted Napoleon: "The boundaries of an empire are the graves of her soldiers." We weren't really surprised at his farewell, but I don't think either of us quite believed him.

Ma and Georgie got to California to a native-son hero welcome, and he continued to say tactless things that got him in more trouble. What made the trouble was that what he said was true. But we had just completed another war to end all wars, and no one wanted to hear him say what he had to say. In fact, very few of his old friends and his family could hear what he was trying to tell them, as they had not seen what he had seen, or could even conceive of his experiences. He felt very lonely. Ma understood. Ma knew what he had been doing all of his life—word, verse, chapter, and book. She agonized with him. He talked to her a lot about retiring, and sailing around the world in the *When and If*. He said that he was not going to write his memoirs—that the truth was never known about a war until one hundred years after it was over, until everyone who had fought in it was dead. He said that most military memoirs were *apologia pro sua vita*. He went back to Europe and had a pretty good time, the highlight being his visit to Sweden and meeting men with whom he had competed in the Olympics thirty-three years before.

Ma was staying with us in Washington when the inevitable happened. I can see it now. Ma was writing letters at my desk in the den, and I was on my knees in the front hall trying to mend the hinge on the door of a corner cabinet that she had given us. The phone rang with a voice of authority asking to speak to Ma. I called out, "It's the War Department for you!" She got up from the desk: "Something has happened to your father."

Georgie had asked for leave to come home for Christmas. He was going to bring Ma a wonderful portrait he had had done of himself by Czedekowski, but at the last minute he thought he would like to bring her some pheasant skins, so that she could have a little pheasant feather hat made—like the one she had loved when she was a bride. He had gone hunting with his friend and chief of staff General Hap Gay, and they were returning with the pheasant. Sergeant Mimms, Georgie's regular driver, was in the hospital, and there was a substitute driver on duty. They were proceeding down the Autobahn at about thirty-five miles an hour when an Army truck came out of a side road at about eighteen miles per hour, and there was a glancing collision. Georgie was thrown up against the roof of the car and fell forward against the glass partition between the driver's seat and the rear. When it was all sorted out, Georgie found he could not move his arms or legs. He said to Hap Gay, "This is a helluva way to die."

He was taken right to the hospital and the wheels were put in motion to do all that could be done. Georgie realized how this might affect the future life of his driver, especially if the worst happened, so he ordered that this same young soldier be sent to the airport to meet Ma when she was flown in. Georgie was a gentleman—as Stevenson said, "One all the world over, and in every relation and grade of society."

The wheels to get Ma to Georgie in Europe were instantly activated. Everyone was splendid from General Eisenhower to Philip Coffin, the head of the Bell Telephone Company, to taxi drivers, to even the vultures of the press. Ma took off for Germany with a famous nerve specialist who had been yanked off a train on his way to his own home and told to accompany Ma to Europe, and see what he could do for General Patton who had broken his neck in a car accident. The British had already sent their foremost expert to Georgie's side.

Jim Totten was in Brazil, liberating trains that we had loaned the Brazilians. Johnnie Waters was at home convalescing. George was at West Point. The War Department called us every day to report on Georgie's progress and we, in turn, called Levin Waters, Johnnie's doctor brother, a pathologist, who could translate the reports for us. One evening the report came through as prognosis negative and even we could understand that. Ma's brother, Fred, had left for Europe to be with her. We stayed in Washington with our own responsibilities.

Bee and I did see and hear Georgie once more. Knowing him, it was only to be expected. The night he died (we all knew he was dying but we had not heard that it was over), I was sound asleep in my bedroom. The room had a bay in it with a window seat opposite the beds. I woke up with a start, wide awake, to see a room full of light and Georgie lying in the bay. He had his head propped on his hand. He was in full uniform and looking at me fixedly. I sat up in bed—I could see him plainly. When he saw I was looking at him, he gave me the sweetest smile I have ever seen. It was loving, and reassuring, and his very own. Then, he wasn't there. I turned on the light and looked at the clock and saw it was about 2:10 a.m. I almost called my sister then, but I knew she had trouble sleeping, and was worried about Johnnie, so I waited. In fact, I felt as if some burden had been lifted, and I went back to sleep.

I called my sister the next morning about half past seven and she answered the phone right away, saying, "Hi, I was just going to call you. The strangest thing happened last night." She said that she had been fast asleep when the phone by her bed rang. She picked it up and there was a lot of static, as if it were an overseas call, and she heard Georgie's voice ask, "Little Bee, are you all right?" Then it was cut off. She called the overseas operator who said there had been no call. She said that she sighed and turned over and went back to sleep. I told her what had happened to me. One of us said, I guess he's dead then, and poor Ma!

The War Department sent an officer to tell us that he had died. We never checked to see if we had heard from him as he died, or later. It didn't seem important.

When you are expecting something, it is not the shock it would be if it were a bolt from the blue. But I think his conditioning of us since childhood in the inevitability, and the acceptability, of death kept us from a feeling of total loss, which is the lot of some.

As only expected, Ma was magnificent. She comforted others; made arrangements for the people in charge who were too shaken to do what they were supposed to do; acted her part, wherein all honor lay.

She told us later that several days before Georgie died they were alone talking, and he said, "I guess I wasn't good enough." She knew he was referring to his often-expressed desire to die from the last bullet in the last battle, or as one of his heroes, the Confederate general Barnard Bee, had died. General Bee, seeing his green troops wavering in the first battle of Manassas, stood up in his saddle, sword held on high, and shouted, "There stands Jackson like a stone wall! Rally behind the Virginians!"—a second later a bullet struck him dead from his horse.

She was very concise and calm when she told us about his death. She had been reading aloud to him from a book called *The Red Pony,* and he had asked her what the time was. She told him, and he said that he felt tired and for her to go and get her dinner, and they would finish the chapter when she got back. She went to the dining room, leaving the duty nurse with him. The nurse suddenly noticed that there was no sound in the room. Georgie had stopped breathing. They sent for Ma. Georgie was gone. They have put lots of last words in Georgie's mouth, some rather good copy, but that is the way it actually happened.

Ma came back to Washington after the funeral. She arrived on Christmas Day 1945, in terrible weather. We all met her at the airport and she went to Bee's, where we all joined her in the afternoon. She looked very small and somehow old, but she kept Christmas, and had somehow found a little trinket for each of us. Mine was a wartime Christmas tree angel made out of straw. She was gay and Christmasy because she said that she didn't want to upset the grandchildren. I remembered back to 1918, when my sister and I were taken in to see Ma's mother, Ellie, after Granfer Ayer died, and Ellie was wearing a fresh flower in her hair in order not to frighten the little girls.

> The heart that has truly loved never forgets
> But as truly loves on to the close
> As the sunflower turns to her God when he sets
> The same look that she turned when He rose.

Ma never did take on about it, but afterwards she was somehow diminished, as if she had lost a part of herself. Of course, she had.

In the most ancient times, the peoples on the edge of the Mediterranean Sea and in that area believed God to be a female, the Great Goddess. As the mystery of procreation took thousands of years to come into focus, the mystery that was accepted was that Woman produced Child. The Supreme Deity was the Great Goddess, equated with the Moon, which is mystically and actually connected to the planting of the crops, and the tide of woman's productivity and the drawing of the waters. In her new moon phase, the Goddess was the Virgin, the learner; in her full moon phase, the Goddess was the Nymph, the doer; and in her waning moon aspect, she was the Crone, the teacher. In the dark of the moon, the Goddess was equated with death, rest, and renewal. Ma entered into the Crone state of her life when Georgie died. She had always been a teacher, but now people saw her as she really was, and not just as an appendage of the Great Man. She was recognized as a person in herself, with a great deal to offer.

Chapter 18

I Hide in Songs

Ma made her base at Green Meadows and involved herself in editing papers that Georgie had sent home to her through the hands of friends. This journal was later published as *War As I Knew It.* She also, with the invaluable and sympathetic aid of her brother-in-law, Keith Merrill, filed the literally thousands of notes and papers left by Georgie—now in the Library of Congress.

Georgie's diary, which was dynamite at that, and which he had kept against all rules, had to be translated. Georgie's handwriting was so eccentric and his spelling was so original that there were very few people who could decipher it. With the help of Georgie's confidential military secretary, Ma got it all down in readable form, and then locked it away. The secretary was everybody's dream employee. Georgie told Ma a story about her that sums her up. When they were finally ordered to land in France, and it was the top-est top secret of all, the secretary, who had typed it all out, said, weeping, "Oh, I would feel so much better if I knew where you boys were going!"

After the papers came the statue that Ma had decided was to be erected at West Point. She chose the most famous sculptor in America, James E. Frazier, who had done the superb Appeal to the Great Spirit that stands in front of the Museum of Fine Arts in Boston. This fine man came to visit and studied photographs, writings, and talked a lot with Ma about Georgie, as he said he wanted to do the statue from the inside out. He had my brother, George, pose in the clothes he planned to put on the statue, and he borrowed from me the snake ring that Georgie had always worn since his Aunt Nanny had given it to him on his twelfth birthday, in order to get even that detail exactly right.

Ma wanted a good biography of Georgie written, so she interviewed authors of all kinds. The immortal Douglas Southall Freeman, who had written master biographies of George Washington, Robert E. Lee, and a follow-up of the latter called *Lee's Lieutenants,* told Ma that as soon as he finished his current book, he would do Georgie's biography but, alas, he died before he could fulfill his promise.

Ma's sister Ellen had been a victim of mediums and people peddling the supernatural after the deaths of two of her four children. Some years later her practical Ayer blood started to boil and she made an abrupt about-face and started having such hoaxes investigated because she felt sorry for their victims. The one medium that no investigation disqualified was Maud Piper of Boston. She and Ellen Wood became fast friends, and one of Ellen's few excursions away from her home in Prides Crossing—the one with the red brocade wallpaper and the staring marble busts of her dead children—was to lunch with Mrs. Piper. A prophet is not without honor except in his own country, and so it was with Mrs. Piper. She had very little money and was totally blind, and lived poorly with her daughter, Minerva; Aunt Ellen helped them out. On the way home from one of her weekly luncheons with Mrs. Piper, Aunt Ellen had her chauffeur drive her to Green Meadows and asked Ma to give her something of Georgie's to take to Mrs. Piper. She said that she would not tell Mrs. Piper whose it was. Ma was very reluctant—the whole idea made her flesh crawl— but Ellen said that it would mean a great deal to her. She had always adored Georgie. So, Ma gave her the glove Georgie had on when his car was struck. Later, she gave Ellen some letters from Georgie to herself. These things were wrapped in paper when Mrs. Piper handled them, but as she was blind, she could not have seen them anyhow. What follows is copied directly from Minerva Piper's letter to Ellen Wood. Ma gave them to me to keep. She said that she could not bear to have them in the house—they scared her.

Suite Four
54 Dwight St.
Brookline, Mass.   May 9, 1946

Dear Mrs. Wood:

I send the enclosed and hope that it may have some meaning for someone.

This time I cannot place any blame for failures on the article [she is referring to the maid's hairpins] which is an excellent one! I seem to feel two influences but one much more strongly than the other; the article may have been handled by more than the owner.

At your convenience you will, let me know if the enclosed is incorrect when I will try again.

With every expression of gratitude and affection,

                    Faithfully yours,
                    Maud Piper

(Minerva took notes while her mother was entranced, and here are the notes from this séance.)

I feel a sudden separation—I feel, that to this person the separation was extra-ordinary—when he awoke—from this life—in the spirit—he was amazed and tried to find—well, he calls, B—I can't quite get it but he says, B, so I'll stick to it.

My happiness—my great happiness, was in the awakening of my spirit and the realization that the faith, trust and sincerity of the life that exists in the mortal body has been continued in the spirit—it is a Divine and peaceful atmosphere impossible to describe through mortal tongue but that I am here in thought, af-fection and devotion—there can be *no* question and B. we are still together per-haps unknown to you but I am at your sides even though you are unconscious of it. I am there with you when the day closes and the night appears to fall—wher-ever you go, I join you and the happiest thoughts go through my mind of the great love in the mortal wound—and the boy—and all that life meant to us there. I shall be with you constantly until we meet again—God be with you dar-ling, my own, and keep you safe and well in His Holy Keeping. (Rector came and stood by him and helped him finish those few words to his dear one.)

All love and devotion and do not worry, darling, we shall meet again in God's own time and way. Be happy—get all you can out of life and think of me as near you. I am thinking of you constantly and loving you with all my heart. Adieu. (Rector says he's a great man).

This may sound general, but the best that I can do and it is I saying it, and no one *but* myself!

I see the letter P and he's tried to write it out for me but I don't get anything but P. I am very fond of that influence (points to package on lap) it brings the spiritual influence magnificently.

The next letter is dated May 21, 1946:

Here are a few more impressions, dear Mrs. Wood, which Mama sends for what they may or may not be worth to your friend.

I want to assure you that the letter, while it had to be opened, of course, to get the contact clear from other influences, has at no time been *seen* by Mama, only *felt,* as is her custom. As a matter of fact, at the distance the letter was placed on her lap, had her eyes been open, she had not the vision to have read a word. And, needless to say, I, myself, have not opened the letter—writing-side up at any time. I am sorry that these things cannot be done under the usual supervision of trained minds to eliminate any possible doubt, but, know you know us, and something of Mama's long and harrowing investigation, I expect you will be willing to accept results at their face value; otherwise, you would not have asked that we try it under the present conditions. And, as a matter of fact, anything more rigid now would, I think, not be possible in view of lowered vitality, etc.

The letter I am returning to you, under separate cover, today for I do not like to have it in my possession since it may be both personal and of value to your friend. The first article I am certain could be returned to you by first class mail, or insured parcel post, quite safely, but I will await your instructions regarding it, of course, before doing anything further than to keep it safely wrapped, and under lock and key.

You know you have all our grateful thanks for the blessing are and ever have been since you came like an angel on high into our lives, so here's our love and hopes that you are taking care of yourself and keeping well. We are, as usual, rather wobbly at times, but still navigating at that!

Affectionately,

Minerva Piper

The notes of the second séance:

My head feels strange—well, that's funny—here's the great big B again—oh, I get the strongest personality—the most determined mind and brain and activity and yet a heart of gold.

I have awakened to a reality that I could hardly have realized in the mortal life but it was to be—there's a smile on this face, very unusual and attractive—there's a determination in the disposition of this person to carry out an idea or efforts to do something and it cannot be squelched—I haven't felt such a determined personality in a long time, a ball of dynamite, but he's gone into a quiet peaceful atmosphere that has toned him down so that he's calm and peaceful, but his love is unbounded. I haven't felt anything so typical of an affectionate nature—there is a—Did he have a son? He wants—he has a desire—for his achievements—wants him to carry out for the betterment of whatever he undertakes.

This personality has an extraordinary combination of power and a warm heart, and his love for a lady who is in the mortal world is unbounded and with the character and will such as he has is most unusual—he wouldn't hesitate to say that whatever he pictured in his mind that a person was—he wouldn't hesitate to say it and yet he wouldn't hurt anyone consciously—now the B comes again—his heart is very warm and very touched by the conditions into which he's moved because he was uncertain because he didn't take to spiritual things as a good many. Oh, such an active personality and determined willpower yet the most delightful and genuine heart that ever anyone possessed!

I'm happy as I can be in that I am living in another sphere and have met some of my own but the happiness I had with my dear ones is almost unspeakable, and will always be to the end of the world the star of my life—I'm not too strong just now in the (use of this power) but I'm taking advantage of what I can get. After all is said and done, it's a beautiful world and I'm thankful for my experiences and my affections were placed in the right channel. Well, I shall go on living—waiting and I know we shall meet again and all will yet be well. I'm sorry when I entered and awoke here that my expression could not have been more Christian-like and beautiful but I was I and I'm still I!—My love was unbounded and still is and ever will be, and I await the day patiently, earnestly and with a knowledge that all will be well. I cannot say more, the light begins to fade and I'm not wholly accustomed to revealing my thoughts through a channel of this sort . . .

He puts up his hand this way (raises right arm straight up and waves hand) and says, "Adios to my darling, we shall meet again as sure as the sun in your world rises and sets."

The last letter from Minerva is dated June 28, 1946.

Dear Mrs. Wood:
I enclose just a few more impressions apropos of the package we still have. They seem to be nothing new but, anyway, they are not for me to *question*—only to pass on to whom they may concern.

It has been so warm we waited a bit, hoping for cooler weather, but this morning the enclosed came and, brief though it is, it may be better than nothing.

We are as usual. Mama had a birthday yesterday, and seemed a bit discouraged over having to consider the swift passing of the years, but today she is again making the best of what she cannot help and aside from the fact that she does not feel like attempting a summer at Annisquam, and the doctor thinks she is better off here, there is no news.

However, the summer isn't far advanced, and we may get there yet, though what is safest for this great lady is all that really matters to me, unless I add another great lady to whom I send my love and all the prayers for her welfare, and all the appreciation a grateful heart can hold.

Mama joins me in every expression of affection and gratitude.

The notes from the third and last seance:

(Holding the letter face down in lap eyes closed the entire time).

This is from a gentleman, the same personality I felt before. A most natural person, upright—straightforward—affectionate and free from the meanness and small trivial things in life that people count as being important, as it would be possible to image. Perfectly fearless—would take chances where few would have ventured—I repeat, that he feared nothing and cared less for people's opinion.

I get a most strong influence—a heart full of love that could scarcely be duplicated—there seems to be (I don't know why) almost two influences here. I can't account for this unless a lady has handled it. If sorrows appeared, they were deeply hidden by the writer who tried to bear these things alone. Impulsive at times and when so there was a little tendency to lack of judgement, but I never could express the benefits of generosity and unselfishness held by the heart of this person. The lines of justice, forbearance, generosity, and the most genuine and faithful of souls, are most apparent—he carried on in his own way, doing what he thought was for the best with a heart full of admiration for the one he loved dearly—a lady connected with this (hand on letter) I think, his companion, she is most understanding, sympathetic, with a heart as large and kindly as his own.

This person would have a capacity along the lines of leadership, and would fight for truth, honor, uprightness and justice from beginning to end.

Painstaking—a very marked personality equally balanced in affection, justice, uprightness, honor and sincerity.

He enjoyed physical comforts but took insufficient rest and, it seems to me hastened on to an end.

I think I never felt greater admiration for this person for the one—the one who should receive the benefit of anything—this seems to refer to unfinished things from which benefits should—as he recalls it—come to her, the climax, he feels, has not been reached and things not wholly adjusted. I am almost overcome by the affection given him by his companion—had a habit of patting this lady, or she pats him—one of the two—I feel it on my face.

(Letter again on lap. Head back on pillow, eyes closed and first influence [the glove and letters] also on lap).

Funny thing—I feel the writing on this is almost of a feminine quality—but the tone of the man expresses exactly what I thought about him, a very remarkable man. He has gone on to his reward and it is better so because his health would have been against him, he had lived—

The devotion—the affection and unlimited interest behind this of the man and his wife is something beautiful and seldom seen . . . It's a glorious life and nothing should be regretted about his going . . . he doesn't want it and wants her to be free until they meet again. (Now I'll open this and put my finger in between the pages). (Proceeds to do this without moving head or opening eyes. MP)

Oh, yes, very powerful influence—seems rather magnificent so true and sincere. This gentleman knew his own mind—loved his wife beyond expression—was happiest when with her and he says she is not to miss him—he doesn't *want* her to miss him—he must progress in his own life until they meet again as they surely will.

He's a character and would never hesitate to say what he thought under any circumstances—noble minded—love in abundance exists between those two, and his affection did not wane when he passed from this world. He went on rather suddenly—I can't say exactly how but he says that he felt dizzy and that he began to lose his hold on himself and just slipped out, but he sends love in abundance (I repeat) and says they will meet again in another life here and be together through all the coming ages. He wants her to be brave and peaceful—and think of their lives together here—she loved him dearly—he's so frank and outspoken I get very clear ideas about that—

Time and conditions are such I cannot go into minute details but if she will accept what I say in general, I shall be grateful for it is very clear and the influence is very powerful—love that nothing can change—he says he will be waiting for her when the Lord wills.

What I have said about this influence (now has first influence in hand M.P.) is gospel as near as I can get it. He says he wants her to be as brave as she is good and there's no real separation and never will be and he'll watch over her as he leaves conditions here himself—eternal life is a fact beyond question, and as Browning said, 'God's in His Heaven, all's right with the world!'

Endless love, darling, don't worry, it had to be and I was tired anyway—tired of all the wickedness of the battles and the unnecessary taking of other people's lives on earth—God love you, darling, and keep you in His holy keeping—I'm talking to Big *B*—my Big *B*—Blessed one.

There are some curious coincidences in this collection of notes. Mrs. Piper did not know that Ellen Wood was Georgie's sister-in-law, and being such a very old and blind and physically limited lady, Mrs. Piper may not even have known who Georgie was. But Georgie nearly always said Adios instead of good-bye, having been raised among California-Mexicans. It came through to Mrs. Piper as Adieu but she may not have been familiar with Spanish. Also, Georgie and Ma never passed each other, sitting or standing, without giving a little pat to the cheek, or the top of head, or the shoulder—it was a sort of recognition signal. And Ma, although half Bee's size, was always known as Big Bee, as my sister was known as Little Bee.

I never understood why Ma did not want those notes of Mrs. Piper's around. They should have comforted her. Perhaps she was made uncomfortable by the unknown.

There was another strange letter which gave her a great deal of comfort and that she kept with her until she died. It was from Mary Gordon Reifsnider, the sister of Louise Ayer's first husband, who had died of leukemia in 1923. Old Doctor Gordon, Donald's and Mary's father, had been a bishop, and Mary was the wife of Charles Reifsnider, the Bishop of Japan.

All Saints Day 3:00 a.m.

Dearest Bee:

Last night when I went to bed, I thought of all my dear ones in Heaven, and of many others who were dear to my friends and me. I thought especially of you and Georgie, and the question in your last letter, "Why?" and "Charlie is Bishop and ought to know the answer." It has been coming back and back to me and to Charlie.

Suddenly, I seem to be in Heaven myself—such confusion—and depression. So many boys and young men milling around with such sad, confused faces; some looking at nothing, others with tears rolling down their exhausted faces. I said to the guide, whom I could not see, "This is no Heaven" and the voice said, This is a picture of Heaven a few years ago—two years ago. So many of these boys came at once. We found they had so little spiritual life to start their life here. From school and college they stepped into the horrors of war. God thought and thought what could be done for these millions. Then He called for some scales and weighed the needs of the world in one side and of the young, confused soul in the other. Then He said "What of the beloved wife? She has always given so much, in all the wars, and is dear, very dear to Me, too."

Then suddenly there was a great light and Georgie appeared in a shining uniform. Instantly the vast crowd of pathetic boys leaped to their feet and saluted. Georgie looked like his portrait only his face shone with glory. "Our General!" came the shout. "He never asked us to do anything he didn't or wouldn't do himself. He always led us straight. Now he has come to us again. Where to?" Georgie just stood and looked at them with love in his eyes, before my eyes those boys changed into happy boys and men again as they looked at their beloved leader. Heaven was ablaze with light.

Then, Georgie said, "I came to lead you again—blessed are the pure in heart for they shall see God—not only see God—but know and love him. Jesus said, 'In my Father's house are many mansions. I go to prepare a place for you that where I am ye may be also.' Come, boys."

Darling Bee. It was so vivid I got right up and wrote it down for I thought that perhaps, somewhere, there might be the answer. I had the vision for some reason but I shall keep this letter for some days before mailing. I love you dearly so forgive me if I am wrong in sending the letter.

> Devotedly,
> Mary

Ma came to Washington often and visited either my sister or me, not only to see us but to consult with various people about the statue of Georgie for West Point and *War As I Knew It*. Many people came to see her and ask her opinion about books and articles they were writing.

We went to Green Meadows to see Ma as often as we could. The four grandchildren adored her, and she really came alive for them for, in spite of everything, she never lost her vitality or her intense curiosity. Young George was to graduate in June of 1946—a long-awaited thrill for all of us, especially George himself. He had spent four years doing the three-year, hurry-up wartime course, just as Georgie had spent five years doing the four-year course. The superintendent of the Corps of Cadets invited Ma to sit on the reviewing stand, and to hand George his hard-won diploma when he came by, nearly at the end. The sign of relief that went up from our section could have been heard in Times Square! Jim whispered to me, "Thank God, that's over! You girls can dust off your knees now!"

It was a great day, but it was saddened for us because Georgie would have so loved to have seen his only son make the grade.

Ma's profound grief, assimilated, became part of her, but she didn't go around being sad and grand and making people uncomfortable, à la Aunt

Elma Totten. One night when I was visiting her at Green Meadows, she went into the library where her desk was, and stayed there for some time. When she came out, she was wiping tears away from her eyes. I asked her if anything was wrong and she said, no, that she had just finally brought herself to the point of burning some of Georgie's letters to her: "There will be a lot of people who will want to dig into his life, and there are some things that were just between your father and myself and they are nobody else's business. I made up my mind that I didn't need to keep the letters because what was written in them is written in my heart."

Many friends, whom she had always humbly accepted as admirers of Georgie, came forward and did nice things for her. Ambassador and Mrs. Kirk invited her to visit them in Moscow, and the Russians gave her a lifetime pass on their subway, which tickled her sense of humor. Perle Mesta, socialite supreme and ambassador to Luxembourg, invited Ma for a visit. Everywhere she went in France, she made speeches, laid wreaths on statues, was eulogized by the mayor and corporation of all the towns, and had a wonderful time. She had a great affinity for France and the French people, which was returned with interest.

She had always had poor eyesight and a dicky heart, neither of which slowed her down any, but she began to worry a bit about her mortality. Some of her friends were approaching senility and a few were in nursing homes, and she viewed that with horror. She was determined not to be a burden on the family. She would say, "I hope someone loves me enough to bring me the black bottle when I can't get it for myself." I know she never contemplated suicide because she thought it was cowardly, but she thought there must be some way to avoid the living death of tubes, transfusions, and intravenous feeding. She finally asked Jim Totten to promise to bring her the black bottle if she ever got in that kind of shape, and to my amazement, he promised. She said that her children loved her too much to bring it to her, but that she trusted Jim because he had never avoided an issue or fabricated a story. After she died, I asked him if he really would have provided the means of exit for her, and he said that he would have thought of something because he respected her too much to let her become a vegetable, but that he had always had enough faith in God to feel sure he would not have to do it.

I was agitating for another baby, although Ma and Jim were not as enthusiastic about a third one. I was so insistent that Jim, who thought he was going to be ordered overseas, told me that if he got a stateside station, I could have another baby, but if we went overseas, there was no way because the foreign hospitals were too risky. God and I won that round. Jim was ordered to the Command and Staff College at Fort Leavenworth, Kansas, a nine-month school tour that had been infamous for years as the great breaker-upper of families, the place where the sheep separated from the goats, and one of the worst tours in Army life. He gave me three months in which to get pregnant, so that the baby would be born about the end of the Leavenworth tour—we still had three months to go on the tour in the Pentagon. The baby, waiting on the cloud, was very obliging, and I was pregnant by the time we got to Leavenworth. There were no quarters available, and almost no housing in town, but Ma still had a hat full of rabbits, and she managed to get for us the downstairs of a very old house that belonged to the ancient mother of one of Georgie's captains. Dear old Mrs. Barth had turned her ancestral home into four apartments, and we had the one she had kept for herself when she was not on a visit to one of her sons. The apartment consisted of the living room and dining room with a kitchenette on what used to be the back entry. It was fully furnished in the early Kansas style. Mrs. Barth had left her own kitchen supplies locked into a cupboard under the stairs, so we had an unbelievable population of mice. I had to read with my feet up on the sofa and Jim had to study with his feet on a box under the desk, while the mice ran in and out like Grand Central Station. We borrowed a cat, but it was out-moused and left.

However, we were able to be together. Ma kept the children until we finally moved into quarters on the post. They were World War II sixty-three–man barracks, hastily constructed into four apartments per building. They had a front door, a back door, and a bathroom door, but no bedroom doors as building supplies were in short order because of the war. We got doors from a junk-yard and were able to bring the children west before the snow fell. It was an experience in community living.

Very intelligently, Jim took on a Top Secret project so that he had to study in his office at night with armed guards at the entrances. Thus he kept his sanity. He came in the house one day for lunch and told me that on his way in he had counted seventy-four children and fifty-five dogs playing in the street outside. Our children were too little for school—I did not believe in nursery school or kindergarten, having taught same before I was married, so we had all of ours at home until they were six years old.

Ma came out during the dreadful Kansas winter for a visit, and had a wonderful time. She knew so many people, and so many of her friends' children were classmates of Jim's, that she was out nearly every night. She loved being back in the Army again: "Sergeant, out of the cold and the rain, yes, back to the Army again." She had so many stories about the hardship tour she had had at Leavenworth, and so many stories about the "Old Army" in general, that she braced up the spirits of a lot of wives with the winter blues. People came to see her every day.

While she was there, our Mike got very sick with an intestinal virus that produced vomiting and a temperature of about 104 degrees. I called the dispensary and was told to bring him in next morning when sick call was on. I was sure he would be dead by that time, but Ma said, "Just leave it to me. This is ridiculous." She called the commanding general and asked to speak to him directly. When he came on the phone she said, "Johnnie, this is Beatrice Patton. I am sure you're not aware that the young people are being told to keep dispensary hours with their very sick children. I know no one has told you." There was a good deal of noise from the other end. "Yes, I know, they never tell the commanding officer these little things, they think they are too trivial. Yes, I was sure you'd feel that way. I know Georgie always did." Well, we not only got a call from the doctor within about ten minutes, but it was published in the daily bulletin that the doctor would come to quarters if the patient was a child. Everybody loved Ma even more after that.

In April of '47, I went home to Green Meadows with the two and eight-ninths children, leaving Jim to finish the course and pack for our next station in Panama.

James Patton Totten was born May 15, 1947, in the Boston Lying-In Hospital. Jim came back for the event—it was the only child he ever had, the other two had been telegrams. We all went into Boston the night before the event—me to the hospital, and Ma and Jim to a hotel. I had gotten them tickets to a good play, but they never remembered what it was. With a Caesarian section, the parents are allowed to pick a birth date within about a week's framework, and for some reason—to be recalled eighteen years later—I picked May 15. None of us realized, until I went to the Virginia Military Institute all the way from Brazil to be with Jamie on his birthday, that it was New Market Day at VMI, the day in 1864 that the cadets were marched to the battlefield at New Market, Virginia, to the tune of fife and drum playing "Will you come to the bower I have builded for you, its bed shall be of roses, bespangled with dew!" The bed for many of the cadets was the cold, cold ground, and VMI never forgot that sacred date and every May 15 since then they have had a dress parade, and as the Old Grads choked down bourbon whiskey along with their tears, the names of the dead are called out and some cadet steps forward, saying: "Dead upon the field of honor, sir!" Of course, I had been brainwashed as a child by Aunt Susie Patton Wills and Aunt Nellie Patton Brown, as one of their uncles had been a New Market cadet, and their father and stepfather had both fought gallantly at New Market.[1] It made it pretty tough on Jamie, though!

As soon as Jamie was delivered, the hospital called Ma and Jim and when I

---

1. George Smith Patton commanded the 22nd Virginia Infantry. George Hugh Smith commanded the 62nd Virginia Mounted Infantry.

came to, Ma was standing beside me looking radiant and telling me it was a ten-and-a-half-pound boy. I asked her where Jim was, and she said, "He is in the next room lying down. He paid you the most wonderful compliment. We were looking in the window of the nursery when they brought the baby to show us, and I heard this little sigh, and Jim had just fainted dead away on the floor."

At this point, some official came in and demanded the baby's name for the hospital record. Jim had wanted to call it Jocelyn, whether it was a boy or girl, because he liked the name, but Ma took charge: "His name is James Patton Totten." I was trying to revive, and started protesting feebly, but she said, "I knew you and Jim didn't want another Jim, so we will call him Jamie after my dear brother." And so we did.

The children and I waited with Ma for four months until Jim could get quarters at Quarry Heights in the Canal Zone in Panama. It gave Jamie and me a good start, as I had a small setback when he was a week old and got phlebitis and had to have a very scary midnight operation to remove a clot. Ma was in Richmond when it happened, seeing Douglas Southall Freeman about Georgie's papers, and she never forgave herself for not being there. She kept saying, "I should have *known*—it was just all *too easy.*"

I was so pleased to have my figure back—a ten-and-a-half-pound baby makes for the unfashionable grotesque look—that I spent a lot of time getting a brand new wardrobe of pretty summer dresses suitable for the tropics. I should have known better.

Panama was everything anyone could ask for: mysterious, beautiful, historic, another world. Jim's parents had been stationed there when he and his brother, Jack, were little boys, and when there was still a mutual love affair between Panama and the U.S.A.—so we had many built-in friends waiting to greet us. There was the Old Guard, who had built the Canal and were running it, and the French and Spanish Panamanian families, who owned the country. The climate was not and is not and will never be good, but you can adjust to anything if you are not in a hurry. And it was so very beautiful! Jim had gotten a houseful of servants, which ran as well as could be expected. He told them when he hired them that if there was any fighting or any one of them gave me any trouble, they would all be fired, no matter whose fault it was. I went there with an Irish nursemaid from Boston, and she was the only one who ever gave me trouble. The Panamanians knew a good thing.

All the Army ladies warned me that the servants would eat me out of house and home, and to ration them, but Ma had always said to feed people well and they would settle in to their accustomed diet as soon as they had sampled yours. So I followed her advice, and after about a month of hog-wallowing, they came and asked me to get them the salt cod and rice that they had always lived on. The only thing they never got enough of was mayonnaise. They put in on everything—even their hair.

Jim had found a man who had once worked for his parents, a most culti- vated and delightful old gentleman named Angus McNeil. He gardened for us and did the shoes, and he found the other servants, beginning with Rebecca Gonzales, the cook, who was a thrice-baptized Baptist working up to her fourth baptism. She had been baptized in the Pacific, the Atlantic, and the Chagres River, and was preparing for Gatun Lake and salvation. Rosetta, the maid, was very pretty with lots of relatives; Josefa, the laundress, was a storm cloud and finally had to go—she had worked too long in the insane asylum. After Josefa went, McNeil brought us a dear old lady who had been a corpse-washer, but did a fine job on three or four white uniforms that Jim wore daily.

My lovely summer clothes had to be mostly put away. We had, by virtue of Jim's job, to see a lot of the Panamanians and, as all Spanish peoples are always in some degree of mourning, I had to redo my wardrobe in white, black and white, or shades of lavender and gray. Jim had been sent there to be on the staff, but the commanding general, Willis Crittenberger, a close friend of Georgie's, asked him to take the job of provost marshal. Jim was outraged, as he had never been a military policeman, but the Panamanian Army was also the Pana- manian police force and the chief of police was also the commanding general, and General Crittenberger thought, very correctly, that a West Point graduate of Jim's quality would be more acceptable than someone less accredited; also, Jim spoke Spanish. Actually, it was a super job and worked both ways, and the chief of police, Colonel José Remon, and his wife, Cecilia, became two of our lifelong friends.

Ma came to visit via the Panama Ship Line, very nice banana boats that car- ried bananas and Canal Zone personnel, mail, supplies, and a few lucky tourists to and from New York. She shared the cabin with Mrs. T. Q. Donaldson, an old Army friend, who was coming to visit her children—also stationed at Quarry Heights. The canal steamers docked in Colon on the Atlantic side, and you had to take the railway to the Pacific side, where we lived, or drive. The drive was spectacular, and the train ride was historic.

Shortly before Ma got there, I bought a cage of mixed birds at the open mar- ket, which was in downtown Panama, right on the sea, where we bought our fresh fish and vegetables. I had about a dozen birds, including a bugle bird, and the cage hung under the eaves outside the lower veranda. The verandas went around three sides of the house on both stories. During Ma's first meal, which was luncheon, we heard a very plaintive and alarming series of cries from the birds. Jim went to investigate and saw that a tree snake had slithered up the porch railing and gotten its head and a third of its leaf-green body in through the wires of the cage. It had swallowed several of the little birds, and the upper part of its body was too swollen to retreat. Jim took the cage down and chopped the snake in half with a machete. The inside of its mouth and gullet were a lovely shade of orchid. The birds that were left all died within a few days—maybe from shock. Ma took it all very well, but it was an unusual sort of welcome.

Equipped with her unceasing curiosity and enthusiasm, Ma was right into the life around us. She adored going to the open market—the children called it the Pew Market, and for good reason. It was a huge ramshackle building, built out over the muddy tide flats on the waterfront. The owners of the stalls hosed it down every day before noon (by law), but the smell of rotting fish and meat and fruit, and the pungent mud beneath, was ineradicable. I shopped there twice a week to buy the vegetables and to see the sights. The Indians from up-country came there in their dugout canoes with whatever they had to sell. The fishing boats tied up there and sold fish from the boat. The Cunva Indians from the San Blas Islands on the Atlantic side were there with their wares. These Indians were a strange sight. They were from a canoe-oriented society, and spent much of their lives paddling their boats. Both men and women were about four feet tall and built like blocks. Their backs and shoulders were tremendously broad and strong; their hips and legs slender. The richer women wore gold nose rings and the typical costume of their people, which was a wrap-around skirt and a shirt called a mola, made of two squares of marvelous appliquéd and cut-out cloth in many layers, embroidered and decorated, and telling stories or legends in pictures. It is a unique folk art, and the ones we bought in Panama for a few dollars are now collectors' items. Ma was crazy about them and bought them for everyone.

The Cunya Indians are interesting—and mysterious. No woman of the tribe was allowed to spend a night off-island. If she did, she could never come back to San Blas. She was an outcast. Because of centuries of inbreeding, there were quite a few albinos in the tribe. It was considered an honor for a woman to bear an albino child, because it was believed to be a moon child—the moon having condescended to come down from the skies and mate with the mother.

Few of the Army wives would go to the Pew Market, preferring frozen stuff from the commissary, or the occasional vegetables we could get from the Chinese gardens along the highway, but Ma loved the market, and spoke to everyone in Spanish mixed with French, and most of the stall keepers got to know her. We had permission to park near the market, under the most fashionable store in town, the French Bazaar, which was owned by the Huertematte family. One day the Grand Old Man, Don Julio Huertematte, saw Ma and me coming back up the alley from the market with full baskets. He was too polite to show his feelings (a Panamanian lady would have had her maid do the marketing), but came down to meet us, dressed in his immaculate white linen suit and white suede shoes, and insisted on taking Ma's basket. I was embarrassed, but Ma took such courteous attentions for granted, and asked such intelligent questions in such perfect French about the secret life of Panama that she got more out of Don Julio in half an hour than most people could have learned in a lifetime. The Huertemattes had been there since before the Canal days and he was a mine of ethnological, geological, and mythological information. Shortly after this, he gave a big party in Ma's honor to which the oldest and best families—many of whom we had never met—were invited.

This was a sit-down dinner for about forty people. The service plates were all of beaten Peruvian silver, coin silver rather than sterling. The chandeliers, table ornaments, platters, and candlesticks were all of the same silver. The china was Sevres and the glasses were Waterford crystal. The dinner was French, with a tropical flair. It was like being in a novel! Ma was perfectly at home in this setting, and they all knew it. How she sparkled!

The Indians shot any jungle animal that was edible, and if there were any young attached, they would be brought to market to be sold or to die of neglect. The children were dying to have a monkey, but Jim, who had trafficked with monkeys as a little boy in Panama, said no, so they finally stopped asking. However, every time Ma went with me to the market, we saw a very small, filthy baby monkey crouched in the corner of a fruit stand in a puddle of its own filth. When it saw us it would make a feeble twitter and look at us with hopeless filming eyes. It got thinner and thinner, and more and more hairless, until, one day Ma said, "I certainly can't stand this any longer. Here, buy it." The little chap—it was a male—was too feeble to protest being put into a paper bag and taken home with the fruit. Ma wouldn't touch him—she was never really mad about animals—but she was fascinated by him. She kept saying he reminded her of someone, but she couldn't remember who it might be.

After about a week of Gerber's baby food, clean water, the tender, loving care of every kid in Quarry Heights, and an old mailbox to call his home, the poor little monkey turned into a fiend from hell with all the vices of men and animals, and a very strong character—a bad character, too. He had a white mask in a soot-black face. His eyes were perfectly round, and although his mind was preoccupied with evil mischief, he had a perpetually worried look—like an old maid about to roll a tennis ball under the bed before getting in it. Ma was watching him one day when she suddenly exclaimed, "I know who he remind me of. He looks just like your Great Aunt Nannie!" Poor Aunt Nannie had spent her life being desperately afraid of things, especially leprosy, and actually, except for the fact that Aunt Nannie wore a chestnut fringe of hair, they did look alike—she even had a faint dark mustache when she was older. But Ma said that we couldn't call him Aunt Nannie as someone's feelings might get hurt, so we called him Cousin, and he lived for wicked years.

Cousin seemed to realize that Ma was his savior. She fascinated him. Whenever he caught sight of her, he would caper obscenely at the end of his chain, making unspeakable suggestions to her in monkey language. Once he got close enough to her to snatch her little blue denim sun hat. We washed it carefully, but she would never wear it again, so Cousin had it for his very own, and wore it a great deal of the time, although it completely covered his head and came down over his chin. When he wasn't wearing it or sleeping in it, he was making love to it. Ma absolutely loathed him, but he fascinated her too. She said that he was mankind in microcosm.

Cousin's arrival opened the floodgates, and over a period of time we had several marmosets, the head of the clan being named George Meeks; a gentle spider monkey named Topsy; a howler monkey that came to us under false colors, but soon revealed its talents by making a noise like a lion and scaring half the post; a one-eyed armadillo; a night monkey; a coati mundi; and a kinkajou named Poor Boy (because that's what he seemed to be saying), who took to drink and had to be carried to the top of Ancon Hill and abandoned. He spent his evenings—he was a night person—pushing the liquor bottles off the bar, but he would only drink the puddles of sweet liqueurs, like Southern Comfort or creme de menthe. We had several parrots, and a huge red macaw that only knew one word, which was a filthy one. They all came from the Pew Market or from departing friends.

Ma was appalled by our zoo, but she was interested too. Some of Jim's parents' old friends, who ran the railroad, took pity on our plight and once a week they sent us a whole stem of bananas. These hung on the back porch and were used by animals, birds, servants, children, and neighbors. George Meeks Marmoset lived in another mailbox near the bananas, and his harem, who were all wild marmosets, came down early in the morning and stole bananas while he chattered and growled and threatened anyone who tried to interfere. As he weighed less than half a pound, he wasn't very frightening—except to other marmosets.

We had a fishing boat on which we used to visit Taboga, which was nearby, or the Pearl Islands, about sixty miles offshore. Ma loved that best of all. She had done a lot of deep-sea fishing with Georgie—it was one of his passions. Ma gave, or rather loaned, us his superb fishing tackle. Many of his reels were of German silver, and the guides on his fishing rods were lined with polished carnelian rings so that the lines would not be frayed.

The game fishing off Panama was almost the best in the world—it certainly compared with New Zealand and Baja, California. Even if you didn't catch many fish, you saw the most extraordinary sights. Once a young whale played with our boat, scratching his back on the keel, and breeching and blowing first on one side and then the other. It is fun to look back on, but it was a terrifying experience at the time. Incredibly huge manta rays would jump out of the water and flap down again, with the sound of a cannon going off—we were told they did this to rid themselves of parasites. Ma caught a record sailfish, which thrilled her to the core, but she enjoyed the things she saw as much as the things she caught. She also liked the men who fished with us. There was a master electrician from the Zone who kept the old engine working. He didn't know too much about fishing, but he liked the camaraderie and the beer. There was also a Zone policeman who made and tied all the baits with masterful artistry, but who suffered from chronic seasickness and was always so full of dramamine that he could never stay awake long enough to fish. The British minister to Panama, Jack Greenway, was almost a permanent fixture and, aside from being an expert fisherman, he was wonderful company and could always be counted on to say extraordinary things.

One morning when Ma was there, we had anchored overnight in the Pearl Islands and were up getting ready to join a fishing tournament at 4 a.m. Jack had taken a sleeping pill the night before so that he would not be able to stand watch. When we were anchored in Las Perlas, we had to keep a watch, as the local indios would glide out in their canoes and creep on board and remove your socks without taking off your shoes. Jack woke up hard, because of his pill, but when he finally did, he looked around the rolling cabin with the coffee sloshing out of the pot, and the fried eggs sliding from side to side in the skillet, and said in a despairing voice, "This is the way the world ends—not with a bang, but with a whimper!" The rest of the crew didn't understand him—they never did—but Ma did, and she chuckled about it the rest of the day.

Another time we were out on a wild day when the clouds were scudding across a sky that was wedgwood blue—Jack's description—and he looked down into the galley and asked what there was for lunch. When I told him we were having clam chowder, he sighed, "Oh, dear, do you suppose I shall look down into my cup and see their sad little blue fringes waving at me?" I never have eaten clam chowder since without wondering.

Another weekend we took a very dear friend out on the boat: Sandy Fairchild, a bug hunter at the Gorgas Memorial Laboratory, where they studied the effects of and cures for insect-borne tropical diseases. Sandy didn't care for fishing, but he was mad about catching bugs, of which there were plenty in Panama. Jim didn't usually anchor near Taboga because of the mosquitoes, but

Sandy wanted to go ashore after dark and hunt insects, so we anchored there for the night. It was beautiful and mysterious—the lip-lipping of the waves on the keel, the stillness that let you hear the rustle of the palm fronds on shore, and the scurrying of the jungle people in the rocks and trees.

Presently, Sandy came back with a case full of specimens and we sat for awhile in the cockpit, talking and enjoying the cool. The moon was reflected in the water, and around the boat there was a faintly luminous cloud of phosphorescence that winked and sparkled with a million infinitesimal eyes. Sandy was very taken with this, and getting out his net he scooped up about two cupsful of plankton, which, on closer inspection, appeared to be the tiniest of shrimps— each about the size of a grain of coarse sand. He asked me to heat up some milk and boil the plankton, which I did, and then he offered around a cup of the hot broth. Ma and Sandy and I were the only people that would touch it. It was quite tasty, like a gritty clam juice. About half an hour later we got ready to turn in and Sandy looked at us with a happy expression, the moonlight glinting off his glasses, and said, "I *told* the fellows at the laboratory that those brine shrimp were only poisonous at certain times of the year. Now, maybe, they will believe me!"

Ma and I, two still-living proofs of his theory, looked at each other with wild surmise. Jim laughed about it for days.

Ma loved the Las Perlas; she said that they were everyman's dream of the island. She had brought us the records from *South Pacific,* which was the big hit musical back home, and there was one island, little more than a rock among Las Perlas, that she swore was Bali Hai. The islet was shaped like a comma, and had three palm trees growing on it, but on the port side there were always tremendous glassy combers breaking—possibly over a hidden reef; that water was so clear in the curling rise that it was like an aquamarine. I never heard that anyone went ashore on Galera—it would have been too hard to get to it on a boat with those huge waves—so it exists still as a dream island in a strange sea.

Everyone in Panama liked Ma, and she met everybody there was to meet, including a lot of oddballs. Her ethnology started showing again and strange elderly scientists appeared at the door and took her to unheard-of places. Sandy Fairchild took her on an all-day trip up the Chagres River to a cave where there were white bats. Ma was excited about this, as the only other place in the world where there were white bats was a cave near the Temple of Abu Simbel in Egypt, which she had visited as a child. Sandy had an ulterior motive. In the cave dwelt a certain white cockroach with pink spots that lived on the white-bat dung and that had the longest spinal cord, or whatever passes for a spinal cord in an insect, of any comparable roach, and Dr. Mann, head of the Washington Zoo, wanted some live specimens. Sandy had tried to ship some of these bugs by air to Dr. Mann with no success, as they are very delicate creatures and need to be fed every four hours and kept warm and dark. So Sandy was hoping Ma would carry some by hand to Dr. Mann when she went back to the States. Ma was dying to see the white bats. So she said in a resigned way that she would take the roaches. She also said that if you lived long enough, you saw that life made a complete circle, and that after sixty years of killing roaches in every way she could devise, Fate had ordained that she make it up to the legions of dead roaches by caring tenderly for live ones. Que sera sera. She also remarked that no wonder roaches were one of the oldest forms of life.

Her trip up the Chagres River was only part way by canoe. The rest of the way, they waded upstream over large and slippery rocks. When Ma got home that night, exhausted, she was so covered with little tiny ticks that we had to wash her and her hair in kerosene before we could put her to bed. The children were thrilled, and said next morning, "Grandma smells like Dracula from being with the bats!" I wonder if they still associate the fading fumes of kerosene with Vlad the Impaler?

Her wonderful zest and curiosity got us another trip. One of the scientists (Panama was full of them) had been at a dig on the northern border of Panama. He went into an Indian house for some reason, and saw a strange little footstool. In fact, he was invited to sit on it. He asked the owner where it came from and was told that there were a whole lot of the same lying on a nearby hill. On reaching the hill, the scientist found the partially exposed fossilized skeleton of a huge dimetrodon—an early kind of sloth—entangled with the smaller skeleton of a carnivorous dinosaur, where they had fallen in combat millions of years before. Erosion had uncovered the skeletons and the Indians were taking the vertebrae as sitting stools. Ma simply had to see this, so she and I and a friend who spoke the local Spanish took off on an overnight trip to see the dinosaurs.

We stayed in a primitive little bodega in a nearby town. Everywhere we went we were followed by a respectful crowd of Indians. They even waited outside the privy while we were inside. Ma spoke to them cheerfully in Castilian Spanish, and they all smiled and applauded politely whenever she spoke. With some thought of classifying them when she got home, Ma started picking plants and flowers on her way to the bone pile, and all the little Indian children immediately began to do the same, and filled her arms with every sort of weed and plant—all smiling and nodding sagely, as if she was doing exactly what they thought she should be doing and doing it well. The bones were a little bit of a disappointment as most of them had been carried off by the authorities, but the trip was a wild success.

Ma never could see enough of the ruins of Old Panama, the city that was sacked by Sir Henry Morgan, the pirate. It is a haunting ruin, the strangler figs trying to finish what Morgan started so many years ago, and odd broken towers rearing up as if in pain from the encroaching plants and vines. There is a thin and stained beach running alongside the falling buildings, and a river runs through the dead city on the Panama side, under a little bridge and out onto the sand. The site had been inhabited by Indians since the beginning, and we never walked along the beach without Ma finding some artifact.

One day she found a leaf-shaped arrowhead, and one joyous day, after a high tide, we found a large burial urn partially exposed in the waterworn bank. The Panamanians would kick anything of that nature to pieces, if they happened onto it, from superstition or fear of ghosts. This one was a large round clay vessel in nearly perfect condition, with at least four skeletons showing through the sand inside of it. Ma insisted that I get in touch with the museum before the natives found it, or the tide came in. The policia, at the main gate, very politely refused to let me use their phone as my business was not official, so I ran back along the beach and Ma told me to take the children and drive back to Panama; she and our big boxer dog, Brandy, would stay with the urn. The natives were terrified of Brandy, who had a heart like a bowl of custard, but the Spaniards had kept the Indians in line with mastiff dogs and the racial memory persisted.

I had never had any trouble with people in Panama. I had always been treated with consideration and politeness, but there was talk, and I was very upset at leaving her there alone. However, she insisted.

When I got back, followed by the museum director, about an hour later, Ma and the urn and the dog were sitting surrounded by a fascinated group of natives—mostly young people—and she was telling them stories. How they understood her, I will never know. She spoke German, French, a smattering of Castilian, Spanish, some Italian, a little Hawaiian, but I suppose it was really heart talking to heart in this case. They followed us back to the car and all waved madly as we drove off, some of the bigger boys even running along beside the car.

Fifteen years later, when we stopped in Panama on our way to station in Brazil, I went to the museum and was overjoyed to see Ma's urn in a prominent place, with the skeletons neatly cleaned and classified. It didn't say anything about her finding it, but I am sure she knew.

One of Ma's conquests was a dear little old bachelor named Johnnie Ehrmann. He was a Panamanian from the word go, although his grandfather had been a German sea captain. He was one of eleven children, but only one of his brothers and sisters ever married, and that one produced one child, always known as "Mother's Grandchild." Johnnie had known Jim when he was a little boy, and he became a dropping-in friend. He always came with a present of fruit or flowers or some little thing for the children. His mother called him Poor Juan. Johnnie was fascinated by Ma, and he asked his mother to invite her for tea. This Madame Ehrmann did by a hand-delivered note with complete instructions on how to get to her house. I think she thought some poor widow was after her Poor Juan.

The Ehrmanns lived in a most unprepossessing building down near the Pew Market. The building was a wreck from the outside, but once within, it was the best-kept secret in Panama City. The light fixtures, switch plates, doorknobs, and the like were all of coin silver, polished to a degree; the teakwood floors were covered with a fortune in Oriental rugs; the walls were hung with gloomy old Spanish paintings, too soiled by age and candle smoke to do anything but hint at the great riches of saint and sinner they portrayed, and the furniture was teak inlaid with mother of pearl. Over all hung the overpowering odor of stale incense and mildew.

Madame Ehrmann was about four feet high with flashing black eyes and a pile of snow-white hair. It only took her a minute to take Ma's measure—and vice versa—and they practically fell into each other's arms. Poor Juan was left to deal out tea and cakes while Mama regaled Ma with ancient scandals. Prides Crossing had never been closer in spirit to New Panama as small-town leader spoke to small-town girl. The high point of the visit was a visit to Madame's bedroom to see her collection of saints. She had a legion of beautiful hand-carved saints, some of papier mâché, some of plaster, and some of great antiquity. Some had eyes of jet and real human hair, and some were of yellowed ivory. There was a Madonna with tears of real diamonds, and a Christ Crucified with rubies as drops of blood. In front of them all was a ten-inch statuette of a gentleman saint in a brown robe, wearing a large bishop's hat, made of silver—so much too big that it concealed his features. Ma said right away that she knew it was Saint Anthony, and the Senora was delighted. She took off his hat and showed it to Ma, saying, "You see, my dear Donna Beatriz, as I get older I get forgetful, and I have to send San Antonio out on so many little errands for me to find the things that I have misplaced that I had this hat made for him in Peru to keep him dry when he is out in the rain looking for my little things."

Ma and the Senora became great friends and had Poor Juan drive them about in the Senora's ancient car to see the sights, accompanied by a running commentary that was as good as a novel. They saw the Cold Altar that had been in the church in Old Panama. When the monks knew Sir Henry Morgan was coming, they had no time to move it so they whitewashed it and the pirates missed it. They saw the little barred alcove in the cathedral that has the tossed-about bones of two saints in it—a very holy relic. They saw the church consecrated to the Black Mary, the saint of the gypsies about whom there are legions of stories and who is very dear to the hearts of the black Panamanians. The Senora herself swept out the foyer of the church of the Black Mary, once a week, "As penance, dear Dona Beatriz, for the sins that I may have committed but which I have forgotten." That is, the Senora's maid swept out the foyer while she gave directions. She also worked very hard for the Poor Box, called the Pac de San Antonio, meaning the bread of Saint Anthony. Saint Anthony is also the patron of children, which may have meant something to the mother of eleven.

At this time, Ma pointed out to us a fact that we all know subconsciously: the hand that rocks the cradle really does rule the world. Here was Senora Ehrmann, a very small, old, and fragile lady living a fairly reclusive life in a circle of family and friends in a small town in a small country, and yet she had her fingers on the pulse of that country and its powers and politics and knew a good deal more about what went on and why it did than the macho male presidents and policia. A whisper from that inner circle could rig an election, make a marriage, call for an execution, or put someone in limbo, socially, spiritually, or economically. Ma always said that the thousands of years that women had spent in harems, or the equivalent thereof, had hardened them for the battle of life far more than the male hunter and killer. In the harem, Ma said, a whisper was louder than a shout and the pressure of a finger in a certain area of the body was as final as the thrust of a sword, and the baby of a rival might never draw its first breath. She said that if women only took time to realize that, they would not go around being discontented and trying to be equal to men. We are a different species; there is no question of equality, simply of quality. Ma said that she never liked women until they turned into people and some of them never made it.

Ma was also the moving spirit behind our trip to Nombre de Dios Bay. This was brought on by a family outing to Fort San Lorenzo on the Atlantic side. Jim had been to the fort, Sir Henry Morgan's old stronghold, as a little boy, but nobody much went there any more. We had to park the car several miles from the fort and walk down a terribly overgrown path that had ominous rustlings on both sides. The view of the river was splendid, and Ma and Mike found some cannonballs, one of which she and Mike took turns carrying all the way back to the car. After that, she felt she had to see Nombre de Dios Bay. Jim had also been there as a child, but no one seemed to know anything about it any more—how far it was or how to get there. The governor of the Canal was a retired engineer and somehow the idea was implanted in his head that a trip to the bay would be a great event, so we found ourselves, and about forty other families, being taken on an all-day picnic on one of the Canal Zone tugs to the place where Sir Francis Drake had fought and died. One of the poems that

Georgie had often recited to us was a stirring one called "Drake's Drum." By the time we were halfway to Nombre de Dios, Ma had all the kids on the tug singing along with her to the goose-bumpy rhythm of

> Drake is in his hammock, a thousand leagues away
> (Captain, art tha' sleepin' there below?)
> Slung atween the round shot in Nombre de Dios Bay
> Dreamin' all the time o' Plymouth Ho.
> Take my drum to England, hang it by the shore
> Beat it when the powder's gettin' low
> If the Don strikes Devon, I'll quit the port o' Heaven
> And we'll drum them down the channel as we did so long ago!

By the time she had chanted it all, she had the children and some of the adults listening for the drum!

The little village of Nombre de Dios is sad and gray, and looks as if it might be absorbed back into the jungle at any time. Buzzards lined the roof trees, and the cannons of the fort lie with their noses propped in the gun ports, their wooden carriages long ago rotted into the ground. The only thing that stood entirely upright and undecayed was the church, the famous shrine of the Black Christ. When Spain ruled the Southern Seas, the king sent to Panama and the other South American countries for religious statues carved from the extraordinarily hard wood of these forests. The Black Christ had been carved from nazarino wood, one of the hardest woods known—so hard it can be enameled like metal, and too heavy to float in water. The statue was commissioned and shipped to Spain on a galleon that was either taken by pirates or wrecked. In any case, everything was lost. However, one day about a year after it disappeared, the Black Christ was washed up on the beach at Nombre de Dios, and so His church was built there and there He stays. He is not really black. Under his fleshy tints, worn by time and seawater, He has a purplish tinge where the natural color of the wood comes through. The indios there have a horrendous ceremony once a year when they haul the statue through the town on a wagon, and lash themselves into a frenzy with whips.

Ma visited us in Panama three times. The second time she came she had a bout with tropical pneumonia that put her into Gorgas Memorial Hospital. Our house was two-thirds porch, and there was no way to control dampness or temperatures, and so we felt the hospital would give her a better environment. She was there ten days, and had everyone from the chief surgeon to the cleaning woman walking in and out of her room, which was full of fruit and flowers.

In what little spare time she had from visitors, she wrote some enchanting Panama stories for our children.

The last time she visited us, we had moved from Quarry Heights to Albrook Field because the number one general and the number two general couldn't decide for whom Jim, as provost marshal of the Canal Zone and Puerto Rico, was working. Albrook Field was all new and lacked the inconvenient charm of Quarry Heights, but we had a lot of interesting young Air Force neighbors with children the same age as ours.

Ma knew everybody by this time, and so spent a lot of time with her friends as well as with us. Our children adored her, as did the neighboring children, and in the cool of the early morning or evening, she would take them on walks that always turned into exciting expeditions.

Our little Beatrice longed for a horse, so Ma found a five-dollar horse for her—a bag of bones named Dynamite, who lived in a paddock with the other riding horses and was frequently bitten by vampire bats. The horses ran loose, and you had to catch them to ride them, but this was no problem as they were always hungry. Dynamite would come to the fence with clotted blood on his neck, which Bea would wash off with a sponge. His saddle had cost twenty dollars, and she would ride him up and down the fence line urging him on. Fortunately, he rarely had the energy to go out of a slow trot—mostly he walked. Beatrice was the proudest five-year-old on the post.

Just before Ma left to go back to the States, we decided to have a real party for her, and invite all the people she really liked. She wanted a Panamanian party with local food, so everyone conspired. The first course would be, of course, ceviche, which is raw fish marinated overnight with lime juice, onions, and hot peppers and tomatoes. Our electrician sailing friend produced a fine red snapper for this. Our Zone policeman went to a lot of pains to shoot a wild canejo for the main dish. A canejo belongs to the guinea pig family, but is about the size of a dog, with long legs, and it tastes like the best pork. We provided all the native root vegetables—yucca and yami, strange gnarled things with bark that have a nutty taste and few calories. There was a heart of palm salad, the palms having been cut down the morning of the party, and all the wonderful native fruits. Poor Juan brought sopa borracho, drunken soup, on a huge platter of Peruvian silver. This is a trifle made with rum, sloppy and delicious.

The company was a mixed bag. Jack Greenway came, of course, and turned out to be a red-hot jazz piano player. There were Panamanians, Zone-ites, service friends, fishing friends, scientists, authors, the governor of the Zone, and the director of the museum. Several of the men we knew only as fishing friends, and had not met their wives. These ladies had never met Ma, but they had heard all about Georgie, and were slightly overwhelmed at meeting his widow—from Boston too! They came in their very best dresses, sparkling with their very best rhinestones, and their hair all done that very day.

Ma was unusually late in making her appearance. The children were running around giggling and nudging each other and calling her, obviously part of a rehearsed act. Jim and I noticed at about the same time a little old lady, wearing a straw boater and carrying two live chickens in a string bag, who was wandering around the house, apparently looking for someone. She was quite a spectacle, dressed in a red and white native print that dragged on the ground, wearing black cotton gloves, and when she smiled we saw she had no front teeth. I was about to ask her whom she wanted to see, when I realized it was Ma. She came up the steps, chickens and all, and started talking about her scool-teacha-datta, and what a hard time she had had to find a place, and how she had brought along two chickens for the pot. Everyone was embarrassed for me, as they thought some old lady had lost her way and was butting into the party—until Jim and I started to laugh. Then, they realized it was Ma, and they all burst out with laughter—all except the two ladies who had dressed up for a real high-class elegant party. I don't think they ever got over it. For the rest of us, it was one of the greatest parties we ever had and lasted until all hours, with eating and drinking and singing and playing—Ma peeled the black electric tape off her front teeth and took turns with Jack Greenway at the piano, trying to outdo each other in ragtime rhythm and old-time vaudeville songs: Ma with her "Bird in the Gilded Cage" and "She Is More to Be Pitied Than Censured," and Jack with his "How We Knocked 'Em in the Old Kent Road" and "She Was Pore but She Was 'Onest." A night to remember.

Our super tour in Panama came to a reluctant close. Just before Christmas, Beatrice came down with the mumps on one side. Jim and the little boys and I had never had the mumps, and Jim was in an absolute decline about it. There was no way to quarantine anyone as the rooms in the quarters were thoroughly modern and thoroughly unsatisfactory, with walls that only went to within a foot of the ceilings. This was supposed to circulate air, but of course it also circulated the germs, and there was no privacy whatsoever.

We had planned a large Christmas dinner, as always, to include our friends who either had no families or whose families were not with them, but the only person who came was Jack Greenway, who said he didn't care if he got the mumps as he didn't want any more children anyway. As he was a lifelong bachelor in his sixties, this was understandable.

It was a time of harassment—all moves are, actually. Mike had a mosquito bite that turned into blood poisoning with the frightening red streaks up the forearm and all the rest. They gave him shots at the hospital and told me to soak him in hot water several times a day, but he was a very sick little boy. I was just getting over a third bout of tropical pneumonia, so did not feel very lively. There was all the packing and farewelling to do, and Jim had to report to the Armed Forces Staff College in Norfolk, Virginia, for the class that started in February, and if he or the boys got the mumps, we would all be quarantined and that would upset his career schedule. Then Ma wired and said that the children should be sent to her immediately before any of the rest of us got the mumps, and she would cope. We sent them off practically in the clothes they had on when her telegram arrived with our wonderful babysitter, Mrs. Anne Main, and her husband who was on vacation at the time. Mr. Main was a CPO for the various fruit companies. They had no children, and Mrs. Main, who lived in the hotel when Mr. Main was off working, had been a real member of our family for two years and the children adored them both. They were both from Broughty Ferry in Scotland and had lived in Latin America for years and could do, and had done, everything.

Ma met the whole group in New York and kept them all with her at Green Meadows until Jim and I could pack, move, and find a house near Norfolk. This was typical of Ma. When I asked her, after the hurly-burly was over and done with, how Jim and I could ever repay her, she told me what our grandmother had said to her years before when she tried to thank her for taking care of Bee and me: "Don't think of repaying me, just do the same thing for your grandchildren when you have them. Pass it along."

There were no more mumps after the children got to Green Meadows, but a lot of tropical infections that had been lurking in the children's systems, held at bay by the numberless shots we had to take in Panama, surfaced, and Ma and the doctor had quite a time dealing with them. Another strain on her was the fact that young George had sustained multiple leg fractures while at the Army Ski School in Germany, and he had written her and asked her to come and sit it out with him. I know she would have loved to have done that as not only was George the apple of her eye, but she had so many friends still on active duty in Germany that she would have had a great time, but she said that there were three grandchildren, and only one George—and he was in good hands.

Chapter 19
Happy Days

Our five months at Virginia Beach, where we found a house right on the beach, were great fun, but we saw little of Ma as she took off for Germany as soon as we were settled. From the Staff College we were sucked back into the tentacles of the Pentagon, and Ma and Colonel and Mrs. Totten found us a very nice house near the Washington Cathedral. (Someone always did our house hunting for us.) Ma came quite often for visits, and spent time with Bee and Johnnie Waters at West Point where Johnnie was commandant of cadets. She took all five grandchildren to Green Meadows for the summer and gave them memories that are still very much alive.

One of our most successful visits from Ma included a massive fossil hunt at Bull Bluffs on the Potomac River. She had given us a book years before called *Potomac Landings* that listed all the sites of the old houses and river ports from Washington to the sea. We had a small motor boat called *Perrachola,* on which we spent the weekends in the spring and summer. It was small and tinny and slid sideways like a Dixie cup, but it got Jim away from the Pentagon and the telephone and the heat. One of the chapters in the book described Bull Bluff as a fossil deposit, and we found on going ashore that this was true. The beachy shore was littered with fossil oyster shells the size of soup tureens, and the bluff, which seemed to be streaked with white lines, really showed layers of pointed shells that we found out, from a visit to the fossil room at the Smithsonian, were Turitella Mortoni. The beach was speckled with small black sharks' teeth.

We took Ma and our children and the Waters boys on an all-day picnic to Bull Bluff and made fossil addicts of the children. Ma was on cloud nine. She had her little fossil pick with her and she collected a crocker sack full of shells and teeth with the help of the wildly enthusiastic recruits. She always used to say, "Open all the doors for the children, and even if they don't go through the doors at that time, if they have been opened some day they will come back and go through them."

More than twenty years after Ma died, I went to visit a married son at Fort Knox, Kentucky. The first thing he and his bride took me to see—before I even unpacked—was a deposit of fossil shells in and near a stream where they exercised their dog. Our son was just as excited at finding that open door as when it had first been opened for him at Bull Bluffs.

The Washington years are always very speedy ones. In addition to school, scouts, entertaining, and just keeping head above water, my brother, George, who had been a fascinating bachelor for about five years, came back to Washington. He had written to us from Germany and told us that he wanted to meet a girl who was a college graduate, a good dancer, beautiful, well-dressed, a good cook, potentially a good mother and, if possible, an Army brat. When Jim looked at the list, he said, "All he wants is Thuvia of Mars!" We introduced him to Joanne Holbrook, a daughter and granddaughter of dear old friends and great-granddaughter of Ma's own Mrs. Hoyle. If ever there was a marriage meant to be, this was it. Joanne was still in college when they met, but they were married a year and a week later, right after her graduation. Joanne was everything that, and more than, he had on his list.

It was at the parties before the wedding that we saw George Meeks for the last time. Jim and I were having a big luncheon before the wedding and George Meeks appeared in his white jacket and black trousers and gleaming black shoes, and took over the bar and buffet as if he had been long expected. We were all very glad to see him and asked him how he was, and where he had been, and why we never saw him. George Meeks replied, "Not much go on about The Family that ol' George don' know. Miss Ruthie, I was mighty glad to hear about this wedding. Seem like the Genrul, himself might be here." He stayed until the end of the party, but would not come to the church with us. He would not take any money but accepted, very graciously, a bottle of Johnnie Walker Black Label.

Next time I saw Fanny Harden, our laundress, I asked her about George Meeks and she said, "He just hole up, tryin' to drink he self to death. When Genrul, he die, it bruk George's heart, but he too tough to die quick."

Ma was supremely happy about the wedding. She never looked more beautiful than when she danced with George at the reception—she looked like a girl in her twenties. She had a lavender chiffon dress and a little hat made of violets, and she really was the best-looking woman at the wedding, which included some of the most beautiful women in the Army—so that is saying it all.

In recollection, I could almost say, So like a dolphin, dies the day. Ma would understand that, as she had caught many of the great Pacific dolphins when she had been with us in Panama, and had seen them as they lay dying, flushed with every exquisite color of the sea and the sky.

Fred Ayer's wife, Hilda, always called Ma Fred's cruising wife. Hilda Ayer really didn't like sailing or cruising—she was a farm and horse person—but she cruised faithfully with her Fred, complaining every splash of the way, but ever game until after Georgie died; then she more or less turned the sailing over to Ma. Ma gave Fred the *When and If,* or rather, they shared it and they had a great time. They took a long cruise to the Barbados—to Nevis and the other islands—to see Nelson's *pied-à-terre.* She loved the sightseeing and marketing and cooking the tropical groceries for the crew. She had picked up a taste for that kind of food in Panama, and she loved to show off her knowledge.

It came very gradually to our attention that Ma was not driving herself in her car any more. She had kept Georgie's car after he died. It was a flashy red and gray sporty sort of car and far too big for Ma, but she had persisted in driving it, literally peering out the windshield from between the spokes of the steering wheel. We asked her if she wanted another car, and she said, no, that she didn't drive much any more because she thought her eyesight was getting worse and that she was a menace on the highway. She had always been a safe driver, although she was the only person I ever knew who made a car leap forward in short, gasping bounds—like a greyhound on a leash with a rabbit in sight. She had Reggie, who had been with us in every capacity for nearly twenty years, to drive her, so we didn't worry too much. She had never been one to drive just for the fun of it.

She continued to ride cross country and ride to hounds. Her faithful steed, Quicksilver, finally had to be put to sleep, and we went to a great deal of thought to get her a new horse, a really good one like the kind Georgie had always provided. Theo Randolph, Chilly Ayer's older daughter, who lived in Virginia, found us a lovely horse, a Trakehner named Formaloup. Ma was particularly pleased at having a Trakehner as Georgie had been keen on their history. They were a breed of German warhorse, carefully bred for quality, courage, and endurance. Ma's horse was out of a famous mare named LaLoupe, and his sire was the well-known stud Format. He was a small, beautifully put-together chestnut, and could and would jump anything. He was not a quiet horse; he had spirit, but he was well-trained. The last letter I had from her was written after she had hunted him all afternoon, and she said, "If he did not have already such a distinguished name, I would christen him Happy Days."[1]

---

1. Fourmaloup lived to a grand old age and taught all the grandchildren to ride and fox hunt.

Johnnie Waters received his well-deserved promotion to general officer and was, in practically the same breath, sent off to war in Korea. The Waters had been at West Point for some time—both the little boys were at school there. They had many friends both on and off the post, so they decided to buy a house in Highland Falls, just outside the Academy grounds, where Bee would live while Johnnie was off to the wars.

Johnnie's going back to action was a deep shock to my sister. I don't think anyone realized at the time what a shock it was. She had been through so much when he was missing in action and a prisoner of war. She was a shy and sensitive person underneath her charm and ability, and she needed loving support for whatever she did. Ma and I were sensitive to the fact that she was not herself, but she had her own sense of privacy, and her doctor didn't see fit to tell us just how ill she really was.

When she was finally ready to move from the commandant's quarters to her house in Highland Falls, Jim suggested that as I had her so much on my mind, I go and help her. I went to West Point for a week, and even talked to her doctor, who told me that he had the situation well in hand and that my sister was getting vitamin shots and the proper medication. He was a lovely man—old enough to be our father—and had taken care of the Waterses for years, and I believed him. Ma had had a feeling about Bee also, and wanted her to come home to Green Meadows, but Bee had run her own home for too long and liked being her own Ol' Mis'.

Jim and I were in a rented house in Washington that we liked very much, but it was being attacked by termites, and the owners, old friends, said that they would not mind canceling our lease as the house really needed drastic treatment. We looked around in the neighborhood where Bee had lived before, and which we both liked—up near the cathedral and Ward Circle—and found a grand big house that we all got together and bought as an investment in the future, as with both of our husbands and young George in the service, chances were that one or more of us would be stationed in Washington frequently.

Jim and I were very anxious to move, not only because of the termites but also because he had started building a boat in the cellar, and had found out that if he finished it there, he would not be able to get it out. There was a great double garage in the new house where we could finish the boat in comfort.

We were in the process of moving when my aunt, Nita Patton, came to Washington on some church business, and also for the Colonial Dames annual meeting, and she urged us to take a weekend off and go to New York, and meet Bee there and take her to the theater and a football game while she superintended the children—which she loved to do. She was my sister's godmother, and she felt very tenderly toward Bee and her being left alone in Highland Falls.

Friday afternoon I was out in the garden building a barbecue on the ruins of an old playhouse, and having a lot of messy fun laying bricks and mixing cement when, all of a sudden, a chill like some wind from outer space, cold and desolate and despairing, blew through me—a feeling of total depression—so tangible it was as if a drain had been opened inside somewhere and all the life and luster were running out. The words of an old song from the "Water Babies" started going through my head, almost as if someone far away was singing it— and only the last verse, over and over.

> When all the world is old, lads, and all the trees are brown
> And every sport is stale, lads, and all the wheels run down
> Come home and take your place, lads, the old and sad among
> God grant you find some face there you loved when all was young.

My aunt came out into the yard to call me in for dinner and I was just standing there with the tears running down my face. She said, "Oh, dear, what is the matter?" "Something terrible is happening." She answered sadly, "Yes, I feel it too."

Jim and I were all packed to take off the next morning early. At about 2 a.m. the telephone rang, and before I answered it, I knew what it was going to be. The voice on the other end said, "Mrs. Totten, this is Doctor Mac. Mrs. Waters just died; I am here with her and the boys." Jim took the phone from me and after a short conversation, we were off on the 4 a.m. flight to New York, leaving the children with my aunt.

Ma was out on the *When and If,* somewhere in New York Harbor with her brother, Fred, and we didn't know how to reach her. Jim called the Department of Defense and arranged for Johnnie Waters to be notified, and then arranged for an indefinite leave for himself. He also called the Coast Guard and told them to look for the schooner.

My sister was only forty-one years old. It isn't only soldiers who are casualties of war.

When Ma finally got to Highland Falls with Fred and the rest of the family, she looked smaller and more transparent than I had ever seen her even when she came back after Georgie's funeral. She looked completely defenseless. All I could think of was what she had said to her brother, Chilly Ayer, when his daughter, Anne Steward, had been killed by a horse: "This is the one thing we don't expect, Chill. We know our parents will die, and we are somewhat prepared for that, but we always expect our children to outlive us. The death of your child is the worst grief of all."

After the barbaric carnival of death was over, Johnnie Waters went back to Korea to finish his tour, and Ma took the Waters boys home with her to Green

Meadows. Johnnie and Ma, each in their own way, were given a palliative for their sorrow in that they were needed—they did not have time for sackcloth and ashes.

Ma and the boys came to Washington and had Christmas with us. We were packed in like sardines, but it was warm and friendly, and as much fun as it could be. We had whole roast pig with an apple in its mouth for Christmas dinner, and we put on a play called "Dry Gulching of Santa Claus," which gave all five children personally hand-tailored parts, and was a riot. Mike Totten was Rusty Dusty Frelinghuysen; Pat Waters was Hopalong Fink; Jamie Totten was Rainbow Manoukian; Bea Totten was Pokebonnet Potsy; and young John Waters was the hero, Sandy Claws. The commercial advertised Easy-Erpsie-Oatsies, the cereal that tastes just as good coming up as it does going down. The stage effects included twittering birds, flushing toilets, and cap pistols. It certainly took everyone's mind off the absent members, at least for a while.

We moved into the new house in the spring, but the year brought a change of station and another move to the Army War College at Carlisle, Pennsylvania. Johnnie Waters came back from Korea and was ordered to Norfolk, taking the boys with him. Joanne and George Patton had their first child, Margaret de Russy Patton. That was the best thing that had happened to Ma since Bee died.

In August of 1953, just before Jim had to report for duty to Carlisle, he took three weeks leave and we all went cruising on the *When and If* with Uncle Fred. Mike Totten, almost twelve, was old enough to go along as cabin boy, and was the most important and the busiest hand on the schooner. We have seventeen days of cruising down Maine. It was all new to Jim and Mike and me; and Ma just loved showing us their gunk holes and special places, and taking us ashore in the dinghy—rowed by Mike, of course. Uncle Fred and I had cooking contests so that we ate like the crew on the Walloping Windowblind. Ma seemed almost herself again.

It was a blessed cruise; the weather was lovely, and we only went aground once. This was almost a record, as Uncle Fred was always fightin' them charts.

Ma and I did a lot of talking. Some of the things she wanted to talk about seemed almost like a last will and testament to me. She kept harping on the fact that I must never fight with young George, that as brother and sister we were the closest kin there is, and that as we grew older we would find out more and more surely that family loyalty was the most important thing in life. I didn't fight with George any more than any sister fights with her brother. In fact, I love him with all my heart and admire him greatly, but she kept bringing it up.

She said that I was going to see a lot of changes in my lifetime. This particular series of conversations has come back to me more and more as the years go by. Ma said that nature became aware of the dangers of a population explosion much sooner than man did, and that she started taking her own steps before it entered men's minds to do something about it. She said that in my lifetime I would see many people who couldn't have children; many people who didn't want children; legalized abortion; an increase in and an acceptance of lesbians and homosexuals; more automobile deaths; more senseless crimes; more little wars.

She said that nature removed some sort of censor from men's minds at these times, and that the only trouble was that the good suffered along with the bad because nature took the long view and didn't make exceptions. Ma thought that people would begin to develop the psychic side of their natures and become less materialistic because they would realize that possessions were not the be-all and end-all of life, that it was what a person had inside that mattered to God, not what they owned. She repeated several times something that she had always told us—that you own nothing until you have given it away freely. When your children grow up, she said, don't try to keep them at home or by your side, open the cage door and let them fly away, and if you leave it open, they will come back when they are ready. But, if you try to keep them, or possess them, they will fly away and never come back. They can take away your goods and chattels, and they can say all sorts of things about you, but they can never take away your memories, so be sure you have lots of lovely ones.

She copied out on a page from the grocery list a little poem she had written and gave it to me.

> I will remember happy times—not sad ones;
> I will remember good people—not bad ones;
> Forgetting hurts, scar tissue is the strongest;
> Remembering love—'tis love that lasts the longest.

She talked like this so much that finally I said to her, "Ma, you sound as if you were trying to tell me something. You are sort of sending out signals. What's the trouble, you have me scared!" She looked at me very thoughtfully, and said, "Well, I *am* sending out signals. It's the truth. I am not going to live very much longer."

I was appalled. In fact, I started to cry. I asked her if the doctor had told her anything she hadn't told us. I reminded her that she was greatly needed; that the Waters boys needed her; that George and Joanne needed her; and that I needed her most of all, but she said very calmly, "No, I am not really needed any more. Johnnie is a wonderful father, and Jim takes very good care of you and I trust him, and now George has Joanne, so I'm really not needed any more. The doctor hasn't told me anything new. It's just that I have lost my zest. Things are too much of an effort. Things are just not very interesting any more." After that conversation, which took place near the end of the cruise, she didn't talk along that line again, and I didn't bring it up because I was deeply disturbed. I told Jim about it, and he replied, "Well, she knows how she feels; she knows her own mind. Aunt Bee can take care of herself. This is a private thing."

We got down to Carlisle Barracks in time for Jim's course to start, and to get the children enrolled in the local schools. Ma planned to come and visit as soon as we were settled, and she telephoned quite often. She was enjoying hunting Formaloup. She was knitting bulky sweaters for the children for Christmas— she was a masterful knitter. Her last letter contained a sample of blue wool in it for Beatrice to approve.

The letter came in the afternoon mail. The next morning the kids had gotten off to school and so had Jim. I was washing the breakfast dishes when the phone rang. I knew it was long distance before I picked it up, and a great tide of feeling went right through me: "All is finished." The caller was Aunt Kay Merrill. She said, in her lovely precise voice, "Good morning, dear. Are you alone?" "Yes, I am. Something has happened to Ma." She sounded a little taken aback, as she replied, "I'm calling from the Beverly Hospital. Your mother had a fall out hunting this morning." I interrupted her: "Ma's dead." Again, Aunt Kay paused: "Yes, she was riding right in front of Freddy and the horse gave a little kick which seemed to unbalance her and she slipped off. She was dead when she hit the ground." I heard myself say, "Thank God." This upset Aunt Kay, although she took it very well. She didn't know that what I meant was, "Ma was good enough. In her own way, she died in battle."

With the help of all our friends and Ma's innumerable friends in high places we got off to Massachusetts that night. Joanne came up from Washington. Young George in Korea was on his way home. The whole family gathered somehow under the one roof.

At just about the time everyone arrived, the cook gave notice, which was the one thing we needed to break the tension. I was able to give her a piece of my mind that I didn't even know I had, and she left immediately by taxi, saying that she had never, no, never been spoken to like that, that she had always worked for nice people.

The George S. Patton, Jr., rose, given Ma by the grower, was in bloom for the first time, and we laid three of the blossoms on her coffin at the crematorium. None of us ever saw her dead. We had insisted on an autopsy so that there would be no doubt in anyone's mind—particularly in that of her beloved brother, Fred, who had lifted her up from the ground where she lay—of the cause of death. Ma had had an aneurysm about which she had been well informed. We found a letter in her desk from the famous heart specialist, Dr.

Charles Dudley White, telling her of her condition, and apparently answering a question by saying that she could live a day, a week, a month, a year, whether she took to her bed or led a normal life, but that having known her for years, he suggested that she should give up driving her own car in case she died at the wheel and was the cause of an accident.

She was buried under the elm tree by the wing at Green Meadows that she had built for Georgie where the children love to play around the cannon Georgie sent her from Fort Lyautey. Rosemary and pansies are planted there. She is really buried in many places, especially in the hearts and minds of those who loved her. She is most apparent in the five grandchildren that knew her—in the turn of the head, the gesture of the hand, the dramatic scene and the meaningful pause. Her opinions are still quoted.

Grandma said the jewel weed grows next to the poison ivy because God put it there for a cure.

Grandma's favorite meal was fish chowder and sliced oranges.

Grandma didn't let us get tired. She said, "A merry heart sings all the way, the sad tires in a mile."

No matter how close one is to another person, each one of us is a sealed book at the end. Ma missed Georgie more and more. She didn't like things to go on that she couldn't share with him, and she felt he had missed a lot of living. He had so looked forward to going around the world in the *When and If,* and he had so many hobbies and enthusiasms, and yet she once said, "Georgie would have ended up hating retirement." Again: "It would have given Georgie so much satisfaction to know how right he was about the Russians, but it would have made him awfully angry too. And Georgie would have hated the way things are changing. He never realized that he was a patriot until nearly the end of his life, but then he did realize it, and everything changed for him."

It is as hard to end a book as it is to begin one, although Ma, in her way, is a book that will never really be written, and a story that will never really end. There is a quotation that fits Ma and Georgie, and with it, I will close my box of memories.

They were lovely and pleasant in their lives, and in their death they were not divided: they were swifter than eagles: they were stronger than lions. (2 Samuel 1:20)

My hiding place is an old law. Holla! I hide in songs!

July 4, 1979